Before the Welfare State

Themes in British Social History

edited by Dr J. Stevenson

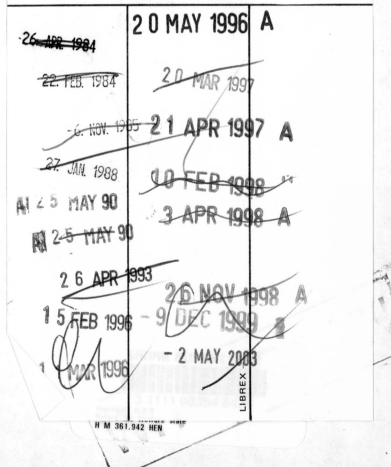

Before the Welfare State

Social administration
in early industrial Britain

Ursula R. Q. Henriques

Longman
London and New York

To Octavia Adler, in memoriam

Longman Group Limited London

Associated companies, branches and representatives
throughout the world

Published in the United States of America
by Longman Inc., New York

© Longman Group Limited 1979

First published 1979
ISBN 0 582 48594 0 cased
ISBN 0 582 48595 9 paper

Henriques, Ursula Ruth Quixano
  Before the Welfare State. – (Themes in British
  social history).
  1. Public welfare – Great Britain – History
  18th century
  2. Public welfare – Great Britain – History
  19th century
  I. Title   II. Series
  361'.941   HV245   78-40336

  ISBN 0-582-48594-0
  ISBN 0-582-48595-9   Pbk.

Printed in Great Britain by Richard Clay (The Chaucer Press) Ltd, Bungay, Suffolk

Contents

Acknowledgements

I should like to acknowledge with thanks the help of the Humanities and Social Sciences Library of University College, Cardiff, the Cardiff City Library, Reference Section, the D. M. S. Watson Library, University College, London, the British Library and the Public Record Office. I should especially like to thank my colleagues Professor Gwyn A. Williams, Professor H. R. Loyn, Dr Clive Knowles and Mr Brian James who have read parts of the book at various stages; also Mrs Patricia Moffatt, History Department Secretary, who has given a great deal of help and Mrs Gladys Takata who wrestled successfully with a very difficult typescript. The book owes much to unpublished postgraduate theses and I have referred further to these and to their authors in the bibliography.

1 Introduction

Social administration grew in the last years of the eighteenth century and the first half of the nineteenth in response to the challenge of the Industrial Revolution. By this term is intended not merely the changes brought about by technical inventions and the rapid application of power to industrial production, but also the contemporary agrarian revolution, and the population explosion which, beginning independently of industrialisation, became a vital element in its continuation.[1]

The changes in economic and social structure produced a massive demand for the intervention of the community, local or central, to mitigate their social effects and provide for their casualties. But of course the demand developed unevenly and in many different ways.

The effects of the wave of parliamentary enclosures of whole parishes, including the wastelands (itself part of the long-drawn-out process of absorption of small freeholds and copyholds by larger estates), were felt firstly by the Poor Law. This code, along with its accompanying settlement and bastardy laws, was by far the most important aggregate of social provisions and regulations which survived into the nineteenth century. Originating in Tudor times, when England and Wales, apart from London, were almost wholly rural and agricultural, the law was centred firmly on the compact parish. In the eighteenth century the parish, consisting of the village and its surrounding open fields, still survived as a geographical community and a natural administrative centre in many areas. Enclosures, which picked up speed around 1760 and reached their climax during the Napoleonic wars, upset this geography, enclosing the fields, pushing farmers out to live in scattered farmhouses, promoting at first the custom of farm servants living with the families of the tenant farmers and later the custom of hiring labourers who walked out to work from the villages. It has been observed that the enclosures promoted employment, in hedging, ditching, ploughing, and similar employments. They also brought about the eviction of squatters on the waste, produced a landless proletariat, and created an over-stocked rural labour market. The Poor Law (when private charity failed) was the last resort of the orphan and deserted child, the old and infirm, the unemployed, the under-employed and the low paid, and it had to adapt itself to these changes. We shall see how, as rural over-population increased and farming collapsed with the end of the wars, the adaptation became explosive.

Unlike the effects of agrarian changes on the Poor Law, industrialisation generated demands for kinds of social regulation which had not existed before. The result of the introduction of early textile machinery was an enormous increase in the numbers of domestic outworkers. The industry grew in new areas such as Lancashire, Cheshire and southwest Scotland (cotton), the West Riding of Yorkshire (wool and flax), Macclesfield (silk), Nottinghamshire (hosiery), east Wales (flannel), etc, but most of the operations were on a domestic scale until well into the nineteenth century. Even in Lancashire the spinning mills were surrounded by combing and carding workshops and villages of handloom weavers. It took generations to gather all these operations under the same or related factory roofs. Meantime the prosperous outworkers required no social administration. But when, from about the turn of the century, the handloom weavers (to take the most famous example) began to suffer from over-stocking with cheap labour followed by growing competition from the power looms, they were disqualified from public intervention by their domestic nature. No doubt the conditions of work in most weaving cottages were worse than in many factories, and child assistants, where employed, worked longer hours. But there was no large conglomeration of workers in weaving cottages, or in nail-making workshops, to unionise and demand reform, and the state had neither the inclination nor the organisation to invade the privacy of the home. Thus attempts to regulate hours, conditions and safety began first in the factories which, even towards the end of the first Industrial Revolution around 1840, employed only about one-half of the industrial workers.[2] But when the demand began, and it was as early as the 1780s, it began in several directions simultaneously. Early spinning mills posed a series of threats to the well-being of factory children – to their health from long hours, over-crowding and dangerous machines, to their education (specially noticed in Scotland, where literacy declined), and to the surrounding districts from the spread of infectious diseases bred in the mills. Industrial control, public health and education were all involved.

It has been noticed that one of the great changes of the Industrial Revolution period was the increase in scale of almost everything.[3] Although many smallholdings survived, even the average farm got bigger. Small workshops grew into factories employing hundreds of people, mines got deeper, production and overseas trade increased as never before, and towns suddenly appeared with the building of a factory, or doubled their size within a decade. The main reason for this was the massive, and as yet not fully understood, increase in population. Between 1781 and 1851 the population grew from nearly 9 million to 20 million.[4] Because of the pull of industrialisation this increase led to the rapid growth of towns, especially in the industrial areas, without, however, emptying the country. In agriculture over-population was added to changes in agrarian structure. In the industrial towns the numbers affected by the cyclical depressions which began to appear, grew beyond Poor Law control. In all towns the hazards to public health from unplanned speculative building, lack of sanitation and the uncontrolled creation of slums were recognised as a serious problem by the second quarter of the nineteenth century. So was crime as a secondary effect of the same causes. Low wages and seasonal employment, encouraged by over-population and soured by the enclosure of wastes and the restriction of diet in the households of landless men, stimulated poaching. Unemployment due to the introduction of new machines, whether stocking frames, power looms or mechanical threshers, produced Luddite-type attacks especially on isolated factories and farms, and these were not distinguishable in contemporary eyes from the more ordinary civil crimes such as robbery. Bad housing, casual employment and cyclical unemployment, the increasing but unnumbered presence of deserted orphan and bastard children, spawned the gangs of urban thieves noted by many witnesses to select committees on crime. Highwaymen and footpads lurked in the approaches to London, pickpockets and thieves in the city. The Fielding brothers had begun their efforts at policing the city in the mid-eighteenth century, but by the beginning of the nineteenth century the increase of scale in crime was creating the need for a wider and more systematic attempt to reform the administration of law and order, on its police or catching side, in its criminal procedures, and its punishments.

In a rural and reasonably stable agricultural society with a traditional culture of festivals, ceremonies and songs, illiteracy among the lower orders would hardly seem a problem. In an unstable, rapidly expanding and discontented population the demand for measures to ensure mass literacy was voiced among evangelicals and middle-class reformers, as an insurance against crime and violent unrest. Again the scale of the problem increased, along with population and urbanisation.

To some extent the problems of destitution, bad health, child labour, illiteracy and crime could be left either to charity or to private enterprise. As well as dame schools and other small private schools, the education of the poor had long been provided for by charitable endowments or by such voluntary societies as the Society for Promoting Christian Knowledge, and by the efforts of some local clergymen. The population rise and urbanisation rendered them insufficient. Private charity for the deserving poor increased in the nineteenth century with the evangelisation of the middle classes and some of the gentry. The Poor Law relieved only those whom charity had failed. Yet with the growth of population and urbanisation, charity was plainly not enough, and this was reluctantly realised even when, after 1815, the Malthusians launched their attack on most kinds of charitable giving as well as on the Poor Law. Paving, lighting and scavenging in the growing towns could be profitably undertaken by private enterprise, but only for those who could pay for it. There was no private inducement to speculative builders who were creating slums to pave, light or drain them.

Millowners, compelled by the technology of their industry to employ the mass labour of children and youths, were deterred by the exigencies of private competition from regulating the working lives of their own workforce. Moreover, the conditions of industrial competition rapidly set up norms which habit and use disabled millowners from recognising as abusive. Neither charity nor unchecked private enterprise was able to deal effectively with the problems created by the growth of scale. Nor was the existing public provision. Village idiots had long been (as modern jargon would have it) 'retained within the community'; dangerous madmen, if not sent to private asylums, were chained up in ruins. With increasing population and increasing numbers of mental cases this primitive treatment became unacceptable. Something on a larger scale had to be done about lunacy, especially among the poor.

The increase in scale meant that the organisation of the village community was being outgrown. Public social administration, to be effective, could hardly help becoming larger. Everywhere the increasing scale and complexity of life called for the reform or the creation of systematic public intervention and administration. And everywhere the price to be paid, if slowly and unevenly, was an increasing impersonality and remoteness from the small-community relations of the past.

The decay of public administration

The need for social administration came at a time when the political and administrative system was singularly ill-fitted to deal with it. During the eighteenth century public administration decayed. This was at least partly the result of reaction from the venal paternalism of the Stuart Kings, and of the victory of the landed upper classes after the civil wars. In 1660 the Poor Law escaped from all central direction and came under the domination of the Justices of the Peace. The supremacy of parish interests was confirmed by the Settlement Act of 1662, but the legal administration of settlement and bastardy went to Petty or Quarter Sessions, while Justices in their own parlours heard appeals from the verdicts of overseers about relief to individuals. In the later eighteenth and early nineteenth century the administration of county gaols and county asylums (when they came to be built) was in the hands of visiting committees of Justices. When Quarter Sessions were concerned Justice of the Peace control was already a widening from the purely parish basis of administration, but it was also a recipe for local diversity, and in many cases, neglect or maladministration. Moreover, towards the end of the century the country gentlemen from whom the vast majority of Justices were appointed showed a growing disinclination to take responsibility for regulating the wages and working conditions and ensuring the well-being of the lower orders.[5] After 1790, while the apprenticeship and the wage-fixing laws were steadily abolished by a gentry-dominated parliament, the Poor Law was brought in to ensure, by means of scaled allowances, some sort of survival subsistence in the agricultural districts. The doubtless unforeseen result was, as we shall see, to enable the working farmers to control the labour market to their own advantage.

The new industrial towns when they came to be built had no government of their own, apart from county officials whose offices often descended in one or two families, while the older boroughs, released from the fear of Stuart attacks on their charters, sank into oligarchy and somnolence. The City of London, despite its elected Common Council, was a byword for the squalor of its prisons and the filth of its slums. Local Acts setting up paving and drainage boards were procured by the inhabitants of wealthy districts. Elsewhere the Commissioners of Sewers and the unstrengthened laws of nuisance were inadequate to protect poor populations from the private vested interests in bad building, bad drainage and dear water.

If the Whig factions which controlled eighteenth-century government would do nothing to improve public administration, the radical groups which from the time of Wilkes (around 1760 onwards) began to appear, promised little better; for they, as much as the gentry, feared strong government more than corrupt government, or no government. For instance, generations of radical politicians resisted the formation of an efficient police. We shall see that the efforts of reformers in social administration were continually hampered by outcries against 'centralisation.'

Being reluctant and stagnant, social administration, along with other branches of public administration, was inevitably corrupt. This corruption was facilitated and augmented by the condition of the political constitution. The decayed franchise in the boroughs ensured political corruption. But the franchise with all its anomalies was defended by contemporary writers as maintaining a balanced constitution of King, Lords and Commons, each with an independent power base in the monarchy, the aristocracy and the people respectively (the 'people' meaning property owners, not the common people, who were more often termed the 'mob'). Liberty, consisting largely in the minimum of government control, was secured by the checking action of the parts of the legislature upon each other, rather than by the representation of individuals or, as Edmund Burke expressed it, of 'a multitude told by the head.'[6] If this mutual limitation was not to become paralysis, some way of harmonising the action of the three houses of parliament and maintaining parliamentary support for the King's ministers had to be found. So patronage and influence were justified as the cement of government.[7] This stratified constitutional system of estates seemed to conflict with the structure of society in pyramids, or rather vertical chains of dependence widening down from the head of the noble family at the top to the many humble dependants at the bottom.[8] At Westminster those chains of influence appeared as parliamentary factions or parties, running through the upper and lower houses, and held together by the cement. Thus patronage in government appointments, from the sinecures of the Board of Green Cloth, through the allocation of government contracts to merchant members of parliament, down to the appointment of tide waiters in the Customs and part-time Receivers of the Land Tax were the perquisite and tool of political faction leaders. The government departments, even when not subjected to party purges following general elections as in 1763, were recruited by patronage (or occasionally, by reaction, by purchase of offices as freeholds), and promoted through patronage, purchase, or rigid seniority. Patronage and favour as a means of influence[9] were generally not considered corrupt or illegitimate as were bribes by cash or public contract; nor did patronage necessarily entail 'jobbery' or the appointment of unsuitable officers for private advantage.[10] Yet the system condoned appointment to public office on criteria and for ends other than those of administrative efficiency. Administration had been sacrificed to the political system, and the whole climate was unfavourable to the development of an upright and zealous public service. Inevitably the attention of critics was focused on limiting the use of public offices for the private or political advantage of the King and other leading politicians, rather than on the development of a necessary and constructive public administration. In the long run the structure of the constitution would have to change, the apparent balance of power be resolved in favour of a more representative and powerful lower house, before the 'cement' could be dispensed with and the extension of administration be contemplated as a necessity of adequate government rather than a tool of factional power-seeking.[11]

Corruption and suspicion of corruption reinforced a long-standing loathing of taxation. Probably in no eighteenth-century European country was taxation considered by ordinary people in any light but that of payment to a ruler for his own purposes. In Stuart England this had been a major problem, with a gentry-dominated parliament resisting taxation for royal policies with which the Commons did not agree. Walpole under the first two Hanoverians had sought at all costs to keep taxation low. When, on the accession of George III, the King's Civil List was separated from the funds for the major expenses of government, politicians continued to attack it as a suspected means for George III's attempt to build up his own political connection. Their attacks gained teeth from the loss of the American colonies and led to Burke's Economical Reform Act. The demand for cheap government, along with the demand for minimum government, was reinforced by centuries of alienation between the central government and the various ranks of the governed. Although there was no *taille* nor *gabelle* in Britain, radicals such as Thomas Paine believed the hardships of the poor were mainly due to taxes, and would be removed if the taxes were repealed. Paine did not think this incompatible even with his remarkable Welfare State programme of 1792. Peace with France and disarmament would allow the army to be paid off, the Poor Rate abolished, taxes cut and a full programme of social payments for old age, marriage, childbirth and education to be made, all at the same time.[12] Jeremy Bentham in his *Constitutional Code* at length realised that the benefits of public administration entailed a cost, which must be weighed against them when their value was estimated.[13] But he showed the deepest suspicion of all who handled power or public money, and sought to impose the tightest curbs upon them. Corruption, alienation and the belief that taxation was an abuse rather than an instrument of government placed shackles on the advance of social administration which survived until the end of the nineteenth century. These attitudes were independent of theories of economic *laisser faire*, or of a free labour market, although they harmonised with them. Economic dogmas, however, reinforced them in debates over poor relief, or state intervention to protect the wages of handloom weavers, and other victims of economic and technical change.

Similar alienation, but this time from the Established Church inhibited the spread of popular education. The most vigorous reformers, the Nonconformists, especially the Rational Dissenters and their deist or atheist allies, were frightened of Church domination backed by the Anglican majority in parliament. Education was weakened by sectarian strife which led to voluntarist attitudes, because the state appeared not as an instrument of aid but of partiality and oppression.

Fortunately for the growth of social administration, complacency with the corruption of the civil service was shattered by the loss of the American colonies. In 1780 Lord North, under pressure from the Rockingham Whigs, appointed six Commissioners to Examine the Public Accounts. This commission, which was far more important than Burke's initiative, lasted seven years and issued fifteen reports. It was followed by a Commission for Inquiring into Fees in the Public Offices, and by House of Commons Select Committees on Finance in 1782, 1786, 1791 and 1797.[14] The Commission on Public Accounts which went systematically through the departments, identifying and reporting abuses, and the Select Committees, cleansed the Augean stable. Despite backslidings during the Napoleonic wars and the persistence of appointment by patronage, this slow purification enabled the central administration to support the immense additions of the 1830s and 1840s, whether by the foundation of new Boards, or by the development of sections of such departments as the Home Office to supervise factory and prison inspectors. Social administration (voluntary organisations apart) was part of local and central government, and waned and waxed with them. The purification of the public service of its worse abuses (facilitated also by its gradual separation from political office) so that by 1830 it was notably less corrupt than the franchise, allowed the employment of zealots and enthusiasts for reform, alongside the residue of the dimmer sons of the nobility. The enormous obstacles in the path of public health administration were at least partly due to the slow progress in the revival of local government, not only through the domination of Tory oligarchies before 1835, but in the ascendancy of ratepayer interests after the Municipal Corporations Act of that year.

Social class and social administration

The Industrial Revolution, which so increased the need for social administration, also created the class structure and the class feelings which were to bedevil it. Class feeling has perhaps never again been so bitter as it was in the 1830s and 1840s. The new men of the industrial and professional middle classes were, on the one hand, frustrated by the social and political privileges of the landed gentry, and on the other hand, increasingly fearful of the nascent working classes they saw forming below them. Philanthropic gentlemen such as M. T. Sadler or Lord Shaftesbury were equally apprehensive of danger from the neglected and embittered poor, although in more kindly mood. They bewailed the passing of the paternal relationship between upper and lower orders which had sweetened the dependence of the poor on their social superiors. Many kinds of social administration, from poor relief to police, prisons and schools, were obvious instruments of social control. That these instruments were grasped and indeed developed at least partly with this end in view was natural and inevitable. But how far this was done consciously and how far the class character of the various kinds of social administration was simply the unconscious result (and sometimes the buttress) of the class structure itself must always be arguable.

Certainly the class dimension was inescapable. But it was also extremely complicated, since administration grew at a time of change in the class structure as well as social mobility between classes. In the agricultural areas, even if we grossly oversimplify the relationships, there were at least three strata; landowners, tenant farmers and smallholders, and landless labourers. There was recognised strife between industrial town and agricultural county, but some of the greatest mills were built, with their own villages, deep in the country, and their owners ran country estates. Industries became capitalised at different times and in different places. In 1830–32 it was easier for Birmingham, where most small iron products were still in their workshop phase, to co-operate in a common political end than for Manchester, where textiles were already made in factories, and owners and workmen were self-consciously opposing each other. Class hostility was as much due to social instability as social rigidity. In advanced industries such as cotton and flax spinning it was possible for the successful entrepreneur to climb from the lower orders to gentry status in two generations, especially if he invested in land and his sons lost interest in the mill (*vide* the Marshalls of Leeds).[15] On the other hand, there was constant danger of losing capital and property in a trade slump, and descending into the amorphous mass of the poor.[16] In such circumstances, most were content to adopt the typical defensive attitudes of their industry and their class. Others were assisted by coincidence of interest to retain and exercise their social conscience. There were always industrialists who, preferring regulation to cut-throat competition, looked to legislation to enable them to reduce the hours of labour and force their rivals to do the same. A landowner as large as the Earl of Westmorland could afford to offer his labourers allotments as an alternative to the Poor Law. Upper- and middle-class attitudes can be identified, but they were never monolithic; the same was true of working-class attitudes. Economic arguments in conflict with those of the classical economists, class organisations such as trade unions, class attitudes, especially in the industrial areas, can be identified. They also were never monolithic. There was much divergence among millworkers between those who grasped the arguments for the value of limiting work hours and those who sought overtime for themselves or their children. The working class was as stratified, sectionalised, unstable and divided as the upper and middle classes; and it has been recently suggested that the unified, class-conscious working-class movement, then as now, was a myth.[17]

Class feeling was compounded by sectarian feeling; class and religion being interrelated in complicated ways which varied from region to region; having, for instance, special significance in ethnically different parts of the country, such as Wales. But even in national politics there was no simple construction of political party based on economic and social interest. Whig and Tory differences over Church and Franchise were bisected by divisions over economic and social policy. Against such a complex background the historian must beware of simple explanations. With this in mind, the ensuing chapters attempt to describe how some of the main branches of social administration developed amid such stresses and strains.

Sources and references

1. **Perkin, Harold,** *The Origins of Modern English Society, 1780–1880.* Routledge, 1969, *passim.*
2. Perkin, *op. cit.,* p. 14.
3. Perkin, *op. cit.,* pp. 107–24.
4. **Dean, P.** and **Cole, G. D. H.,** *British Economic Growth.* C.U.P., 1964, p. 8.
5. Professor Perkin has traced this 'abdication on the part of the governors'. Perkin, *op. cit.,* pp. 183–95.
6. The few populous open boroughs were cited as 'virtual representation' of the lower orders. **Burke, Edmund,** *An Appeal from the New to the Old Whigs,* 1791, p. 183; *Writings and Speeches,* 1887, iv.
7. 'Parliaments have ever been influenced, and by that means our constitution has so long subsisted.' **Jenyns, Soame,** *Thoughts on Parliamentary Reform.* London, 1784, p. 22.
8. Cf. Perkin, *op. cit., passim.*
9. Patronage was part of the legitimate influence which nobles and gentry exercised on their tenants or others in their entourage, including influence in voting for parliament.
10. Further facility for corruption on one hand and suspicion on the other was the payment of many civil servants by fees.
11. But 'deference' politics and chains of influence lasted long into the nineteenth century. Cf. **Moore, D. C.,** *The Politics of Deference.* Harvester Press, 1976, *passim.*
12. **Paine, Thomas,** *Rights of Man,* part II. Everyman edition, pp. 238–70.

13. **Bentham, Jeremy,** *Constitutional Code. Works,* Bowring (ed.), 1842. Vol. ix, Sections I and II, pp. 269–74.
14. **Binney, J. E. D.,** *British Public Finance and Administration, 1774–92.* Clarendon Press, 1958, pp. 15–19.
15. It had been possible to effect a similar transition in the eighteenth century through success in overseas trade or through central politics (*vide* the Jenkins family who became Earls of Liverpool). The growth of industry made it more frequent.
16. Vide. The struggle of the Scottish Whig journalist and businessman James Stuart to keep his head above water before he became a factory inspector. **Henriques, U. R. Q.,** 'An early factory inspector: James Stuart of Dunearn', *Scottish Historical Review,* P. I. No. 149. April 1971, pp. 22–3.
17. **Musson, A. E.,** *Trade Union and Social History.* Cass, 1974, pp. 4–5.

2 The old Poor Law

The parish basis: settlement, bastards, workhouses

Eighteenth-century poor relief included a number of disparate elements, connected in that they were wholly or partly administered by the parish. Pauper relief proper was usually classified into outdoor and indoor relief, but other administrative activities also affected the lives of the poor. They included the enforcement of the apprenticeship, bastardy, settlement and vagrancy laws. The parishioner who became unable to maintain himself or his family could expect to receive outdoor relief – a small pension, exemption from rates and assistance with his rent – or indoor relief, in the workhouse or poorhouse. He could expect to be helped in sickness, infirmity and old age, in unemployment or inadequate wages. He could expect to be buried, his children to be apprenticed, his wife to be assisted in childbirth, and his daughter helped to recover payments from the putative father of her illegitimate child. But he was secure of all this only in the parish where he had established a 'settlement.' Since the sixteenth century or before, the parish as the community had sunk deeply into the consciousness of the people. Attempts to widen the basis of Poor Law administration by grouping parishes, setting up large Houses of Industry, etc, always seemed, after the first flush of enthusiasm, to give way, and the parish to reassert itself.

Parish poor relief in the small farming community provided a personal service in which the pauper was relieved in familiar surroundings among his neighbours. A great deal of the poor rate was spent on small pensions. A. W. Ashby who as long ago as 1912 published a detailed study of Poor Law administration in the Warwickshire village of Tysoe, lists many such payments. In July 1727 three widows were receiving 1s 6d each, fortnightly. In January 1728 two of them were still receiving 1s 6d, while another woman was paid 8s and another widow 8s 6d.[1] The real meaning of these payments is unclear, as some may have maintained several dependants of the recipient. A recent study of the neighbouring village of Butlers Marston some 45 years later gives further details. In 1771 two men and one woman were being paid 1s a week each, one man 2s, another 3s, a woman 3s 6d, a man 2s 6d to 4s. The periods of receipt varied between nine weeks and more than a year.[2] Most of these sums were so small that they must have supplemented some other source of income. Probably some of the pensioners were partly supported by friends or relatives or patrons, but many of them may have had some way of scraping a part-living. This was not stated in the overseer's accounts, but the custom of supplementing inadequate casual earnings by parish payments seems to have been so well accepted as to require no special explanation.

The weekly pension was only part of the story. There were extensive lists of occasional payments and payments in kind. Funerals gave rise to such entries in the parish accounts as; 'Wm Haynes for ringen the bell for 2 berens – 4s.'[3] Then there were apprenticeship fees of £8 or more together with an outfit of clothes.[4] Sickness and childbirth produced entries for nurse, doctor or midwife.

In 1775 the Collins family was subsidised during the illness of Mrs Collins to the amount of £18 11s 1d. The children were boarded at the blacksmith's; they were shod and the boy breeched. Fuel, soap and meat were provided. Mrs Collins had a nurse (who was supplied with 'bear' at 10s, as much as the family's meat for six weeks), wine and brandy (eighteenth-century invalid foods) and oatmeal. Evidently she died, for her funeral cost £1 – after which Mr Collins was removed to another parish.[5]

Among payments in kind a main item was the subsidising of rents, another the provision of fuel. When Tysoe was enclosed, eighteen acres of 'fuel land' were set aside, the produce of which helped to buy coal for needy villagers. Payment in food was comparatively rare, but bread was sometimes provided, or later, bread money. Some Cambridgeshire villages distributed wheat, maslin (mixed corn), barley or rye. Essential articles of clothing included shifts and stays, bodices, petticoats, gowns, frocks and aprons, shoes, hats and gloves for women; leather shoes, shirts, breeches, smocks, and re-footed stockings for men. There were occasional overcoats or waistcoats.[6] There was also basic cottage furniture – 'Two chamber pots, 1s 6d '. Beds, straw mattresses, blankets, sheets, pots and pans, chairs, crockery, trenchers and candlesticks all figured in the lists.[7] The small parish provided for its poor without frills; but it provided on the basis of personal knowledge of immediate needs.

The parish basis which allowed poor relief to rest so securely on the local community had gross disadvantages. Under 43 Elizabeth both rating and expenditure were carried out by unpaid overseers, annually appointed by the Justices or elected at the vestry meeting. These burdensome offices which carried neither reward (if one excepts the rare cases of settlement gained in this way) nor social prestige, and which could render the occupant liable to be punished for negligence or surcharged for expenditure which displeased the local Justice of the Peace, were inevitably unpopular. Little seems to be known about the real ways in which overseers were selected, nor what inducements or methods of coercion were used to fill the offices. The list of overseers at Butlers Marston from 1713 to 1822 shows many overseers performing two-year stints, and the same names appearing repeatedly on the lists.[8] It was inevitable that many of those willing to serve were people who could make something out of it. The paupers in Bottisham workhouse, Cambridgeshire, in 1789 lived on a generous diet of cheese and beer purchased from the two overseers, while young Thomas Skipper was put to bird-scaring on one overseer's land at parish expense.[9] The Poor Law Commissioners of 1834 complained bitterly of the corruption in workhouse expenditure, when the local tradesmen sold food and other commodities to the workhouse masters unaudited and almost unchecked.[10] When roundsmen and other 'make work' (or work-spreading) systems developed, the overseers exercised an intolerable degree of personal power over labourers and small farmers. Where assessments to rates were not purely customary or 'frozen' there was also opportunity for fiscal bullying. The Poor Law Commissioners noted cases of high-rating unpopular clergy, probably in revenge for their taking of tithes.[11] Thus the parish was a source not only of intimacy but also of corruption.

The smallness of the normal parish mattered comparatively little in sparsely populated rural areas, but by the later eighteenth century it was adding to the inequalities of poor relief in towns, or growing industrial places. In many ports or manufacturing towns the industrial centres and middle-class suburbs were already under different parish administrations, and the wealthier ones could not be rated to help the poorer parts. In South Shields, already full of working-class tenements, the lower-middle-class dwellers in rented houses resented having to maintain the wives and children of seamen brought in to man the ships owned by the residents of wealthy neighbouring Westoe.[12]

If the reverse side of the intimacy of parish relief was the liability to corruption or victimisation, the most obvious cruelties of the old Poor Law appeared in the treatment of 'strangers' to the parish. It was embodied in the supervision of the settlement and bastardy laws.

The laws of settlement and removal went back at least to the sixteenth century. Provision for whipping sturdy beggars and removing them to their parish of settlement was included in the complex of social laws of 1597-1601. They drew their continuing vigour from the desire of every overseer to save the parish funds, but they were obviously rooted in the age-old suspicion of 'foreigners'. They tended to confuse labourers genuinely looking for work with tramps and vagrants, and to depress them into the vagrant class. They also threatened the stability of ordinary people and families living outside their legal parish. The Webbs suggest that respectable working men were being removed even in the early seventeenth century.[13] The practice was standardised by the Law of Settlement and Removal, 1662, under which the church-wardens and overseers, by warrant of two Justices, could remove any newcomer whom they thought likely to become a burden on the parish, unless he could give security to indemnify the parish, or owned property worth at least £10 a year. Although a newcomer could only be removed within forty days of his arrival, this protection was nullified by an Act of 1683 which provided that the forty days should be counted from the time the overseer received written notice of his presence. During the eighteenth century constant attempts to define settlement produced an increasingly complicated code of laws and practices. By the end of the century children up to the age of sixteen followed the settlement of their father, or if he died, that of their mother. Illegitimate children were settled in the parish in which they were born. Later in life, settlement could be acquired by residence, by apprenticeship, by being hired for a year, by paying parish rates or serving a parish office. A woman followed the settlement of her husband. According to figures from Cambridge and East Yorkshire, the majority of settlements were obtained by hiring and apprenticeship.[14]

The administration of the settlement laws showed the parish officer at his most oppressive. The overseers removed as many paupers, actual or potential, as they could, sometimes with callous disregard of their livelihood, happiness and health. Since removal was carried out before appeal against it to Quarter Sessions could be heard, families were sometimes removed in the overseer's cart backward and forward between reluctant parishes. In one case a mother and three children were removed seven times.[15] And removals were no rarity. Between 1730 and 1832 Butlers Marston, with a fairly constant population of about 300, had many removals both out of and into the village, while a number of settlement claims were confirmed.[16] Between 1759 and 1830 the East Yorkshire Magistrates heard 759 settlement cases, confirming 282 removals; and these were only the cases which were appealed.[17] Removal was a source of expense rather than saving, and settlement laws seem to have been the largest single source of inter-parochial litigation. In the four years 1831–34 the Chester Local Act Incorporation spent £82 19s 6d on uncontested removals alone.[18] The average annual cost of removal in Cambridgeshire Quarter Sessions was £9 12s 10d, but one case reached £29.[19] The lawyers, of course, had a vested interest in perpetuating this work, but many poor families could have been supported on less than it cost to remove them.

To the hardships of removal from work or the splitting of families[20] was added the injustice that the threat bore unequally on different classes of the population. Single women, widows with children, and deserted wives with families were most often removed. These were the most defenceless, and the most burdensome people. Next came men with families. Single men were more favoured, being a useful addition to the labour force, in some places taking lower wages than married men, and being less likely to burden the rates. Because of this it has been suggested that the settlement laws hindered marriage and encouraged illicit unions and the multiplication of illegitimate children.[21] But the provision that an illegitimate child followed its mother's settlement produced one of the most scandalous features of the old Poor Law, the shifting of women in the last stages of pregnancy from parish to parish in a kind of heartless game of 'Lose the Slipper'. Dr Marshall quotes an entry for 1722; 'To a big bellyd woman several days and nights at nursing at Robinsons, and conveying her to Chigivell after she had gathered strength to prevent her lying in here, she fell to pieces in two or three days there ... 17s 7d.'[22]

The settlement laws had other harmful results, many of them listed in the Royal Commission Report of 1834. Houses were pulled down behind migrating labourers to prevent newcomers gaining a settlement in the parish, with consequent housing shortages and overcrowding. Employers forced their farm hands to live across the parish border and walk long distances to work. Farmers turned their hands off just short of the year to prevent them gaining settlement. Overseers apprenticed children away from the parish, where they could acquire a new settlement and safely be forgotten.

The laws of settlement and removal came under powerful criticism from contemporary observers. Adam Smith thought that the variation of wages in different districts was 'probably owing to the obstruction which the law of settlements gives to a poor man who would carry his industry from one parish to another without a certificate'. He added that to remove a man who had committed no misdemeanour from the parish where he chose to reside was 'an evident violation of natural liberty and justice'.[23] The Poor Law Commissioners of 1834 characterised the rural labourers as serfs *adscripti glebae*.[24] And in 1836 Assistant Poor Law Commissioner Revans grumbled that the redundant population of Bishops Burton would not seek work in the wolds, where labour was scarce and wages high.[25]

Modern historians have been moved to ask whether these complaints that the laws of settlement tied men to the parish and prevented mobility of labour were justified. But they have found no simple answer. Most removals were between neighbouring parishes and over short distances.[26] But this could still prevent people from seeking work across the parish border unless it could be reached daily on foot. However, in the course of time, ways had been found of mitigating some of the effects of the settlement laws. The Act of 1662 had authorised the issue of certificates to workmen going to other parishes for harvesting. In the later eighteenth century these were increasingly extended to facilitate the migration of men seeking work outside their own parish. Provided they could get the overseer's agreement, the migrants thus preserved their original settlement rights, but the need for a certificate subjected the labourers to the control of the overseer, or of the farmers acting through him.[27] There were also increasing numbers of agreements between parishes to relieve either their own non-resident poor or each other's poor, so that the labourer who fell on hard times might be supported in the parish to which he had migrated. Such agreements mitigated the settlement laws. Moreover, it is unlikely that overseers in districts urgently in need of factory hands insisted too rigidly on the law of settlement, although in trade depressions some of them required that the unemployed should be supported by their parish of settlement, or even packed them off home. Again, much of the migrant labour was Irish, and as there was no law of settlement in Ireland, Irish families could only be removed under the Vagrancy Acts. Some were so removed, and simply dumped in the Irish ports.

The first serious attempt to loosen the grip of parish settlement was Pitt's Act of 1795 prohibiting the removal of labourers until they actually became chargeable to parish funds. This must have lifted the shadow of arbitrary removal from a number of individuals. However, continuing removals indicate that the Act was but a palliative.

To assess in detail the effects of settlement on the mobility of labour would require examination in a large sample number of parishes, not only of the removal cases but also of all other circumstances tending to discourage the unemployed and the inadequately paid from seeking work elsewhere. And this would be a well-nigh impossible task.[28]

The bastardy laws were involved with the Poor Law because, once the Church Courts had relinquished their grip, unmarried mothers who could not support their children were punished not for the sin of unchastity but for the crime of burdening the parish.[29] An Act of James I modified by another of 1810 authorised Justices to commit to prison 'a lewd woman who shall have a bastard which may be chargeable to the parish', but enforcement was patchy. In the later eighteenth century, few women were sent to prison, at least for having one illegitimate child. Instead the parish officials set about relieving the rates of the cost of mother and baby. The pregnant woman might be dumped over the parish border. If this was likely to be impossible a forced marriage might be arranged, especially if the putative father came from another parish, so that removal swiftly followed the dismal wedding. If this was impossible the woman could be urged to name the father so that he could be arrested and compelled to give a bond to indemnify the parish against the costs of the child, or failing this, a recognisance with security to appear at the next Quarter Sessions. A poor and friendless man unable to give bond or surety would find himself in gaol waiting the birth of the baby, so that the Justices could have the two brought into court to see if there was a family likeness. The forced marriages, with the man brought shackled to the church door, were recognised as scandalous. So was the opportunity afforded to 'loose' women to swear their children, rightly or wrongly, to rich employers' sons. The parish authorities rarely recovered the whole cost of supporting an unmarried mother, but they did recover a substantial part of it. Between 1829 and 1834 the parish of Leven, East Yorkshire, recovered about one-half of its annual expenditure of some £35 on chargeable bastards from the putative fathers.[30] In many parishes the weekly payments awarded by Quarter Sessions against the father (and these varied with his apparent ability to pay) were handed over to the mother in the form of a pension. This might make her better off than an honest widow left destitute with children, and might even provide her with some kind of dowry for a legal marriage. In these strange commercial proceedings there was too much to excite jealousy and affront common morality. Nor was the threat of the punishment of putative fathers, which facilitated blackmail, an idle one. In Cambridgeshire between 1760 and

1770 ten out of thirty men charged at Quarter Sessions as putative fathers went to the House of Correction. Between 1796 and 1834 eighty-nine were committed for failing to indemnify the parish.[31]

The parish unit hindered the development of the most notorious Poor Law institution, the workhouse. The aim of 'setting the poor on work' went back to 43 Elizabeth, but if a workhouse or House of Industry was even to cover its costs it needed a labour force worth organising, and this in turn required a grouping of parishes. Since the initiative of John Carey in obtaining in 1696 a local Act incorporating the Bristol City parishes into a union for the purpose of building a workhouse, there were periodical waves of enthusiasm for creating large pauper units, usually in the hope that they could be made to yield a profit,[32] Knatchbull's general Workhouse Act of 1723 empowered parishes singly or jointly to build workhouses. In the 1750s the example of a House of Industry at Nacton, South Suffolk, in which the poor were set to work weaving hemp corn sacks, making cordages and plough lines, and spinning wool for the Norwich weavers, led to the incorporation of more East Anglian parishes into hundreds to build Houses of Industry. In the 1770s Shrewsbury's new House of Industry started a wave of interest in the West Country. Gilbert's Act of 1782 was unusual in that it authorised unions to build workhouses for those who were not able-bodied labourers or their families (who could be relieved outside). In an age of female and infant labour this was not necessarily in conflict with the aim of covering costs. Then there was Bentham's plan for Panopticon workhouses, also intended to extract profitable labour from the poor.

Apart from making money the purpose of the founders of these schemes varied with contemporary attitudes towards the poor. If Carey was a philanthropist, the 1720s saw the beginning of the deterrent workhouse, and the 'offer' of the workhouse as a condition of relief, to drive idle paupers off the rates. The General Workhouse Act of 1723 provided that a person refusing to be relieved in a workhouse was to be 'put out of the book.'[33]

All these initiatives encountered the same stumbling blocks: that labour not engaged for its suitability for the tasks could not be made to pay, especially in an institution devised to keep out all but the most unfortunate or helpless; that if it did pay it would undercut the local industries; that large committees of local gentry were inefficient and quickly lost enthusiasm. Surviving workhouses tended to fall into the absolute power of workhouse masters, who secured continually varying contracts from the parishes or unions, mismanaged the houses until the inmates rioted, and then sought relief from the burden of administering pauper labour by hiring out their paupers to private employers. Thus most of these schemes collapsed, and the small parish unit reasserted itself.[34] In 1786 Bottisham in Cambridgeshire consisted of six adjoining cottages and the old poorhouse. In 1776 Soham, the largest workhouse in the county, had 60 residents. Royston had 26, 14 of them children; the 34 parishes of the Isle of Ely had 19 workhouses. There were various Schools of Industry in Cambridgeshire employing in all 140 children, but the largest had only 10 inmates.[35] Only in a few rural areas and in the big cities, especially London, were there workhouses with really large numbers. But in London, as elsewhere, the general mixed workhouse, or poorhouse, became a squalid dwelling rather than a place of labour.

Wars and enclosures

From about the 1760s onwards the conditions in which the poor law had to operate began to change. The end of the eighteenth and beginning of the nineteenth centuries saw a coincidence of various factors which influenced agriculture and the life of the rural (as well as the urban) poor in different ways. There were wars, especially the long French wars of 1793–1815, which on the one hand kept a more or less sheltered home market for food, but on the other hand reduced the possibility of mitigating the effects of bad harvests by imports. The French wars kept farm wages, as well as the incomes of small farmers, at a reasonable level,[36] but when there were bad years as in 1795, 1800, 1801 and 1812, prices rose above the rate at which poor people could buy sufficient food.[37] Poor relief was then required to relieve near-famine conditions due to scarcity. More far-reaching if, for a long time, less obvious was the growth of population which set in around 1760, and between 1781 and 1851 had swollen the total population of England and Wales from about 8,900,000 to about 20,000,000.[38] Whatever the reasons – and they are still disputed – and whatever the distribution, over-population of the countryside was an inescapable long-term cause of rural distress. Finally there were the enclosures of whole villages and their common lands which came to a peak towards the end of the French wars.

With prices of the staple food fluctuating violently from year to year, relief on a scale which took into consideration the price of bread and the number of mouths to feed would not seem inappropriate. Indeed, it probably fitted the case better than the less elastic method of wage-fixing by the Justices then being abandoned. In 1783 the Justices of the Cambridgeshire Hundred of Whittlesford met and decided that 'every man who has a family and behaves himself seemly, be allowed the price of five quartern loaves per week, with two quartern loaves added for each member of his family.'[39] Here was an early example of what later became known as the 'Speenhamland System', i.e. formal relief scales based on the price of bread and the number of children under seven years old in the family.[40] The degree to which Speenhamland dominated poor relief – its extent and its periodisation – have been subject to considerable dispute. There are now indications that it waned some time after 1818. Following the rates crisis of that year, and the report of Sturges Bourne's Select Committee, Poor Law expenditure decreased and for a time levelled off. The chief cause of distress after the end of the Napoleonic wars was less violent changes in food prices than continuing un- and under-employment. Family allowances, devised to keep the income of poor families at some locally fixed subsistence level, seem at least partly to have taken the place of bread scales.[41]

The effects of enclosure on the standard of living of the rural poor have been much disputed. But it is difficult to believe that loss of access to commons and wastes did not inflict hardship on smallholders (why else were 'fuel fields' established by the more far-sighted enclosers?). The squatters without title to part of the land, and those who could not afford to enclose their share, came into the labour market when labour was becoming over-plentiful. Mrs Lane has shown from the overseers' accounts at Butlers Marston that within two years of the enclosure of the parish new families came into the relief list, while items for winter fuel appeared among the payments.[42]

During the French wars these effects were mitigated by the continuing demand for food and therefore for labourers on the new enclosures, especially on arable lands. When expansion collapsed after the war, the results of enclosure coinciding with over-population were revealed in an almost inexhaustible reservoir of surplus labour.

The paternalist phase. Pitt's Poor Bill

From the 1770s onwards the Poor Rate grew, slowly at first, rapidly during the French wars. Between 1792 and 1812 it almost trebled, rising from £2,600,000 to £6,500,000. By 1818 it had reached nearly £8,000,000.[43] Public attitudes moved with it; in the 1780s a trend towards a practical sympathetic paternalism is discernible. Miss Hampson writes, 'It is impossible to peruse, for example, the voluminous interparochial correspondence of this period arising specially over questions of settlement – without recognising a more frequent note of spontaneous kindliness than in the early part of the century.'[44] In bastardy cases too, there is some evidence that overseers were not unhelpful to unmarried mothers, and did not go out of their way to press charges which would result in the imprisonment of one or both parents.[45] This phase of opinion was reflected in Gilbert's Act of 1782, encouraging parishes to form unions to set up workhouses. These were to be emptied of able-bodied labourers (the element always used to justify a deterrent workhouse), and rendered fitting homes for the orphans, aged and sick poor. The able-bodied were to be found work near their own homes. This, as the Webbs pointed out, 'almost necessarily' involved the free use by the Justices of their power of ordering outdoor relief.[46] Thus the phase was associated with the increasing domination of Poor Law administration by the Justices of the Peace. It reached its culmination in the Speenhamland decision of 1795 and Pitt's unsuccessful Poor Bill of 1797.

The phase saw a search for methods of helping the poor other than conventional poor relief, and a number of remedies for extreme poverty were canvassed. Among these were Friendly Societies of which, according to a parliamentary report of 1803, there were some 9,672 in England and Wales, with 704,350 members, or 8 per cent of the population.[47] Gilbert's Act included a clause for contributions for the support of these societies by county committees; and under the same inspiration between 1780 and 1820 a succession of plans for social insurance were laid before parliament.[48] Some of them were surprisingly sophisticated in detail, one proposing that employers should levy graded contributions from their employees' wages,[49] another proposing a nation-wide society with compulsory contributions and payments on an actuarial basis to be supplied by Dr Richard Price.[50] After the war such schemes were revived, the most interesting being John Curwen's plan for a national Friendly Society which would raise contributions from employers and workmen, to be supplemented up to one-third from the Poor Rate.[51] As late as 1833 George Poulett Scrope, the leader of the rather feeble opposition to the Poor Law Amendment Bill in the House of Commons, was proposing an employers' fund to insure their labourers against destitution; 'a measure which would throw the expense of maintaining the aged, impotent, and destitute poor precisely upon those persons who have profited by their labour'.[52]

Along with Friendly Societies and their later alternative (and to some extent rival) the Savings Bank movement, there were suggestions for making the rural poor self-sufficient by means of allotments. Arthur Young, the champion of cottage smallholding, wanted every labourer with three or more children to have half an acre of land on which to grow potatoes or to graze cows. In 1801 he put forward an ambitious plan to settle a million families on waste lands, each with a cottage and one acre.[53] Sir Thomas Bernard and William Wilberforce's Society for Bettering the Conditions and Increasing the Comforts of the Poor made suggestions for leased family smallholdings.[54] Robert Owen's 'Pauper Parallelograms' only differed in that they were communal rather than individual, and the tradition can be followed through the Chartist O'Connor's land scheme even up to proposals in the 1930s that the Welsh unemployed should be set to work on smallholdings.

Clauses in Pitt's Poor Bill for Friendly Societies (an Act had been passed in 1793 protecting their funds) as well as those for a cow, or cow money which excited Bentham's derision, were part of the same body of suggestions. It is important to emphasise them since they disprove the impression fostered by the reformers of 1834 and long preserved in the canon of Poor Law history, that no alternative was offered to the perpetuation of a deterrent Poor Law. Whether they could ever have provided a comprehensive alternative to poor relief is another question. Social insurance contributions were probably not possible from the very low wages of farm labourers and contributory pensions were furthest from the reach of those who might need them most. Something as radical if much more carefully worked out than Tom Paine's extraordinarily modern-seeming proposals for state-financed welfare went nearer to meeting the case, but was politically impossible.[55] Allotments were common in the South although some farmers discouraged them as diversions from the proper use of labour – on the farmers' land. But it is doubtful whether smallholdings could have survived in an age when farming was rapidly increasing in scale. They would also have exposed their occupiers to all the old hazards of bad weather and failed crops.

As the Poor Rate continued to rise, predictably (at least in the light of hindsight), sympathy with the suffering and costly poor began to wear out. It would be impossible to date such a swing of opinion, which was never complete, always patchy, and began in different places at different times. But it can be detected in the pronouncements of intellectuals such as Bentham, and in the administration of parishes by overseers and Justices. Bentham's attack on Pitt's Poor Bill is an early example of the change of tone.[56] Bentham agreed with the abolition of wage-fixing, which, he considered, was an intervention in the labour market calculated to drive men out of employment. But he disagreed with the allowance system because it offered the idle and the negligent exactly the same economic rewards as the diligent and the industrious. The child allowance was mere profusion, which would encourage parents to keep their children idle in order to claim it. Schools of Industry proposed in the Bill would be too costly for a parish and too remote for the children to attend if built by a union. 'First comes the pay of the *idler*, made up to an *equality* with the *earnings* of the *industrious*; then come the *extra children* of the idler to be put in whatsoever number upon the *pension-list*.' As for the cow-money clause, it was profusion in capital, which would be given through favouritism, or to buy votes at an election. The cows would graze on an over-stocked common, go off milk, and die. A General Enclosure Bill which would profit the rich and raise the wages of labour would do more. The clauses offering help in the apprenticing of poor children (which seem to have done little more than continue traditional parish practices) he objected to as putting people of inferior class into positions which would have been occupied by those of superior class. The whole Bill was just an excuse for spending, which would throw more industrious hands on the parish. 'To banish not only indigence but dependence it would be necessary to banish not only misfortune but improvidence.'[57]

Bentham was at this time occupied in drawing up plans for his own 'Pauper Kingdom', and there were large areas on which he and Pitt agreed, such as education and apprenticeship (despite his grouching), savings schemes and savings banks. Both, too, believed pauper labour could be made to pay. But the change of tone and emphasis were ominous. Pitt's Houses of Industry were to be replaced by a systematic network of 'Panopticon' workhouses into which the indigent were to be swept by force and retained on a minimum diet until they could earn their release by profitable labour.[58] Bentham was busy reviving the principle of the old deterrent workhouse under the catch-formula 'less eligibility'. He had private reasons for his sour tone towards Pitt himself, whom he believed responsible for the delay in accepting his plans for a panopticon prison, but his pamphlet (whether or not, as he claimed, it had an influence in securing the rejection of Pitt's Bill) did mark the beginning of a change of attitude towards the poor.

The practical effects of this change were apparent later. By 1818 the first of the new 'well-regulated' workhouses on which the 1834 model was to be based, was already in being, at Bingham, Lincolnshire.[59] After the rates crisis of 1817–19 more of these were founded. By 1834 many parishes could object to the new Act on the ground that they had already got rid of allowances in aid of wages and cut down the rates. After 1818 the Bingham overseers (and it must have been with Justices' approval) ceased to assist unmarried mothers and brought increasing numbers of bastardy cases which resulted in putative fathers going to gaol.[60] In Lindsey generally, bastardy orders multiplied after 1800. The permissive and paternal phase of the old Poor Law, which Pitt would not have dared to challenge in face of French war and working-class unrest, was receding piecemeal.

Arguments and attitudes

The swing in attitudes and administration was reflected in the writings of social philosophers. Throughout the eighteenth century there had been dual lines of argument. These were not about poverty. All but a few eccentric radicals accepted the fact that in all societies the vast majority would be poor. Contemporaries like Paine and later Owen had to be eccentrics to oppose the accepted realities of the age, for no society had ever experienced anything different. Moreover, it was also accepted that the civilisation of the higher orders was supported by the labour of the lower ones. The differences were about the destitute poor, the casualties of the economic and social system. To oversimplify, there were those who believed in the duty of the privileged to look after the unprivileged; and there were those who saw destitution as a consequence of if not a punishment for personal and social inadequacies.[61]

The first attitude was strikingly expressed in a quotation from the Bishop of Cloyne given in Sir Frederick Eden's *State of the Poor*. 'How can they justify their exclusive property in the *common heritage* of mankind, unless they consent, in return, to provide for the subsistence of the Poor, who were excluded from those common rights by the laws of the Rich, to which they were never parties?'[62] It might be proper to call such an attitude the conscience of landed property; and whatever may be considered about its practical effects, it enshrined a long-lived theme, perpetuating itself in the often-expressed regrets of Victorian Tory philanthropists that the rich had lost their personal connection with and concern for the poor.[63] Its influence was, however, partly counter-balanced by a lively fear that the poor might be too easily convinced that they would never be allowed to become destitute, and relax their labour, or even ape their betters and get ideas above their station. Nevertheless, the idea of a right to subsistence for the less fortunate accorded well with the older practices of parish relief, of which it was in part a rationalisation; and it was important enough to draw a barrage of contemptuous criticism from the Commissioners of 1834.

The second attitude, a kind of secular puritanism in which destitution was the reward of idleness on this earth as damnation might be the reward of sin in the next, was also a conscience-quietener.[64] The emotive association of the words 'improvidence', 'idleness', 'vice' and 'crime', in various permutations and combinations with the word 'poverty', went back at least to Defoe. 'The distresses of the Poor', Defoe had written, 'are either owing to their infirmities merely providential, as sickness and old age, or to the improvidence of the labouring classes.'[65] People find it hard to accept that avoidable suffering is the consequence of their own meanness or timidity, and prefer to impute blame where they are unwilling to offer help, or willing only to offer it on penal terms.[66] The association of words which implied that the destitute, especially those who could be called 'able-bodied', were destitute by their own fault, quietened the conscience of those who suffered from or feared the growing cost of poor relief, and discouraged attempts to find the deeper causes of destitution. Or when the causes were found it created an invisible barrier between the finding and its practical application. Bentham himself constructed an elaborate 'Table of Cases calling for Relief' as a guide to the classification of paupers in his proposed workhouses. In this he devoted one column to accidental causes of worklessness such as bad weather and trade recession, and another to avoidable causes such as improvidence and bad character. A copy of this paper found its way into Chadwick's papers. There is no doubt that Bentham and his successors in Poor Law reform recognised the existence of involuntary unemployment through lack of jobs. Yet the whole moral justification of the deterrent workhouse was that it would drive those able to work into finding employment. It was striking that Bentham's supporter and associate in police and prison reform, Patrick Colquhoun, who also made an analysis of causes of destitution, or 'indigence', disagreed with the idea of deterrent workhouses, calling them 'gaols without guilt.'[67] Bentham's main contribution to Poor Law reform was in encouraging statements of feeling which clouded analysis. He also devised formulae which enabled Poor Law policy to be based on this feeling even while they disguised harsh intentions under strange terminology. They included the distinction between poverty and destitution, which he called 'indigence', and the test of indigence, that relief should be offered on terms 'less eligible' than the conditions of life available to the 'free' labourer. Apart from these definitions, Bentham's Pauper Kingdom was mainly an advertisement for the Panopticon workhouse, or another of the many schemes advanced by social planners which littered the decades preceding 1834.

The growing influence of punitive or deterrent thinking on the Poor

Law was greatly reinforced by the political economists, who began to find a wide readership towards the end of the Napoleonic war. Thomas Malthus' *Essay on Population*, published in 1798, was aimed both at puncturing Pitt's Poor Bill and at quenching the euphoric utopianism of radical supporters of the idea of progress as embodied in the French Revolution. Malthus saw all diversion of scarce resources to unproductive mouths as an acceleration of the day when population would outstrip the supply of food and other essentials. Malthus' thesis, whatever its later modifications, was a stronger argument than that of the Benthamites, undermining all charitable relief, not only public but private, not only to the able-bodied but to the sick and helpless. The association of poverty with vice and crime reappeared, but this time vice and crime were the agents of inevitable destruction. There was an eschatological flavour about Malthus' arguments which promoted an entire quiescence in the face of social distress from whatever cause. Along with the wages-fund theory, the so-called iron law of wages, in which not only higher wages but all poor relief diverted capital from its constructive task of creating commodities and ensuring employment, Malthusianism envisaged any Poor Law as a positively harmful agent. Malthusian influence, at its strongest during the rates crisis and the Select Committees of 1817–19, nearly brought about the destruction of the Poor Law. If such a solution was politically intolerable, so that the Select Committee of 1818 did not even dare to recommend it clearly, Malthusian influence never really died out of Poor Law thinking.[68] It was revealed in the appointment of Sturges Bourne, Chairman of the Select Committee of 1817 to the Royal Commission of 1832 (although he did not take an active part in it); in the speeches of Lord Brougham on the Poor Law Amendment Bill, in the avowed opinions of various Assistant Commissioners, and in some of the Poor Law Commission's regulations after 1834.

Thus deterrent attitudes to poor relief waxed and covered themselves with powerful theoretical justifications. Inevitably these attitudes were class-based, for the social gulf between rich and very poor presented an almost impassable barrier to imagination. But they were not wholly attributable to class, for the conflict between paternalist and deterrent or punitive thinking caused divisions within the professional and gentry classes. Moreover, harsh attitudes were commonest among the lesser ratepayers, the smallholders, the artisans, shopkeepers and clerks, who had the greatest inducements to them in the fear of rising taxes, fear of the mob, and above all, fear of being themselves sucked down into the indigent. This 'petty bourgeoisie' had the strongest temptation to repudiate those whom the cost of helping was high. This was well understood by the Poor Law reformers of 1834, who built their new Poor Law administration upon it.

Select Committees

Between 1817 and 1832 few years passed without some Select Committee or parliamentary enquiry upon some aspect of the problems of labourers' wages and poor relief. The 1824 Select Committee on Labourers' Wages was the most openly Malthusian in its arguments, attributing the current distress to over-population directly encouraged by children's allowances and the supplementation of wages from the rates. However, after 1819 the demand for repeal of the old Poor Law gave way to less radical demands for its reform. Many of the practical recommendations of the Royal Commission report of 1834 were foreshadowed in these committees. The Committee of 1818 proposed select vestries (soon embodied in an enabling Act) and paid Assistant Overseers. A Lords' Committee of 1831 complained about the lack of systematic information about expenditure of the Poor Rate. Committees of 1824 and 1828 wanted to distinguish between the unemployed and the low paid by cutting off the allowance system and occupying those without work in parish employment. However, from 1828 onwards reference began to be heard to the repression of pauperism by 'well-regulated' workhouses. The influence of the Nottingham reformers was spreading.[69] In 1831 the Lords' Committee heard evidence from the Rev J. T. Becher, magistrate, prison reformer, workhouse manager and pamphleteer, about his 'anti-pauper' system, whereby Southwell workhouse had been devised not to keep the poor in but to drive them out. By this means the inferior classes were constrained 'to know and feel how demoralising and degrading is the compulsory relief drawn from the parish to silence the clamour and to satisfy the cravings of wilful and woeful indigence; but how sweet and wholesome is that food, and how honourable is that independence, which is earned by persevering and honest industry.'[70]

In these committee reports Friendly Society schemes and allotments continued to be recommended, but with declining conviction and emphasis. Friendly Societies, savings banks and other self-help activities were still encouraged by the government, but not as substitutes for the Poor Law. The mass augmentation of contributions from public finance necessary to make these institutions reach down to the bottom of the economic and social scale where dwelt the mass of day labourers and agricultural workers was unacceptable. Moreover, it threatened to change them from realisations of the principle of self-help into vehicles of state support.[71] By 1831 two events had occurred which made it possible to bring the long and hesitant search of the governing classes for a solution to the Poor Law problem to an active conclusion. The Whigs had come to power, faced by a Conservative opposition of which the most influential, Peelite section was in substantial agreement with the government on fundamental economic and social policies. And the labourers' revolt had removed the scruples of country gentry about severe measures to abolish allowances, roundsmen, and bastardy cases. Indeed, they were ready to grasp at any plan which they could be persuaded would reduce pauperism and curb agrarian sedition.

The Royal Commission of 1832

In February 1832 the Chancellor of the Exchequer, Lord Althorp, announced the setting up of a Royal Commission to enquire into the operation of the Poor Laws. The enquiry was evidently considered important, for it was initiated in the middle of the struggle for the Reform Bill. An all-party commission of nine members was appointed, including Bishop Blomfield of London, the Bishop of Chester, William Sturges Bourne of the 1817 Select Committee, and Nassau William Senior, Professor of Political Economy at Oxford; William Coulson and Edwin Chadwick, a young barrister suggested by Senior, were both protégés of the aged Jeremy Bentham (who died that year). The work of gathering information was directed by Senior and Chadwick, who also wrote the report. Twenty-six travelling Assistant Commissioners armed with questionnaires visited between them 3,000 out of the 15,000 parishes and townships in England and Wales. Chadwick served as Assistant Commissioner for East London and Berkshire, a role which enabled him to inspect both rural and urban poverty and fortify his opinion that a reformed Poor Law would suit both types of area; as well as enabling him to draw a salary.

The final report, evidence and answers to the questionnaires, filled seven large volumes, but as historians have noticed, the Commissioners had made up their minds upon the drift of their proposals long before all the information had been gathered or the report written.[72] Nassau Senior was writing to Brougham with suggestions for radical alterations in Poor Law administration as early as September 1832, while Chadwick's report on East London and Berkshire was published, along with other 'extracts of information' from the Assistant Commissioners a year before the final report was drafted. This report was eventually written in a hurry, at Cabinet behest, which may account for the state of confusion which characterised its construction, and which makes orderly description of it difficult.[73]

The Royal Commission Report differed from the reports of the preceding parliamentary Select Committees chiefly in its greater length, deeper analysis and its air of self-confidence. Each section opened with an historical survey of the statutes governing the administration of the particular branch of the Poor Law it purported to examine, and the whole was neatly divided by headings. However, on further examination the marks of haste appear; for the headings do not always relate to the subject matter, while the same topics are often discussed in separate parts of the report, reflecting, no doubt, the division of authorship between Senior and Chadwick. It must be added that the Commissioners stated their case with great cogency, illustrating each point with a string of quotations from the answers to their questionnaire or from the Assistant Commissioners' reports. They did not offer statistical evidence. It is improbable that their conclusions would have been different if they had.[74]

The report began with a history of poor relief, in the course of which the Commissioners emphasised that they were not attacking the Elizabethan Poor Law, but attempting to purify it of the abuses of the last two centuries. Their section on definitions accepted the old statutes' separation of paupers into the able-bodied and the impotent, and then proceeded to discover the source of contemporary abuses principally in the outdoor relief afforded to the able-bodied on account of themselves or their families. An attack followed on relief in kind, identified largely as exemption from rates on cottage property, and help with rent and on 'what are called pensions of from 1s to 3s a week' given to widows 'without any reference to their age or strength, or powers of obtaining an independent subsistance, but simply as widows'.[75]

The report discussed relief given to the workless, in the form of money paid without requirement to work ('a bounty on idleness and crime'), or in return for answering a daily roll call or for nominal labour in a parish gravel pit.[76] The sections which followed, on allowances in aid of wages, on the various roundsman systems and on the Labour Rate were the most detailed and among the most difficult and interesting in the report. They examined the abuses which the Commissioners hoped to abolish.

In describing allowances in aid of wages the report gave several examples of bread scales (the 'Speenhamland System') mostly from the year 1821, but devoted more attention to family allowances (or children's allowances), giving examples of more recent date.[77] There is no indication that the Commissioners failed to see the difference. Their fundamental objection was to any division of wages between the employer and payer of Poor Rate. This created what would nowadays be called a 'poverty trap', in which the labourer received the same whether he worked well or ill, with special skill or without it. He soon became demoralised and pauperised,[78] and this pauperisation spread wherever the division was maintained. Equally serious was the fact that the system encouraged early marriages and large families, since the pauper could claim additional allowance with each child, and thus the surplus labour was increased.

In many places (and unfortunately the Commissioners provided no means by which it could easily be ascertained how far they coincided with the allowance areas) the parishes operated what have since been called 'make-work' devices, although 'work-spreading' devices would be an equally appropriate name.[79] These included various forms of the roundsman system, of which the Commissioners identified two. By one (known as the ticket or stem system from the ticket carried by the pauper to authorise his employment, and signed by the employer to inform the overseer that he had fulfilled his conditions of relief) the labour of one or more paupers was sold to an employer. He paid the wages, and received back, under contract, part of what he had paid. By the other form of the system, the pauper received part of his wages from the employer and part from the overseer direct.[80] The Labour Rate, which seems to have been a later replacement for the roundsman system, and had been legalised by an Act of 1832, provided for the employment of applicants for relief by private employers, in place of or in supplement to, their Poor Rate.[81] The Commissioners identified at least three kinds. By one each ratepayer had to employ labourers in proportion to his assessment to the Poor Rate. By another, and the most frequent, the farmers shared among them all the labour, including the surplus of the parish. By the third and least usual, all the occupiers had to employ labour according not to their rate assessment but their rent.

Each of these work-spreading devices carried abuses, in addition to those of the ordinary allowance in aid of wages. The labour of roundsmen was sold at periodical intervals, on market days or fairs. Apart from this humiliating procedure, roundsmen provided a threat to the security of other labourers, especially those employed on small farms. In 1835 Assistant Commissioner Revans reported that in Patrington, East Yorkshire, twelve of the principal farmers had gradually dismissed their workmen to make a bargain with the parish to pay part of their wages from the rates.

> To such a degree had this system proceeded that the overseer used to put up the Labour of a number of them for Sale, for the coming week or fortnight; and it has frequently happened that those who had previously received and are now receiving 14 or 15 shillings a week, were sold at these parish auctions for 3 shillings: the difference between which, and a sufficiency to maintain their families was given by the parish, principally Shopkeepers in the Town.[82]

The various forms of roundsman system which enabled the richer farmers to obtain their unskilled labour at half price must have compelled the small man faced with a roundsman he couldn't employ to dismiss his own workman, and then perhaps take him back on half pay and the allowance.

The Labour Rate differed from the roundsman system principally in that while the labour was shared out, the labourer was paid entirely by his employer. It was therefore outside the allowance system.[83] But it invited an abuse common to both, that of spreading the cost of surplus labour onto the weakest parishioners. Allowance and roundsman systems enabled the wealthier employers of labour to get varying portions of their wages expenditure paid by their neighbours in the form of rates. Chief targets for this shifting of burdens were the smallholders, shopkeepers in the small town or village, and the parish clergyman, especially if he was unpopular through taking tithes. A parish whose dominating clique adopted the Labour Rate spread its burden not by driving up rates in order to pay what should have been wages, but by compelling small men to take on hands they didn't need and couldn't employ, or pay instead. The report gives a long list of such cases, concluding that Labour Rate might have worked if some way of ensuring that labour was allocated fairly had been found, but that it was impossible to prevent the strong and wealthy burdening the defenceless by it.[84] And in addition to this abuse, where labour was shared out within the parish, those working in the parish whose legal settlements were elsewhere were dismissed and removed to make way for the local labourers, regardless of ability or desert. In all these work-spreading devices to save the Poor Rate, preference was given to the man with a family to support, and thus the unmarried worker found himself at the back of the queue, both for relief and employment.

These sections of the Poor Law Commission Report amounted to an indictment, not of the pauper, who the Commissioners admitted was a helpless victim, but specifically of the wealthy tenant farmers who often controlled the rural vestries. These used their power on the one hand to burden their weaker neighbours, on the other to keep and even create a pool of labour, half-paid, or paid one day and discharged the next, for their own advantage. They explained through the mouths of witnesses, how industrious workmen who had saved their earnings to obtain a comfortable cottage and a little property were denied employment by the farmers until they had consumed all their savings and were forced onto relief. Yet the Commissioners never denounced the greed and selfishness of farmers in the emotive words they used of paupers. This harsher tone reappeared in the section on the effects of the Poor Law on those actually relieved, in which they described the idle, feckless and insubordinate habits, the dirty cottages and ragged children of the pauperised labourers.[85]

The Commissioners saw less harm in the relief of the non-able-bodied, since these were no part of the labour force, but their discussion of the effects of the Poor Law on the old, the young, the sick and the disabled provided opportunity for an attack on the family morals of the lower orders. If the deficiencies of filial and parental affection were to be supplied by the parish, and the natural motives for the exercise of these virtues thus withdrawn, we must replace them with artificial stimulants, and make 'fines, distress warrants, or imprisonment act as substitutes for gratitude and love'.[86] They rejected the conventional distinction between deserving and undeserving poor, claiming that attempts to base relief upon it led merely to favouritism, discontent, clamour, intimidation, greater profusion, and the encouragement of all the poor to claim a *right* to a reasonable, fair or adequate subsistence, which could never be defined or settled.[87] Of those parents who took advantage of indoor relief to shift responsibility for some of their children by putting them in the workhouse, they declared, 'It appears to the pauper that the Government has undertaken to repeal, in his favour, the ordinary laws of nature: to enact that the children shall not suffer from the misconduct of their parents, the wife for that of the husband, or the husband for that of the wife!'[88]

A similar moralism pervaded the section on bastardy. The Commissioners proposed to repeal the Acts under which the parents of illegitimate children could be sent to prison, and stop the actions of prospective or actual mothers of bastards against putative fathers for the maintenance of the child. 'As a further step towards the natural state of things' the support of the child would fall on the mother, or her relatives, and if she could not support it she would have to go to the workhouse. A bastard would then be 'what Providence appears to have ordained that it should be, a burthen on its mother, and, where she cannot maintain it, on her parents'.[89] In future the penalties of illegitimacy would fall on the woman instead of on the man.

Apart from paupers and unmarried mothers, the class which incurred the Commissioners' disapprobation was that of the large landowners. These, especially in their role as Justices, they held responsible for debauching Poor Law administration by encouraging the allowance system and by reversing the verdicts of overseers who refused individual applications for relief. They castigated the magistrates who felt themselves entitled to settle the weekly income of labourers and act as their protectors,[90] even though, as they pointed out, the landowner was the greatest loser by profusion, the occupier passing on the cost of his rates in reduced rent.

After dealing faithfully with the corrupt practices of open vestries and unpaid overseers, the Commissioners spent some time rejecting allotment schemes as alternatives to the Poor Law. Allotments were dangerous in times of bad harvest. They should be left to private contract. But despite all this Senior and Chadwick would not recommend the abolition of relief to destitute able-bodied paupers. Refusal was 'repugnant to the common sentiments of mankind'. The spread of pauperism could be stopped by administering it on the first principle of sound administration, that the situation of the relieved 'shall not be made really or apparently so eligible as the situation of the independent labourer of the lowest class'.[91] As the means of enforcing the principle they turned to the deterrent workhouse of the early eighteenth century as revived in the Model Houses of the Nottinghamshire and Berkshire reformers.[92] They recommended that, after a specific period, no further relief to able-bodied persons should be given except in a well-regulated workhouse. Relief to children under sixteen should be considered as relief to their parents.

Far the most original section of the report lay in its recommendations for enforcement machinery. There would be a Central Board of three Commissioners, directed to frame regulations for the workhouses, for the amount and nature of the relief to be given and the labour to be exacted in them. As far as practicable, these were to be uniform throughout the country.[93] Because the parishes were too small, the Central Board would be empowered to incorporate groups of them into units large enough to provide four or more workhouses. These would be classified to provide for: (1) the aged and really impotent; (2) the children; (3) able-bodied females; and (4) able-bodied males, each in separate houses. Each class could then receive appropriate treatment, and an enthusiastic picture was painted of the old enjoying their indulgences without torment from the boisterous, the children properly educated, and the able-bodied subjected to such courses of labour as would repel the indolent and vicious.[94] Useful work would be provided in making essential goods for the workhouse, or in drainage or roadmaking. All workhouses would be provisioned by tender under free competition, and a strict system of accounts would be enforced.[95] The Central Board, although not appointing the workhouse officials, would specify their qualifications and dismiss those found unsatisfactory. It was hoped they would be free from local ties and politics, chosen, perhaps, from army NCOs or from the poorer clergy.[96] Having rested the cure of pauperism on a penal workhouse regime, the Commissioners now contrived to make their system sound 'salutary', if not positively cosy.

Since the object of the deterrent workhouse was avowedly to drive the able-bodied adult out to seek independent work, a key recommendation should have been abolition or radical reform of the settlement laws. But while denouncing settlement the Commissioners did little to end it. In fact settlement reform fell victim to the high priority given to the workhouse system and the machinery devised to support it. Settlement was the guardian of the parish, and Senior at least shared the popular belief that it could only be done away with by abolishing the parish as the financial basis of the Poor Law. So long as a parish had to pay for its own poor, it would seek to repel and remove the poor of other parishes. The obvious remedy was to do away with the parish fund and transform the Poor Rate into a tax centrally collected for the relief of the nation's poor. But here the Commissioners came up against the prevailing belief that local assessment and collection of the Poor Rate was the only real safeguard against 'profusion'. Moreover, Senior believed that local rating would be an insurance against the gradual erosion of the severities he was proposing, by central politicians seeking popularity and votes.[97] When the matter was discussed Chadwick suggested a compromise by which rating and therefore settlement would be transferred to the new Union, an area big enough to do away with the majority of settlement cases.[98] But both men realised that the new Unions would be dangerously unpopular, and that they (however irrationally) as well as the Central Board would be subject to the cry of 'centralisation'. For the sake of Union administration of poor relief, they let go the chance of transferring the machinery of rate collection away from the parish, and of abolishing or reducing settlement at the same time. They were content to propose, for the time being, the abolition of settlement by hiring and residence (both sources of abuse) and the reduction of the means of acquiring it to birth and marriage. To simplify matters, children would in future follow their parents' settlement until they reached the age of sixteen. Illegitimate children would have the settlement of the mother.[99]

In the last few pages of the report the Commissioners recommended a uniform system of rating assessed on rental value, and devoted some attention to 'collateral aids', notably assisted emigration and a general system of religious and moral education for the labouring classes.[100] It was usual for reformers to include large items of this sort in their schemes, and while Chadwick was an enthusiastic educationist it seems most unlikely that he expected an immediate outcome to his suggestions.[101] They could hardly be said to mitigate the general harshness in tone and purpose of the Poor Law Commission Report.[102]

Despite its length and detail, the report barely touched on some of the Commissioners' plans which were to be important in the new Poor Law. Nothing was said about the nature or constitution of the Unions, although these were already being worked out by consultation and private debate. Senior had originally contemplated a hierarchy of paid state officials, from the three members of a Central Commission through a corps of 200 centrally appointed and paid inspectors, down to some 4,700 full-time overseers, each administering a group of three parishes. This highly centralised service would terminate the rule of the JPs, which Senior considered the source of all abuses.[103] However, Chadwick substituted the large Unions, reduced the inspectors (an expensive item) to nine, and proposed to administer the Unions by boards of guardians elected on the same lines as the contemporary Select Vestries. There would be a great reduction in cost, and he believed, apparently, that with a Central Board laying down regulations and empowered to dismiss or even appoint the Union officials, the guardians would have little significant power.[104] These provisions were established during the preparation of the Bill and during the early days of the operation of the Act.

In producing their report Senior and Chadwick undoubtedly intended a revolution in the Poor Law. They purposed to abolish relief in aid of wages. They managed by their constant propaganda to create a long-lived historical tradition that, while their methods were harsh, the allowance system was so harmful that they were necessary. This became historical orthodoxy until it was challenged in 1963 by a famous article written by Mark Blaug entitled 'The Myth of the old Poor Law'.[105] Blaug argued that the allowance system (in its Speenhamland form almost ended by 1834) had not created poverty, but had mitigated it. Like all historical theories which challenge orthodoxy, this thesis has attracted critics, who have whittled away at it – thus does history progress. It now looks as though Blaug's claim may stand up when applied to the family allowance seen in isolation. But when the allowances are considered in conjunction with their accompaniments, the roundsmen and the Labour Rate, and the laws of settlement, a rather different picture emerges. The old Poor Law's work-spreading devices, once intended as a means of mitigating the hardships of unemployment, had almost imperceptibly turned into a means by which farmers dominated and oppressed their workforce. Chadwick and Senior were not fools, and they intended to break those bonds. They proposed by the workhouse test to separate the employed from the unemployed, thereby forcing the farmers to engage their workers full-time and to pay them a full wage. That they refused to believe that a determined man would be unable to find employment (although they must have known about the seasonality especially in the wheat-growing areas) can be accounted for by their reliance on the wages–fund theory. They believed that, as the rates went down, so the money in the fund available for employing labour would go up. So they underrated the over-population of the countryside in relation to the work available, probably overrated the elasticity of demand for agricultural products, and possibly failed to consider their own argument that income left by lower rates would be drained off as higher rents to the landlord. In consequence they ignored the extent to which rural employment was dependent simply on the supply of and demand for labour.

It could be argued that the employed and unemployed, as the Select Committee of 1824 had suggested, could have been separated just as well by insisting on full-time work for the parish as a condition of relief. Admittedly, the example of the parish gravel pit and the stone yard was not promising, and the revolt of 1830 was believed to have been hatched in such places. However, the Commissioners did not even examine the possibility of a centrally inspected programme of local public works or road-building. Nor did they examine any method of exerting direct pressure on the farmers to pay a proper wage, preferring to get at the employers by penalising the labourers. They were wedded to the deterrent workhouse, as were the village reformers whose institutions they held up as models. In this as in the tone of their writings, they revealed the ambiguity of their attitudes and their intentions.

The passing of the Poor Law Amendment Act

The Royal Commission Report was so successful that, by March, Lord Melbourne had directed Senior to prepare the heads of a Bill. This he did, with Chadwick's somewhat overwhelming assistance, after both had consulted a number of people experienced in pauper management, and generally of their own way of thinking.[106] Thereafter a Cabinet committee made some alterations, specifying that the general orders of the administrative Commission should be laid before parliament by the Secretary of State before becoming operative, and omitting the date for the cessation of outdoor relief to the able-bodied, which had been proposed for two years' time. Meanwhile, the propaganda of the Commissioners had publicised the Bill, and probably helped to raise the beginnings of opposition to it. However, it passed through parliament with ease, for most of the landowners were only too pleased to listen to promises of 'depauperisation', lower rates and a quiet countryside, while the alliance of Whigs and Peelites on social matters disarmed opposition in the House of Commons. A tiny group of dissidents led by Poulett Scrope and William Cobbett succeeded in limiting the duration of the Act to five years. The Commons restored the right of the parish to procure a Magistrates' Order forcing a putative father (but not the mother) to indemnify it. But the Lords limited bastardy cases to Quarter Sessions, and demanded corroborative evidence to the woman's story, thus putting paternity actions largely out of her reach. Despite a rather more determined resistance in the Lords than in the Commons, by July the Bill was law, slipped through (as the Webbs thought) before the rising tide of opposition in the country could become effective.[107]

Sources and references

1. **Ashby, A. W.,** *One hundred years of Poor Law administration in a Warwickshire village,* in **Vinagradoff** (ed.), *Oxford Studies in Social and Legal History.* 1912, III pp. 115-17. 1*s* equals roughly 5p.

2. **Lane, Joan,** 'Administration of the Poor Law in Butlers Marston, Warwickshire, 1713-1822', Wales (Cardiff) M.A., 1970, p. 30. See table of 10 regular recipients.

3. *Ibid.,* p. 30. For more detailed accounts of burials, including hospitality at the funeral, see pp. 157-62.

4. For table of pauper apprentices, *ibid.* p. 137.

5. *Ibid.,* pp. 34-5. For further detailed case histories, see App. I. pp. 217-51.

6. For a detailed discussion of clothes provided, *ibid.,* pp. 76-96.

7. *Ibid.,* pp. 101-6.

8. *Ibid.,* pp. 50-4.

9. **Hampson, E. M.,** *The Treatment of Poverty in Cambridgeshire.* C.U.P., 1934, p. 114.

10. *Report from H.M.'s Commissioners for Inquiring into the Administration and Practical Operation of the Poor Laws,* C. 1834 (hereafter called *Poor Law Commission Report*), pp. 55-9, 181-2.

11. *Ibid.,* p. 62.

12. **Mawson, Pamela,** 'Poor Law Administration in South Shields 1830-1930.' Newcastle on Tyne M.A., 1971, p. 15.

13. **Webb, S.** and **B.,** *English Poor Law History.* Part I, *The Old Poor Law.* Longmans Green & Co., 1927, p. 320.

14. In East Yorkshire 98 persons including 17 women claimed settlement by hiring, 58 by apprenticeship, 12 by birth, 8 by father's settlement, 6 by marriage, 13 by owning or renting land, 1 by residence, 1 by service as overseer of the poor, and some by two of these. **Hopkin, N. D.,** 'The Old and the New Poor Law in East Yorkshire, *c.* 1760-1850', Leeds M. Phil., 1968, p. 356. In Cambridgeshire between 1753 and 1823, 221 claimed by hiring, 101 by apprenticeship, 55 by renting and 35 by marriage. *Ibid.;* Hampson, *op. cit.,* p. 279. These eighteenth-century provisions have been called 'Settlement by Merit'. See **Taylor, James Stephen,** 'The impact of pauper settlement 1691-1834', *Past and Present,* **73,** Nov. 1976, pp. 42-74. There seems to be an exaggerated contrast between residence and 'merit', since apprenticeship and hiring implied residence, and an adult working man would scarcely reside without working.

15. Hampson, *op. cit.,* pp. 129-30.

16. Lane. *op. cit.,* pp. 178-84.

17. Hopkin, *op. cit.,* App. K, p. 560, Table of Cases.

18. **Handley, M. D.,** 'Local Administration of the Poor Law in Great Broughton and

Wirral Unions and the Chester Local Act Incorporation, 1834–71'. Wales (Bangor) M.A., 1969, pp. 50–1.

19. Hampson, *op. cit.*, p. 137. One late case in East Yorkshire (1840–41) was recorded as costing £132 0s 8d. Hopkin, *op. cit.*, p. 390.

20. Hampson instances the case of Thomas Hampson, removed from his employment in Royston to Lee. Perhaps somebody wanted his job. The East Yorkshire Justices several times removed men while their families stayed behind, and there were cases of single women being separated from their babies. A stepchild could have a different settlement from his stepfather, and a widow who remarried got a different settlement from that of her children. Hampson, *op. cit.*, pp. 137–41.

21. **Chambers, J. D.**, *Nottinghamshire in the Eighteenth Century*. 1932, p. 273.

22. **Marshall, Dorothy,** *The English Poor in the Eighteenth Century*. Routledge, 1926, p. 212.

23. **Smith, Adam.** *The Wealth of Nations* (1776). Clarendon Press, 1880, pp. 148–9.

24. 'He has all a slave's security for subsistence without his liability to punishment.' *The Poor Law Commission Report*, p. 32.

25. Hopkin, *op. cit.*, p. 341. Cf. **Rose, M. E.** 'Settlement, Removal and the New Poor Law' in Derek Fraser (ed.), *The New Poor Law in the Nineteenth Century*, Macmillan, 1976, p. 32.

26. The average distance in Cambridgeshire was just over 8 miles, in East Yorkshire 7½ miles. But between 1821 and 1830 the number of removals from more distant areas rose sharply. Hopkin, *op. cit.*, pp. 352–3.

27. Without such a certificate the labourer could be in difficulties. Ashby describes the case of Jack Lenten, a thatcher, who went off in the hay-making season to earn money. The farmers refused to let him have settlement in the winter, and he had to live miles away from the parish. Eventually he got work as a ganger on the railways, discovered an improved method of tipping for embankments, and became a rich man. Ashby, *op. cit.*, p. 80.

28. I am indebted for this point to Mr Gerald Lewis who has been investigating the effects of settlement in three parishes.

29. For a more detailed account of these laws and practices, see **Henriques, U.,** 'Bastardy and the new Poor Law', *Past and Present*, **37,** July 1967, pp. 103–29.

30. Hopkin, *op. cit.*, p. 424. The parish of Sutton recovered £442 of its expenditure in one year of £601 5s 0d on 22 bastards. But Hull had a deficit of £1,928 on similar transactions. The overseers often contented themselves with lump sums in full settlement. A bird in the hand was worth two in the bush.

31. Hampson, *op. cit.*, p. 168.

32. Webb, S. and B., *op. cit.*, Part I, p. 102.

33. i.e. The Relief Register. Hampson, *op. cit.*, p. 73.

34. Hampson gives examples of the constantly changing terms of contract with the same master, or different masters in the same workhouse, including one at Royston, Cambridgeshire. The master of the large joint workhouse set up by Royston, Cambridgeshire, and Royston, Hertfordshire, had, in 1784, £260 a year plus 2s a week per pauper above the number of 50, as well as the proceeds of the inmates' labour. In return he was to provide food, materials and all the costs of keeping the paupers, including legal, burial and medical expenses (except in cases of smallpox or broken bones). By 1790 another master was running the house on a cheaper contract of £212 per year, but he managed it so badly that the inmates rioted. After this the paupers were maintained by outdoor relief until the advent of a new workhouse master, who let out their labour to farms 20 miles away. Hampson, *op. cit.*, pp. 106–12.

35. Hampson, *op. cit., passim.* The Isle of Ely houses were much larger, averaging over 60 per workhouse. *Op. cit.*, p. 100.

36. It is generally argued that money wages rose, but real wages declined over the period of the wars.

37. In 1750 the price of wheat was 26s to 36s per quarter. In the late 1780s it fluctuated between 45s and 60s. In 1795 it rose to 90s, in 1800 it was 113s 10d,

in 1801, 119s 6d. It then fell but rose again to 126s 6d in 1812. **Chambers, J. D.** and **Mingay, G. E.,** *The Agricultural Revolution. 1750–1880*, Batsford, 1966, pp. 110–13.

38. **Deane, P.** and **Cole, G. D. H.,** *British Economic Growth 1688–1959*. C.U.P., 1964, p. 8.
39. Hampson, *op. cit.*, pp. 189–90.
40. Decision of the Justices at Speenhamland (Newbury) Berkshire, 1795 ratified by an enabling Act in 1796.
41. **Baugh, D. A.,** 'The cost of poor relief in S.E. England, 1790–1834,' *Econ. Hist. Review*. 2nd series XXVIII No. 1, Feb. 1975, pp. 50–68.
42. Lane, Joan, *op. cit.* pp. 187–9.
43. Hampson, *op. cit.*, p. 216. **Webb, S.** and **B.,** *English Poor Law History* Part 2, Vol. 1, Cass, 1963, p. 2. In Butlers Marston expenditure rose gradually and irregularly from £61 in 1770 to over £100 in 1780. The parish was enclosed during that decade. In 1783 it leaped to £184, then fell, though not to its former level. In the famine year 1800 it jumped to £384. Between 1801 and 1812 it fluctuated between £276 and £312. Lane, Joan, *op. cit.*, Table p. 28. In East Yorkshire Poor Law expenditure climbed from £4,110, the average for the three years 1748-49-50 through £11,036 in the year ending at Easter 1776, and £15,499 averaged over 1783-84-85, to £41,388 in 1803. In the year ending Easter 1819 it reached £114,314. Hopkin, *op. cit.*, p. 3. The same thing happened in London, where population and prices were rising fast. Cf. **Froshaug, Ann,** 'Poor Law Administration in Selected London Parishes between 1750 and 1850', Nottingham M.A., 1969, p. 165 *et seq.*, for a discussion of the movement of population, numbers relieved and expenditure.
44. Hampson, *op. cit.*, p. 102.
45. **Couth, William,** 'The Development of the Town of Gainsborough. 1750–1850', Wales (Cardiff) M.A., 1975, pp. 199–201.
46. Webb, S. and B., *op. cit.*, p. 171.
47. Figures are from **Colquhoun, Patrick,** *A Treatise on Indigence*. London 1806, p. 116.
48. For a good account of these schemes and for the allotment schemes, see **Barnett, D. C.,** 'Ideas on Social Welfare with Special Reference to Friendly Societies and Allotment Schemes. 1780–1834', Nottingham M.A., 1961, *passim*. Cf. **Barnett, D. C.,** 'Allotment and the problem of rural poverty, 1780–1840' in **Jones, E. L.** and **Mingay, G. E.,** (eds), *Land, Labour and Population in the Industrial Revolution*. Edward Arnold, 1967, pp. 162–83.
49. Richard Pew's system. Barnett, *op. cit.*, pp. 50–2.
50. John Acland's scheme. *Ibid.*, p. 52. Richard Price was the well-known Radical Dissenting minister who was also a pioneer in working out the actuarial basis of insurance. He supplied Pitt with several alternative schemes for his sinking fund. But his tables for the probability of sickness devised for the friendly societies were unreliable. **Gosden, R. H. J. H.,** *Self Help*. Batsford, 1973, pp. 18–19.
51. Barnett, *op. cit.*, p. 60.
52. *Ibid.*, p. 63.
53. *Ibid.*, p. 131.
54. *Ibid.*, p. 109. This society later turned into a philanthropic housing association.
55. See the final section of Part II of his *Rights of Man*. But there was a 'soak the rich' element about Paine's scheme which inevitably put it outside the pale of contemporary practical politics.
56. **Bentham, Jeremy,** *Observation on the Poor Bill introduced by the Rt. Hon. William Pitt*. The pamphlet was circulated privately, not published until Chadwick rescued it from oblivion to justify the new Poor Law in 1839.
57. *Ibid.* See Bentham's *Works*, edited by Bowring. Edinburgh, 1843. Vol. VIII, pp. 440–61.
58. For Bentham's tracts on Pauper Management see his *Works*, Vol. VIII.
59. **Marshall, J. D.** 'The Nottinghamshire reformers and their contribution to the

new Poor Law', *Econ. Hist. Review*, II, 13, 1960–61, p. 389.

60. Couth, William, *op. cit.*, p. 201.

61. Attitudes both to poverty and to the destitute have been examined in detail and with great ability in **Poynter, J. R.,** *Society and Pauperism*. Routledge, 1969. It seems unnecessary to repeat the detail here.

62. **Eden, Sir F. M.,** *The State of the Poor: A History of the Labouring Classes in England, etc.*, 1797. Rogers, A. G. L. (ed.), 1928, pp. 86–7. Eden summarised these views very fairly, but was on the other side himself.

63. See, for instance, the writings of Disraeli.

64. This attitude has been attributed to the belief that poverty (like lunacy) was a part of Divine Providence, a sign and consequence of God's judgement on the wicked. Equally it could have sprung from the eighteenth-century view of moral cause and effect, in which (reflecting the social habits of some of the rich) the content of immorality was seen largely in terms of idleness and reckless extravagance which led to the debtors' ward, the madhouse and the gallows. See *The Rake's Progress*, and Bishop Butler.

65. Quoted in Eden, *op. cit.*, p. 44.

66. The writings of Marx and his successors are riddled with similar thought processes, in which the oppression exercised by capitalists is argued to be the result of a system over which they have no control, in language of the strongest condemnation.

67. **Colquhoun, Patrick,** *op. cit.*, p. 223. Colquhoun stressed the traditional distinction between deserving and undeserving poor. He was referring to contract workhouses set up under the Act of 1722 (9 Geo I c. 7).

68. The Select Committee in 1817 bitterly criticised 43 Elizabeth, the very foundation of the Poor Law. It went as far as recommending the gradual withdrawal of parish relief from able-bodied adults. But if this was impossible (which the Committee plainly thought it was) then parishes should be left to provide work for their own paupers, taking care to withhold from idleness 'the wages that should be due to industry alone'. *House of Commons Select Committee on the Poor Laws. PP* 1819, II, pp. 17–20.

69. Marshall, J. D., *op. cit.*, pp. 382–96.

70. *Report from the Select Committee of the House of Lords appointed to consider of the Poor Law. PP* 1831, VIII. Minutes of Evidence, p. 219.

71. Gosden, R. H. J. H., *op. cit.*, pp. 69, 215–18. Gosden suggests that, on their own evidence, the Commissioners failed to prove their contention that the undoubted increase in savings in the 1830s and 1840s was the result of the Poor Law Amendment Act, or was largely contributed to by those who would otherwise have claimed poor relief.

72. The Royal Commission Report is very well known. For accounts of it, see **Finer, S. E.,** *The Life and Times of Sir Edwin Chadwick*. Methuen, 1952, pp. 69–95; **Bamford, G. B. A. M.,** *England in the Eighteen Thirties*, Edward Arnold, 1969, pp. 54–58; **MacDonagh, O.,** *Early Victorian Government*. Weidenfeld & Nicolson, 1977, pp. 99–103. A Pelican paperback edition of the Report appeared in 1974, edited by S. G. and E. O. A. Checkland. Unfortunately the editors saw fit to tidy it up under their own headings, thus altering its structure.

73. **Lewis, R. A.,** *Edwin Chadwick and the Public Health Movement*. Longman, 1952, p. 18.

74. The Poor Law Administrative Commission proved adept at using figures to support its contentions in controversial matters.

75. *Poor Law Commission Report*, p. 24.

76. *Ibid.*, pp. 11–12.

77. *Ibid.*, pp. 12–18.

78. *Ibid.*, pp. 49–55.

79. The name 'make-work' system seems to have originated with Poynter, *op. cit.*, *passim*.

80. *Poor Law Commission Report*, pp. 18–21.

81. *Ibid.*, pp. 24, 108, 126. The Act of 1832 (2 & 3 Wm IV, c. 96) authorised a vestry by majority decision to compel dissenting occupiers to share a parish Labour Rate. See **Digby, Anne,** 'The labour market and the continuity of social policy after 1834: the case of the Eastern Counties', *Econ. Hist. Review*, 2nd series, XXVIII No. 1, 1975, pp. 69–83.
82. Quoted in Hopkin, *op. cit.*, p. 48.
83. Anne Digby notes that in many East Anglian areas there were elements of both
   • systems. Digby, *op. cit.*, p. 78.
84. *Poor Law Commission Report*, pp. 108–126.
85. *Ibid.*, pp. 49–54.
86. *Ibid.*, p. 25.
87. *Ibid.*, pp. 28–9.
88. *Ibid.*, p. 34.
89. *Ibid.*, pp. 196, 197.
90. *Ibid.*, pp. 74–9. They made the connection between magistrates' rule and the allowance system.
91. *Ibid.*, p. 127.
92. Examples cited were Southwell in Nottinghamshire and Bingham in Lincolnshire, Hatfield in Hertfordshire, where the Marquis of Salisbury had installed a drill sergeant from the Grenadier Guards as Workhouse Master, Thomas Whately's parish of Cookham, Berkshire, and Swallowfield, Berkshire, where John Walter of *The Times* was fighting a pamphlet war with the manager over the harshness of the workhouse regime.
93. *Poor Law Commission Report*, p. 167.
94. *Ibid.*, pp. 429–30; pp. 172–3.
95. *Ibid.*, p. 180.
96. *Ibid.*, pp. 183–5.
97. **Senior, Nassau W.,** Second Letter to the Lord Chancellor, January 1833. Chadwick papers, 18. D. M. S. Watson Library, University College, London.
98. I am indebted for much of this information to Mr Gerald Lewis.
99. *Poor Law Commission Report*, pp. 193–5.
100. *Ibid.* Chadwick also proposed public parks and zoos, museums and theatres to educate the poor. Finer, *op. cit.*, p. 70.
101. National education was also included in Colquhoun's Pauper Kingdom.
102. Lewis, R. A., *op. cit.*, p. 19. Dr Lewis makes the point that parts of Chadwick's project were omitted from the Report but there is little evidence that the scheme was harsher than intended – least of all in Chadwick's behaviour as Secretary of the Poor Law Commission.
103. Senior, Second Letter to the Lord Chancellor. *Chadwick Papers*, 18.
104. **Chadwick, E.,** *Measures proposed with Relation to the Administration of the Poor Laws.* *Chadwick Papers*, 18. There are five printed versions of the *Measures*, undated, and differing slightly from each other. They also have different MS descriptions.
105. *Journal of Economic History*, Vol. 23, 1963, pp. 151–84.
106. Thomas Whately of Cookham, Berkshire, Henry Russell of Swallowfield, Berkshire, and William Day of Uckfield, Sussex, were among those consulted. George Nicholls, manager of Southwell, Nottinghamshire, became a Commissioner after the Act. Tidd Pratt, the Registrar of Friendly Societies, whom the Commissioners praised as a model of rigid administration of friendly society funds, was also consulted. James Stephen, who would have preferred the administration of poor relief to remain with the Justices, was consulted, but his advice was ignored.
107. For an account of the influence of the classical political economists and social scientists on the development of the poor law roughly between 1780 and 1834, see **Cowherd, R. G.,** *Political Economists and the English Poor Laws.* Ohio U.P., 1978, showing that Bentham exercised an important influence in retaining relief to the able-bodied but in such a way (as he thought) as to check population and pauperism. I regret this book appeared too late for proper consideration here.

3 The new Poor Law

The Poor Law Amendment Act

The Poor Law Amendment Act (4 & 5 Wm IV, c. 87) established the constitutional machinery of Victorian poor relief. It constituted a very careful dovetailing of new institutions with survivals from the old order. The central supervisory organ was a Commission of three members in London, reporting annually to the Secretary of State for the Home Department.[1] The appointments were administrative, and none of the members had seats in parliament, a provision which no doubt reflected the concern of Chadwick and Senior to keep Poor Law administration away from the day-to-day pressures of politics. The Commissioners could without further Treasury consent appoint up to nine Assistant Commissioners (or Inspectors) to carry out their work in the field.[2] With this assistance they were empowered to unite parishes into Unions, to be administered by Boards of Guardians.[3] These were to be elected by the ratepayers and property owners, with multiple votes for the larger proprietors. The annual elections in March were to be semi-secret, the voting papers being left at the homes of the electors and collected from them.[4] The Commissioners could also prescribe the number and property qualifications of the guardians, up to a £40 rental, and their duties.[5] Once a Union was established, the Commissioners could order the building of workhouses, with the consent of the guardians or a majority of the voters. Without it they could only order the alteration or enlargement of existing workhouses up to a total sum of £50.[6] The workhouses could be financed by loans from the Poor Rate, repayable in instalments spread over ten years. The work of the Union would be performed by paid officials, of whom those superintending the relief of the poor (the future Relieving Officers) and the auditor were specified. The Commissioners were empowered to order overseers and guardians to appoint them, and to lay down their qualifications, duties and salaries (paid from the Poor Rate). They could dismiss Union officials,[7] but the actual appointments were left in the hands of the guardians, a piece of valuable patronage well calculated to win their attachment to the new system. While the administration of poor relief was transferred to the Unions, the assessment and collection of the Poor Rate was left with the parish overseers, who were to render quarterly accounts to the Union auditor and guardians, or in their default to the JPs.[8] Later in the Act a clause forbade any person connected with the administration of poor relief to supply any goods, materials or provisions for the relief of the poor.[9]

The Commissioners were to administer the Act by means of General Orders, which had to be reported to the Home Secretary forty days before coming into effect and to lie on the table of both Houses (where they might be challenged).[10] But they could also communicate with individual Unions by letter, and issue orders by circularising the Assistant Commissioners, both convenient ways of circumventing the forty days rule. They could make regulations for workhouses and amend Union by-laws; while Commissioners as well as Assistant Commissioners could attend meetings of Boards of Guardians and vestries, although they could not vote at them.[11]

In setting up these brand new authorities some care was taken to mollify the feelings of the Justices of the Peace who, representing the powerful landowners, could not lightly be superseded. The JPs within each Union were made guardians *ex officio*.[12] Although they lost the vital power to order relief to applicants refused by overseers (or guardians) they were allowed to order outdoor relief in kind for non-settled paupers in case of emergency and medical relief for all paupers in cases of sudden and dangerous illness.[13] Along with the guardians, they were made visitors to the new workhouses with responsibility for enforcing the Commissioners' regulations.[14] And of course they retained judicial functions in settlement and bastardy cases. But henceforth their control of poor relief would depend largely on their position on the Boards of Guardians, or their private influence as landowners and employers.

The Act gave the Commissioners certain powers to regulate poor relief. They could lay down the condition under which relief outside the workhouse was to be granted to able-bodied paupers and their families, although the actual date for the imposition of the workhouse test was not specified.[15] They could disallow payments to paupers which infringed their regulations, one of the few real 'teeth' conferred on the Commissioners.[16] But in emergency cases, relief could be granted by guardians or overseers, provided it was reported within fifteen days, or was only in food, lodging or medicine.[17]

The Act also embodied some general rules – such as, that help to any one member of a family was to be considered relief to all.[18] Relief could be treated as a loan, and recovered direct from the recipient's employer.[19] No workhouse inmate was to be compelled to attend any religious service contrary to his principles,[20] a conscience clause which revealed the liberal provenance of the Act, and the only clause to safeguard any of the indoor paupers' rights.

The sections of the Act on Settlement and Bastardy followed fairly closely the recommendations of the Poor Law Commissioners' Report. Settlement by hiring and service or by residence in any tenement which did not pay rates was abolished, leaving birth and marriage as the main source of settlement.[21] Children would then take their parents' settlement, and illegitimate children were to follow the settlement of the mother to the age of sixteen, a provision which ended the motive for the removal of pregnant women.[22] Guardians, by unanimous agreement, could take over the rate-collecting powers of the parishes, and the Union would become the unit of settlement. But few Boards wished to do this, or parishes to allow it. The bastardy clauses repealed the laws for the imprisonment of 'lewd' women, but removed the mother's right to sue the putative father of her illegitimate child for maintenance, except with corroborative evidence (which would usually be impossible to obtain) and at the costly Quarter Sessions. No money recovered by the parish from the putative father at Quarter Sessions could be paid over to the mother, and any man who married her had to be responsible for the maintenance of all her children. Thus the full economic consequences of illegitimacy were heaped on the mother.[23]

There were some significant omissions in the Act. Nothing was said about the actual administration of the workhouses, nor was any reference made to the principle of 'less eligibility'. It was obviously assumed that the principle would be assured by the Commissioners' control, combined with the self-interest of ratepayer-elected guardians.[24] No guarantee of multiple classified workhouses was included. Evidently Chadwick had not gained the support needed to embody it in the Act. Nothing was said about the education of pauper children, although this was soon to become a leading interest to some of the Poor Law administrators. The Act was to last initially for five years;[25] this limitation in time being one of the few successes won by the parliamentary opposition.

The Poor Law Commission and unionisation

The Poor Law Amendment Act was implemented with speed and determination. The Commission of three appointed in July was busy in October and November interviewing and appointing its Assistant Commissioners and office staff. But the seeds of disharmony were already sown in that Chadwick, warmly recommended by Senior for a place on the Commission, had been passed over. He became Secretary with a salary of £1,200 a year compared with the Commissioners' £2,000. And Althorp's assurance that he was immovable, and equal in power to a Commissioner, was not communicated to Nicholls and Lewis.[26]

Although the trouble on the Poor Law Commission, which rent it apart and later caused Chadwick to devote himself to the cause of public health, was partly due to pique and to clash of personalities, there were also differences of principle and policy. Chadwick considered the Commissioners, and especially the Tory squire Frankland Lewis, unsuitable to carry through a policy of 'thorough'. Lewis, once on Sturges Bourne's committee of 1817, now thought mainly in terms of reducing the

Poor Rate. Here he resembled many gentlemen whose co-operation would have to be won if the new law was to be enforced, and who thought about poor relief in terms of economy tempered by expediency. But although economy and depauperisation or the restoration of self-dependence among the poor were twin aims, and frequently referred to as complementary, they could conflict whenever depauperisation required specialised institutions entailing expense. Moreover, 'thorough' was a dangerous attitude. What would have happened if Chadwick, as a full Commissioner, had had *carte blanche* to impose the workhouse test in its full rigour on the industrial areas during the distress of 1837? In preferring Shaw Lefevre, Frankland Lewis and George Nicholls to Chadwick, Althorp has been accused of snobbery and jobbery.[27] But Chadwick was by now known, and it is possible that his exclusion included an element of political self-preservation.

With the help of nine Assistant Commissioners (who rose in number within a year to sixteen)[28] Poor Law Unions were created with a rapidity which gave the illusion of some sort of semi-automatic and uniform process. By the end of 1835 the Commissioners reported that they had already combined 2,066 parishes into 112 Unions, covering about one-tenth of the total population and about one-sixth of the local rates in England and Wales.[29] These were in a wide band of counties in south and central England, from Kent and Suffolk in the east to Somerset and Wiltshire in the west, an area roughly coinciding with the main disturbances of 1830. In 1836 the Commissioners' score reached 365 Unions (including 14 single parishes under Boards of Guardians) incorporating 7,915 parishes.[30] Thereafter progress slowed down as attempts to unionise the industrial north coincided with trade depression, and resistance was encountered all over the country from Gilbert Act and Local Act Unions, which the Commissioners had no power to dissolve.[31] Despite these difficulties, by December 1839, 13,691 parishes out of some 15,000 had been incorporated into 583 Unions, leaving 799, mostly Local Act or Gilbert Act Unions, outside. The new Poor Law territorial system was nearly as complete as it would be until 1871, although some splitting and reconstituting of Unions occurred later.[32]

According to the Commissioners the results were gratifying; by 1838 the country had been relieved of 'direct annual taxation' by nearly £2,300,000.[33] Between 1834 and 1839 a saving of £10,933,013 compared with the expenditure of the five previous years had been made.[34] Although after 1837 the costs began to climb again, it was long before they reached the level of 1834. Mitchell and Deane have given figures to show that from 1813 to 1834 Poor Law expenditure averaged some £6,300,000; between 1835 and 1860 some £5,200,000.[35]

For those who aimed chiefly at reducing the Poor Rate the new law was a success. For those who propagated it as a measure of social rehabilitation it was also claimed as a success. Already in 1835 the Commissioners were announcing that it had brought more prompt and adequate relief to the aged, infirm and sick; was improving the education of pauper children; was encouraging industry and moral habits in the able-bodied and thereby increasing their welfare; was helping the farmers to provide more employment and higher wages; was improving the relationship between rural employers and their workers; and was increasing the deposits of the benefit societies. Moreover, there was a decline in chargeable bastardy, and better sexual morals in the countryside.[36] The Commissioners found that the law was essentially of popular tendency (although of unpopular appearance), conditioning the masses to frugality, forethought and self-dependence, and protecting them from contrivances to lower wages and the caprice of employers.[37] Thus did the Secretary of the Poor Law Commission construct from the communications of his Assistant Commissioners reports from which the attacks of prejudiced opponents could be repelled and a case made for continuing the discretionary powers of the Commissioners. All the propaganda features of the report of 1834 reappeared in annual reports of the administrators of the Poor Law Amendment Act. It remains, with the help of some regional studies, to see how far their claims were justified.

Implementation: the Unions

The southern counties of England felt the impact of the Poor Law Amendment Act even before the new Unions were created. In some places it was welcomed as an opportunity to reduce poor relief wholesale, or even stop it altogether. When Winchester willingly abandoned its Gilbert Act Union for a Poor Law Union, the weekly poor lists vanished. Three parishes discontinued outdoor relief, and the new Union had to be cautioned against this radical economy.[38] The chairman of Uckfield Union in Sussex (the 3rd Lord Liverpool) claimed that within one year of its creation, expenditure had dropped from £16,643 to £8,733, of which (since the workhouse was being refurnished) only £5,675 was actually spent on the poor. About half the Poor Rate had been saved; '. . . and this had not produced the slightest riot or confusion, but on the contrary, . . . few or no able-bodied labourers have been out of work, as may be seen from the very small number of able-bodied men at the most unfavourable time in the workhouses of Mayfield and Marshfield.'[39]

Immediate reductions, if not all as extreme as this, occurred in widely separated areas. In East Yorkshire, expenditure, reduced from its 1819 peak, fell a further 13 per cent in 1835 and had again diminished by 27 per cent from 1834 by 1837.[40] This eagerness to cut costs, with its threat of local reprisals may have been one reason why the Commissioners proceeded so rapidly with unionisation. But although, as the Commissioners reported, the Assistant Commissioners were received without hostility in many rural areas, the impression of easy and uniform unionisation was wide of the truth.

On arrival the Assistant Commissioners surveyed the local

situation, reported back to the Commissioners, and then called meetings of the principal owners, ratepayers and parish officers, at which they explained their plans and invited comments.[41] But eventually the size and shape of the Unions were the result of negotiations between the Assistant Commissioners and the local bosses. The Commissioners wanted the Unions to consist in a circle of parishes round a market town. This would be convenient for the attendance of officials and guardians, while discouraging applications from paupers living far from the union workhouse.[42] And some Unions did conform to this natural geographical pattern, which facilitated the attendance of guardians at Boards held on market days.[43] But in some places geography confused the pattern, as in Anglesey, most of which formed a large Union of 53 parishes, while 5 parishes in the east of the island were attached to Caernarvon to which they were linked by ferry, and 16 more were attached to Bangor across the Menai straits.[44] Elsewhere the construction of Unions was affected by existing Gilbert Act and Local Act Unions. Assistant Commissioner William Day encountered Local Act Unions at Shrewsbury, Atcham, Oswestry, Ellesmere, and Whitchurch. He extended Atcham into a new Union of 45 parishes entirely surrounding the 6 parishes of the Shrewsbury incorporation.[45] Similarly, a Chester Local Act incorporation of 9 parishes was surrounded by Great Boughton Poor Law Union, comprising 101 townships, whose guardians insisted on using the Chester workhouse.[46]

In some rural areas the Assistant Commissioners were compelled to purchase the support of the landed nobility by drawing the boundaries of Unions around their estates. Dr Anthony Brundage has drawn attention to a number of these Unions in Northamptonshire, including Potterspury (the Duke of Grafton's interest), Aynho (the Cartwrights' interest) and Daventry (Charles Knightly's interest). Northampton then became a kind of residue, consisting of four town parishes and thirteen rural parishes without major landowners. Thus, in Dr Brundage's view, the great landowners had the Unions gerrymandered to suit their interests, overwhelmed the elected representation of populous town parishes by rural *ex officio* guardians, and successfully maintained their control of Poor Law administration.[47] The view has been challenged by Mr Peter Dunkley, who observes that in urban areas, and in some rural districts lacking great landowners, yeoman farmers or town shopkeepers and artisans secured control of the Boards of Guardians.[48] This controversy is likely to continue until surveys of the political and social geography of many more Unions have been completed and collated. Meantime the obvious feature of the new Unions is their diversity.[49] Some of them were indeed geographical and administrative nonsenses. The rector of Petworth pointed out that the poor of Graffham had no medical help, as their doctor lived in Chichester, ten miles away over the downs.[50]

This disparity was exhibited in the size, shape, population and wealth of the Unions. The great City of London Union included 57,100 people in 98 parishes.[51] Presteigne Union, combining parts of Radnor and Hereford, contained 3,441 people and 16 parishes.[52] Bath Union was even more populous than the City, with 64,230 people though only 24 parishes; while Dulverton, also in Somerset, contained 4,951 people in 11 parishes.[53] Despite the Commissioners' pious hope that distance would deter the idle applicant, they were compelled to sanction the subdivision of Unions into relief districts and medical districts. Far from uniformity, the Poor Law Amendment Act inaugurated a period of the most variegated experiments in local administrative areas.

The Commissioners' intention of rescuing the Poor Law from the control of large landowners and Justices, evident both in the Commission Report and in the Act, was embodied in the ratepayers' franchise for the Boards of Guardians. The type of control aimed at seems to have been that of the Select Vestries, much praised by Chadwick. It was, however, impossible to pursue a policy of 'thorough' in rural local government. Since to conciliate the JPs they (though not the urban magistrates) were allowed on to the Union Boards as *ex officio* guardians, in mainly rural areas, where small towns were under-represented, or where a really large property owner could get his steward and other minions on to the Board, the Union went back into landowner control.[54] In more populated areas the *ex officio* guardians could find themselves outnumbered by the elected representatives of an inferior social class, whereupon they not infrequently walked out altogether.[55] The transfer of power can, at best, have been patchy. If it did occur in rural districts there was the danger (from the Commissioners' point of view) that control would fall, not as they wished, to artisans, shopkeepers and smallholders who had suffered most from the soaring rates of the old Poor Law, but into the hands of the large tenant farmers who had so successfully spread the burden of their wages bill. Whatever happened (and we do not yet know all), the construction and constitution of each Union probably had some relevance to the degree of central control enjoyed by the Commissioners.[56] That was also conditioned by the terms of the Act, from which the Cabinet had removed the proposed power of the Commissioners to commit for contempt of their orders, or even to compel the levying of a Poor Rate or the building of a workhouse. It followed that they could prevent expenditure – largely through their ability to disallow disbursements contrary to their regulations, and to surcharge Boards – but not enforce it. It was also conditioned by the fact that local Boards financed by local taxes had an independent power base which preserved their independence from central dictation. Not only was the prospect of uniformity precluded from the start; when the Boards concentrated on reducing rates and refused to finance the more constructive projects of the new Poor Law, such as proper medical services, pauper schools and classified workhouses, the Commissioners could do nothing about it. In the 1840s the Commissioners found themselves fighting in vain against the negative attitudes of Boards of Guardians whose sole concern was to save the rates.

The Poor Law administrative services

The success of the Commissioners' policies was bound to depend largely on the character and efficiency of the Poor Law Union officials. The new local government service, whose inspiration was the paid Assistant Overseer of the larger parishes before 1834, included Clerks to the Boards, Relieving Officers, Workhouse Masters, and Medical Officers. Some of these posts, including the much sought-after clerkships, and most of the medical posts, were part time. The salaries varied widely, but generally bore some sort of relationship to the size and population of the Union.[57] The officials in the front line of the new Poor Law were the Relieving Officer and the Workhouse Master, sometimes one person holding the two posts. The Relieving Officer decided (subject to the confirmation of the guardians) the fate of applicants for relief; whether they should be relieved at home, enjoy free medical treatment, be sent to task work, or 'offered' the workhouse. He was supposed to supervise outdoor relief, while the Workhouse Master (who could also admit emergency cases on his own) ran the House. He served two masters, the Commission and the Board of Guardians, who not infrequently issued conflicting orders.[58] He was required to fulfil the demands of Medical Officers for the supply and treatment of pauper patients, and if he obstructed or delayed, they might retaliate by ordering expensive invalid foods off the rates.[59] He incurred the fury of disappointed applicants while the guardians to whom they appealed could shelter behind him.[60] He needed to be of firm character; and the Commissioners hoped that guardians would use their patronage to appoint both Relieving Officers and Workhouse Masters from the police or military NCOs. Some attempts were made to do this,[61] and if the new Poor Law had come ten or twelve years earlier, employment for many discharged soldiers might have been found. But by 1834 it was difficult to find such men locally for Relieving Officers, or men and their wives to be Master and Matron of the workhouse; and strangers were not always satisfactory. The inevitable result of local patronage was that officials displaced from the parish regime of the old Poor Law were re-appointed and survived into the new. The only real hope of revolution in Poor Law administration was by purging 'jobs' and up-grading salaries. The former was impossible because the Commissioners, who could veto but not appoint, never had sufficient time to exercise even their limited powers fully; the latter was precluded by the demand for economy. Relieving Officers' pay of course varied enormously. In Bridlington, East Yorkshire, the post of Relieving Officer and Workhouse Master was offered at £60 a year, with board, lodging and stable, but on separation of the posts the Relieving Officer got £80. At Howden Union the Relieving Officer received £90, later increased to £110.[62] This was non-resident, and a horse had to be kept; it was not above the pay of an adult textile spinner. A resident Workhouse Master, in addition to his board and lodging, might get £35 to £50 according to the size of the House.[63] With such salaries, literate, honest and experienced persons were not easy to find. Between 1835 and 1841 ninety Relieving Officers had to be discharged, and others asked to resign, for malversation of funds, neglect of duty, misconduct or drunkenness.[64] The Workhouse Masters, as before 1834, continued to be continually dismissed and changed. Some of the better ones, while capable of running a deterrent workhouse, were quite incapable of responding to the higher policies of the Poor Law Commissioners. They fought with the resident schoolmasters, and Chadwick's hopes of a better education for pauper children were not fulfilled. Some workhouses were honestly run and kindly governed. In others well-attested scandals about the treatment of children or sick paupers were disclosed.

Similar difficulties beset the Commissioners' attempts to establish professional Poor Law medical services.[65] It is difficult to know whether these improved or deteriorated after the Poor Law Amendment Act, but deterioration seems most likely, at least in the first eight years after 1834. Medical attention was the Commissioners' main target for relief by loan, repayable when the patient recovered. This was probably unenforceable, but the paupers lost the right to choose their own medical attendants (if in many cases these were anything better than Wise Women) and had to rely on physicians appointed by the guardians. At first the Commissioners encouraged Boards of Guardians to offer part-time medical posts for competition at lowest tender, a method sanctioned by Bentham, but likely to attract horse leeches and other unqualified practitioners.[66] As a result many complaints of neglect and ill-treatment were ventilated before the Select Committee of 1837. Thereafter the Commissioners pressed the Boards to appoint qualified doctors at reasonable wages according to the population served, with extra fees for maternity and other special cases.[67] They then encountered the resistance of guardians, especially in poor areas such as south Wales, where small farmers on the Boards bitterly resented paying their officials more than they themselves earned, and providing medical attention they themselves could not afford.[68]

From 1842, when the first General Medical Order was issued, attempts were made by the Commissioners to regulate and improve the service. Unions were to be divided into medical districts of not more than 15,000 acres or with a population not exceeding 15,000.[69] In each district a Medical Officer was to provide medical treatment to paupers on outdoor relief on the order of the Relieving Officer, and to look after sick paupers in the workhouse. This has been hailed as a remarkable service, and the more so in that (unlike most Poor Law services) it extended to the pauper on outdoor relief and even, in practice, to the poor who, except in time of illness, were independent of the parish.[70] But despite the attempts of Chadwick and the Commissioners to build up the Poor Law medical service, it continued to be haunted both by the doctrine of less eligibility and the ambivalent Poor Law attitude which underlay it, and by the parsimony of ratepayers. In many Unions the limitations on the size of medical districts were ignored. Even in 1861 there were districts containing populations of up to 40,000.[71] Respectable people who applied for medical help were stigmatised as paupers and deprived of civil rights, which after 1867 could include the parliamentary franchise.[72] The applicants had to get an order to see the doctor from the Relieving Officer, which placed that official with his arbitrary powers between doctor and patient, to the detriment of both. The money allocated to the medical service was totally and permanently inadequate.[73] Although the workhouse infirmaries providing indoor medical treatment grew rapidly, they were places of overcrowding, squalor, and penny-pinching misery, without adequate furniture, chairs, pillows, soap, towels, or other equipment. And they were staffed by untrained nurses. The persistent efforts of reformers, including Chadwick and his friend Florence Nightingale, and of the Poor Law doctors through their organisations, supplemented by the British Medical Association, made little headway against the inertia of the Poor Law Unions.[74] The infirmaries failed to improve until 1867, when the Metropolitan Poor Law Act[75] began the process of taking the London infirmaries out of Union control. Hospitals for infectious diseases were placed under the supervision of a Metropolitan Asylums Board financed by a Common Poor Fund, and the rest under amalgamated districts in which they were separated from the workhouses. The provinces followed in due course. Thus was inaugurated an attempt to introduce a more liberal and less penal policy towards the sick poor. Yet judging from the state of some municipal (ex-Poor Law) hospitals as late as the 1940s, the flavour of 'less eligibility' never died out of Poor Law indoor medical relief.[76]

A key figure in the new system was the Union auditor. Under guardians' control the auditor was comparatively innocuous; but when ingenuous boards, doubtless hoping to save a fee, invited the Assistant Commissioner to audit their accounts,[77] they delivered themselves into the Poor Law Commissioners' hands. The auditor, with his powers of disallowance and surcharge, could stop guardians paying widows' pensions, subsiding rents, and continuing outdoor relief to able-bodied people and their families who should have been sent to the workhouse. The Act of 1844 which enabled the Commissioners to combine Unions into audit districts with the Union chairmen and vice-chairmen electing the auditor was a landmark in the enforcement of the new law. Yet, overall, the picture of Poor Law officials, as far as we can see it, and allowing for all the diversity, does not suggest that the Commissioners possessed the means to carry out a thorough revolution in administration, either in incorruptible severity towards the able-bodied or in the care of the young, old and helpless.

The workhouses

The centrepiece of the new Poor Law was the well-regulated workhouse, which was to care for the orphans, the old and infirm, while driving the able-bodied labourer to provide for himself and his family without help from the parish. Chadwick intended to use the existing parish workhouses included in the Unions for the separate treatment of classified paupers, the old, the young, and the able-bodied. He hoped to extend this principle to the separate housing of lunatics, the blind, and other special categories.[78] In the circumstances of 1834 this was impracticable, as Chadwick had been warned by William Day. A single large workhouse would enable a salary to be offered sufficient to command the services of an efficient officer. With half a dozen different houses the governors would 'hardly be removed above the condition of the paupers they would be called on to controul'. Furthermore, if families were split up among houses in different parishes, there would be 'considerable opposition'.[79] Day might have gone on to ask how, with families thus scattered, the Commissioners' policy that families must go in and come out together was to be operated.

There were some attempts to promote separate classified workhouses, including one in Day's own Union of Uckfield, where existing houses were adapted, one for the old and infirm, one for the sick, one for the able-bodied women (in fact, unmarried mothers), a girls' school, a boys' school, and a workhouse for able-bodied males.[80] This was claimed to be successful at a cost of only £465; but in East Yorkshire attempts to adapt old workhouses had to be abandoned in favour of building new ones.[81] In fact, most old poorhouses were dilapidated beyond cheap repair, and quite unsuitable for the new purposes. Already in 1835 the Commissioners were promoting the building of large Union workhouses, publishing model plans for the use of guardians.[82]

The Poor Law Commissioners had never intended, even in the accommodation for able-bodied males, that food and comforts should be reduced below 'the lowest point at which existence may be maintained'.[83] Paupers might be better fed and housed than in a labourer's cottage. But they would be put to heavy work and subjected to discipline, including the denial of tobacco and fermented liquors, the separation of men from women, and enclosure in the house without leave to go out or to receive visitors. The Commissioners did not mention bone crushing, or high walls, or silence at meals, which already prevailed at Southwell. But they intended 'prisons without crime'.[84] The model Union houses were carefully designed for internal classification, with wards for men and for women (an arrangement soon justified by a General Order for the separation of married couples under 60), a separate ward for the infirmary, and quarters for children. There were no private rooms for the older married couples, and the Commissioners replied to criticisms about this with comments that the aged preferred living apart, that they were dirty, and that they were more easily looked after in separate wards.[85] Dietaries published by the Commissioners were not wholly insufficient, and took some notice of local eating habits, providing for lobscouse (stew) in the north, and endless bread and cheese in the south.[86] But the food was coarse, stodgy and monotonous, and when bread was dear the

Commissioners caused resentment by ordering the dilution of the wheaten loaf with barley or rye. Inmates had to wear workhouse uniform, drab and no doubt ill fitting, but to the benefit of the ragged and filthy and their neighbours. But the Commissioners resisted the attempts of some guardians to clothe unmarried mothers in yellow, as a badge of shame.

The picture of a stern but salutary and healthy uniform regime in the workhouse was, of course, belied by the facts. There were reasonable houses such as that at Chatham, with some accommodation for aged couples, a fair diet, extra food for the old, good medical attendance, a school (with pauper teachers), and regular leave for the young, the old and the infirm to go outside.[87] There were others like Neath workhouse, into which the paupers were moved when it was 'all naked, damp and cold, as when the mason left - undried - unaired - unventilated - unwarmed', and permanently cold and dirty.[88] Or like Swansea, with a crowded verminous fever ward and a Master who had to be suspended for making a female inmate pregnant.[89] The most common complaint was overcrowding. 'Pauper palaces' had plenty of room between floor and ceiling, but little on the ground.

The actual conduct of the workhouses (as well as the treatment of outdoor paupers) was regulated by the character of the Master and Matron, the Union board, and the regional Assistant Poor Law Commissioner. In the North East, where the comparatively liberal Sir John Walsham was Assistant Commissioner, and was more than usually influential with the local guardians because of his social rank, the new regime showed, on the whole, a kindly face.[90] Enlightened guardians at South Shields were allowed to pay the fees of the workhouse children at a local school, 'placing them on the *same* footing in the school as the *free* children'.[91] In Fareham workhouse, Surrey, children were starved, beaten and put in the stocks all day for bedwetting.[92] A rule-of-thumb indicator of the attitude towards and treatment of workhouse inmates is provided by the local provisions for Christmas. At South Shields the guardians, with the Assistant Commissioner's approval, provided (presumably from their own pockets), roast beef, plum pudding and ale for all workhouse paupers at Christmas, New Year, and the anniversary of the Queen's coronation and marriage days.[93] When a lady offered a Christmas dinner to the children at Petworth, West Sussex, the guardians consulted Assistant Commissioner Hawley, who 'did not think proper to allow it'.[94]

One cause of the wide diversity of pauper treatment was the ambivalence of the Commissioner's own attitudes (including those of Chadwick). For instance workhouses were visualised as 'refuges' for the aged, in which they would have favourable diet and treatment - usually, in fact, a little bread and butter and tea in place of gruel - and leave to go out on Sunday afternoons. On the other hand, old age in the workhouse was seen as the result of earlier improvidence or filial undutifulness. The workhouse must always be 'less eligible' to make the poor save for their declining years and the children look after their parents.[95]

The same ambivalence beset the treatment of pauper children. The workhouses had more of these (mostly orphans and illegitimates) than of any other class of pauper, and from the outset the Commissioners had good intentions towards them. As J. Phillips Kay put it in his *Report on the Training of Pauper Children*; 'The pauper children maintained in Union workhouses are dependent, not as a consequence of their errors, but of their misfortunes. They have not necessarily contracted any of the taint of pauperism.[96] 'He explained that while their food, clothes and lodging should not be above that of the children of free labourers, it was impossible to confine their moral, religious or secular instruction within the limits prevalent among the working classes. Education was the best means of eradicating the germ of pauperism from the rising generation, 'and of securing in the minds and in the morals of the people the best protection for the institutions of society'.[97] So the Commissioners waged a long-drawn-out battle with Boards of Guardians who cared about rates and not about education, to get pauper children into separate workhouse or special district schools, and under the tuition of trained and qualified teachers. And yet Phillips Kay, who pioneered this movement and passed from it to working-class primary education, never succeeded (never, it seems, attempted) to assimilate workhouse education to that of primary day schools. The emphasis on 'industrial' training, the special training school at Kneller Hall, the attempts to push teachers from the workhouse back into workhouse teaching, all made Poor Law education 'less eligible' than that of free labourers' children. Again the ambiguity appeared in the Commissioners' attitude to pauper apprenticeship. They wanted to end it because of the appalling abuses which their regulations were unable to check. Guardians too often failed to inspect the places in which pauper children were apprenticed, and scandalous cases of cruelty and neglect emerged from time to time, which were probably only a small proportion of those which occurred. Yet the Commissioners also complained that guardians who paid apprentice fees for their paupers tended to place pauper children in a better position than the children of independent labourers. When they succeeded in procuring the abolition of compulsory apprenticeship in 1844, they promoted the sending of workhouse children into the army or navy or domestic service; occupations which carried the lowest pay and status.

The 'less eligible' or deterrent workhouse was supposed to apply only to able-bodied adult paupers. But the ambiguous attitudes of the Poor Law reformers encouraged the immediate application of the principle of less eligibility to all workhouse inmates. There were other reasons for the failure of the hopeful initiatives to apply special and indeed philanthropic treatment to the other classes of pauper. They included the constant use for economy reasons of pauper servants, nurses and teachers, which made it impossible to segregate the children from pauper influence; the refusal of guardians to send idiots and lunatics out of the workhouses to county asylums, places which were much more expensive than workhouse places; and the existence of problem families which constantly moved in and out of the Houses. The slide back towards the general mixed workhouse was probably inevitable; but the one possible obstacle, a whole-hearted determination by the Commissioners that the Houses should aim at the welfare of their more helpless inmates, was lacking.

Opposition to the new Poor Law

The unpopularity of the Poor Law Amendment Act, which Senior and Chadwick had foreseen, was soon manifest. In some villages in the South (including the model, Uckfield), the villagers rose to prevent their paupers being removed out of the parish to the Union workhouses, or rioted to get them back.[98] Dr Edsall has shown how the enforcement of the Act early in 1835 was followed by waves of spontaneous rioting in parts of Kent, Sussex and the Home Counties.[99] Hard winter weather which put ploughmen out of work caused particular hardship, when applicants for relief were offered the House. It was not unusual for the farmworkers, abetted by the local parson, to go to the House in a body in order to swamp it out.[100] The new workhouse regime produced great resentment. The Commissioners' excuses for the separation of families were obviously not believed; parting man and wife was seen as part of a Malthusian plot to reduce the population. Wild rumours circulated about workhouse food, which was believed to be doctored with an anti-fertility substance. An anti-Poor Law guardian at Bridgwater, Somerset, declared that the gruel had spread an outbreak of diarrhoea, at that time generally believed to be a prelude to cholera.[101] In the winter of 1835-36 more serious disturbances in East Anglia culminated in a general rising in East Suffolk, which did not subside until London police and troops had been brought in. In February, more rioting broke out in Devon and Cornwall, a very low-wage area, and the building of Camelford workhouse had to be delayed. This was the Commissioners' first defeat.[102]

Local discontent produced a stream of petitions to parliament. These, of course, came from the more literate, usually the Justices or local gentry. They put forward two main objections to the new law; its harshness, and its centralising tendencies. The town and parish of Tiverton, Devon, complained about the building of a new workhouse because it was costly and would resemble a House of Correction, 'Thereby constituting poverty a crime, repugnant to the feelings of your petitioners'.[103] They denounced the cruel separation of husband and wife in the workhouse, attacked the bastardy clauses, and demanded the restoration of outdoor relief. A more extreme, and sophisticated, petition from industrial Salford claimed that 'The title of landlords to their estates and of Peers to hereditary Possessions rests on the same foundations as the title of the Poor to a maintenance in exchange for their labour from the soil that gave them birth'. It demanded the repeal of the Act, the punishment of its authors, and the repeal of all other acts tending to remove the 'guardianship of the poor from their neighbours, and to place it in the hands of hired overseers or of strangers, and (to) allow the humane 43 Elisabeth again to come into full operation'.[104] This was a Tory–Radical effusion from the northern anti–Poor Law movement. Objections to centralisation were more often expressed on the grounds that the new law was unnecessary, since the system of relief in the petitioners' district had already been reformed, and the rates reduced. The deep cleavage in the opposition between those who repudiated the law's attitude towards pauperism and those who agreed with it in principle but wanted no meddling with their local autonomy, boded no good to the attempt to get it repealed. There was no unity in the opposition, even though many more petitions attacked the Act than supported it, and those in favour were almost all from the new Boards of Guardians. The new order had already set up its own vested interest.

From the start, Tory newspapers, led by *The Times*, had opposed the new Poor Law in principle and practice. They were soon joined by the radical and unstamped press. But the journalists defeated their own ends by concentrating on atrocity stories, which often proved to be insufficiently verified, and exaggerated or false.[105] None the less, by 1837 the continuing agitation by petition, pamphlet and newspaper, combined with the disturbances, had made enough headway to persuade Lord Melbourne to set up Select Committees in both Houses of Parliament to inquire into the operation of the new law.

In 1837 the mood of government and parliament had not changed since 1834. The Commons Committee was packed by Lord John Russell, then Home Secretary, with supporters of the Amendment Act.[106] It is difficult to discover how the Lords Committee was constituted, but its attitude was the same as that of the lower house. The Lords examined complaints of neglect and cruelty in the Unions, especially from persons of rank or note, such as General Johnson, Earl Stanhope, and the Rev. George Stringer Bull. They concluded that almost all the cases cited were of people who had refused to go into the workhouse, and they deduced that, to persons of dissolute and drunken habits, who, if industrious would have had the means of providing for their families and themselves 'The Confinement and Restrictions of the Workhouse are irksome and disagreeable'.[107] After this blinding discovery they attacked Bull for presenting cases which were either fraudulent or taken from the newspapers without verification, criticised Stanhope for presenting cases found for him by an ex-overseer employed by a society in London to collect cases of alleged hardship under the new law, and denounced General Johnson for failing as *ex officio* guardian to attend his own Board meetings at Bourne Union. Bull, in particular, was scolded for stirring up excitement at Bradford, and lending his authority as a clergyman to inflammatory statements the truth of which he had not ascertained.[108]

While the Lords Committee discredited the critics, the Commons

Committee vindicated the new system. It was prepared to admit that labourers with large families were 'said to feel severely the loss of allowances', but claimed that this had been met by judicious relaxations of the rule against taking some children from existing families into the workhouse.[109] After examining witnesses from Petworth, it concluded that the new law had been 'attended with considerable improvement in the character and condition of the poor.... The Employment of agricultural labour appears to be greater; ... the morals and conduct of the labouring poor are said to be improved: ... they have become more provident, and more anxious to obtain and keep their places.'[110] When the Committee re-met in the autumn of 1837, John Walter's place as leader of the opposition had been taken by the much tougher and more radical John Fielden of Todmorden. Fielden attacked the Committee's report with a succession of amending resolutions. But he carried none of them, and the Committee repeated the Lords' criticisms of parson Bull, and confirmed the Assistant Commissioners' 'Strong and uniform conviction of the beneficial effects of the new law'.[111]

Both Committees had swallowed the Commissioners' propaganda whole. The critics had prejudiced their cause by carelessness and exaggeration, but it is doubtful whether the most accomplished testimony could have overturned a system which had become, with remarkable speed, a going concern or *status quo*.

The Commissioners met no really effective opposition until their emissaries, in 1837, began to apply the new law in the industrial towns of the North. It is unnecessary to recount in detail the struggle which has been very well described in Nicholas Edsall's *The Anti-Poor Law Movement*. The Commissioners cannily used the Registration Act of 1837 to set up innocuous Registration Districts, which they could later turn into Poor Law Unions.[112] The dissident industrial towns either refused to elect Boards of Guardians, or chose their guardians specifically to refuse to build workhouses. In the event, the workhouse test was never fully applied in the northern textile districts. In place of the Outdoor Relief Prohibitory Order they remained subject to the Outdoor Labour Test Order of April 1842 and the Outdoor Relief Regulation Order of 1852 which added to the imposition of task work as a condition of relief, the proviso that able-bodied males should not be relieved while employed for wages, and should receive half their grant in kind.[113] Determined and often riotous opposition enabled the industrial counties to ride out the initial period of 'thorough' until half-measures crystallised in the calmer period of the Poor Law Board. But in any case it is difficult to see how the workhouse test could have been applied in towns where, in prosperous days the Houses stood half-empty, while in trade recessions they could not, however large, contain the thousands of unemployed.

In Wales there was resistance mainly because of the poverty of many of the guardians, their conservatism, and their dislike of English administration. They could not be persuaded to reform or rebuild the workhouses,[114] and in 1843 Assistant Commissioner William Day, from

Sussex, having expressed his opinion of the Welsh rather too freely, was made the scapegoat and dismissed.[115] He was unfairly treated, but it is pertinent to speculate whether Poor Law Commissioner Frankland Lewis may have known better than he did how *not* to treat dissenting Welsh hill farmers.

By 1843-44 resistance to the Poor Law in Wales had merged into the Rebecca Riots. 'Rebecca' attacked workhouses, and it was evident from the statements of witnesses before the 1844 Commission of Enquiry that the rural Welsh communities had been deeply upset by the bastardy clauses of the Poor Law Amendment Act.

Indeed, of all the provisions of the new law, the bastardy clauses were probably the most unpopular. A stream of petitions flowed into parliament, complaining that bastardy cases in Quarter Sessions were far too expensive; that affiliation orders were only enforceable against propertied men, so that only the rich could be made to pay for fathering bastards; that parishes were prevented from recovering the cost of supporting mother and child; that the law dealt severely with the weaker party and overlooked the stronger and generally more blameable one; and that, relieved of the fear of punishment, the men did what they pleased.[116] The Commissioners' attempts to show that illegitimate births were decreasing by publishing the figures of bastard babies reaching the workhouses, and affiliation actions in Quarter Sessions, were challenged by the Registrar General.[117] By 1844 the bastardy clauses had already been partially repealed. They were one part of the Poor Law Amendment Act which did not survive the 1870s.

In 1845 a great scandal broke about the treatment of the paupers in Andover workhouse. These unfortunates were found to be supplementing their diet with raw potatoes, hogwash and chicken feed, and to be eating gristle and marrow from bones supplied for crushing. An investigation by Assistant Commissioner Parker failed to quiet the public, and he was dismissed. This attempt of the authorities to divert attention onto a scapegoat produced such a row that Peel's Home Secretary, Sir James Graham, was forced to set up a Select Committee of the House of Commons to investigate. The Committee found a long list of cruelties and mismanagements in the workhouse, but refused to put all the blame on the Workhouse Master. It found that the dietary was below that recommended by the Commissioners, and it blamed the Andover guardians both for the mismanagement of the workhouse and for the rigour with which (generally acting in accordance with the frequently published views of the Poor Law Commissioners) they had carried out the law. Moreover, it listened to the evidence that this had often been the means of inducing labourers to take reduced wages in order to avoid the workhouse.[118]

The Select Committee accepted the kind of evidence which the committee members of 1837 had brushed aside, and its report was, in substance and in tone, in striking contrast to theirs. It blamed Chadwick and Nicholls for their rigour, and the other Commissioners for their slackness and neglect, and it blamed the Treasury for reducing the number of Assistant Commissioners from twenty-one in 1839 to a wholly inadequate nine in 1842.[119] It did everything but demand the repeal of the Poor Law Amendment Act, a demand which Lord John Russell hastened to forestall by replacing the Poor Law Commission in 1847 with a Poor Law Board, of which the two senior members had seats in parliament. This was a means of securing the continuation of the Poor Law central administrative machinery rather than of changing its policy. As Bagehot said, parliament would continue to 'poke at' the Poor Law until it was represented in parliament,[120] and there is no indication that this direct ministerial responsibility made any substantial difference to the conduct of the Victorian Poor Law. But at least for the time being, the days of 'thorough' were over.

Effects of the new Poor Law

In 1837 Chadwick told the House of Commons Select Committee that it was generally acquiesced in that 'relief in the workhouse to the aged destitute persons is so humane a course compared with any other, that we constantly persuade them to accept that mode of relief; and, in fact, the refusal of the workhouse under such circumstances by the aged and infirm person, the refusal of this very careful provision and attendance, may be compared to the refusal of an abode in a well-arranged hospital by a sick or lame person.'[121] Enough is now known about the administration of the new Poor Law to identify this speech as a typical Chadwickian exercise in wishful thinking. But the question remains, how far was the Amendment Act a success?

The Act was intended to do away with the allowance system, and in so doing, to raise wages. In the first flush of enthusiasm many parishes, and Unions when formed, cut off allowances. Yet they tended to reappear, especially in the form of help to ill-paid widows, casual or sporadically employed labourers and town workers. In East Anglia and in many other counties they reappeared as sick relief, especially to the parents of large families, or as payments from the highway rate.[122] The custom of taking one or two children into the workhouse to keep the rest of the family out was soon re-established. Indeed, it has been argued that relief in aid of inadequate wages was actually extended.[123] Outdoor relief cost the ratepayer much less than keeping families in the workhouse, and as long as this was so the workhouse test could never be universally enforced.[124] Thus Chadwick and Senior's intention that wages should be paid to the single man according to his ability (so that he would be encouraged to save and marry late) rather than to the married man according to his family's needs, was not realised. In the 1840s it was reported that the East Anglian workhouses in the winter were full of single men, as well as of those of indifferent character.[125] Even the abuses which accompanied the allowance system, the roundsman and the Labour Rate survived, in the shape of ticket or 'stem' systems by which the farmers delayed relief and drove down farm wages.[126] In bad weather fear of the workhouse goaded men into a desperate search for employment, a situation which tended to drive down wages further. In general, real wages did not rise until free trade and low prices combined with high farming in the 1850s gave the farm labourers a modest share in mid-Victorian prosperity.

With the privilege of hindsight this can be seen as inevitable, since the Poor Law Commissioners refused to admit that the root cause of rural poverty was over-population combined with seasonality, which created the pool of un- and under-employment. At least they implicitly contradicted their own assertions that all who really tried could get work by their strong encouragement of emigration abroad as well as migration to the industrial areas. But the migration schemes were inadequate and unpopular.[127] As long as labour was cheap and labourers so powerless, the farmers would be at their old tricks of using Poor Relief to organise the pool of surplus and seasonal labour for their own convenience.

It may be argued that the Commissioners' fatal mistake was their failure to abolish parish settlement, at least by making the Union rather than the parish responsible for the cost of all those relieved by it. As long as the parishes had to pay for their own paupers, whether on outdoor relief or in the Union workhouse, their overseers would attempt to remove the burdensome newcomer, and the mobility of labour would be hindered. The abolition of apprenticeship and hiring as a means of gaining a new settlement may well have increased the number of removals. There were more after 1834, and the Commissioners increased them further by disallowing the payment of outdoor relief to persons living outside their parish, a vicious outpost as they thought, of the allowance system. But the attempt to put a stop to such payments was unrealistic. The practice of agricultural parishes supporting migrants to industrial towns who had become unemployed could not be suppressed, because the urban parish authorities insisted on it, threatening in industrial depressions to ship whole families back to their place of origin.[128] Nor did the 'Irrèmovability Act' of 1846, which secured from removal persons resident for five years in a new parish, make much difference.[129] As before 1834, the settlement laws were mitigated mainly by 'understandings' between industrial parishes which needed to recruit and retain workers, and rural parishes with insufficient employment opportunities. Employers tended to favour workers whose settlement was elsewhere as more highly motivated to work hard and keep their jobs, and overseers kept them off the relief books by threatening them with removal.[130] Thus the settlement laws continued to bear arbitrarily and sometimes harshly on individuals. They reinforced the power of overseers and of employers over the workforce, both in town and in country.[131] How far they prevented labour mobility may never be finally agreed. A recent writer has concluded that settlement and removal as it was practised, was no great barrier to mobility.[132] It may be surmised that (as might have happened anyway) the more enterprising country dwellers moved in search of higher wages while the more apathetic and less capable remained behind, deterred not so much by the threat of removal as by the knowledge that they could rely on relief only in their own parish.[133]

The complicated problems of settlement dragged on, despite repeated complaints and enquiries, until the Union Chargeability Act of 1865 at last transferred the cost of poor relief from the parish to the Union. This put a stop to the removal of pauper families from one parish to another within the same Union. But removals between different Unions continued right up into the twentieth century.[134]

An important object of the Act, and in particular of the workhouse test, was to force the poor into self-reliance instead of dependence on the parish. But the effect of the unsuccessful attempt to enforce the law in the north was to promote Chartism, a consequence certainly not envisaged by Chadwick. In the south it may have compelled some labourers to be more dependent on and outwardly more subservient to their employers. This was included in the Commissioners' definition of 'independent', so here they scored a limited success, at the probable cost of deep disaffection and bad industrial relations later on. In its aim of 'depauperisation' the new Poor Law can hardly be considered successful.

The use of the workhouse test as a simple means of identifying indigence, invented by Bentham as a substitute for the distinction between the deserving and the undeserving poor, had a short life. An efficient Relieving Officer was nothing if not an investigator, whose main role was to distinguish real need from fraud. By 1870 he was being instructed by the government to hand over cases of genuine misfortune to the Charity Organisation Society, keeping the residue for poor relief.[135] The distinction between deserving and undeserving poor was a very old tradition in English private and public charity, and it returned to take its place in the administration of the nineteenth-century Poor Law.

The bastardy clauses of the Amendment Act were intended to reduce illegitimacy as well as to improve sexual morals. They did nothing of the sort; they probably increased illegitimacy (since they relieved men of responsibility without decreasing the need of women to get themselves married) and they may – although this is difficult to prove – have increased the number of infanticides by desperate mothers.[136]

Conclusion

In methods of administration, except in the degree of attempted central direction, the main feature of the new Poor Law was continuity with the old. Dr Michael Rose has described the large parish of Leeds in the early 1830s, divided into 7 townships for poor relief, employing 20 officers including a clerk and treasurer at £250 a year, and 3 Assistant Overseers. They were praised by Assistant Commissioner Alfred Power as 'equal to the best officers that can be obtained under any management'.[137] There was continuity in the best local management which the Commissioners tried to copy, as well as in the worst, which survived their attempts to change it. Although London workhouses in the 1840s were recognised as feeding institutions for the London prisons, the provincial areas which most scandalously neglected their poor were those whose authorities successfully refused to build new workhouses.[138]

Looking at the development of the Poor Law as a whole, although we can see its outlines but dimly, it appears that from the end of the Napoleonic war new attitudes and a new system were being developed. The rates crisis of 1817–18; the prevalence of Malthusian thinking in the Select Committees of those years; the multiplication of select vestries; paid overseers and Local Act Unions in the 1820s; the foundation of 'well-regulated' workhouses; and the reduction in many parishes of expenditure on the poor; all point in the same direction. The problem of poor relief was outgrowing the capacity of the small parish to deal with it, and neighbourhood care was doomed. A larger unit in the interests of scale and efficiency was becoming necessary, although the separation of financial liability for the pauper from the administration of relief to him by the parish Union compromise of 1834 was a bad way of initiating it. But independently of administrative changes paternalist attitudes were being overwhelmed by population growth, financial instability and new middle-class moralities.

It has been suggested in a recent article by Dr Peter Dunkley that these were developments in which the Amendment Act played no part. He has shown how an attitude of comparative generosity which distinguished Poor Law administration in the North East after 1834 failed in the 1840s under pressure of economic recession, unemployment and rising rates. A change towards meaner, sterner and more censorious attitudes occurred independently of and out of step with the Poor Law Commission and its policies.[139] It would be easy to claim that the Poor Law Amendment Act was of no significance, to submerge it under the tide of historical inevitability, and bury it out of sight. I believe this would be a mistake. Even if the Commissioners did not establish full control over provincial poor relief, nor uniformity in the policies of their assistants; even if, in many places, the law produced harshness without efficiency, it constituted the focal point in the process of change. In 1834 the new development was given a scope, a momentum and a character which made it irreversible. The change was more immediate and more complete in the south than in the north, but it was lasting. Indeed, 'thorough' returned for a time in the 1870s. The Victorian workhouse and all it stood for, including the tainted reforms in medical and educational services which grew from it, was perhaps the most permanent and binding institution of Victorian England. Not until the working class had obtained the vote and entirely different attitudes towards poverty in general and unemployment in particular began to creep in at the turn of the century did the principles of 1834 start to lose their grip.[140]

Sources and references

1. 4 & 5 Wm IV, c. 76, Clauses I-V.
2. *Ibid.*, Cl. VII.
3. *Ibid.*, Cl. XXVI, XXXVIII.
4. *Ibid.*, Cl. XXXVIII, XL. Ratepayers with less than £200 worth of property had a single vote, and those with more had a further vote for each extra £200, up to three votes. Property owners had votes in accordance with Sturges Bourne's (Vestries Regulation) Act - 58 George II, c. 69. The arrangements were a hybrid between Gilbert's Act of 1782 and Sturges Bourne's Act of 1818, where the franchise weighting was 1-6 votes, according to rates paid.
5. *Ibid.*, Cl. XXXVIII.
6. *Ibid.*, Cl. XXIII, XXV.
7. *Ibid.*, Cl. XLVI, XLVIII. The officials dismissable included assistant overseers and Workhouse Masters.
8. *Ibid.*, Cl. XLVII.
9. *Ibid.*, Cl. LXXVII.
10. *Ibid.*, Cl. XV, XVI, XVII.
11. *Ibid.*, Cl. XLII, LXXI.
12. *Ibid.*, Cl. XXXVIII.
13. *Ibid.*, Cl. LIV.
14. *Ibid.*, Cl. XLIII.
15. *Ibid.*, Cl. LII. The Commissioners were already aware that the workhouse test in all its simplicity (rigidity) could not be imposed suddenly on the most pauperised districts, where the allowance system, along with roundsmen or Labour Rate prevailed. This was stated in a memorandum included in the Commissioners' official minutes for 4 November 1834. Task work, hard and low paid, was proposed as an intermediate stage. 'Preliminary Considerations and memorandums (sic) of Essentials with reference to Workhouses and the discipline to be observed in them.' (presumably by Chadwick) PRO, MH1, Vol. 1, pp. 68-9.
16. *Ibid.*, Cl. LII.
17. *Ibid.*, Cl. LII.
18. *Ibid.*, Cl. LVI. Relief to a child was to be considered relief to the mother if she was widowed. But the practice of taking poor families into workhouse schools by day and feeding them there was soon encouraged by the Commissioners as a way of mitigating hardship without destroying the responsibility of parents for their children. Commissioners' Minutes, MH1, Vol. 1, p. 71.
19. *Ibid.*, Cl. LVIII, LIX.
20. *Ibid.*, Cl. XIX.
21. *Ibid.*, Cl. LXIV.
22. *Ibid.*, Cl. LXXI.
23. *Ibid.*, The bastardy clauses were those from LXIX to LXXVI. The right of the woman to sue at least in Quarter Sessions had been maintained by the Lords.
24. The principle of 'less eligibility', only it was carefully referred to as making subsistence in the workhouse 'less desirable' than that obtained by independent exertion, was laid down in the 'Preliminary Considerations' in the Commissioners' Minutes of 4 November, 1834. PRO MH1, Vol. 1, p. 68 *et seq.* This included detailed instructions about separating the sexes, refusing temporary leave, licensing visits, types of suitable work, etc. Presumably it was written by Chadwick, although signed by the three Commissioners.
25. 4 & 5 Wm IV, c. 76, Cl. X.
26. **Finer, S. E.,** *The Life and Times of Sir Edwin Chadwick.* Methuen, 1952, pp. 108-11. **Webb, S.** and **B.** *English Poor Law History* pt. II, Vol. I, p. 105.
27. The Commissioners were not undistinguished. T. G. Shaw Lefevre, an under-secretary at the Colonial Office appointed by Althorp for family reasons, was a Senior Wrangler, Fellow of Trinity College, Cambridge, a traveller and a

linguist. He was a member of the Political Economy Club, which suggests that his views were not far from those of the 'Benthamites'. Brougham's nominee, George Nicholls, was known as a promoter of the model workhouse at Southwell. Frankland Lewis was believed to have drafted the report of Sturges Bourne's committee. Finer, *op. cit.*, pp. 108-9. Webb, S. and B., *op. cit.*, part II, Vol. I, pp. 105-7. **Lewis, R. A.,** *Edwin Chadwick and the Public Health Movement.* Longman, 1952, pp. 20-21. Brundage, *op. cit.* (n. 140 below) pp. 77-9.

28. From 1836 to 1839 the number of Assistant Commissioners stood at 21 before it began to decline. *Select Committee of House of Commons on Andover Union. PP* 1846, V, p. vii.

29. *First Annual Report of Poor Law Commissioners,* 1835. p. 42. (HMSO quarto edition).

30. *Second Annual Report of Poor Law Commissioners,* 1836, p. 3.

31. *Third Annual Report of Poor Law Commissioners,* 1837, pp. 64-9.

32. *Report of the Poor Law Commissioners . . . on the Continuance of the Poor Law Commission,* 1840. More Unions were formed in the West Riding between 1849 and 1854. Unions were split and reconstituted e.g. in West Riding, Lancashire and Cheshire. **Rose, M. E.,** 'Poor Law Administration in the West Riding of Yorkshire (1820-1855)'. Oxford D. Phil., 1965, pp. 98, 121-2.

33. *Fourth Annual Report of Poor Law Commissioners,* 1838. p. 73.

34. *Report of the Poor Law Commissioners . . . on the Continuance of the Poor Law Commission,* 1840 (HMSO quarto edition), p. 26.

35. Figures roughly averaged from table of Poor Law expenditure in **Mitchell, B. R.** and **Deane, Phyllis,** *Abstract of British Historical Statistics.* C.U.P., 1962, p. 410.

36. *First Annual Report of the Poor Law Commissioners,* 1835, pp. 47-57.

37. *Report of the Poor Law Commissioners . . ., on the Continuance of the Poor Law Commission,* p. 28.

38. **Pack, L. F. C.,** 'A Study of the Evolution of the Methods of Poor Relief in the Winchester Area, 1720-1845'. Southampton M.A., 1967, pp. 135-6, 158.

39. *An account of the operation of the Poor Law Amendment in the Uckfield Union . . . by the Earl of Liverpool, Chairman of that Union.* 1836, pp. 11-14. But there were riots later.

40. **Hopkin, N. D.,** 'The Old and New Poor Law in East Yorkshire, *c.* 1760-1850.' Leeds M.Phil., 1968, p. 73.

41. *First Annual Report of the Poor Law Commissioners,* p. 14.

42. *Ibid.,* p. 19.

43. Hopkin, *op. cit.,* p. 80.

44. **Lewis, R. A.,** 'William Day and the Poor Law Commissioners', *University of Birmingham Historical Journal,* **9,** 1964, p. 178.

45. *Ibid.,* p. 172.

46. **Handley, M. D.,** 'Local Administration of the Poor Law in Great Boughton and Wirral Unions and the Chester Local Act Incorporation, 1834-71.' Wales (Bangor) M.A., 1969, pp. 7-8, Map 1.

47. **Brundage, Anthony,** 'The landed interest and the new Poor Law', *Eng. Hist. Review,* LXXXVII, 1972, pp. 27-48.

48. **Dunkley, Peter,** 'The landed interest and the new Poor Law: a critical note', *Eng. Hist. Review,* LXXXVIII, Oct. 1973, pp. 836-41.

49. Sometimes political; there were Whig and Tory Unions.

50. *First Report from the Select Committee on the Poor Law Amendment Act,* Minutes of Evidence. *PP* 1837, XVII, I. pp. 6-7.

51. *Third Annual Report of the Poor Law Commissioners,* 1837. App. C, No. 9, pp. 258-9. The population figures were taken from the 1831 census.

52. *Ibid.,* pp. 308-9.

53. *Second Annual Report of the Poor Law Commissioners,* 1836. App. D, No. 6, pp. 608, 609.

54. For example, the Marquis of Bute had a representative on the Cardiff Union Board.

55. **Brooks, Clive,** 'The Poor in the Medway Towns of Kent, 1832-7'. Uncompleted M.A. thesis.

56. Where there were great landowners, local opposition would obviously be more effective than where Assistant Commissioners only had lesser gentry or tradesmen to deal with.

57. In Surrey the Clerks were paid £80 to £150 according to the population of the Union. They were legal advisers to the Guardians, but not always lawyers. See **Pike, Walter,** 'The Administration of the Poor Law in the Rural Areas of Surrey, 1830-1850'. London (Birkbeck) M.A., 1950, pp. 132-3.

58. For a full account of the duties of Relieving Officers see **Mishra, R. C.,** 'A History of the Relieving Officer in England and Wales, from 1834 to 1948'. London Ph. D., 1969, *passim.*

59. Mishra, *op. cit.,* pp. 49-50.

60. The Chairman of Uckfield Union, the 3rd Earl of Liverpool, maintained that the good conduct of the Union depended on the guardians' strict examination of the Relieving Officer's request and relief books, avoiding as much as possible any direct communication between the Board and the paupers. **The Earl of Liverpool,** *An Account . . . of the Poor Law Amendment in Uckfield Union . . .,* pp. 14-15. Enraged paupers sometimes attacked the Relieving Officers in spontaneous rioting. **Edsall, Nicholas,** *The Anti Poor Law Movement, 1834-44.* Manchester U.P., 1971, p. 31.

61. See **Brundage, Anthony,** 'The English Poor Law of 1834 and the cohesion of agricultural society', *Agricultural History,* **48,** 1974, pp. 405-417. At Brackley and Towcester, Northamptonshire, the landed gentry insisted on London policemen, while the farmers resisted.

62. In Uckfield Union the salaries of Relieving Officers and Workhouse governors (often coupled) varied from £30 to £80. See The Earl of Liverpool, *op. cit.,* p. 37. The latter workhouse was in Howden Union, East Yorkshire. The Relieving Officer at Howden was found to be embezzling money and falsifying his accounts, and had to resign. Hopkin, *op. cit.,* pp. 81-2.

63. Bridlington offered £20 a year each for Master and Matron. Howden, £35 for the Master and £15 for his wife. The big Workhouse at Beverley carried a salary of £50. Hopkin, *op. cit.,* pp. 246-50.

64. Mishra, *op. cit.,* p. 37.

65. For a detailed, if somewhat confused description of Poor Law Medical services see **Hodgkinson, Ruth,** *The Origins of the National Health Service.* Wellcome Historical Medical Library, 1967, *passim.* This is a somewhat euphoric account. Flinn, M., 'Medical Services under the New Poor Law', in Fraser, D. (ed.), *The New Poor Law in the Nineteenth Century.* Macmillan, 1976, pp. 45-66. Flinn is more critical, but omits developments between 1834 and 1842.

66. The Medical Officer was usually paid a fixed salary and was required to provide medical attendance and medicine to all sent to him by the Relieving Officer. He was feed for midwifery cases. Mishra, *op. cit.,* pp. 48-50. Hopkin, *op. cit.,* pp. 165-75.

67. Flinn points out that a part-time Poor Law engagement helped doctors to build up their private practice. It seems improbable that the best qualified and most successful doctors resorted to this ill-paid and unprestigious service.

68. **Lewis, R. A.** 'William Day and the Poor Law Commissioners', *University of Birmingham Historical Journal,* **9,** 1963-64, pp. 185-6.

69. Flinn, *op. cit.,* p. 54.

70. Flinn, *op. cit.,* pp. 48-9.

71. Flinn, *op. cit.,* p. 54. The Unions objected strongly to this rule, and between 20 and 30 obtained exemption from it. Hodgkinson, *op. cit.,* p. 14.

72. An Act of 1885 abolished this disability.

73. Flinn, *op. cit.,* p. 51. Out of a total expenditure of £4.5 million in 1840, medical relief accounted for £150,000. In 1871 out of a total of just under £8 million, medical relief accounted for less than £300,000.

74. These associations of Poor Law doctors went through various phases. The Provincial Medical and Surgical Association and the first British Medical

Association were followed by the Convention of Poor Law Medical Officers and the Poor Law Medical Officers' Association. *Ibid.*, pp. 59-60.

75. The Act was given various names.

76. The author served briefly as a Red Cross auxiliary nurse in one of these hospitals during the last war. The patients all had bedsores, and the food was uneatable.

77. Pike, *op. cit.*, pp. 133-4.

78. *Poor Law Commission Report*, p. 173.

79. Poor Law Remedial Measures. Comments of Mr Day of Uckfield. *Chadwick Papers*, 18.

80. *An Account of . . . the Poor Law Amendment in Uckfield Union*, pp. 21, 27-32.

81. Hopkin, *op. cit.*, pp. 227 *et seq.*

82. *First Annual Report of the Poor Law Commissioners*, App., p. 407 *et. seq.*

83. *Poor Law Commission Report*, p. 129.

84. Intentions are to be found in the 'Preliminary Considerations' in the Commissioners' Minutes of 4 November 1834. PRO MH1, Vol. 1. Hand mills for corn grinding were commended as specially suitable for pauper labour in a list of occupations identical with those of contemporary prisons, with the possible exception of the treadmill grinding air.

85. *First Annual Report of the Poor Law Commissioners*, 1835, pp. 34-5.

86. Rose, *op. cit.*, pp. 243-4.

87. Brooks, *op. cit.*

88. **Thomas, J. E.,** 'Poor Law Administration in West Glamorgan from 1834 to 1930'. Wales (Swansea) M.A., 1951, p. 29.

89. *Ibid.*, pp. 54, 84.

90. See **McCord, N.,** 'The implementation of the Poor Law Amendment Act on Tyneside, *International Review of Social History*, XIV 1969, Pt. 1, pp. 90-108. Professor McCord makes the usual mistake of thinking that the new law which was kindly in his area was kindly everywhere else. Mr Peter Dunkley has since shown that favourable attitudes towards the very poor waned under the pressure of the Hungry Forties. **Dunkley, P.,** 'The Hungry Forties and the New Poor Law: a Case Study', *The Historical Journal*, XVII, 2, 1974, pp. 329-46.

91. **Mawson, P.,** 'Poor Law Administration in South Shields, 1830-1930'. Newcastle on Tyne M.A., 1971, p. 28.

92. *Third Report of the Select Committee on the Poor Law Amendment Act*, 1837. pp. 28-9. *PP* 1837, XVII, 1.

93. Mawson, *op. cit.*, p. 29. The same was true of Newport Pagnell Workhouse, Buckinghamshire.

94. *First Report of the Select Committee, etc.*, p. 39. *PP* 1837, XVII. 1.

95. **Henriques, U.** 'How cruel was the Victorian Poor Law?', *The Historical Journal*, XI, 1968, 365-71. This view was expressed in the 'Preliminary Considerations' in The Commissioners' Minutes, 4 November 1834.

96. *Fourth Annual Report of the Poor Law Commissioners*, 1838. App. B3, p. 228. In 1838 it was discovered that, of 97,510 workhouse inmates in 478 Unions in England and Wales, 42,767, or nearly half, were children (presumably under 16). *Report of the Poor Law Commissioners . . . on the continuance of the Poor Law Commission*, 1840, p. 56.

97. *Fourth Annual Report of the Poor Law Commissioners*, 1838. App. B.3, p. 229.

98. Edsall, N., *op. cit.*, pp. 30-31.

99. *Ibid.*, pp. 27-32.

100. *Fourth Report from the Select Committee on the Poor Law Amendment Act*, 1837. *PP* 1837, XVII, p. 6. The clergy were thoroughly divided on the new Poor Law.

101. **Bowen, John,** *Refutation of the Charges Against the Poor*, 2nd ed. London, 1837, p. 10.

102. Edsall, *op. cit.*, pp. 35-6, 39.

103. *Appendix to the 9th Report on Public Petitions*, 4041.

104. *Ibid.*, 160.

105. **Roberts, David,** 'How cruel was the new Poor Law', *Historical Journal*, VI, 1963, pp. 97-107.

106. **Henriques, U.** 'Jeremy Bentham and the Machinery of Reform', in *British Government and Administration*, Hearder, H. and Loyn, H. R. (eds.), University of Wales Press, 1974, p. 171. Cf. Finer, *op. cit.*, pp. 129-37.

107. *Report from the Select committee of the House of Lords on the Poor Law Amendment Act. PP* 1837-38, XIX. I, p. VII.

108. *Ibid.*, p. ix.

109. *Report from the Select Committee of the House of Commons on the Poor Law Amendment Act. PP* 1837, XVII.I, pp. 7-8. Quoted in Finer, *op. cit.*, pp. 136-9. Chadwick persuaded Russell to cancel the General Order permitting this relaxation.

110. *Ibid.*, p. 7.

111. *Report from the Select Committee, etc.*, 1838. *PP* 1837-38, XVIII. I, p. 12.

112. However, M. E. Rose points out that this Act produced over-haste and disastrous blunders in setting up Unions in the West Riding. Rose, *op. cit.*, pp. 107-12.

113. **Rose, M. E.** 'The allowance system under the new Poor Law', *Econ. Hist. Review*, 2nd series XIX, 1966, pp. 607-20.

114. **Jones, Tydfil Davies,** 'Poor Law and Public Health Administration in the area of Merthyr Tydfil Union 1834-1894'. Wales (Cardiff) M.A., 1961, *passim*.

115. Lewis, R. A., *op. cit.*, pp. 163-95.

116. *Appendix to the 11th Report on Public Petitions*, 4557. Hopkin, *op. cit.*, p. 455.

117. **Henriques, U.,** 'Bastardy and the new Poor Law', *Past and Present*, **37,** July 1967 pp. 122-3.

118. *Report of the Select Committee on the Andover Union. PP* 1846, V. I, pp. iii-x, and Minutes of evidence, p. 9. Cf. **Webb, S.** and **B.,** *Poor Law History* Part 2, Vol. 1, pp. 179-82.

119. *Select Committee on the Andover Union*, p. viii.

120. **Bagehot, Walter,** *The English Constitution.* Quoted in Webb, S. and B., *op. cit.*, p. 184.

121. *Twenty-first report from the Select Committee on the Poor Law Amendment Act. PP* 1837, XVII. II, p. 50.

122. **Digby, Anne,** 'The labour market and the continuity of social policy after 1934: the case of the Eastern Counties', *Econ. Hist. Review*, 2nd series XXVIII no. 1, pp. 78-79. **Digby, Anne,** 'The Rural Poor Law', in Fraser, D. (ed.), *The New Poor Law in the Nineteenth Century*, Macmillan 1976, pp. 157-8.

123. Rose, M.E ., 'The allowance system under the new Poor Law', *op. cit.*, pp. 607-20.

124. Digby, Anne, 'The Rural Poor Law', *op. cit.*, pp. 149-70. It was estimated that the cost of relieving a rural labourer with his family in the workhouse was double his wages.

125. *ibid.* Digby, Anne, *'The labour market, etc.'*, *op. cit.*, p. 74.

126. *Ibid.*, pp. 69-83.

127. **Redford, A.,** *Labour Migration in England, 1800-1850.* Manchester U.P., 1926, *passim.* The migration of large families from East Anglia to the textile towns was enthusiastically promoted by J. Phillips Kay - later J. Kay-Shuttleworth - at that time Assistant Poor Law Commissioner for the area. But it ran into the trade recession of 1837, and many of the migrants were removed. They had been regarded by the textile workers as a strike-breaking force.

128. **Rose, M. E.,** 'Settlement, removal and the New Poor Law', in Fraser (ed.), *The New Poor Law in the Nineteenth Century.* Macmillan, 1976, pp. 35-6.

129. *Ibid.*, p. 36. It did however, suddenly burden some industrial parishes with the support of numbers of poor families hitherto supported from outside. In 1847 Bodkin's Act transferred this cost from parish funds to the Common Fund of the Union.

130. *Ibid.*, p. 37.

131. Overseers in northern industrial towns regularly refused poor relief to operatives on strike.

132. Rose, M. E., *op. cit.*, p. 36.

133. I am indebted for this point to Mr Gerald Lewis. James Stephen Taylor agrees,

and goes on to argue that the settlement law provided industrial towns and (sometimes) sparsely populated agricultural areas with an élite force of the more vigorous and enterprising labourers, while the others remained in their parishes of settlement. **Taylor, James Stephen,** 'The impact of pauper settlement 1691–1834', *Past and Present,* **73,** Nov. 1976, p. 67.

134. Rose, M. E., *op. cit.,* p. 31. The Settlement Law was not finally repealed until 1948.
135. *Relief to the Poor in the Metropolis* – Minute of The Poor Law Board, 1869. In **Rose, M. E.,** *The English Poor Law 1780–1930.* David & Charles, 1971, pp. 226–28.
136. Henriques, U., 'Bastardy and the new Poor Law', *op. cit.,* p. 125.
137. Rose, M. E., 'Poor Law Administration in the West Riding of Yorkshire', p. 26.
138. Jones, Tydfil Davies, *op. cit., passim.*
139. Dunkley, Peter, *'The Hungry Forties and the New Poor Law: A Case Study'.,* pp. 329–46.
140. For a detailed account of the passing of the Poor Law Amendment Act and its enforcement, especially in East Anglia and the East Midlands, see **Brundage, Anthony,** *The Making of the New Poor Law.* Rutgers U.P., 1978. I regret that this book appeared too late for proper consideration in this work.

4 The Factory Acts: I

Early attempts at regulation

Before the Industrial Revolution it was taken for granted that the children of the lower orders should work as soon as they could be of use to their parents. Child labour was part of the domestic economy. Little Bo Peep lost her sheep in many an open field, while her brother started bird-scaring at the age of seven. In the so-called 'developing countries' child labour is still commonplace. Tiny children stand all day long in the *suk* of Fez holding the threads for adult lacemakers, and small boys sit hammering patterns into brass plates for the tourist trade. Small shepherds watch their flocks by day and night on the plains of North Africa. In eighteenth-century Britain nobody thought it necessary or desirable to protect children from the tyranny of their parents, who were applauded for accustoming them early to habits of industry.

While all worked if they could, those who suffered most were the pauper children, deprived of family protection. They were presumed to be growing up idle, improvident and dissolute, and were sent to 'schools of industry', where industrial training was too often sacrificed to semi-skilled production for the sake of self-sufficiency, or to workhouses which have been described as 'loosely conducted and highly inefficient factories for the preliminary processes of the textile trades'.[1] Here, where the children were already working twelve hours a day exclusive of meal breaks, it was a short step to sending pauper apprentices to fill the demand for child labour in the early factories.

The application of power to industrial machinery first created the demand for the control of child labour. This in its long-drawn-out initial phases created the market for light, semi-skilled labour, which produced a rapid rise in the number of children employed outside their own homes. Then local epidemics drew attention to the conditions in which they worked.[2] The novelty and abuses of the factory rather than the fact of child labour shocked disinterested contemporaries.

There were two strands in the struggle for factory legislation. Middle-class humanitarians sought state intervention to control not the existence but the abuses of child labour, and their prime interest was child welfare. Among adult factory workers the control of child exploitation was part of the maintenance of their own security, wages and conditions of employment; and this much less publicised aspect of the factory movement was present throughout. It has been shown that a 'normal' working day, from 6 a.m. to 6 p.m. including two one-hour meal breaks, had become established among the artisans of most trades in the early eighteenth century.[3] This tradition was being destroyed in the textile manufacture of the late eighteenth and early nineteenth centuries, where technical changes, transference to new geographical areas and the introduction of cheap female and child labour were accompanied by varying but extensive lengthening of working hours. By the 1830s other industries such as coalmining were also extending hours, although others, usually through trade union pressure, had maintained the norm of the ten-hour day. This would explain the obsession of the Yorkshire factory movement with ten-hour bills. Adult labour depended very largely on the assistance of children and young persons, and the demand for the regulation of children's hours was partly a respectable front for other aims. Before parliamentary committees concealment was advisable because of the growing dominance of economic theories insisting on a 'free' labour market, not only among factory owners, but throughout the ruling and middle classes. Factory legislation was second only to the wages struggle in provoking conflict of interest, ideas and feelings between capital and labour. This was augmented by the close and known connection between the trade union leaders and the organisers of short-time committees in the textile districts, and the fact that the demand for factory bills was often put forward in the middle of wages strikes.[4] On the other hand it was partly mitigated by the fact that, from the beginning, the operatives were helped and sometimes inspired by a small proportion of benevolent millowners, of all political persuasions. These masters, who had their employees' welfare at heart, were encouraged in supporting limited hours and other factory regulation by the wish to prevent their rivals undercutting and underselling them by overworking and exploiting the more defenceless of their workers.

The question of regulating the hours and conditions of children's employment first arose in textile manufacture because of its lead in the development of British industry. By 1780, Arkwright, his partners and other proprietors were reported to have erected some fifteen or twenty water-powered spinning rollers in the northern counties, which were estimated to drive some 30,000 spindles.[5] Smaller carding machines and jenny factories were also being established on the banks of Pennine streams. Power-driven machinery was introduced in Nottingham, which came to specialise in lace and hosiery, and more gradually in the well-established Yorkshire woollen and worsted industry.[6] Cotton proved specially adaptable to machines originally devised for wool, and attention was drawn to its rapid development by an outbreak of machine-breaking in Lancashire in 1779. But the industry was too profitable to be stopped. When in 1785 Arkwright's patent was ended while Crompton's mule combining roller and jenny spinning came into operation, cotton manufacture got into its stride. Between 1785 and 1795 the official value (based on quantity) of cotton goods exported rose from £864,710 to £2,433,331 per year. By 1830 it had reached £35,395,400.[7]

The first warning was heard in 1784, when a group of physicians was commissioned by the Lancashire Magistrates to investigate an epidemic at Sir Robert Peel's mill at Ratcliffe Bridge. The report, written by Dr Thomas Percival who was already well known for his pamphlets on the state of the manufacturing population, attributed the fever to long hours of work, filthy conditions and bad ventilation. As a consequence the magistrates (presumably not millowners or their friends) resolved not to apprentice parish children to the owners of cotton mills where they would have to work at night or for more than ten hours in the day.[8] If this policy had spread, or had even been maintained in Manchester, the whole history of industrial relations might have been different; but it ran in the face of growing economic power. Twelve years later, the same group of doctors, now organised in what they called a 'Board of Health', discussed a list of resolutions culled from an investigation of the local mills. The resolutions included a declaration that children and other workers crowded in large cotton factories were particularly liable to fever, which then spread through the neighbourhood; that child workers suffered in health from close confinement, hot or impure air, and want of appropriate exercise, as well as from working at night and protracted working by day; that factory children were deprived of moral and religious education; and that parliament should be asked 'to establish a general system of laws for the wise, humane, and equal government of all such works'.[9] The main demands of the middle-class factory reformers were thus early formulated.

The Manchester doctors had little success in arousing public opinion, although they may have been instrumental in inducing Peel to take up the question of the factory apprentices. Many of the early water mills were built by remote Pennine streams or Midland mill ponds. This was the era of apprentice labour, because the rural population detested factory discipline, and the proprietors could not find enough young workers to service their water-frame machines. They were driven to import workhouse orphans from as far away as Bristol or London, and to become responsible for building apprentice houses, and boarding, clothing and educating their workforce. Inevitably these children, sent away by the Poor Law authorities to get their settlement elsewhere, were poor, sickly and ungovernable. More than a third of the apprentices in Midland mills absconded, died, or for some reason had to be returned to those who sent them.[10] Robert Owen referred to a report that the London overseers compelled the proprietors to accept one idiot in each batch of twenty children.[11] He had found at Lanark some 500 workhouse children from Edinburgh aged between 5 and 8 years. They were working a thirteen-hour day with one and a half hours off for meals, and the well-intentioned proprietor David Dale had had to accept them at that early age or he could get none.[12] Because Peel noticed that the many parish children employed at his Tamworth works were unhealthy and stunted, he sponsored the Health and Morals of Apprentices Act in 1802.[13]

Peel's first Act, for cotton factories only, was an attempt to generalise the treatment afforded to apprentices by the most responsible and philanthropic of the millowners. Boys and girls must have separate accommodation, with no more than two to a bed. All were to have two suits of clothes a year. There was to be daily instruction in reading, writing and arithmetic at the owner's expense. All night working of children was to stop, and they were not to work more than twelve hours a day, exclusive of meals. A local magistrate and clergyman, not being millowners, appointed by the magistrates at Quarter Sessions would act as visitors to enforce the law.

The main importance of this Act was as a precedent. The responsibility forced on masters because the children were their living-in apprentices was later transferred to 'free' child labour. The prohibition of night work, and the limitation of day-work hours, although inadequate for health and useless for the purpose of education, set another precedent. Exactly how far this Act was effective is difficult to say. The main problem in all factory legislation was its enforcement.

Peel's Act of 1802 rapidly became irrelevant, as technical advances changed the organisation of the textile industry. The utilisation of steam ensured that the cotton industry would develop near the great coalfields of Lancashire and Glasgow.[14] Yorkshire developed its long-standing woollen and worsted manufacture, with some flax spinning,[15] while Macclesfield specialised in silk, to the detriment of the old London Spitalfields trade. Industrial towns and villages grew round the new factories, sometimes of superior two-bedroomed cottages supplied by the more responsible masters such as the Ashtons of Hyde, the Gregs of Styal, and Robert Owen of New Lanark, but more often run up by the speculative builder. Young workers, while still outnumbering the adult males, were now 'free', i.e. non-apprentice labour, living at home and hired by master, overlooker or adult operative, by agreement with their parents. They were outside the scope of Peel's Health and Morals of Apprentices Act.

New technology, especially the development of mule spinning which combined rollers with jennies, also altered work organisation within the mills. In 1833 there were still water-frame or throstle mills, turning out coarse yarn for warps, and employing a large number of women and young persons, usually engaged direct by the master.[16] But the bulk of the fine spinning was performed by mules, and in these mills a varying but large proportion of the young workers were hired and paid by the adult male operatives, whom they assisted. Each operative required three or four children. The youngest, often between 7 and 10 years old, served as scavenger, retrieving ends from beneath the mule, where the threads were only about 18 inches off the ground so that the operative could reach the top of the machine. The others were 'piecers', or 'pieceners', who followed the mule carriage in and out, tying broken threads. In woollen mills most of the family teams seem to have been employed on the hand-operated slubbing machine or 'billy' which took the thick band of wool from the carding machine and drew it into a thread fine enough to go onto the power-driven spinning machine. The piecers' job was to tie the ends of the wool from the cards on to that on the billy.[17] At 13 or 14 the piecers might graduate to other processes for which they were hired by the manager. The boys might be employed in the washing and finishing sheds, on heavy men's work to which masters assigned adolescent boys or other cheap labour if they could. Some eventually became comparatively well-paid male operatives, both skilful and strong, pushing the heavy mule carriages in and out. For the less fortunate boys, piecening was a dead-end job which left them on the streets at fourteen. Young women might find work in the carding and combing sheds. In general there were more jobs for young people than for adult males. Some wealthy or careful employers might seek to attract families by offering the fathers places as porters, or even gardeners, but many were left earning a pittance as handloom weavers working for the local factory, or unemployed and dependent on the incomes of their children.

The most fortunate families were those which might work as a team. A father with three children close together in age might be employed as an adult mule spinner, earning 25s 8d a week, with an additional 13s for the earnings of the children, at 2s 10¾d for the youngest (scavenger) and 5s 4¾d each for the two older pieceners.[18] Obviously when the children grew up the team would have to split; and in families where there were more children or the father was not employed as a spinner they had to be hired out to strangers. These sometimes paid them more, but treated them with less than parental care.[19]

The system was essentially unstable, both as to wages and employment. Apart from booms and recessions, profits declined between 1815 and 1832, and wages with them. A fine spinner who in 1814 could earn up to 32s a week, in 1833 could earn only 20s to 25s. But prices had also fallen, so that Baines could set out to prove statistically that real wages had actually risen.[20] In the early 1830s employers discovered that they could couple the mules, dismissing half the operatives and retaining the strongest men to manipulate the linked machines. The same number of pieceners was required as before.[21] At about the same time the self-acting or automatic mule, patented in 1825, was coming into use;[22] so that the requirement for adult males in proportion to young people and children declined still further. Peel's second Act, prompted by Robert Owen, and subsequent Acts were devised to meet this new situation.

Beginnings of the Factory Movement

The period 1815–31 saw a series of Factory Regulation Bills; three quite important Acts, to wit, Peel's of 1819, Hobhouse's of 1825, and

Hobhouse's second Act of 1831; also a House of Commons Select Committee from 25 April to 18 June 1816, and a Committee of the Whole House in 1819. This progression has long since been described by M. W. Thomas in *The Early Factory Legislation*,[23] as has been the struggle for the Ten Hour Bill in Yorkshire in the 1830s and 1840s, by Cecil Driver in his life of Robert Oastler,[24] and J. T. Ward in his work on the Factory Movement.[25] Only in 1975 however, have the details of the agitation behind the legislation and enquiries between 1815 and 1831 been elucidated by R. G. Kirby and A. E. Musson.[26] It is now apparent that the Factory Movement began, as might have been expected, in Lancashire where the great cotton industry began. The first short-time committee dates as far back as 1814, when it was financed by spinners' contributions with the help of a local merchant, Nathaniel Gould.[27] Robert Owen, who devised Peel's Bill, and lobbied for it, was supported by petitions from Manchester and the surrounding cotton towns.[28] Owen was anxious to raise the minimum age of children working in textile mills to 10 (12 if he could have managed it), extend protection to children in silk and flax mills, abolish night working, limit the hours of adolescents as well as children, and use the time thus gained for education. His plans were not all that radical, coming at a time when conditions in many mills were approaching their worst. They would have procured a ten-and-a-half-hour day exclusive of meal breaks; but provisions for making up time lost in water mills through shortage of water and in steam mills through the breakdown of steam engines would probably have allowed owners to circumvent them. As it was, the masters had now organised a parliamentary lobby which succeeded in emasculating Owen's proposals. In the Committee each side used medical evidence. The masters relied on practitioners who depended on their patronage, to assert that thirteen hours of light labour in a warm and airy textile mill was good for the health of young children. The reformers produced physicians from the local dispensaries and independent medical pundits from London to contradict them. Peel gave in to pressure, and the 1819 Act offered nothing better than a twelve-hour day for children between 9 and 18 in cotton mills only, without time for education. Hobhouse's Act of 1825 had behind it the force of the militant Manchester Cotton Spinners' Union, encouraged by the recent repeal of the Combination Acts, but somewhat divided in its priorities between wage demands, petitioning against the probable restoration of the Combination laws, and factory regulation. The Bill itself was (as he claimed) drafted by Francis Place[29] and introduced by John Cam Hobhouse, a middle-class radical who, like Place, believed in the laws of political economy and the free labour market, and was unlikely to sponsor a revolutionary measure. It extended the night hours when work was forbidden, and introduced the principle of a shorter (nine hours) Saturday.

Some attempts were already being made at solving the difficult problem of enforcement. Owen had proposed Visitors, appointed by the local Clerk of the Peace or County Magistrates, supplementing an annual written declaration by the factory owners that they had observed the Act. This has been hailed as an early use of inspectors, but was much more probably connected with the tendency of operatives to appeal from borough magistrates, many of whom were involved in the cotton industry, or related to those who were, to county JPs who were often landowning gentry. The 1819 and 1825 Acts relied on informers, encouraged by an award of half of the fine on securing a conviction. This apparently primitive method was the most promising which could be conceived at the time. Millowners could see what their rivals were doing, even if only because the neighbouring mills were lit up at night. Enforcement by informers encouraged John Doherty of the Manchester Spinners' Union to found his Society for the Protection of Children Employed in Cotton Factories. The central society in Manchester was soon copied by local societies in the surrounding cotton towns. Between 1829 and 1831 Doherty and Thomas Foster, on behalf of the Manchester Society, travelled round the mills bringing court actions against recalcitrant millowners and managers who overworked their children against the law, trying to enforce Hobhouse's Act.[30] If they were not very successful (Doherty reported to a meeting of the society in April 1830 that of 187 cases brought against the masters they had secured only 27 convictions) they made enough impression to secure by agreement with the larger millowners a standard twelve-hour day in Manchester itself. Some of the more benevolent masters themselves organised a similar committee to enforce Hobhouse's second Act in 1831.[31] During these attempts at enforcement by voluntary associations, many of the problems later to become familiar to the Factory Inspectors declared themselves. There were the poor, and unco-operative parents, the hostile magistrates who regularly dismissed cases on grounds of minor technical errors, the inadequate fines, and the intimidation of witnesses, who could expect dismissal if they gave evidence against their masters. Undoubtedly their experiences in these enforcement attempts built up the resentment against the millowners which induced the operatives to get tough with the employers in Sadler's Bill of 1832, and led to their defeat.

The new feature of the Factory Movement after 1830 was the temporary transference of its leadership from Lancashire to the West Riding. The Lancashire operatives and their friends were disillusioned and disheartened both by their failures in getting the law enforced and by the collapse of the strikes against lower wages, as the trade recession of 1830 reduced both hours and piecework wage lists.[32] There were also developments in the woollen industry which had led to urgent demands for factory regulation among its operatives.

By 1830 mechanisation in wool spinning and weaving seems to have caught up with that in the cotton trade. At the same time the market for wool was poor, and competition for orders was producing desperate overtime working in some mills alongside unemployment in others. Wool, flax and silk had never enjoyed the unrivalled predominance in world markets of British spun cottons, and foreign competition was feared, possibly with more justification among wool than among cotton manufacturers. It was known that France, Austria, Switzerland and North America were all building textile mills.[33] This coincided with a decline in profits since 1825 which had enhanced competition between millowners, and forced them to improve and extend their machinery.[34] The temptation to use this valuable capital to its utmost before it fell out of date was great, even while saving in manpower through the new machines caused unemployment. The millowners sought to stay solvent by speeding up the machinery, installing longer mules with double the number of spindles, lengthening hours of work, and engaging as much cheap, i.e. woman and child, labour as possible. 'Spare sets' of hands, which had been kept in reserve in some mills to take the place of young workers who became sick or exhausted, disappeared.[35] All such pressures helped to sour industrial relations. In addition, some of the machinery in use in Yorkshire in the 1820s deformed those who worked with it, especially the young. The throstle spinner gradually lamed young people who stopped the machines by repeatedly raising one knee. Bradford at this time was a town of crippled adolescents.

Hobhouse's Act of 1831, promoted by three Bradford millowners, John Wood, John Rand and Matthew Thompson, banned night work for all under 21 while limiting working hours for those under 18 to twelve a day including meal hours (in effect a ten-and-a-half-hour day). But it allowed more latitude than before for making up time lost by accident or water shortage. It continued the requirement for age certificates already specified in the Act of 1825, and introduced a time book in which masters must enter the children's working hours, and which, following written notice, would be subject to inspection by the magistrates. But it applied only to cotton mills, and in disgust, the Yorkshire woollen operatives turned to a more whole-hearted parliamentary champion.[36] Within two months the Tory Evangelical M. T. Sadler's Ten Hour Bill had been introduced in the House of Commons amid unprecedented agitation.

The Factory Movement occurred in the context not only of the struggle between capital and labour but in that of other economic and social rivalries. There was jealousy between industrialists and the surrounding landed gentry, a rift which had encouraged operatives to look for protection from millowner to county JPs. The crisis of 1831–32 overcame the hostility towards Tory philanthropists of working-class agitators such as Doherty who were demanding a democratic franchise, and resulted in a 'Tory–Radical alliance'. This alliance produced many of the local and national leaders of the Factory Movement, including Oastler, Bull, Ferrand and (in parliament) Sadler and Lord Ashley. Tory radicals were not beguiled by the tenets of political economy and were not committed to the doctrine of the free labour market. They were therefore less inhibited in their support of the industrial worker – and to a lesser degree, the rural poor – than were Whig Radicals such as Hobhouse, or Benthamites such as Francis Place. They led the Short Time Movement until the alliance weakened under the strain of differences about the

Reform Bill and later and more seriously about Chartism. Those who left were replaced by Nonconformists of the extreme radical brand such as Rayner Stephens,[37] while a group of philanthropic millowners of diverse political affiliations supported them rather erratically in parliament. At the political centre this combination was hardly strong enough to outweigh the main body of industrialists (the more impressive in that some could claim to be providers of good housing and education to their own workpeople) with their allies among the 'centrists', i.e. Whigs and Peelites. But it was too strong to be ignored, even during the struggle for the Reform Bill.

Because many millowners were Dissenters, the Short Time Movement acquired a tinge of Anglican intolerance. Because they included anti-slavery enthusiasts its spokesmen, from Doherty in Lancashire to Oastler in Yorkshire, expressed contempt for the fight against West Indian slavery. There was continual comparison of the harsh treatment meted out to British 'factory slaves' with the short working day and comfortable conditions believed to be secured by legislation to the West Indian negroes. Thus dissenting hypocrisy was a favourite theme of Short Time polemics. Oastler attacked it in a famous passage of invective:

> Yes, Mr Baines, this master, John Schofield must be a *very*
> 'pious', 'respectable', 'humane', 'charitable' man. He is quite a
> 'pillar' in the dissenting church. . . . 'Satan is pleased such
> saintship to behold', and so, Baines are you. Your Dissenters
> may call such as these 'saints' and 'pillars' and 'deacons', but as
> long as I have pen or tongue to use I will denounce them as
> Cardinal Legates from the Court of Hell.[38]

The Ten Hour Bill and Sadler's committee

Sadler's Ten Hour Bill contained little new; nor did it promise to be particularly effective. It retained most of Hobhouse's 1831 Act, including age certificates and time books. The ten-hour limitation was to apply to all under 18. Education was dropped.[39] Ashley's Ten Hour Bill was novel largely in its proposals for enforcement by draconian punishments. Millowners would be subject to a fine of £20 for a first offence, doubled on second conviction and trebled on the third. For the latter they would also be imprisoned for a term ranging from three to twelve months.[40] They could be fined £100 for making false entries in the time book[41] (which had to be certified correct on oath to the Justices), or for procuring false age certificates.[42] The parents' penalty for signing a false certificate remained, as before, a fine of up to £5.[43] There were intermediate penalties for foremen and overlookers. The masters were made responsible for accidents. Fatalities caused by unfenced machinery and certified by the coroner, would be automatically followed by an action for man-slaughter,[44] and injuries would carry a penalty of £50 to £200, to be paid to the injured.[45] This loading of heavy penalties on the masters was bound to provoke a confrontation, which was probably what the exasperated operatives desired.

The second reading of Sadler's Bill took place on 16 March 1832. Its supporters leaned heavily on an emotional appeal.

> Our ancestors could not have supposed it possible . . . that a generation of Englishmen could exist, and had existed, that would task lisping infancy, of a few summers old regardless alike of its smiles or tears, and unmoved by its unresisting weakness, eleven, twelve, thirteen, fourteen, sixteen hours a day, and through the weary night also, until, in the dewy morn of existence, the bud of youth faded, and fell ere it was unfolded. . . .[46]

Sadler argued in substance that children were not free agents, and their parents, helpless to resist a system which forced them to surrender their children to the factories on pain of starvation, were not free agents either. This was an attempt to counter the free trade–free labour arguments of the factory lobby. The masters' spokesmen maintained that economic and social evils were bound to follow any attempt to interfere with the labour market. Shortened working hours could only result in the triumph of foreign competition, producing lower wages and unemployment. Moreover, legislation could not substitute for the protection parents ought to give their own children. If a child had to work half-time in one factory, he would certainly be sent to complete the day in another. They relied on evidence from the Lords' committee of 1819 to show that factory workers enjoyed a low death rate, were healthy, and rarely applied for parish relief.[47]

Lord Althorp, Chancellor of the Exchequer, who was handling the factory question, had probably been got at by the factory lobby. When the Bill passed its second reading, it was referred to a Select Committee, which ensured that it would not be completed before parliament dissolved. This manoeuvre provoked angry protests,[48] yet Sadler and his supporters made good use of the Select Committee. Its thirty-seven members comprised representatives from both sides, including Poulett Thomson, the strongly free-trade President of the Board of Trade, Lord Morpeth, a Whig member of the government, and the younger Peel, conservative devotee of political economy. But the Committee was dominated by people to whom the factory system was suspect; the Tory Evangelical chairman, M. T. Sadler, the Tory Evangelical philanthropist, Sir Robert Inglis, J. C. Hobhouse, author of the Acts of 1825 and 1831, George Strickland, one of the Yorkshire county members and sympathetic to the workers rather than the *nouveaux-riches* industrialists of the West Riding; and Thomas Attwood, Tory Radical of the Birmingham Political Union. These manipulated the Committee by intervewing witnesses who had been selected, financed and coached by the short-time committees, and asking them leading questions.

As Commissioner Drinkwater (who was admittedly biased against the Ten Hour Movement) wrote indignantly in his report to the Royal Commission:

> I conceive that it is not possible for any unprejudiced person to peruse the evidence contained in the volume ordered to be printed on 8th August 1832, on the Factories Labour Regulation Bill, without being forcibly struck by the extraordinary manner in which a great number of the questions appear to have been put, leading the witnesses in a degree seldom, if ever equalled, even in parliamentary evidence, and frequently supplying circumstances to the previous answers which otherwise, as it would seem, were not in the contemplation of the answerer.[49]

The text of the evidence confirms Drinkwater's complaint: the degree of prompting was remarkable. 'Is it your impression that your growth has been very much stunted, your health injured, and your constitution thus early destroyed by excessive labour?' 'Yes it is.'[50]

The organisers of this testimony appear to have had two ends in view. They wanted to expose the physical and moral damage inflicted by the factory system on the child workers, preferably in such a way as to publicise the greed, negligence, callousness and cruelty of the millowners. They also wanted to use this evidence to secure the ten-hour day for all workers, juvenile and adult. A succession of young people from the Yorkshire mills crippled by industrial deformities passed before the Committee.

James Kirk, 17½, explained how the masters had put boys onto men's work because they were cheaper. He had worked all day and all night three times a week, gigging, i.e. turning over heavy pieces of wet cloth, until his knees bent up and his health collapsed.[51]

Elizabeth Bentley said she had started at 6 in a flax mill. She had had to pull heavy baskets until eventually she became deformed in her shoulders. Now at 23, deserted by her employer and unemployable, she was in Hunslet poorhouse.[52]

John Hall, overlooker from John Wood's Mill at Bradford, and Secretary of the Bradford Short Time Committee, explained how piecening on a throstle spinning machine turned healthy children into cripples. They had to throw the left shoulder up and the right knee forward; and they always bent at the right knee. One youth had already been bent when he came to the factory. First he became straight in the right knee, then he became crooked in it the other way.[53]

As well as deformities from these repetitive movements, there were accidents and industrial diseases. Machines were too close together (even Drinkwater confirmed this), and children drowsy from fatigue, caught their hands, or lost their fingers while cleaning moving machinery during mealtimes. Cotton and flax were more unhealthy than woollen mills. Flax carding rooms were full of floating particles of dust and hair, which coated the food brought in for the workers' meals, and induced asthma and other respiratory diseases. Wet flax spinning machines continually threw up hot spray. The operators had to plunge their arms into hot water, and when they went out into the street their clothes froze upon them.[54] Fine cotton spinning had to be done in overheated rooms, at a temperature of 80 degrees or more.[55]

The evidence of the mill workers was reinforced by that of some of the local doctors. Thomas Young, physician, of Bolton had examined the local Sunday Schools. In a Methodist school, 165 out of 446 boys under the age of 16 were factory workers. Of these, 46 had been injured by machinery, 3 losing fingers, 3 were deformed at the knees, 17 complained of coughs, 6 of loss of appetite, and 9 were scrofulous (consumptive). Of the girls, 171 out of 458 were factory workers. Of these, 27 had been injured by machinery, 5 were deformed at the knees, 19 complained of coughs, 31 of loss of appetite, and 9 were scrofulous.[56] Although no comparable figures were given for children who did not work in factories, the casualty rate was compelling enough. There was also general testimony that the factory children were pale and sallow, stunted in growth and lacking in vigour. They were 'more like dogs dozing upon a warm hearthstone than like children', said an operative whose three daughters worked in the mills.[57]

There were many complaints of ill-treatment. Sometimes over-lookers were blamed, while the master was a remote figure, who neither knew nor cared. Sometimes the owner himself was accused of kicking and beating the children. Hanna Brown, who worked in a Bradford factory from 6 a.m. to 8 p.m. without meal breaks, claimed that the master dragged her about by her hair.[58] Eliza Marshall, who had become lame in a spinning mill, said the children were strapped and kicked by the master to get more work out of them. When the parliament gentlemen inspected the factory the sick children were sent away and the others sent home to put on their Sunday best.[59]

Several overlookers claimed they were forced to flog the children when they were late in the morning, and to keep them awake at the end of the day. Operatives who hired their own pieceners, including fathers with their own children, had to beat them to keep them up to their work.[60] Mr Abraham Whitehead, a clothier (domestic clothworker) living near the mills at Holmfirth, claimed that children aged 5 or 6 working from 5 or 6 a.m. until 9 or 10 p.m. were beaten or poked with the billy roller, a detachable iron rod from the top of a slubbing machine.[61] Some had died and others had been blind for two or three days; but if a parent invoked the law the child would lose its situation.[62] Whitehead gave no actual cases.

The witnesses insisted that these evils were either created or intensified by the long working hours. They quoted examples of the effect of the over-long day on small children. Thomas Bennett's eight children worked in the factories from 6 or 7 in the morning, or when 'throng' (in a rush of orders) from 4 or 5 in the morning, to 9 or 10 at night. The children cried when taken from their beds, and moved their hands when almost asleep. They were too tired to eat at night, dropping asleep with their victuals in their hands. He had to carry the lesser child home half a mile on his back. He had to beat his pieceners to keep them awake, or when they spoiled his work.[63] Stephen Binns, at one time overlooker at Marshall's Water Lane flax mill, said the last but one hour of the day was the worst. The children were going to see what time it was every five minutes. He stood in the dark and gave them a good lacing.[64]

The witnesses stressed that pressures were increasing. There were more spindles, and finer thread which broke more often. The masters who fined their workers for being late also fiddled with the factory clock to bring them in early, or to cut three minutes off their thirty-minute lunch break.[65] They agreed that the children were very unhappy. 'I have seen at that mill, and I have experienced and mentioned it with grief', said Thomas Bennett, 'that the English children were enslaved worse than the Africans.'[66] They also expressed concern about the decline of education, feeling that an hour's instruction after a twelve-hour day was useless. Short-time committees maintained that the children were longing for a ten-hour day so that they could be educated. When Abraham Whitehead went to the mills the children gathered round him, saying, 'When shall we have to work ten hours a day. Will you get the Ten Hour Bill? We shall have a rare time then; surely somebody will set up a neet (night) school; I will learn to write, that I will.'[67] This picture of virtue was slightly spoiled by William Kenworthy's evidence that he had run away from school to go to the mill.[68]

Some parents tried to get their children educated by sending them to Sunday school, and a number expressed resentment that the Methodists now refused to teach their Sunday-school pupils to write.[69] But others recognised that the children were too exhausted to learn on Sundays. Joseph Firth thought it 'a stain upon this nation, to think that the children should be laboured to such an extent during the six days, that they must be bound again upon the seventh'.[70] Some Sunday schools were being used hypocritically, or for political purposes. Ashley in a later pamphlet complained of a master who pushed his workmen's labour until midnight on Saturday and commanded its renewal at 1 a.m. on Monday, yet drove the unhappy children to a Sunday school.[71] Thomas Daniel found Sunday schools were being used by their managers to preach obedience to the masters during a strike.[72] Dr Charles Thackrah, the Leeds dispensary physician, with more common sense than most, thought that, if children had to work, which he deplored, then six hours was better than ten. 'Though intellectual and moral education should be regarded, and I should be glad if there were time for both, I think, in the present state of things, that physical education or the improvement of health is most urgently required. Children want that fresh air and recreation which could not be enjoyed in school.'[73]

Witnesses before the Select Committee hinted at gross immorality. A man of 22 told the Committee that 18 or 19 out of 34 women millworkers he knew had had illegitimate children. They also stole each others' food.[74] Where bastards were few, it was hinted that 'certain books', i.e. manuals on birth control, were being circulated.[75] Fathers complained that their children learned 'everything that is bad' in these 'seminaries of vice'.[76] People would not take a mill girl as a domestic servant. One parent admitted that his children were out of control; 'Impudence and immorality of every description appear to be their growing characteristics'.[77]

Where parents were living on their children's earnings it was inevitable that the children lost their respect for, and obedience to, their parents. Ashley saw this as a veritable reversal of the order of Nature.[78] Yet the parents were helpless. A disgruntled Poor Law overseer confirmed that select vestries would not relieve a family if the children could get work in a mill.[79]

Upper-class sympathisers with the factory movement deplored most of all the loss of female education, which rendered the mill girls unable to make a home for their husbands, or care for their children. Lord Ashley in the ensuing debate told the Commons that the disruption of domestic ties in the factory districts was the most tremendous evil. He would rejoice if his Bill indirectly limited the working hours of adults, if only to promote a return of the working classes to domestic habits and domestic comforts.[80]

The evidence to the Select Committee was a damning indictment of the factory system and of the masters, whom it exhibited grabbing their profits at the cost of the health and happiness of children. Yet the remedy proposed, the ten-hour day, was obviously inadequate. This in itself was enough to alert hostile committee members to the ulterior purposes of the Short Time Movement. They pressed witnesses hard to make them admit they were really seeking to limit the working hours of adults.

Opposition to the regulation of factory hours, as it emerged in the questioning of Select Committee witnesses and in the masters' evidence to the subsequent Royal Commission, rested on four main arguments. One was the practical danger from foreign competition. The second was the argument of classical political economy for a free labour market, and free wages contracts,[81] working hours being recognised as an aspect of wages. The third, arising from this, was the theory of the natural identity of economic interests. Capital, which was stored profit, provided the tools for human labour. The labourer's interest was thus to make ample profits for the master, just as the master's interest was to supply his workmen with all the necessities required to preserve them in vigorous working condition, as well as the leisure to acquire correct views on political economy. To this, a little later, Nassau Senior added a gloss maintaining that, in a twelve-hour day, the workmen's keep was earned in eleven hours, and the master's profit only in the twelfth.[82] Legislative meddling with these natural economic laws was thus unnecessary and mischievous.

The fourth argument, a survival from Enlightenment views on the connection between property and liberty, maintained that the poor man's only property was his labour. He had the right, like any other property owner, to sell it freely, securing the best contract available, as a free agent should. This plausible argument had been put forward by radical thinkers of the last generation such as Tom Paine.[83] It still sounded radical; but it could be said that machinery had destroyed the free agency of the workman.

In the prevailing climate of middle-class opinion, in which these contentions were implicitly accepted, to make the ten-hour representatives admit that they aimed at limiting adult working time would be a tactical victory. When sufficiently pressed, working-class witnesses made the admission. Said David Brook, a cloth dresser and former overlooker, 'I really do think it is absolutely necessary, . . . that children should be protected from excessive labour; that is the first point in my mind; and with a hope, I confess, that it will benefit myself and others as well.' Pressed as to whether he thought a Bill necessary to regulate the employment of men, he added that it wouldn't be necessary if men were free agents, able to move from one job to another, and if machinery did not 'naturally make against us in the way it does, so as to render us at the mercy of our employers . . . but at present I do not know whether it might not be safely extended even to men.'[84]

From the evidence of the working-class witnesses there gradually emerged a fairly coherent set of counter-arguments for the adult ten-hour day. Firstly, they flatly denied free agency, especially with the millowners and the Poor Law vestries allied against them. They must get work, or live on their children's earnings, or starve. Even if they were not, as some argued, chained to the power of the machine, the free labour market was a mockery. Secondly, they denied that state intervention would cripple the textile industry in the face of foreign competition. Two witnesses, William Smith and James McNish, had been sent by the Glasgow Cotton Spinners' Union to look into industrial conditions on the Continent. McNish reported that the French yarns were 40–50 per cent higher in cost and poorer in quality than the British ones.[85] Smith said the French were thirty years behind. Their costs were high partly because they had little coal, but also because they had an undisciplined workforce. Their operatives worked longer hours than the British, and lived on vegetables and cheap wine. The Americans also had inferior machinery and could not compete with British spinners.[86]

There was an implicit conflict of attitude and expectation between, on the one hand, the Tory–Radical leaders and the surviving domestic or workshop workers, and on the other, the factory operatives. The former almost welcomed the disastrous consequences foreseen by the millowners. Abraham Whitehead, the clothier of Holmfirth, rather hoped that some factories would give up. Many that have some small property would begin business. 'It would introduce domestic manufacture, which would be the greatest blessing that could be introduced into Old England.'[87]

Oastler and Bull also dreamed of a return to Old England and to the independent producer, closing the 'immense chasm, a great impassable gulf, between a state of perpetual labour and a state of independence'.[88] The mill operatives, more realistically, lived in the future, not the past. Refusing to be frightened by the masters' threats of installing machines as a substitute for human labour, they latched on to the political economists' argument that capital created employment. Several hoped that a limitation of ten hours would increase machinery, and with it the demand for labour. Some hoped it would lead to the invention of machinery which would restore the work from children to men.[89] A Committee witness John Hannam later told one of the Royal Commission investigators that some thought machinery should be done away with altogether, and some said that only such machinery as took away manual labour should be done away with; 'but I am an advocate for machinery myself; but I want the benefit of it to be that the people who work at it should get part of it. That is one great reason why I want the hours shorter, to give a chance of work for those who are willing and able to work.'[90]

The positive thrust of the short-time committeemen's arguments was away from foreign markets to home markets, and from competition to work-sharing. The operatives diagnosed the ills of the textile industry as over-production (they called it an over-stocked market) brought about by unbridled internal competition. Because of the masters' competition for orders, operatives were working sixteen hours a day surrounded by unemployment. Because of over-production, profits had declined and wages with them. Where hours were longest wages were lowest. The millowners claimed that shorter hours would mean a corresponding (or because of the high overheads) an even greater reduction in wages. When asked whether they would accept this cut in pay, nearly all the working-class witnesses said they would prefer the shorter hours with less pay, but most expected wages to stay the same, or even to rise. David Brook said, 'If the hours of labour were regulated, it would in some measure destroy undue competition for labour, and the wages would be more likely to rise than to fall.'[91] Wages were regulated by the demand for labour and regulation would take the edge off competition and share out the available work between more men, as well as ironing out the alternations between rushes of work and idleness. In later evidence to the Royal Commission, John Hannam proposed that hours should be reduced successively from ten to nine or eight, and so on, until the pool of unemployment was mopped up.[92] It was agreed that with shorter hours the prices of manufactured goods would rise. But the rise would not be excessive, since operatives would produce more and better-quality goods in a reasonable working day, and do more work in ten hours than they now did in twelve or thirteen. Finally, full employment and good wages would ensure a proper home market for the factory products.

The operatives' spokesmen may have been appealing to the old tradition of the ten-hour day. But their sophisticated arguments were really concerned with wages and employment rather than with leisure.

They amounted to a coherent theory of the economics of factory production in rivalry with the millowners' interpretation of the classical political economists. The originator of this theory seems to have been John Doherty, the founder-leader of the Manchester Cotton Spinners' Union. Doherty, who made persistent attempts to weld the industrial Unions into powerful amalgamated combinations, propagated the idea of limiting hours and output to protect the interests of the productive classes in a succession of journals, of which the most famous was the *Voice of the People*.[93] He did not campaign for co-operative production, distribution or exchange, nor, despite some strong language, for the expropriation of the millowners by the operatives. He was not in the full sense a socialist, although he occasionally joined forces with the Owenites. The *Poor Man's Guardian*, organ of the London intellectual working-class Left, was already harping on the theme that property is theft. The Short Timers preferred to express their feeling that the capitalists were stealing the value created by the working men in more archaic terms. They maintained that their labour was their only property, and in a market rigged against them by the technical, economic and political domination of their masters, that property was being violated. However, their aims, if not socialist in the collectivist sense, could be revolutionary; and even the respectful tones of the Select Committee witnesses could contain a hint of menace. James McNish, the Glasgow cotton spinner, said that

> 'the Glasgow combinations for ten hours thought that while slaves were protected they were not; ... that their labour, which forms their principal property, was left completely open to be trampled upon by every avaricious employer as he chose; they were therefore determined to form as extensive a combination as they possibly could to reduce those hours of labour, for the benefit both of themselves and their children.'

These combinations were out to force the town masters to petition for the Ten Hour Bill, 'after starving their operatives, and getting some of themselves murdered for starving these men'. They could fall into the hands of demagogues who might endanger government. Therefore government, in the interests of masters and men alike ought to pass the Bill as soon as possible.[94] After the disappointment of the 1833 Factory Act, Doherty and Fielden, in temporary co-operation with the Owenites, founded the National Regeneration Society to procure an *eight*-hour day for twelve hours' pay. They tried to organise a general strike to enforce it. But the Regeneration Society's branches, many of which joined Owen's Grand National Consolidated Trades Union, never attracted enough support to strike successfully.[95]

If threats of violence before the Select Committee were unusual, there was a strong element of personal antagonism in the evidence. An overlooker and several employees came to London to describe the conditions in the factories of John Marshall, owner of two flax spinning mills in Leeds and one in Shrewsbury, and until 1830 the senior Whig MP for Leeds.[96] The Committee was told that his mill rooms were full of dust or of hot spray; that the child workers were not allowed to sit down nor to speak to each other; that they were beaten with straps of five or six thongs set in a handle; that they were only allowed to go to the 'necessary' three times in a day, and had to ask permission which was often refused, so that they soiled their clothes. It was alleged that a boy had died as a result of this ill treatment. At the Shrewsbury mill a boy had been tied to a pillar and flogged. Drowsy boys were dropped into a cistern or forced to stand on a stool and hold a weight above their heads. Even the school established by Marshall for his Leeds workers was criticised. The operatives had been told that schooling would be free, and when a teacher was ordered to collect fees he lost all his scholars.[97]

This evidence advertised Marshall's unpopularity. But the Committee managers over-reached themselves. On 7 August parliament was dissolved and the Committee automatically broke up without hearing evidence from the masters, or issuing a report. The Minutes of Evidence were published verbatim without comment, and received with fury. The masters would hardly take this treatment lying down, nor permit the passage of the Ten Hour Bill if they could possibly prevent it.

The Factories Commission and the Act of 1833

The Committee's evidence was published in January 1833. By February petitions organised by the short-time committees all over the industrial districts were being received: from Leeds with 16,000 signatures, from Bradford with 12,000, from Huddersfield with 5,000, as well as from Glasgow, Bolton and other textile towns. All demanded the speedy passage of the Ten Hour Bill. The millowners countered by forming an Association of Master Manufacturers, and adopting Lord Morpeth's compromise proposal for an Eleven Hour Bill. They petitioned for a further enquiry to clear their reputation from the aspersions of the Select Committee. When parliament met, Sadler had lost his Leeds seat to Macaulay, and his place as parliamentary spokesman for the Short Time Movement had been taken by the formidable Lord Ashley. On 6 March 1833 Ashley's Ten Hour Bill was introduced in the House of Commons. Immediately Wilson Patten, MP for North Lancashire, proposed a commission of enquiry not, as he said, to cause delay, but in order that the subject should be better understood, and also 'for the purpose of clearing the characters of the masters from those imputations which seemed to be cast upon them by the friends of this measure, but which further evidence would prove to be utterly unjustifiable'.[98] Despite protests from Lord Ashley and Brotherton,[99] the motion was carried on 3 April in a thin house, by 74 votes to 73. Sixteen days later the commission was issued.

The Commission for Inquiring into the Employment of Children in

Factories sat at the same time as the Poor Law Enquiry Commission of 1832, which it closely resembled. Although it had no separate Central Board of Commissioners, a *de facto* Central Board was formed by three of the fifteen appointed Commissioners who remained in London, while the rest, in groups of two civil and one medical Commissioner, toured the factory areas. The three London Commissioners, Edwin Chadwick, Thomas Tooke and Thomas Southwood Smith, were all personally acquainted with the aged Jeremy Bentham.[100] The travelling Commissioners, although said to have been appointed in a 'riot of jobbery' included a number of able men of similar outlook who subsequently made careers as factory or Poor Law inspectors.[101] The only identifiable 'job' was the appointment of James Stuart, a Scottish Whig journalist of doubtful reputation who got his commission by importuning Henry Brougham.[102] The Commission was about as friendly to the Short Time Movement as was the Poor Law Commission to the pauper host. Inevitably it was hailed in the factory districts as a whitewashing job for the millowners.

The London Commissioners made some attempt to conciliate their opponents by asking them to send in suggestions, and inviting Ashley to attend the Board (which he refused to do).[103] Elaborate questionnaires were sent to the millowners and elaborate instructions given to the investigators as to their method of ascertaining the hours of work, the treatment and the morals of the mill hands. They were to make enquiries about the moral character of working youths inside and outside the factories, trace and question the organisers of petitions, and re-examine the Select Committee witnesses, on oath. They were to examine parents and children as to whether any improvements had been made since the Ten Hour Bill came before parliament, find out whether parents had complained about the treatment of their children, or why they had not. After contradictions and difficulties in this evidence had been resolved, the employers would be examined last. In view of the many reports of victimisation, precautions would be taken against publishing names, and a degree of secrecy would be observed.[104]

These instructions show that the Commission was indeed intended as a check on the conduct and evidence of the Select Committee. They do not show that it was a whitewashing exercise on behalf of the millowners, although the order that the employers were to have the last word might justify some suspicion. In effect the travelling Commissioners were received with open hostility. The Yorkshire and Lancashire short-time committees organised protest marches, and had the Commissioners shadowed wherever they went. Thomas Daniel, a leading Lancashire cotton spinner who had given evidence to the Select Committee, refused to meet the Commissioners, while Doherty and Turner who were in London lobbying for the Manchester Central short-time committee refused to appear before the Commission in the Metropolis.[105] The Yorkshire committees demanded that evidence be taken in public, and refused a proposal that it should be heard before equal numbers of representatives of the supporters and opponents of Lord Ashley's Bill.[106] The Lancashire operatives harried the two civil Commissioners Tufnell and Cowell (who disliked each other) until Tufnell walked out on Cowell leaving his hotel bill unpaid.[107] James Stuart, one of the Scottish Commissioners, peppered the Central Commissioners with rude letters, complaints and criticisms, which he printed in his paper, the *Courier*.[108] In the circumstances it was a remarkable achievement that Chadwick was able within two months (by 25 June 1833) to produce a more coherent report than that which he and Senior drew up on the Poor Laws after two years of investigation.

Notwithstanding the local obstruction, the Commissioners succeeded in interviewing many of the Select Committee witnesses. Drinkwater in Yorkshire took statements from ten, including the men from Marshall's mills. Judging from his report, he had already decided that the witnesses had exceeded 'the truth in the evidence they gave', although he threw most of the blame for this on the way in which they had been examined.[109] Some of them stuck to their stories. Eliza Marshall reaffirmed that her lameness was due to stopping the spindle with her knee. The works manager *had* knocked her down, and although he had offered her a job if she got better, he had never given her any money. All she had said in London was true.[110] The witnesses from Marshall's mills repeated that young girls and children were beaten, not allowed to sit down, and prevented from going to the privy. But it emerged that much of this ill-treatment was inflicted by an overlooker, who had been dismissed when it was discovered.[111] The younger Binns insisted that a boy had died, and his sister also, after the overlooker had accidentally hit her with a billy roller and cut her lip. But Binns' father and the local doctor said that both children had been ill for some time, and their deaths were nothing to do with what happened at the mill. Accidents and injuries were confirmed, but attributed less to exhaustion than to children playing 'dares' with their fingers in dangerous machinery.[112] Hannah Brown had indeed been dragged around by her hair, but it was the result of a private quarrel with her master, who had overheard her saying she was going to steal some beans being ground for the horses. Detail by detail the more sensational testimony was weakened, and a slightly less inhuman picture of life in the mills began to emerge. But the evidence of overwork, ill health and deformity was not undermined.[113]

The Ten Hour men at the Select Committee had wanted to show that the big new factories were as bad as the small country mills, and that the pressure of machinery on the workers was increasing. But some Royal Commission witnesses now admitted that the older, smaller and more remote mills were generally worse run than the large new ones, and that some of the machines which had inflicted deformities were now obsolete.[114] They agreed that some improvements had been made at the flax mills at the time of Hobhouse's Bill, when it was not realised that this applied only to cotton. Questioned about victimisation, they confirmed that Committee witnesses had been dismissed, but some had been re-employed, or taken on elsewhere.[115]

The Commissioners discussed with witnesses the possibility of working children in six- or eight-hour shifts, so as to curtail their labour without touching the adult working day. The idea was not new, Robert Owen having suggested six-hour shifts to the Select Committee of 1816. But Thomas Ashton, cotton mill owner at Hyde, Lancashire, told Commissioner Tufnell that it would be opposed by both masters and men.[116] The six-hour shift would cause an acute shortage of juvenile workers, reduce their wages by half, and encourage their parents to send them to complete the day in another mill. The extra hands, if they could be found, would be difficult to train. The eight-hour shift was also opposed, for it would necessitate working by relays, which could extend the adult working day up to sixteen hours. The possibility that the extra demand for children might raise rather than lower their wages was not discussed. But either way, adult workmen stood to lose: if children's wages fell, from the drop in the family income; if they rose, from the fact that many operatives paid their assistants themselves, and might have to pay for double sets as well.

In their evidence the masters beat the drum of foreign competition, and without considering the sophisticated arguments of the short-time committee leaders, asserted that a ten-hour day would mean a drastic fall in wages. They attributed the workmen's confidence in their ability to withstand the effects of new machinery to the obstructive power of the trade unions. Jervase Walker, millowner of Leeds, described how, after a largely successful standstill for higher wages, he had introduced machinery to reduce the hands by half. They had refused to work unless the same number were employed as before, or the remainder given double wages. Supported by a trade union fund, and despite a counter-combination of masters, they had forced Walker's firm to keep on its former number of hands. It was part of their 'system of dictation which is being carried on very generally throughout the kingdom'.[117] The millowners were not in doubt that the Ten Hour Movement was run by the unions, and its work-sharing effects would be secured by union power. The fact that the Lancashire short-time committees were run by leaders of the militant Spinners' Union was well known.

Some of the larger and more reputable owners, like Marshall, bitterly contested the claim that they ill-treated, overworked or exploited their young workers.[118] Others were defiant. Aaron Lees, cotton factory master of Gorton, Lancashire, who maintained that short hours would be unenforceable because the men would be 'unwilling to lose the benefit of moderate long hours', admitted that after the Acts of 1819 and 1831 he had increased the working day because of 'uneasiness', i.e. irritation, that cotton factories should be singled out for legislative restriction. The unions' real motive, he said, was not the benefit of the working classes, but political and private animosity. They made the workpeople their tools.[119]

In one vital particular the masters succeeded in discrediting their opponents. The real intention of the Ten Hour men, they said, was the restriction of their own labour without concern for the children. James Greenhough, overlooker for H. & E. Ashworth at Bolton said, 'I never met one that had that feeling about the children; they all say it would be pleasant to work ten hours, and have the same wages.'[120] Two Rochdale master spinners who had once been journeymen and claimed to be in the confidence of the operatives, were asked if the operatives were motivated by desire to lessen the labour of young children. 'Not in the least'; this reason, they said, was never mentioned.[121]

The Factory Act of 1833

The Report of the Factories Inquiry Commission was written by Edwin Chadwick. As in the Poor Law Report he had certainly decided what he was going to say well before the investigations were completed.[122] The report embodies two main aims; to protect the factory children (and educate them), while leaving unregulated the adult working day, and to discredit the Ten Hour men and their union backing. In attitude and tone the report throughout favoured the masters. Its economic arguments were theirs; it accepted the dangers of foreign competition, accepted that shorter hours meant lower wages, and rejected the need for state regulation. Without denying the existence of squalor, discomfort and callousness, even in the largest mill in Glasgow, it accepted the travelling Commissioners' report that the dirty, ill-ventilated factories where the privies stank and the machines were unguarded were generally the small, remote, and out-of-date ones; while in large and modern mills conditions were improving.[123] It accepted that the beating and ill-treatment of children was now typical only of the small mills, and was usually inflicted by the overlookers or the operatives themselves. It vindicated the regime in Marshall's factories, and especially the company's school. And it quoted extensively and approvingly from the reports of the troublesome James Stuart, who was well in with the owners of the big Scottish country mills, such as Kirkman Finlay's at Deanston, Perth.[124] It bitterly attacked the Ten Hour men, whose efforts at restriction of hours showed how little they cared for justice to the manufacturers, and accused them of hypocrisy in bringing forward a measure which claimed to protect the children and did not do so. The leaders of the factory agitation, in 'rash and headlong strikes', intimidated quiet and contented workmen simply to keep up discontent for their own profit.[125]

Despite all this, Chadwick found that the reports of exhaustion, deformity and ill health among the factory children were well based. The root of the trouble was the tying of children's labour to the working hours of adults. But the factory system which assembled them in large numbers outside their homes afforded an opportunity to regulate their labour without 'such vexatious scrutiny of private dwellings and occupations as could not be borne'.[126] He proposed, therefore to keep them out of the factories until they were 8 or 9 (the prevailing minimum age) and then restrict them to part-time work until they reached the age of puberty, when they began to keep their own wages and to be 'free agents'. To prevent them being sent on to other work and secure their education, he proposed three or four hours daily of compulsory schooling. To limit their hours without touching those of the adults he recommended, in the face of all the arguments against it, a shift system. And after some hesitation between the six- and eight-hour day, to mitigate the demand for more juvenile workers and cut in their wages, he proposed eight hours, worked in relays.[127] To soften the effects of the change, the restrictions would be imposed by yearly stages, and if a shortage of hands did develop, it could be solved by a return to the older system of boarding apprentices from workhouses and pauperised country parishes.[128]

As in the Poor Law Report, Chadwick's most important and original contribution was the enforcement machinery. Age certificates were already required. To prevent falsification they should now be provided by a doctor, and countersigned by a magistrate. There had been talk of 'millwardens' to direct the fencing of dangerous machinery. Chadwick proposed inspectors, armed with wide powers of entry, direction and summary jurisdiction, to enforce the whole scheme.[129] He did not propose a central board, but the inspectors would meet from time to time, as a board, report to government, and suggest amendments to the law.

A weakness in the report was the sudden ending of restrictions on labour on the assumption that children abruptly became adults at the age of 14. Yet the protection of children in a free labour market was exactly what the aroused conscience of middle-class Britain wanted. Chadwick had driven a wedge between the Short Timers' declared aim of protecting the children and their ulterior aim of limiting the adult working day.

To the Whig government, torn between its conviction that the Ten Hour Bill would produce a trade slump, starvation and revolt in the textile districts, and its nervousness of the existing unrest, the Royal Commission's Report came as a lifeline. But Althorp still hesitated, the problem being how he could kill Ashley's Bill before it reached the statute book. Ten days after the Commission reported, through a delay for which Althorp was 'unable to account', no copies of the report had been circulated to MPs. Then, accepting Chadwick's ideas in principle he proposed that the Bill be referred to a Select Committee instructed to provide that no child under its fourteenth year should labour more than eight hours a day, and that there should be arrangements for part-time education, and for a system of inspection.[130]

Ashley saw that his movement had been outmanoeuvred and outbidden. He could only object to the government's attempts at further delay, to the report's lack of provision for the protection of young girls over 13 (who several speakers thought were in greatest need of it), and to the relays in which an eight-hour day for children must be organised. He knew that three travelling Commissioners, Drinkwater, Power, and

Stuart, had disagreed in their proposals while they all opposed relays; and 'how they got blended into two sets was more than he was aware of'.[131] But he was not then aware of Chadwick.

The report, when published, was received with acclamation. Even the editor of the *Poor Man's Guardian*, hopelessly out of touch with opinion in the factory districts, welcomed the ensuing government Bill with a laudatory piece. 'We do think we may congratulate our little friends *under fourteen* years old, in the factories, on a very material improvement indeed in *their* condition, and we hope a quick one.'[132] The more moderate millowners in the Commons rallied to the proposals. Even relays were preferable to a Ten Hour Act. In the debate the supporters of the Ten Hour Bill were caught in the impossible position of calling for an *extension* of children's working hours from eight to ten.[133] On 10 July, at the end of a long debate, Ashley found 'that the noble Lord (Althorp) had completely defeated him. He should, therefore surrender the Bill into the hands of the noble Lord . . . he would only say into whatever hands it might pass, God prosper it.'[134]

The government's Factories Regulation Bill passed rapidly through the House of Commons. It differed materially from Chadwick's proposals only in a clause limiting the work of young persons aged between 13 and 18 in textile mills to 12 hours a day or 69 a week. This concession restoring the hours in Hobhouse's Act of 1831 had been suggested by the conciliator Lord Morpeth, to Chadwick's great disgust.[135] It diminished the operatives' fears of a sixteen-hour day, and without it the Act would probably have been totally unenforceable. In the debates the more violent millowners got nowhere with intransigent opposition to its principles, but the more skilful members of their lobby obtained the partial exclusion of silk factories and the complete exclusion of lace factories from the restrictions of the Act, as well as amendments permitting twelve hours' work on Saturdays and extended hours to make up time lost by accidents.[136] Further attempts to delay the Bill on the grounds (with which Althorp agreed) that relays were harmful, and to limit the powers of the inspectors, were defeated.[137] Later the Lords removed the vital clause empowering the costs of educating factory children to be subsidised from the rates.

The Act to Regulate the Labour of Children and Young Persons in the Mills and Factories of the United Kingdom (3 & 4 William IV, c. 103), with which Chadwick had thwarted the Ten Hour Bill, became known as Althorp's Act. It was a monument which that hesitant politician, who had done everything he could to obstruct and delay legislation, in no way deserved.

Sources and references

1. **Wadsworth, A. P.** and **Mann, M.,** *The Cotton Trade and Industrial Lancashire, 1600-1780.* Manchester U.P., 1931, p. 406.

2. See p. 68.
3. **Bienefeld, M. A.,** *Working Hours in British Industry.* LSE, 1972, *passim.*
4. See **Kirby, R. G.** and **Musson, A. E.,** *The Voice of the People: John Doherty, 1785-1854, Trade Unionist, Radical and Factory Reformer.* Manchester U. P., 1975, *passim,* but especially Ch. X. The Factory Reform Movement, pp. 346-406.
5. Wadsworth and Mann, *op. cit.,* pp. 489-90. There is, of course, a large literature on the growth of the textile industry and its technology.
6. For the early growth of power in West Riding textiles, see **Jenkins, D. T.,** 'Early Factory Development in the West Riding of Yorkshire, 1770 - 1800', in Harte, N. B. and Ponting, K. G. (eds), *Textile History and Economic History.* Manchester U. P., 1973, pp. 247-80.
7. **Baines, Edward, Jnr,** *History of the Cotton Manufacture in Great Britain.* Jackson, 1835, pp. 349-50.
8. **Chapman, S. J.,** *The Lancashire Cotton Industry.* Manchester U. P., 1904, pp. 89-90. Resolutions of the same kind were passed at Pontefract and Birmingham. *Ibid.* p. 90.
9. Evidence of Sir Robert Peel to the *Select Committee on the State of Children employed in the Manufactories of the United Kingdom. PP* 1816, III, pp. 139-40.
10. **Chapman, S. D.,** *The Early Factory Masters.* David and Charles, 1967, pp. 170-1.
11. Evidence of Robert Owen to the Select Committee, 1816, *op. cit.,* p. 39.
12. *Ibid.,* p. 20.
13. Paper exhibited by Sir Robert Peel to the Select Committee of 1816, *op. cit.,* 132. Peel said he employed nearly 1,000 apprentices at Tamworth.
14. Between 1820 and 1832 cotton mills in Manchester and Salford increased from 66 to 96. By 1835 there were 657 mills in Lancashire, many in satellite cotton towns such as Bolton, Rochdale, and Oldham, others in Cheshire such as Stockport and Hyde, and others in the West Riding. Cf. Baines, *op. cit.,* pp. 395. 386-8.
15. Jenkins, D. T., *op. cit.,* pp. 247-80.
16. Where throstles cut out the need for adult spinners, heads of family were sometimes found work on the owners' estates. Chapman, S. D., *op. cit.,* pp. 159-61.
17. Ure, Andrew, *The Philosophy of Manufactures (1835).* Cass, 1967, p. 171. This process was current in Yorkshire, and may be one reason why Yorkshire led the Factory Movement in the early 1830s. It seems to have been largely overlooked by textile historians. The influence of the ever-changing technology of the various textile factories on the size, shape and conditions of the workforce is, of course, important.
18. Baines, *op. cit.,* p. 436. The modern values are approximately £1.28, with 14p for the scavenger, and 27p for the pieceners. There was no uniformity in wage rates. Baines and other sources provide a bewildering variety of figures.
19. The number of family spinning teams in which the adult male operative employed his own children or young relatives is smaller than has sometimes been thought. For proportions of employment of child assistants by operatives and of family employment, see **Edwards, M. M.,** and **Lloyd Jones, R.,** 'J. N. Smelser and the Cotton Factory Family: a Reassessment', in Harte, N. B. and Ponting, K. G. (eds), *Textile History and Economic History.* Manchester U. P., 1973, pp. 304-19.
20. Baines, *op. cit.,* p. 438 table. The wages for fine spinners ends in 1822 at 32*s* (£1.60). The wage for male spinners in Manchester in 1832 is given as 20*s* to 25*s* (£1.00 to £1.25).
21. Evidence of Angus Campbell to the *Select Committee on Combinations of Workmen. PP* 1838, VIII, p. 47.
22. Baines, *op. cit.,* pp. 205-7.
23. Thames Book Publishing Co., Leigh on Sea, 1947.
24. **Driver, Cecil,** *Tory Radical: A Life of Richard Oastler.* O.U.P., 1946.
25. **Ward, J. T.** *The Factory Movement, 1830-1855.* Macmillan, 1962.

26. Kirby and Musson, *op. cit.*, *passim*.
27. *Ibid.*, p. 346.
28. *Ibid.*, pp. 347-8.
29. *Ibid.*, p. 350.
30. *Ibid.*, pp. 353-63. Kirby and Musson point out the considerable importance of this society, which brought together the more enlightened masters with the operatives, and of which the committee eventually turned into the Manchester short-time committee. Cf. p. 366.
31. *Ibid.*, p. 366. It was called the Cotton Factory Time Bill Association, and lasted until 1833, being little more successful than the operatives' societies.
32. Kirby and Musson, *op. cit.*, pp. 62, 67, 360.
33. **Gayer, A. D., Rostow, W. W.** and **Schwartz, A. J.,** *The Growth and Fluctuation of the British Economy, 1740-1850.* Clarendon Press, 1953. I, p. 224.
34. *Ibid.*, pp. 221-4.
35. For the spare or 'billy' set of children, see the evidence of Joshua Drake about Gott's factory at Leeds, to the *Select Committee of 1832 on the Factories' Bill, PP* 1831-32, XV, p. 36, also of John Hall, *ibid.*, p. 115.
36. Kirby and Musson, *op. cit.*, p. 367.
37. A former Wesleyan Methodist who had been expelled for his radical views.
38. **Oastler, Richard,** *Slavery in Yorkshire*, 1835.
39. *PP Bills Public*, 1831-32, II, pp. 1-8.
40. *PP Bills Public*, 1833, II (pp. 263-78), Clause 34.
41. *Ibid.*, Cl. 24-26.
42. *Ibid.*, Cl. 15.
43. *Ibid.*, Cl. 14.
44. *Ibid.*, Cl. 29.
45. *Ibid.*, Cl. 30.
46. *Hansard*, 3rd series X1 (March-April 1832), 349-50.
47. *Ibid.*, pp. 386-98, especially John T. Hope, pp. 386-93.
48. Cf. *Poor Man's Guardian* for 10 March 1832, which pointed out that the manufacturers had carried out the same manoeuvre with Peel's Bill sixteen years ago, the consequence being delay on delay until the most valuable provisions has been frittered away, and the appalling evils of the system remained in full force.
49. *Supplementary Report of the Central Board of H.M. Commissioners for Inquiring into the Employment of Children in Factories etc. PP* 1833, XX. Evidence taken by Mr Drinkwater, p. 157.
50. *Report from the Select Committee on the Bill to regulate the Labour of Children in the Mills and Factories of the United Kingdom.* Evidence of William Cooper. *PP* 1831-32, XV, pp. 8-9.
51. *Ibid.*, pp. 14-15.
52. *Ibid.*, pp. 195-9.
53. *Ibid.*, p. 115. Hall, presumably, gave evidence with the support of his master.
54. Evidence of Mark Best, overlooker in a flax mill. *Ibid.*, p. 170. Wet flax spinning was introduced in Marshall's great Water Lane mill about 1826. Cf. **Rimmer, W. G.,** *Marshalls of Leeds, Flax Spinners 1788-1886.* C.U.P., 1960, p. 175 *et. seq.*
55. Evidence of William Smith, cotton spinner of Glasgow. *Select Committee*, p. 235.
56. *Ibid.*, p. 522.
57. Evidence of Joshua Drake. *Ibid.*, p. 38.
58. *Ibid.*, p. 231.
59. *Ibid.*, p. 150.
60. Evidence of Stephen Binns. *Ibid.*, p. 174.
61. Andrew Ure hastened to point out that the 'billy' was run by the slubbers with their teams of pieceners (who joined the wool from the cards together on the slubber) independently of the power-driven carding engines and spinning machines. Cf. Ure, *op. cit.*, pp. 171-83.
62. *Select Committee*, pp. 19-22.

63. *Ibid.*, p. 102.
64. *Ibid.*, p. 181.
65. *Ibid.*, pp. 177-8.
66. *Ibid.*, p. 103.
67. *Ibid.*, p. 20.
68. *Ibid.*, p. 79.
69. Evidence of John Goodyear, *ibid.*, p. 93. Evidence of Thomas Bennett, *ibid.*, pp. 103-4.
70. *Ibid.*, p. 296.
71. **Lord Ashley,** 'The factory system', *Quarterly Review*, 1836, LVII, p. 442.
72. *Select Committee*, p. 327.
73. *Ibid.*, p. 518.
74. Evidence of Matthew Crabtree, *ibid.*, p. 100.
75. Evidence of Benjamin Bradshaw, *ibid.*, p. 132.
76. Evidence of John Allett, *ibid.*, p. 111.
77. Evidence of William Kershaw, *ibid.*, p. 48.
78. Lord Ashley, *op. cit.*, p. 435.
79. Evidence of Gillett Sharpe. *Select Committee*, pp. 211-12.
80. *Hansard*, 3rd series XIX, 18 July 1833, p. 889.
81. 'Labour, like all other things which are purchased and sold, ... has its natural and its market price.' ... 'Like all other contracts, wages should be left to the fair and free competition of the market, and should never be controlled by the interference of the legislature.' David Ricardo, *Principles of Political Economy, 1817* P. Staffa (ed.), C.U.P., 1951), pp. 93, 105.
82. **Senior, William Nassau,** *Letters on the Factory Act.* London, 1837, pp. 11-13. Col. Torrens, who favoured the regulation of factory labour, gave the argument from natural identity of interests a curious twist when he argued that, as the state had intervened through the Corn Laws to abolish the free market in food, it must also intervene to protect the labourer. *Hansard, op. cit.*, pp. 901-2.
83. **Paine, Thomas,** *The Rights of Man.* Everyman Edition, pp. 265-6.
84. *Select Committee. PP* 1831-2, XV, p. 71.
85. *Ibid.*, p. 262.
86. *Ibid.*, pp. 241-9.
87. *Ibid.*, p. 23.
88. Evidence of George Stringer Bull. *Ibid.*, p. 491.
89. Evidence of Benjamin Bradshaw, cloth dresser and Primitive Methodist preacher. *Ibid.*, pp. 133-4.
90. *Factories Inquiry Commission Report. PP* 1833, XX. Evidence taken by Mr Drinkwater, p. 83.
91. Evidence of David Brook. *Select Committee*, p. 64.
92. *Factories Inquiry Commission. PP* 1833, XX, evidence taken by Mr Drinkwater, pp. 87-8.
93. For the Grand General Union of Cotton Spinners, the National Association for the Protection of Labour, the National Regeneration Society, etc., see Kirby and Musson, *op. cit., passim.* It is evident from this biography that Doherty was a more important and influential working-class leader than has hitherto been realised. His advocacy of the use of combined trade union power to limit hours for the sake of maintaining wages seems to have been his most distinctive contribution to working-class political ideas.
94. *Select Committee*, p. 265. For James McNish, a frequent trade union witness before government enquiries, and later an opponent of James Stuart the factory inspector in Scotland, see **Henriques, U.,** 'An early factory inspector; James Stuart of Dunearn', *Scottish Historical Review*, L, 1. no. 149, April 1971, pp. 23-4, 29-37.
95. **Foster, John,** *Class Struggle and the Industrial Revolution.* Methuen pbk ed. 1977, pp. 110-14. Kirby and Musson, *op. cit.*, 272-301. As Kirby and Musson point out, Foster gives an exaggerated account, coloured by his Marxist bias. The

eight-hour day would have prevented the out-bidding of the Short Time Movement in parliament by those concerned only with child protection, and would have obviated the need for relays. In this sense it included an intention to re-link the labour of adult and child in the factory.

96. Rimmer, W. G., *op. cit.*, *passim*. Attempts to discredit Marshall may have anticipated the election of December 1832, still some months away, in which John Marshall II held the senior seat for Leeds, but Sadler lost the junior seat to Macaulay.

97. Rimmer, *op. cit.*, pp. 215-19. Hostile evidence was given to the Select Committee by Charles Binns, Stephen Binns, Mark Best, Samuel Downe, and Jonathan Downe, prompted by Oastler. An employee of John Wood (the Bradford millowner who had helped to initiate the Ten Hour Movement) and a local physician were brought in to say how kind he was to his mill children. *Select Committee*, pp. 116-22, 300-7.

98. *Hansard*, 3rd series XVI, 14 March 1833, p. 640.

99. Ashley thought that the House ought not to be stopped from legislating 'merely because ten or twelve gentlemen fancied themselves aggrieved by the tendency of the matter already known to the public.' *Ibid.*, p. 641.

100. Tooke was a well-known economist. Dr Southwood Smith, physician at the London Fever Hospital, performed the post-mortem on Bentham's body.

101. For the 'riot of jobbery' cf. **Finer, S. E.,** *The Life and Times of Sir Edwin Chadwick.* Methuen, 1952, p. 52. But L. Horner, E. C. Tufnell, J. W. Cowell, and Alfred Power, despite some distressing experiences in the factory districts, all became well known in the various corps of permanent inspectors later on.

102. Henriques, *op. cit.*, pp. 22-3.

103. Correspondence with Lord Ashley, 20 April (memo). *Chadwick Papers*, 40. D.M.S. Watson Library, University College, London.

104. *First Report of the Central Board of H. M. Commissioners for Inquiring into the Employment of Children in Factories, etc. PP* 1833, XX, pp. 3-6.

105. Kirby and Musson, *op. cit.*, pp. 380-1.

106. Further Report of Mr Drinkwater. *Factories Inquiry Commission.* Evidence taken by Mr Drinkwater, p. 175.

107. Correspondence of the three Commissioners for Lancashire with the Central Board. *Chadwick Papers*, 41. The Medical Commissioner, Dr Bissett Hawkins, seems to have kept out of these quarrels.

108. Henriques, *op. cit.*, pp. 25-6. Doherty was enabled to claim betrayal because of Stuart's accusations. Kirby and Musson, *op. cit.*, p. 383. But the short-time committee men can hardly, at any time, have looked on Stuart as a friend.

109. Mr Drinkwater's Report on Yorkshire. *Factories Inquiry Commission.* Evidence taken by Mr Drinkwater, p. 157.

110. *Factories Inquiry Commission*, evidence taken by Mr Drinkwater, pp. 72-4.

111. Evidence of Charles Binns, *ibid.*, pp. 76-7. Rimmer, W. G., *op. cit.*, pp. 215-16. Marshall's sons neglected the mills, and things happened there without their knowledge.

112. Evidence of William Holden, *Factories Inquiry Commission, ibid.*, p. 79.

113. Ashley claimed that these witnesses (even allowing for the sake of argument that they exaggerated in one or two individual cases) 'confirmed and extended the results of Mr Sadler's investigation'. Lord Ashley, *op. cit.*, p. 413.

114. A point emphasised by Andrew Ure, who discussed some of this evidence with that of Sadler's Committee in *The Philosophy of Manufactures*. The book strongly favoured the masters and praised the factory system. Ure, *op. cit.*, pp. 374-403.

115. John Hannam, who had quarrelled with the Leeds short-time committee when he decided to co-operate with the Royal Commission, thought that fear of victimisation had passed away a good deal. Men had more liberty to express their opinions. *Factories Inquiry Commission*, Evidence taken by Mr Drinkwater, p. 88.

116. *Ibid.* Examinations taken by Mr Tufnell, pp. 84-5.

117. *Ibid.* Evidence taken by Mr Power, pp. 61-2.
118. *Ibid.* Examinations taken by Mr Tufnell, pp. 83-4. Rimmer, *op. cit.*, p. 218.
119. *Factories Inquiry Commission*, examinations taken by Mr Tufnell, pp. 90-1.
120. *Ibid.*, p. 134.
121. *Ibid.*, p. 94.
122. Cowell, who was opposed to relays, while busy collecting information in Manchester actually read in the newspapers that the government had decided to adopt them. Cowell's letters of 20 and 24 June 1833. *Chadwick Papers*, 41.
123. *First Report of the Central Board of H.M. Commissioners for Inquiring into the Employment of Children in Factories etc. PP* 1833, XX, pp. 18-24. This was generally agreed by the operatives themselves. Cf. Kirby and Musson, *op. cit.*
124. Chadwick quoted from Stuart's report, asking whether 'the phraseology of Lord Ashley's Bill, and its severe enactments by penalties, and their payment to common informers, should be applied to individuals who have acted and are acting in the most liberal, disinterested and benevolent manner; or generally against the other proprietors of factories in the great manufacturing districts in Scotland.' *Ibid.*, p. 24. The Finlay-Buchanan cousinry ran 'model' mill communities. So had Robert Owen, whose New Lanark was also praised by Chadwick.
125. *Ibid.*, p. 47. Cf. Kirby and Musson, *op. cit.*, p. 382.
126. *Ibid.*, p. 51.
127. *Ibid.*, pp. 53-8.
128. *Ibid.*, pp. 61-4. This would, of course, favour the large mills whose owners could afford to keep apprentice houses.
129. *Ibid.*, p. 68.
130. *Hansard.* 3rd series XIX, 5 July 1833, pp. 219-27.
131. *Ibid.*, p. 226.
132. *Poor Man's Guardian* Vol 3, 6 July 1833, p. 214.
133. See Brotherton's amendment to extend children's hours to ten, seconded by Hyett, of the master's lobby. *Hansard.* 3rd series XX, 13 August 1833, pp. 577-8.
134. *Hansard.* 3rd series XIX, 18 July 1833, p. 913.
135. *Ibid.*, 5 July 1833, p. 230. Morpeth proposed extending this to all manufacturers, or imposing an 11-hour day. Cf. an undated memorandum in Chadwick's papers inscribed 'On the employment of children in factories and Senior's objection to be combated'. This was mostly devoted to arguing that stretching a day beyond 12 hours merely produced spoiled work, so that there was little danger of it happening (an argument unlikely to convince the operatives). *Chadwick Papers*, 40.
136. *Hansard.* 3rd series XX, 9 August 1833, pp. 450-3.
137. *Ibid.*, 12 August 1833, pp. 528-30; 13 August 1833, p. 583.

5 The Factory Acts: II

The Factory Act of 1833: first attempts at enforcement

The state control of modern private industry began seriously in 1833. But it began reluctantly. There was not the same political consensus on Althorp's Act as there was on the Poor Law Amendment Act. While no independent board stood between the four inspectors and parliament, responsibility for their administration devolving in the first place on an under-secretary of state at the Home Office, control by the politicians was weak and vacillating. Fox Maule (later as Lord Panmure to become Florence Nightingale's 'Bison') was hardly a zealot. Lord John Russell took little interest in the Act. Sir James Graham, Home Secretary under Peel, and Sir George Grey, Home Secretary under Russell in 1846–51, lent a ready ear to the factory lobby. Whigs and Peelites mistrusted state intervention in industry, and did their best to ignore the Act. With Chadwick engrossed in the Poor Law and subsequently in Public Health, the inspectors were left to battle with the problems of enforcing an unpopular law very much on their own.

Four great factory districts were set up, covering the British Isles, including Ireland, and bearing a very rough relation to the regionalisation of the textile industry.[1] An inspector was appointed to each, and the four inspectors were ordered to meet at least twice a year, to co-ordinate their policies. A small section of the Home Department was developed to correspond with them. The districts soon proved grossly inequitable in burden, since the whole of the Lancashire cotton and Yorkshire woollen areas were included in the geographically smallest of them. After Robert Rickards, the first inspector of that district had retired sick and died, leaving chaos behind him, the work had to be redistributed.

The initial appointments were soon made. The Act had received the royal assent on 29 August. By December four inspectors were already sending in reports to the Home Department.[2] Their assistants, or superintendents, authorised under Section 41 of the Act, took longer to materialise. There was speculation about the institution of resident 'millwardens', one Aberdeen industrialist suggesting that their duties be divided between the four surgeons of the Aberdeen dispensary.[3] Horner suggested that the Glasgow millowners should call a general meeting to appoint local committees to investigate the number and size of the Glasgow mills and plan their division into local wards.[4] But the politicians were unwilling to let this extra patronage out of their hands, and by March 1834 Horner had applied to the government and obtained his first superintendent.

Any illusions held by the inspectors as to the difficulties of their task must have been dispelled by the reception given them in the industrial districts. Horner in Scotland, at this stage both optimistic and naïve, did report a general disposition to co-operate on the part of the millowners.[5] But Rickards in the crucial northern textile districts found 'no variation in the language' held to him, 'both by masters and operatives, on the present Factory Act; the former declaring certain parts of it to be impracticable, and the latter apprehensive that it would materially affect the future earnings of themselves and families.'[6] Where the owners appeared co-operative, or at least courteous, it was evidently from relief that the Ten Hour Bill had failed. Mr Joseph Stevenson, proprietor of Springfield mills, Belfast, told Horner that no legislative interference was called for, at least in his part of the United Kingdom, but 'as they were to have an Act, he was very much satisfied with that which had been passed'.[7] It was judiciously framed, and with attention to the interests of the manufacturers.

The masters were most worried about the eight-hour restriction and the education clauses. To maintain eight-hour shifts for children with twelve for adults necessitated a complicated system of relays. Masters pointed out that 'regularity' of labour was essential to their operations. It was difficult enough to get the children punctual in the factory, even if all started at the same time; relays would make it impossible.[8] Then they anticipated a shortage of young workers, which would increase when the parents of children already working withdrew them as their wages fell from 3s to 2s or 1s 6d. Only the great millowners employing apprentices and running their own schools would be able to find juvenile labour.

Relays were also needed so that children could be released at times when the local schools were open. But masters were infuriated by the Act's provision that children were not to be employed without a certificate that they had attended school the necessary number of hours the previous week. This, they said would put their whole business at the mercy of lazy or obstinate teachers who wouldn't sign certificates, or of truant children, or of irresponsible parents who kept their children from school.[9] They would be compelled either to suspend their own workforce or to break the law.

Faced with these hazards, the millowners rapidly became intractable. Many declared their intention of circumventing the Act by dismissing all children subject to the eight-hour restriction and the schooling clauses. Soon all the inspectors were reporting the threatened or actual dismissal from their jobs of the children the Act was intended to protect.[10] Horner thought the threats unlikely to be carried out wholesale, since the masters needed young children, and could re-employ those dismissed from other mills.[11] But a year later, Rickards reported from Leeds that the school clauses had defeated the humane objects of the

Act. They had caused the owners to discharge children under 11 to a distressing extent; 'Turned out on the wide world to seek other employment, or to wander about the streets of towns in idleness and vice.'[12] The story of the unemployed children wandering the streets is well known, and it is worth making some attempt to decide whether it is true. Did the Act have the unforeseen result of depriving children between 9 and 13 of their jobs in regulated factories?

The Factory Act applied to children in stages: to those of 9 and 10 in February 1834, to those of 11 in March 1835, and to those of 12 in March 1836. The immediate threat of dismissal therefore applied only to those under 11. All above that age would be 12 by the following year and 13 by 1836, and would avoid the eight-hour and schooling clauses altogether. The moment of danger, then, was February 1834. Thereafter children of 11 or 12 might find it difficult to obtain jobs in the regulated factories, but those in employment were unlikely to be dismissed. This already limits the probable number of sackings, and it is further limited, if the inspectors' figures are to be believed, by the very small number of children employed under the age of 11. In July 1834, Horner estimated that in Scottish mills (including cotton, wool, flax and silk), employing some 46,825 persons, about 100 had been discharged in favour of older children. These were mostly from mills employing three or four younger children for whom it was not worth altering the working timetable of the mill. Some 1,043 children under 11 remained in the industry.[13]

Moreover, dismissal did not necessarily entail unemployment. While some firms were sacking their youngest workers, others were engaging them as the extra hands needed for relays.

A sudden surplus of unemployed children would, as the millowners predicted, have caused a drop in wages. Did it happen? Rickards commented indignantly on a petition to parliament complaining of the hardship caused to families by children gaining less than 3s a week and having to pay 6d for their age certificates, and instancing the case of a poor mother who had to sell her shift to meet the certifying doctor's demand. Very few children, wrote Rickards, received less than 3s a week. Scavengers usually got between 3s 8d and 4s 2d, while the youngest pieceners were paid extra to do scavenger's work. A husband in the mill would be getting 26s to 30s a week, his wife 12s to 14s, three children as piecentrs 10s, 7s 6d and 5s 6d a week, and 'at these rates, the mother who pawns her shift must have other wants than to pay for her child's certificate'.[14]

No doubt the Act caused some dislocation in the workforce, but the main working-class sufferers were most likely adult operatives compelled to pay higher wages to older assistants, or to pay for double sets of young ones. Where children were dismissed, it was not always to their disadvantage. Howell reported that at Frome (Somerset) the master of a very good National school had found his numbers augmented by children discharged from neighbouring clothing mills.[15]

The last word on this question has not been said. The inspectors periodically collected figures on the factory population. But the lack of standardised categories in their classification makes them difficult to compare. In 1836 the House of Commons, faced with a revolt against the restriction of 12-year-olds, called for a return of children subject to restricted hours and compulsory education *or* dismissal.[16] The number actually dismissed was thus concealed.

In addition to their worries about restricted hours and compulsory education, the millowners feared their businesses would be inspected by 'millwardens' of poor salary and low social status, who would boss them about and betray their business secrets. They had obtained a clause in the Act enabling them to exclude any superintendent not accompanied by an inspector from the working parts of the mill. But their bid to control the appointments (which would have rendered the Act nugatory) failed. The government-appointed superintendents were mostly ex-army or navy paymasters or pursers, with the occasional physician. They ranked as minor civil servants, and, as will be seen, were not very satisfactory.

The final, and in some cases greatest source of worry to millowners, their managers and overlookers, was the spate of certification and form-filling required by the Act. The inspectors required time books informing them of the numbers, ages, hours, etc, of all children and young persons subject to the Act. Three of them issued their own time forms, hoping thus to mollify the millowners, but the numbers of forms and the information demanded tended to grow.[17] In addition there were age certificates signed by doctors and magistrates both for children entering the mill and for those proceeding to the young person's twelve-hour day. And there were the certificates of school attendance, to be presented each Monday. The inspectors' methods of dealing with these forms were not co-ordinated. Some allowed the children to keep their medical age certificates; others required them to be kept in a book at the mill. In some districts the parents paid the doctor's fee, but in Rickards' district the employers paid for the initial certificate (sometimes engaging the doctor to certify their own workers), and retained it, so that a child wishing to change his job would have to procure a new one. Rickards conceived this would keep the children steadily to their work, and prevent capricious removals.[18]

As well as procuring certificates, copies of the inspectors' regulations had to be read and filed, and the Act displayed on the factory walls. Most of this clerical work fell on the shoulders of managers or overlookers, and soon the inspectors were calling for a more precise demarcation of the responsibility between them and their masters. No doubt this paper-work was a leading factor in perpetuating discontent with the factory laws.

As March 1836 approached, the millowners, claiming that they would be unable to find enough children under 13 for relays, and would go bankrupt, persuaded Poulett Thomson, President of the Board of Trade, to introduce an amending Bill to stop the Act applying to children of 12. The four inspectors supported them, signing a joint report that the labour of 12-year-olds could not be restricted to forty-eight hours a week without serious inconvenience to masters and workpeople. Horner was by now becoming wary of the millowners' complaints and forebodings, but Rickards, although he realised the need to protect children from excessive labour imposed by the few millowners 'whose worldly interest is the moloch of their worship', in alliance with greedy parents, thought the cost in industrial disruption of regulating the labour of the 12-year-olds, too high. Like Stuart, he was an instinctive partisan of the masters.[19] Committed to the partial repeal of the Factory Act, and encouraging the millowners to believe the amendment would succeed, he had already tacitly ceased to enforce the school attendance clauses and was probably turning a blind eye to the full-time working of children under the permitted age. Admittedly, even with the help of four superintendents he was finding it impossible to enforce the law in 2,142 mills of various kinds. He retired in June 1836, and died soon after. Horner, on taking over, found 'a very imperfect observance of the law' throughout his district. The millowners were working children of 12 and under, twelve hours a day. Employment without age certificates was common, and those certified as twelve were obviously not more than ten or eleven. The masters who participated in these frauds were 'extremely reprehensible', wrote Horner, who was being educated by experience.[20] He sacked two surgeons and began prosecutions against several masters.

The debate on the second reading of Poulett Thomson's amending Bill contained little new. Bowring maintained that laws regulating wages, hours and conditions of labour were no more than cobwebs, because it was in the interest of master and servant that they should be broken.[21] Ashley treated the millowners' threats of more dismissals with contempt, arguing from the inspectors' reports that new machinery needed more child labour, and the masters could not do without it.[22] But the balance of opinion had not materially changed since 1833. Ashley was still in the false position of introducing Ten Hour Bills which would have prolonged juvenile labour. Poulett Thomson's Bill was carried, but only by two votes; and the government dropped it. The Factory Act had become the *status quo*; it still remained to enforce it.

The Factory Act of 1833: problems of enforcement

After the failure of Poulett Thomson's Bill and the departure of Rickards, and at Horner's insistence, the factory districts were recast.[23] The shady journalist, James Stuart, who had been so troublesome on the Factories Inquiry Commission was, under pressure from Brougham, appointed inspector in Scotland.[24] In January 1837 the inspectors were invited by Russell to draw up the heads of a Bill providing for more effective age certification, proper penalties for lawbreakers, and powers for the superintendents. The only result was two Bills which failed.[25] Meantime the inspectors were accumulating experience in enforcing the

Act, while the masters were exploring, on the whole successfully, its loopholes.

The first basic difficulty in enforcing the Factory Act was the impossibility of discovering the real age of the children. An efficient certifying system was vital; but how was it to be achieved? The pressure came, not at the minimum entry age of 9 (few masters wanting to employ very young children), but at the dividing line of 13 when 'children' became 'Young Persons' and proceeded to the sixty-nine-hour week. The determination of masters to avoid the embarrassments of relay working and school attendance certificates coincided with the desire of parents to get their children on to longer working hours for higher wages, and the wish of the children themselves to avoid 'school' or to reach the wages and status of the senior age groups. All parties had a motive to pretend the children were older than they were, and probably many more became 13 overnight on 1 March 1836 than were dismissed. The same thing happened when, in a flush of orders, millowners wanted extra hours or night working. It was even more difficult to prove the illegal employment of young persons, since no certificate of reaching the age of 18 was required.[26]

The inspectors realised they were being cheated. Horner, still in Scotland in February 1836, thought one-third of the mill children had obtained their age certificates by deceptions practised on the surgeon.[27] This might not have happened if doctors and magistrates had been conscientious. But there was no legal minimum qualification for practising medicine. Rickards noted that a drunken alehouse keeper pretending to be a medical practitioner, and a man trained as a druggist's apprentice were signing certificates.[28] Even genuine doctors were sensitive to pressure from millowners who were their patrons, or from parents who could turn nasty if certificates were refused. Refusal could lose them a lot of 6d fees, and the formula 'of the ordinary strength and appearance' (of nine, or thirteen as the case might be) on the certificate, enabled the less scrupulous to sign, even if they knew the child's real age. Careless or hostile magistrates then signed the certificates in batches, without seeing the children. The legal alternative to these medical age certificates, the baptismal certificate, was even less reliable. Parents supplied children with their older brother's or sister's certificate, or forged a false date of birth on their own.

The inspectors tried to overcome the difficulty of corrupt doctors by selecting reputable surgeons for certifying work in their respective districts. In 1834 Horner appointed 112 surgeons for different parts of his Scottish area,[29] while Rickards divided Manchester into five divisions, and allocated a surgeon recommended by the Manchester Royal Infirmary to each.[30] Thereupon some millowners complained to the government, and the Law Officers of the Crown informed Rickards that the inspectors were not authorised under the Act to appoint surgeons.[31] Yet when Horner moved to Lancashire, he managed, by agreement with the millowners, to obtain control of these appointments.[32] Saunders, who had made no attempt of this kind, reported in 1838 that millowners at Wakefield were sacking their surgeons in favour of a Dr Smith, who would grant false certificates to children under 12.[33] After the amending Act of 1844 he hastened to appoint doctors in his area also.

Even when respectable practitioners could be secured, the problem was not solved. When a child's age was unknown, what was meant by 'ordinary strength and appearance'? Horner, after consultations, told his surgeons not to grant certificates to children claiming to be 9 if they measured, without shoes, less than 3 feet 10 inches, nor to children claiming to be 13 if they measured less than 4 feet $3\frac{1}{2}$ inches.[34] He also sent them forms to record observations as to the stature of working-class children in their districts. The Manchester short-time committee then accused Horner of circumventing parliament's refusal to repeal the clause protecting children of 12 by inventing a formula to conceal the real age of those certified.[35] For a time there were attempts to tell the age of the children (like horses) by their teeth. But no solution to the problem was found until thirteen years after the establishment of the Registrar of Births and Deaths, and the local registration districts, in 1837.

Another obstacle to enforcing the Act was the unpopularity of the education clauses. By vetoing the rate-aiding of factory schools, the Lords had rendered evasion inevitable, but in any case, the millowners so opposed the principle that they, not the parents, should be held legally responsible for their juvenile workers' education that some of those already providing tuition refused to co-operate. Only the very wealthy could provide good schools at their works, and suggestions for central schools serving a group of mills bore little fruit. The relay system was devised to release children at times when the local day schools were open, but they were unwelcome in them. Being part-time in attendance, and generally slower than the rest in progress, they also tended to disrupt the curriculum.

The factory 'school' was too often a bench in the coal cellar, supervised by a broken-down mill hand. Horner admitted that 'schools' were often places of detention for the children when not on work shift, and that they and their parents were being cheated of their 3d school fees.[36] Although the inspectors considered education one of the main purposes of the Act, until 1840 only Saunders took the education clauses seriously. In 1843 his scheme for factory schools on National School lines, controlled by the clergy,[37] was adopted by Graham who incorporated it in his Factory Bill. The result was an explosion from the Nonconformist millowners, and the defeat of the Bill. The faint possibility that the education provisions of the Factory Acts might pioneer a nationwide compulsory school system quietly faded. In 1847 Horner reported that in the Lancashire district 3,746 children attended factory schools, as against 4,355 in National Schools, and 1,211 in British, 2,020 in other public schools, and 3,908 in private and dame schools. Fully half the children in factory schools were as well taught as those in good British (Nonconformist) and National Schools.[38] In reality it was a disappointing outcome of the hopes pinned on the educational effects of the Factory Laws.

The millowners were finding other means of evading the Act. They tinkered with the factory clocks to shorten meal breaks and to bring in the children half an hour early to work.[39] They lengthened hours on the excuse of making up time lost through water shortage or accident. They took advantage of the failure of the Act to specify children's meal times to make them clean machinery during the older workers' meal breaks, often while it was moving. This was one of the most frequent causes of accidents.[40]

The inspectors and their superintendents fought these evasions as best they could. Within four months of his transfer to Lancashire, Horner had prosecuted for 504 offences and obtained 458 convictions. His table of descriptions of offences in his report of 18 January 1837 shows which kinds of offence were most frequent.[41] The figures, however, must be treated with caution since some offences, such as using false age certificates, were more difficult to detect than others.

Table of descriptions of offence

Description of the offence	Informations	Convictions	Withdrawn	Dismissed
1. Employing children under nine years of age	8	6	—	2
2. Employing children under 13 years of age longer than 48 hours in the week	69	58	5	6
3. Employing children in silk-mills more than 10 hours in the day	14	13	1	—
4. Employing children in the night-time	5	4	1	—
5. Employing young persons more than 12 hours in the day	24	19	4	—
6. Employing children without certificates of age	24	18	3	3
7. Employing children without requiring them to attend school	68	55	7	6
8. Not giving the time for meals prescribed by the Act	9	8	—	1
9. Not keeping the register required to be kept, in order to show the workers in the factory who are subject to the Act	32	31	1	—

Table of descriptions of offence

Description of the offence	Informations	Convictions	Withdrawn	Dismissed
10. Not keeping the register of time required to be kept, in order to show the hours when the children and young persons are employed	65	51	10	5
11. Making false entries in these registers	7	6	—	1
12. Giving false certificates of school attendance	2	1	1	—
13. Not fixing up the Abstract of the Act and the Regulations of the Inspectors	10	6	4	—
14. Not whitewashing the interior of the factory for more than 12 months	5	5	—	—
15. Various minor offences	18	10	7	1
	360	291	44	25

As well as these routine cases, Horner recounted one, reminiscent of the marathons reported in the Select Committee of 1832, when work was 'throng'. The owners of a shoddy mill at Batley, Yorkshire, had worked five boys from 6 a.m. on Friday to 4 p.m. on Saturday with only meal breaks and four hours' rest. Prosecutions were useless unless sufficient evidence could be obtained to convict, and there was probably a large hinterland of undisclosed offences. Suspicions were aroused by the discovery of children at odd hours concealed in wool bags, or hidden in the 'necessaries'.[42] There were far too few inspectors, the superintendents could get no further than the counting-house without the millowners' permission, and many places had early-warning systems against the arrival of enforcement officers.

The ultimate obstacle to the enforcement of the Factory Act was the resistance of the local magistrates. Some provisions in the Act allowed the masters to shuffle off their responsibilities on to their subordinates, and Benches to refuse to convict; but on the whole a difficulty greater than securing convictions was securing adequate penalties. The inspectors could sometimes achieve their object by prosecuting for multiple offences, since many masters found overworking their children were also caught without age- and education certificates, and without time books and registers. There were indignant protests at prosecutions for these merely 'formal' offences, which produced accumulated fines. But under Section 43 of the Act no more than one penalty could be imposed for simultaneous breaches of the law, so that many children could be illegally worked on the same day (or night) for the price of one.[43] Under Section 31 an inspector or magistrate who considered an offence not wilful nor grossly negligent could mitigate the penalty below the sum of £1 or dismiss the information. Mitigation seems to have been the Lancashire magistrates' favourite resource. The newly arrived and zealous Horner found that of the 458 convictions he secured, 343 were followed by 20s fines. These fines became known as 'the sovereign remedy'.[44] Even a succession of them constituted a mere pinprick to millowners who could secure lucrative orders by working longer hours than their rivals. Horner pointed out that they would continue to violate the law until the punishment exceeded the profit from doing so.[45]

Under Section 30 of the Act a proprietor's servant could be held responsible for offences committed without the knowledge and consent of the master. This was a gift to magistrates who favoured the owners. There were reports of collusive agreements between proprietors and their overlookers that the latter should stand the fines, at least in court;[46] and there were rumours of operatives being forced to indemnify their masters against penalties incurred under the Act. Thus enforcement depended on the inclinations of magistrates who in the most industrialised areas were least inclined to carry it out.

The obstacle of partial magistrates was of long standing, and was doubtless the reason why under the 1833 Act the inspectors themselves had been given the powers of magistrates, and could fine delinquents 'on view', i.e. summarily. It is difficult to ascertain how these powers were used, since the inspectors were shy of publicising them. Horner maintained that he very seldom convicted 'on view' but always let the accused go before a magistrate if he wished rather than pay a £1 fine to the inspector. The implied assumption was that they were used mainly against operatives. Horner followed his table of offences with the remark: 'Besides the above there have been four instances in which I have convicted upon view; they were cases of operatives whom I found employing children contrary to law, notwithstanding repeated warnings by the master and manager'.[47] Howell also included four convictions on view in a list of twelve prosecutions in 1836.[48] The £1 fine, sometimes with costs, seems to have been a standard penalty for adult operatives discovered employing pieceners without age certificates. Of course this was a far heavier penalty upon a spinner than upon a millowner, and it was more oppressive in that an operative who could not provide his team of child assistants was liable to be discharged.[49] In other ways, too, the Act was more savagely enforced against the less articulate classes. It was not easy to prosecute surgeons for signing false age certificates. Horner could only refuse to accept their certificates and freeze them out. But he admitted that several parents and schoolmasters (a despised race) had been imprisoned for putting false hours on school attendance certificates.[50] Such uneven-handedness may have strengthened the hostility of the short-time committees. Hoping still for a Ten Hour Act, they had adopted an attitude of angry vigilance, maintaining that the 1833 Act could not work, while blaming the inspectors for breaches of it and demanding enforcement by stopping all machinery at the end of a ten-hour day. The committees attempted to elect their own inspectors (which Russell refused) and renewed their activity in bringing informations against factory owners for breaches of age and hours regulations.[51] This could well have backfired in view of the parents and operatives who were themselves supplying under-age assistants, and apparently fizzled out. But it cannot have helped the inspectors, on whose administration the success of the Act depended, to maintain their impartiality and integrity.[52] Without that integrity, as the doings of James Stuart were soon to show, the Act could indeed become an engine of oppression.

All the inspectors started with some predisposition in favour of the millowners, but Stuart, the Whig journalist and politician, had personal friendships and alliances with the Scottish proprietors. He refused to prosecute masters for breaking the law, but instead used the threat of prosecution to make them dismiss operatives who employed assistants without certificates, or with false ones. He then made the masters keep them out of employment until they and their families were starving, and they crawled to the inspector to let them get their jobs back. These methods were facilitated by the absence of parish relief and by the fact that in Scotland, unlike the north of England, a prosecution, quite apart from conviction, was considered shameful.[53] When, despite Stuart's activities, it became apparent that the law was not being observed in Scotland, he continued to send in optimistic reports, suppressing any statements from his superintendents which might throw doubt on his claims. Eventually he tried to cover up his failure, collecting evidence which would throw the blame on the operatives by forcing their children to testify against them in the presence of their masters and of his superintendents.

The whole story came out under cross-examination before the Select Committee of 1840, when it also emerged that Stuart was using his powers to make war on the Glasgow Cotton Spinners' Union, and victimise its leaders.[54]

The situation in Scotland before Stuart received a salutary lesson from Ashley and his supporters at the 1840 Select Committee was exceptional. Horner and the other inspectors were men of integrity, and Horner at least had an open mind which permitted his first-hand observations to cure him of his illusions about the philanthropy of many millowners, and carried him gradually away from the factory lobby and into increasingly sympathetic co-operation with Ashley on behalf of the factory children. But Stuart's case showed the danger that the factory administration could become a mere tool in the embittered struggle between capital and labour.

Early factory inspectors

The enforcement service, struggling to enforce the Factory Act in the teeth of resistance from masters, operatives and parents, was not helped by the divisions in its own ranks. The inspectors remained four in number, while the factories they were to supervise multiplied. However, under their constant demands, the superintendents increased. The four appointed in 1835 had, by 1838, become fifteen, mostly resident in subdivisions of the great factory districts. The Treasury, however, had learned nothing about the payment of civil servants in the field, since Tom Paine's celebrated protest about the remuneration of customs officials. The inspectors, among the most highly paid of their kind, received £1,000 a year each. The superintendents were at first paid £250, of which some £200 was swallowed up in travelling expenses.[55] They were worse off than many operatives, and an obvious target for bribery. After representations by the inspectors, Russell, in 1836, raised the salary of two superintendents in each district to £350. But the lack of travel allowances constituted a standing temptation to the whole service to shirk its duties. The inspectors, not required to reside in their districts, could avoid expensive journeys by sending their superintendents out on tours of inspection. The superintendents, who bitterly resented this, tried to curtail their own journeys. The system taxed the zeal and integrity of the inspectors and the loyalty of the superintendents, and fomented jealousy between the two ranks. In appointing superintendents, patronage was exercised with little attention to character. Several officers justified the millowners' apprehensions about 'millwardens'. Daniel Webster was irresponsible and insolent, and borrowed money from the millowners which he could not repay.[56] Dr Robert Baker supplemented his inadequate salary by signing the age certificates he was also inspecting.[57] John Wood spent his time collecting evidence of the inadequacies and misdoings of the inspectors in order to get them into trouble; he was eventually forced to resign. His fellow superintendent in Scotland, John Beal, embarrassed the government by allowing a confidential letter from his inspector authorising him to spy on Chartist meetings to fall into the hands of Fielden.[58]

The superintendents were not always set a good example by their superiors. James Stuart after his appointment remained in London editing the *Courier*, and making money as chairman of an insurance company. The other three failed to co-ordinate their policies as they were supposed to do. For instance, they had different methods of dealing with age certificates and appointing surgeons. Stuart, as we have seen, tried to enforce the Act in ways entirely his own.

These internal divisions and the complaints of the superintendents were instrumental in obtaining a Select Committee to investigate the service in 1840.[59]

The Select Committee of 1840

On the House of Commons Select Committee, the factory reformers and the factory owners were both well represented.[60] Ashley in the chair ensured that the questioning would be long and fierce. The superintendents were allowed to voice their complaints. The inspectors, especially Horner, were cross-questioned at length. Apart from Stuart, who endured some of the bullying he had meted out to others, they on the whole vindicated themselves. In the upshot, one superintendent resigned and another was dismissed, although he was re-employed later at the lower grade.[61] Stuart apparently was unassailable, but he behaved more cautiously for the next few years. A number of Horner's suggestions were embodied in the Factory Act of 1844.

The evidence taken before the Committee showed clearly that the juvenile eight-hour day applied by relays was, except in a few large mills, not working and not likely to work. The result was a revival of interest in the half-time day; six or seven hours in morning or afternoon shifts. Ashley's attempts to amend government Bills in favour of the ten-hour day were a continuing factor in delaying legislation, but the Committee marked a change in his attitude from confrontation towards co-operation with the inspectors. Removing or chastening trouble-makers, it cleared the air within the enforcement service, and enabled the inspectors to devote more energy to constructive plans for education and factory safety.

The Factory Act of 1844,[62] held up for years by the sectarian strife over factory education, embodied many of the Select Committee's conclusions. It shortened the children's working day to $6\frac{1}{2}$ or 7 hours, worked before or after the dinner break, or to 10 hours on alternate days through the week. The young persons' 69-hour week was extended to women. Alternate 10-hour days, if used, would have secured the 10-hour day for adults, and the 69-hour week for women probably limited adult hours in many factories. The conflict between protecting children and limiting adult hours (though not between the ultimate aims of the government service and the Short Time Movement) was resolving itself.

Most of the Act's other provisions closed loopholes or improved administration. It specified wording and laid down uniform procedures for age and school attendance certificates, and it also gave the inspectors more control over the doctors and schoolteachers. It specified the times and places for meals, and ordered the display of a factory clock, to be approved by the inspectors. But the inspectors lost, willingly, the powers of summary jurisdiction which had made them unpopular prosecutors and judges in their own cause, as well as the power to make independent regulations. The superintendents (now called sub-inspectors) were empowered to enter all parts of a mill, and the children could not be hidden from them. But the millowners managed to defeat a proposal of Horner's that the master should be legally responsible for all offences in his works, recovering from his subordinates if he could make a case against them.

The Act also embodied a number of safety measures, suggested in 1840 by the inspectors, who saw the increasingly ferocious accidents inflicted by new machinery, as ever larger and swifter revolving belts and shafts caught tired or careless millworkers by sleeves or aprons or hair, and tore off limbs or scalps. The cleaning of moving machinery by young workers was at last forbidden, but fencing and safeguarding involved controversial and technical problems. After 1844 the Home Department began paying sub-inspectors' travelling expenses separately from their salaries, and a more harmonious service could give its full attention to solving these difficulties.

Extension of the Acts; mines and printworks

After 1840 Horner and Ashley, acting in concert, turned their attention to removing some of the anomalies set up in 1833, by extending the Factory Acts to children in other industries. Even in textiles, silk mills were allowed to work children up to ten hours a day, and lace factories were totally unregulated. Chadwick had intended the 1833 Act merely as a beginning. There are in his papers at least two lists of industries employing child labour, one forming an appendix to an anonymous pamphlet entitled 'Remarks on the propriety and necessity of making the FACTORY BILL of more general application', dated 1833.[63] In June 1840 Horner wrote to him, suggesting that protection should be extended to other children besides those in factories, asking if the Poor Law Officers could collect information, and proposing a parliamentary commission of inquiry with Ashley on it.[64] Horner backed this up with a pamphlet; 'On the Employment of Children in Factories and other Works in the United Kingdom and in some Foreign Countries'. Ashley reviewed the pamphlet, together with the published minutes of the 1840 Select Committee in an article entitled 'Infant Labour' in the *Quarterly Review*.[65] He drew special attention to Horner's admission before the Select Committee that the restriction of the work hours of 12-year-olds had not, as the millowners had predicted, forced them to close their mills.

Ashley now began a parliamentary campaign to obtain an investigation into the condition of children working in mines and industries not covered by the existing acts. His speeches were powerful and well informed, and they publicised scandals such as the borrowing of money by parents who then sent their children in bond to the masters in the pin trade, to work off their debt; or the spreading of poisonous dyes in the night hours by 7-year-old 'teerers' in printworks. At the second attempt Ashley succeeded. Fox Maule had been squared, and promised government help in the inquiry. The result was the Children's Employment Commission of 1842.

The Children's Employment Commission followed a now familiar pattern. It had a Central Board of four; the factory inspectors Horner and

Saunders, and two survivors of the 1833 Royal Commission, Thomas Tooke and Thomas Southwood Smith. It had a sizeable corps of sub-commissioners appointed by the Home Department, armed with forms and questionnaires, and assigned to collect information in various districts. But it differed from the previous Royal Commission in that it had no ulterior motive. The report started with the statement that the principle of legislative interference on behalf of children and young persons had already been decided and acted on by Acts of Parliament for their protection.[66] It bestowed blame impartially on greedy parents who lived on their children's labour, owners who forced or encouraged them to do so, miners who ill-treated their child assistants, and owners who refused to intervene to prevent them. It refrained from side-kicks at trade unions and from propagating *laisser faire*. It was a genuine piece of humanitarian propaganda.

The first report of the Commission is too familar to need detailed description. It recounted graphically the horrors of infant and female labour in the mines, especially in east Scotland, where children starting at 5 years of age were most numerous. After their time as trappers, sitting alone in the dark from twelve to sixteen hours a day to open the doors for coal carts, they graduated to hauling these carts along tunnels 28 inches high, by means of a girdle round the waist which blistered the sides, and a chain between the legs which rubbed holes in their trousers.[67] Girls and young women did the same work, even when pregnant; or carried baskets of coal weighing up to 2 or 3 cwt along tunnels and up endless ladders.[68]

The Commissioners had an unerring eye for abuses likely to interest and shock a middle-class audience, such as the presence of women in the mines, often half-stripped, and working with men who laboured naked because of the great heat. They described accidents which occurred because the ventilation doors were worked by tiny children, deaths without inquest, deformities from overdeveloped arms and stunted growth, bow legs and curved spines, skin diseases, lung diseases from dust, premature old age and early death. And they illustrated the report with engravings which soon became famous and have since become the stock-in-trade of all school textbooks on nineteenth-century social history.[69]

After this report Ashley had no difficulty in obtaining an Act forbidding the employment of women and girls underground, and the employment of boys under 10. To get it enforced was not so easy: the inspector appointed by the Home Department, H. S. Tremenheere, was another Whig, devoted to political economy, favourable to the employers and hostile to trade unions.[70] He tended to apply the Act selectively, turning a blind eye to the continuing use of little boys to pull trucks in narrow seams. The government dragged its feet, fearing to be saddled with responsibility for mining accidents. Expert underground inspectors were needed, but the first was not appointed until 1850.

The second report of the Children's Employment Commission, while less sensational than the first, covered many more unregulated trades. Ashley followed it up with a demand for control of calico printworks and ropeworks. Printworks were particularly difficult because they were subject to changes of fashion and season which caused rush orders and sudden flushes of work. The government now experimented with more flexible provisions for limiting juvenile work through the medium of education clauses. An Act passed in 1845 imposed a minimum entry age of 8 and forbade night work for all females and for boys up to 13.[71] All children up to 13 were required to attend school for at least thirty days between 1 January and 30 June, and another thirty days between 1 July and 31 December each year. The Act was retrograde in that it allowed children to be worked from 6 a.m. until 10 p.m. when work was 'throng'; and did nothing to protect boys over 13. The masters soon discovered that the Act had failed to specify a minimum time per day to be spent in the schoolroom, and started calling the children out at any time they needed them. This was stopped by an amending Act in 1847, but parents complained that a clause demanding a certificate that the child had had at least thirty days' schooling in the six months before starting work caused them hardship. A real danger of the Printworks Act in its amended form was that it hardened a growing tradition that working-class children should be allowed to start work only after reaching a certain elementary degree of educational proficiency. This fulfilled the Victorian demand for a minimum moral and intellectual education of the lower orders, but it tended to ensure that the brightest children were those who left school earliest.[72]

Relays and the Ten Hour Bill

The period 1845-53 saw the belated realisation of the Ten Hour Act in textile mills. But this was not achieved without a severe struggle. In January 1846 Ashley (thoroughly disillusioned with Peel because of his obstructive attitude to social legislation) resigned his parliamentary seat in protest against the Bill to repeal the Corn Law.[73] Leadership of the Short Time cause in the Commons fell to the Fieldens, father and son, who were both more extreme and less intelligent than Ashley, and who had the backing of the Manchester unions. The initiative for shortening the working day was facilitated by the economic depression which followed the railway crisis of 1845. It was easier to shorten hours when many factories were not working to capacity, and a ten-hour day (excluding meal breaks) could be organised with two shifts of children or one of young persons. Indeed, John Fielden put forward the need to protect young persons in order to obtain the backing of the new Home Secretary, Russell, for the Ten Hour Bill which passed in June 1847. But the factory reformers reckoned without the ingenuity of the millowners. The relay system, so condemned until its suspension in 1844, was now revived to keep the machinery going. With children and young persons organised in two- or two-and-a-half-hour shifts, the adult day could be maintained, or even extended. The children and adolescents could be kept hanging about the factory all day long, and it was by no means certain that any law was being broken.

The revival of relays ruptured the somewhat fragile harmony of the factory inspectors. Horner had been particularly anxious for the young persons to have their evenings free for night school. Stuart once more came out vehemently on the side of the millowners. He argued that, in a recession, the ability to run a few machines for long hours would enable the masters to keep at least a part of their workforce in employment. He even maintained that young women liked having a couple of hours off in the morning, to do their shopping. Unfortunately, his refusal to take action against relays in Scotland undermined the other inspectors' attempts to suppress them elsewhere. It became known that while Horner was taking Lancashire millowners to court, Stuart was encouraging Scottish millowners to organise relays.[74]

In the summer of 1848, when trade was beginning to revive and the 'false' relay system continuing to spread,[75] the trouble came to a head. Horner had prosecuted a number of Lancashire millowners for relays, with conflicting results. While the Manchester Stipendiary Magistrates narrowly convicted the large firm of Messrs Kennedy of illegality in working their children in relays, the Atherton Justices not only dismissed a similar case, but turned up at neighbouring Tyldesley and swamped the bench to do likewise.[76] Russell's Home Secretary, Sir George Grey, besieged by millowners on one side and Horner on the other, pursued a consistent policy of giving way to conflicting pressures.

'Sir George Grey', wrote Cornewall Lewis (now Under Secretary at the Home Office), 'thinks it inexpedient to lay informations against Mill Owners for a breach of the letter of the Act as to the employment of young persons by relays, in cases in which there is no reason to believe that such young persons have been actually employed for a longer time than that sanctioned by law.[77] But Horner's answering broadside pointing out that masters who instituted relays were acting not merely against the letter but the spirit of the factory laws,[78] extracted an assurance that 'Sir George Grey had' no intention of interfering with the discretion of the Inspectors in regard to particular instances of a violation of the law, which might come under their notice. . .'.[79]

Unfortunately, this retreat did not prevent Stuart from using Grey's first letter as authority for his refusal to prosecute for relays in his district; and the inspectors quarrelled furiously at their half-yearly meeting. In this heated atmosphere Horner brought the collusive case of *Ryder* v. *Mills* in order to test the law by appeal to the Court of Exchequer. On 8 February 1850 Mr Justice Parke returned a verdict that, under the Act of 1844 which specified when all should begin work, but not when all should end it, relays were not illegal.[80] Stuart had died in November 1849, but the remaining inspectors were deadlocked in their effort to stop relays, which threatened to become nearly universal.

The situation was resolved by Ashley, now back in the Commons as member for Bath. Ashley was no longer official spokesman for the short-time committees, and was regarded by them with some suspicion, perhaps because of his association with Horner and Chadwick. However, he could still use his enormous prestige to effect a workable compromise which would give the operatives almost a ten-hour day. He would need to move quickly, since the reaction against Peel's repeal of the Corn Law which had induced Tories to vote for the Ten Hour Act in 1847 was declining. He proposed to realise his object by amending the law so as to lengthen the night hours in which young persons were forbidden to work, or shorten the day hours, from the existing 5.30 a.m. – 8.30 p.m. to 6.30 a.m. – 6.30 p.m. A permitted twelve-hour working day with one and a half hours off for meals would produce a ten-and-a-half-hour day with a Saturday half-day. The whole working week would be just two hours longer than that intended by the Ten Hour Act of 1847, and relays would be stopped.

It is not clear why this proposal evoked such an outbreak of wrath from the short-time committees. Certainly it came as no surprise to Ashley, who was hurt rather than astonished at being furiously denounced as a traitor.[81] Presumably the textile unions felt that their former champion was now hand-in-glove with the Chadwick party. They had failed to secure control of the working day as a means of influencing the level of employment and wages.

The amending Act of 1850 did not end the problem of relays. Grey went back on his assurances to Ashley that the section forbidding women and young persons to work between 6 p.m. and 6 a.m. would include children. Thus, if a millowner could hire enough children to make relays of workers under 13 he could still lengthen the adult day. It was done in bad faith, and was Sir George Grey's final obeisance to political economy.

From 1850 until the Act of 1853, when children were included in the 6 a.m. – 6 p.m. day, a sort of limbo existed, with ten and a half hours as the norm and factories here and there working thirteen hours with relays. Palmerston, Ashley's father-in-law and unlikely ally, completed the process of limitation, with the purpose of protecting the children but the consequence of a ten-and-a-half-hour day for all factory workers in the trades regulated by the Act of 1833.[82] The conflict between protecting children and limiting the hours of adults had now vanished, even if the basic conflict between adult workers and their masters remained. The people most affected by the long struggle were the administrators. The inspectors' reports show a gradual disenchantment with the millowners and a growing scepticism about their arguments. 'Nine tenths of the employers of children care nothing about them', wrote Horner to Chadwick in 1859, apropos of a further attempt to extend half-time education.[83]

The factory code established by Chadwick, Ashley and the inspectors was only a beginning. The demand for child labour did not start to decline until the 1860s, and meantime evasions of and insufficiencies in the law remained and abuses tended to overtake remedies. In the 1850s enthusiasm for state action waned, in factory regulation as elsewhere. It took long to become accepted that only a system of full-time compulsory education which took children right out of industry could secure their health and welfare. The plan of part-time factory work and part-time education beloved of Chadwick and Horner never really succeeded. On the other hand, restriction of adult hours turned out to be no panacea for unemployment. It remained, however, one aim of increasingly powerful trade unions.[84]

Sources and references

1. The districts comprised: (1) Scotland, with the northern half of Ireland and the four most northerly English counties; (2) Lancashire, Yorkshire, Cheshire, and a strip along the north coast of Wales; (3) The rest of Wales with the Welsh marches, southern Ireland and some of the English Midland woollen counties such as Gloucestershire and Worcestershire; (4) the rest of England from Cornwall to the Humber. Cf. **Thomas, M. W.** *The Early Factory Legislation.* Thames Book Publishing Co., Leigh on Sea, 1947, pp. 98-100. Thomas gives details of the districts before and after the reorganisation of 1836, with two maps, facing pp. 160 and 224. His excellent chapters on the problems of enforcement leave little scope for more than the provision of some extra details.
2. The inspectors' reports for 1834 and 1835 were omitted from the catalogue of the *Parliamentary Papers.* They were, however, found by Thomas.
3. Report of Leonard Horner, 26 December 1833. *Half Yearly Reports by Inspectors of Factories,* 11 August 1834, p. 4. *PP* 1834, XLIII.
4. *Ibid.*, 4 December p. 3.
5. *Ibid.*, p. 2.
6. Report of Robert Rickards, 24 December 1833, *ibid.*, p. 24.
7. Report of L. Horner, 28 November 1833, *ibid.* p. 1.
8. Report of L. Horner, 26 December, *ibid.*, p. 5.
9. Report of T. Jones Howell, 20 December 1833, *ibid.*, pp. 20-1.
10. Report of R. J. Saunders, 28 December 1833, *ibid.*, p. 61. Report of T. Jones Howell, 20 December, *ibid.*, p. 20.
11. Report of L. Horner, 4 December 1833, *ibid.*, p. 2.
12. Rickards. Answers to queries sent by Vsct Duncannon, 12 August 1834, *ibid.*, p. 39.
13. Report of L. Horner, 21 July 1834, *ibid.*, p. 7.
14. Report of R. Rickards. February 1835 (return dated 1 July 1835) p. 7. *PP* 1835, XL. Rickards presumedly meant drink.
15. Report of T. Jones Howell, February 1835, *ibid.*, p. 5.
16. *PP* 1836, XLV, p. 203.
17. Rickards circulated Time Form No. 1 requiring a statement of the number of hours the machines ran daily, and Time Form No. 2 requiring a statement of the number of hours worked each day by each child and young person, with the times of beginning and ending. The forms were several times revised and the questions increased. However, Horner on taking over Rickards' district issued a simplified time book requiring a general instead of daily entry of the children's hours. Report of R. Rickards, 10 February 1834. App. pp. 31, 33. *PP* 1834, XLIII. Joint Report of L. Horner, R. J. Saunders, J. Stuart, 12 October 1836, p. 33. *PP* 1837, XXXI.
18. Report of R. Rickards, 10 February 1834, p. 28. *PP* 1834, XLIII.
19. Rickards did not actually sign the joint report, as he was away in Manchester. His attitudes are interesting. He observed that the steam engine was 'a relentless

power to which young and old were bound to submit', but he considered work in an up-to-date mill neither unhealthy nor exhausting even full time, for children over the age of 9. He contrasted the 'intelligence, energy and activity' of the manufacturers with 'the coarse habits of the general mass, from want of sound moral and religious education, the slaves of vice, prejudice and passion, easily excited by factious clamour as to real or supposed grievances.' But he noticed the animosity and confrontation in place of friendship and subordination, between masters and men. He proposed the factory inspectors should act as spies for the Home Department, a proposal which led to trouble.

20. Report of L. Horner, 12 October 1836. Inspectors' Reports for half-year ending December 1836, pp. 4-5. *PP* 1837, XXXI.
21. *Hansard.* 3rd series XXXIII, 9 May 1836, pp. 753-4.
22. *Ibid.*, p. 742.
23. According to Kirby and Musson, Horner's transfer to Lancashire under instructions to enforce the Act was the price for Hindley's dropping his Ten Hour Bill in 1836. **Kirby, R. G.** and **Musson, A. E.,** *The Voice of the People: John Doherty, 1798-1854 Trade Unionist, Radical and Factory Reformer.* Manchester U.P., 1975, p. 389.
24. **Henriques, U.,** 'An early factory inspector: James Stuart of Dunearn', *Scottish Hist Review,* Vol. L, 1. No. 149, April 1971, pp. 26-7. The Lancashire district lost North Wales, much of Cheshire with Derbyshire and Staffordshire to Howell's Western district, and the West Riding and other parts of the Midlands to Saunders. Scotland now included all Ireland. Cf. Thomas, M. W., *op. cit.,* pp. 99-100.
25. Thomas, M. W., *op. cit.,* pp. 146-58.
26. Rickards in 1835 extracted from Glossop (notorious for its long hours) 60 cases of children certified in February 1832 to be between 12 and 16, who the following year were 18. Report of R. Rickards, undated. *Reports by Inspectors to Secretary of State,* 1 July 1835, p. 8. *PP* 1835, XL.
27. Report of L. Horner, 24 February 1836. *Half-yearly Reports of Inspectors* dated February 1836, p. 13. *PP* 1836, XLV.
28. Rickards, undated. *Reports of Inspectors,* 1 July 1835, p. 8. *PP* 1835, XL.
29. Report of L. Horner to Vsct Duncannon, 21 July 1834. *Inspectors' Reports* dated 11 August 1834, p. 9. *PP* 1834, XLIII.
30. Rickards to Melbourne, 10 February 1834, *ibid.,* p. 28.
31. Rickards to S. M. Philipps. 22 February 1834, *ibid.,* pp. 34-5.
32. Horner sanctioned surgeons proposed at meetings of the millowners. See his evidence to the Select Committee of 1840, p. 41. *PP* 1840, X.
33. Quarterly Report of R. J. Saunders. 1 October 1838. *Inspectors' Reports for half-year ending 31 December 1838,* pp. 11-12. *PP* 1839, XIX.
34. Supplementary instructions to surgeons. Report of L. Horner, 12 October 1836, App. 6. *Inspectors' Reports for half-year ending 31 December 1836,* p. 21. *PP* 1837, XXXI.
35. Thomas, M. W., *op. cit.,* pp. 128-9. The formula was laid down in the text of the 1833 Act as the means of ascertaining the age of those entering the factories at 9, but not repeated as a test for the 13-year-olds. The inspectors merely applied it to the older group. Fielden and Doherty maintained that the scale of measurements was too low, and was intended to facilitate full-time employment of children under 13. They made no allowance for Horner's difficulties and showed great suspicion of his intentions. For this controversy, cf. Kirby and Musson, *op. cit.,* pp. 390-92.
36. Report of L. Horner, 7 July 1843, *Reports of Inspectors for quarter ending 30 June 1843,* p. 12. *PP* 1843, XXVII.
37. *Report of R. J. Saunders upon the Establishment of Schools in the Factory Districts,* February 1842. Also Report of R. J. Saunders, 25 January 1843. *Inspectors' Reports for Quarter ending 31 December 1842,* pp. 32-9. *PP* 1843, XXVII; and *Inspectors' Reports for Quarter ending 30 June 1843, ibid.,* pp. 20-38. Cf. p. 218 below.

38. L. Horner. Report of 17 May 1847. *Inspectors' Reports for half-year ending 30 April 1847*, p. 5. *PP* 1847.

39. *First Report of S.C. on the Operation of the Act for the Regulation of Mills and Factories. PP* 1840, X. Evidence of M. J. Heathcote, pp. 141-2. *Second Report.* Evidence of T. J. Howell Esq., p. 15.

40. See Table of Accidents from Stockport Infirmary to the Select Committee of 1840. From March 1839 to February 1840, there were 86 accidents to children, of which 36 happened while machines were being cleaned in motion. *Second Report of the Select Committee, etc. PP* 1840, X. Evidence of Mr C. Trimmer, p. 35.

41. Report of L. Horner, 18 January 1837. *Reports of Inspectors for Half-year ending 31 December 1836*, p. 48. *PP* 1837, XXXI.

42. *First Report of Select-committee, etc.* Evidence of L. Horner, p. 29.

43. Thomas, M. W., *op. cit.*, p. 185.

44. *First Report of Select Committee, etc.* Evidence of L. Horner, p. 80. Horner's Superintendent, Mr Heathcote, was in 'open warfare' with the Bury magistrates over this.

45. *Ibid.*, p. 80.

46. *Ibid.*, p. 117.

47. Report of L. Horner, 18 January 1837. *Reports of Inspectors for Half-year ending 31 December 1836*, p. 48. *PP* 1837, XXXI. Horner was accused of fining the manager of a large millowner on view once – to cover up the discovery that he was working children illegally after Horner had publicly praised him for his observance of the education clauses. But William John Wood, the Superintendent who made the accusation, was so soured that his evidence is unreliable. *Second Report of Select Committee, etc. PP* 1840, X, p. 111.

48. Report of James Howell, 12 January 1837, *ibid.*, p. 58. *PP* 1837, XXXI. Howell reports one £2 fine (out of six) on Edward Barnard and Son, which may have been a manufacturing firm.

49. Horner admitted this after pressure from Ashley and Lalor Shiel, in evidence to the Select Committee of 1840, *First Report. PP* 1840, X, p. 75.

50. *Ibid.*, pp. 57, 74.

51. Kirby and Musson, *op. cit.*, pp. 389-90.

52. They actually tried to get Horner dismissed.

53. For the story of James Stuart see Henriques, *op. cit.*, pp. 18-46.

54. *Ibid.*, pp. 34-7, 40.

55. Thomas, M. W., *op. cit.*, pp. 105-6.

56. Thomas, M. W., *op. cit.*, pp. 106-7. See correspondence in PRO Inspectors of Factories No. 1. Webster was finally sacked on 27 July 1840 for circulating a printed paper comparing the duties performed by the Inspectors and Sub-Inspectors (Superintendents).

57. Thomas, M. W., *op. cit.*, pp. 107-8.

58. Henriques, *op. cit.*, p. 39.

59. The immediate occasion of this Committee was the letters written to Ashley and Hindley by some of the superintendents, complaining of the behaviour of their own inspectors. However, these seem to have been inspired by personal discontent rather than by any serious social concern.

60. The Select Committee included Joseph Strutt and R. H. Greg, influential industrialists, Edward Baines of the *Leeds Mercury*, mouthpiece of the Yorkshire woollen manufacturers, and Fox Maule for the government. On the other side it included Hindley, Aglionby, Brotherton and Fielden, Tory Radical millowners.

61. Woods resigned, Beal was sacked, and on eating humble pie was reinstated at £250. The government was remarkably tolerant of indifferent civil servants.

62. 7 and 8 Vict., *c.* 15.

63. Another list is on the back of a copperplate memo of uncertain date, arguing for intervention on behalf of children but not adults. The list, which provides information on geographical distribution of industries, and the age at which children start work in them, includes earthenware and porcelain, nail-making,

iron works and foundries, collieries, glass-blowing, pin and needle-making, calico printing, hand cotton weaving, lace-making and small workshop and domestic manufactures. *Chadwick Papers*, 40.

64. Horner to Chadwick, Rochdale, 21 June 1840. *Chadwick Papers*, 1051.

65. *Quarterly Review*, 1841, LXVII, pp. 171–81. Ashley claimed authorship of this article in his diary. It was intended to extend the protection of children to other trades.

66. *First Report from the Commissioners for inquiring into the employment of Children in Mines and Manufactories. PP* 1842, XV, p. 3.

67. *Ibid.*, pp. 27, 67.

68. *Ibid.*, pp. 28–9, 91–4.

69. *Ibid.*, pp. 135, 173. Illustrations, pp. 78–104. The Commission also dealt with less spectacular but equally important evils, such as the unpaid slavery of Poor Law apprentice miners, the extortions of truck shops in South Wales, the prevalence of bastardy (inevitably) and the existence of illiteracy where child labour was most frequent.

70. Tremenheere had been a school inspector who was transferred to the Home Department to inspect collieries for speaking his mind too freely about the quality of the British and Foreign Society's London schools. Cf. **Webb, R. K.,** 'A Whig inspector', *Journal of Modern History*, XXVII, 1955, pp. 352–64.

71. See Thomas, M. W., *op. cit.*, pp. 276–83.

72. Under later Acts children could not be employed without a certificate not merely of school attendance but of ability to read and write, etc. Cf. **Robson, A. H.,** *The Education of Children engaged in Industry in England, 1833–1876.* Kegan Paul, 1931, pp. 186–7. Cf. p. 219 below.

73. Peel and Graham had obstructed a Ten Hour Bill introduced by Ashley in 1842, and had thereby forfeited Ashley's personal and political loyalty. Cf. Ashley's diary, 18 and 24 February 1842. Historical Manuscripts Commission.

74. Henriques, *op. cit.*, pp. 41–44.

75. Thomas, M. W., *op. cit.*, p. 298 *et. seq.* Thomas gives a detailed account of this complicated struggle. It is not quite clear why he calls the new relays 'false'. They closely resembled the schemes recommended in 1833.

76. *Ibid.*, p. 303.

77. Sir George Cornewall Lewis to Horner, 5 August 1848. PRO, HO 45/OS 2871.

78. L. Horner to Sir George Cornewall Lewis, 10 August. *Ibid.*

79. Sir George Cornewall Lewis to Horner, 12 August. *Ibid.*

80. Thomas, M. W., *op. cit.*, pp. 311–12. The difficulty was that appeals were only allowable where the penalty in each case exceeded £5; but the penalty for working children too long under the 1844 Act was £3.

81. Ashley's letter of 7 May 1850 explaining his reasons for accepting the 10½-hour day to the Lancashire and Yorkshire short-time committees is quoted in full by Thomas, *op. cit.*, pp. 319–21. Ashley knew he would be 'exposed to sad misrepresentations'. Ashley also wrote some bitter comments in his diary, but attempted no explanation of the fury of the attack on him. He did not have an analytical mind.

82. The worldly and irreligious Palmerston listened to Ashley on social matters. Jasper Ridley gives an amusing account of the chairs in the dining room at Carlton Gardens being arranged by a deputation to illustrate the work of pieceners in a mill. It shows how little some professional politicians knew about the conditions for which they were legislating. Cf. **Ridley, J.,** *Lord Palmerston.* Constable, 1970, pp. 293–4.

83. Horner to Chadwick, 24 December 1859. *Chadwick Papers*, 1051.

84. Leonard Horner, younger brother of Francis Horner M.P. co-founder of the *Edinburgh Review*, had studied chemistry at Edinburgh University. He was an ardent geologist, an educational reformer (a founder of Edinburgh Academy) and a not very successful warden of London University. Like the Scottish Whig journalist and shady financier, James Stuart, he owed his inspectorship to the patronage of Henry Brougham.

6 Public health: I

Public health and housing

In the first half of the nineteenth century no aspect of life suffered such cumulative deterioration as did public health. Yet none had to wait so long before it was taken seriously as a ground for public action. This was not because nobody recognised the dangers; even in the late eighteenth century the Manchester 'Board of Health' called for the regulation of child labour in factories on the grounds that children herded together for long hours in insanitary conditions constituted a health hazard.[1] Howard and other prison reformers were concerned with the filth in prisons and the dangers of gaol fever. Dr Jebb devised plans for a well-ventilated model gaol at Ipswich,[2] and Jeremy Bentham's Panopticon prison was planned to have a privy in every cell. Plans for sanitation and ventilation circulated among progressive medical men, especially Rational Dissenters who were practically and educationally the pioneers of the time in pure and applied science.[3] But these were a small minority. Public intervention for health purposes meant intervention in the management of private property, since the seventeenth century the sacred cow of all sacred cows. Moreover, health reform was necessarily a part of the reform of local government, and especially of urban government. Poor Law, prisons or education might all conceivably have been administered by local branches of a central agency; drainage, sanitation and town planning were necessarily the affairs of regional geography and community concern. Drainage and water were needed by everybody, and their regulation if not their provision entailed local responsibility for public services. But this need opposed not only the commercial ethos of the time, but also the long-standing and deeply traditional corruptions and inefficiencies of municipal corporations and other governing bodies. Sanitation and municipal reform waited on each other.

While the development of public health administration is part of the history of local government, it is inextricably tied up with the history of working-class housing. The topics overlap, and if the history of nineteenth-century housing is largely that of sanitation as it applies to domestic building,[4] the history of public health can hardly omit the question of housing. The Poor Law public health enquiries of 1839 and 1840, the House of Commons Select Committee of 1840, Chadwick's Sanitary Report of 1842, and the Health of Towns Commission Report of 1845, which drew forcible attention to the connection between disease and bad drainage, poor ventilation and inadequate living space, all seemed to focus attention on the housing problem. But by the 1840s popular dislike of 'centralisation' (increased by reaction against the new Poor Law), combined with reformers' fear of pauperising the poor by any non-penal provision to inhibit any suggestion of municipally built or even rate-aided housing. So the reports of these early enquiries, which seemed to lead in that direction, resulted only in the voluntary promotion of model housing associations on a 5 per cent philanthropy basis. Chadwick made this clear in a speech of 1843 of which the notes have survived: 'Now it is by enabling us to see what is to be done, and perhaps by giving legislative powers that the government may help us, and then we must help ourselves.'[5] This attitude was shared by all Chadwick's contemporaries, including Lord Shaftesbury, who got no nearer to promoting state provision of homes than advocating rate aid for common lodging houses. So the public health movement concentrated on water, sewerage and the control of nuisances, leaving building regulation to follow in largely separate and later legislation. There was a rapid growth of voluntary building societies in the 1840s, which catered for working-class families who could afford to save up enough to buy or lease their own small property.[6] But municipal housing was not contemplated until the end of the century.

In this chapter it is proposed to take advantage of this historical separation, and concentrate on sanitation.

Urban squalor and disease

The main causes of the cumulative deterioration in living conditions in the first half of the nineteenth century were the rapid growth of population, its concentration in towns, and, in some areas, industrialisation. Of course, filthy housing, dirt and disease were nothing new. Seventeenth-century London, where Pepys complained that his neighbour's cellar was overflowing into his basement, or that he dared not buy a new wig for fear that it was made from the hair of someone dead of the plague, provided no golden age of purity for sanitary reformers to hark back to. Nor did the gin-sodden slums of Defoe's London. Rural labourers whose cottages were pulled down by landlords to prevent them gaining settlement where they worked, or squatters in tumbledown shacks on the waste, were no better housed than the urban poor. But squalor is always intensified by overcrowding, within a building or on a site, by lack of fresh air, outside as well as inside, and by lack of pure water as well as drainage. By 1830 the problem of urban overcrowding had spread from the metropolis to many provincial towns.[7] Its effects could be seen in a levelling of the national rate of population growth, even while the birth rate remained steady, and town populations continued to multiply.[8]

In his introduction to Chadwick's *Report on the Sanitary Condition of the Labouring Population of Great Britain,* M. W. Flinn points out that in the early nineteenth century, the gradual decline in the death rate which had been noticed in the eighteenth century was reversed. Chadwick had demonstrated in his report that the cause was in the towns. Between 1821 and 1831 the population of Manchester and Salford increased by 47 per cent. In 1840 the average age of death in the gentry and professional classes in Manchester was 38 years, in the gentry class of Rutlandshire it was 52 years; the average age of death among Manchester tradesmen was 20 years, among Rutlandshire farmers 41 years; the average age of death among Manchester mechanics and labourers was 17 years, among Rutlandshire mechanics and labourers 38 years.[9]

These figures are misleading as they include the deaths of children under 5, and more than 57 per cent of those born in Manchester failed to reach their fifth year. The survivors of early childhood had a somewhat better chance of growing up. In 1840, 1 child in 1.7 died under the age of 5; 1 in 22 between the age of 5 and 10; 1 in 43 between 10 and 15; and 1 in 34 between 15 and 20.[10] But allowing for some exaggeration, the figures suggest that mortality was far higher in town than in the country, and that the lower the social class the more likely an early death.[11]

Chadwick also demonstrated the prevalence of overcrowding. In his *Report on the Practice of Interment in Towns* he made use of figures provided by the London Statistical Society. In the London ward of St George's Hanover Square, 929 families lived in one room each, 408 in two rooms each, and only 125 enjoyed three or more rooms. Nearly half the families had only one bed. In the poor parish of Marylebone, 159 families and 196 single persons lived in a part of one room, while 382 families and 56 single persons had a whole room to themselves, but few had more.[12] This extraordinary overcrowding in the capital city was partly due to the inability of casual labourers to pay more rent, and partly due to the need of workers to live near their place of work.[13] Suburban trains and electric trams did not appear until the 1880s, when commuting to work began to be possible and working-class suburbs began to grow. Meantime the inflated value of land in town centres, or near large factories and works, produced a bonanza for the speculative builder and the slum landlord. In the 1850s and 1860s overcrowding was further augmented by extensive clearances for railway termini and other commercial purposes. When slum clearance began in the second half of the century, this too increased the pressure of population on housing all round the clearances. The rehousing of tenants evicted from slum sites who could not pay the higher rents for the new tenements built upon them, was the last problem to be tackled, in London, or elsewhere.[14] Until this was solved overcrowding continued. Even if drainage and water supply had been adequate, the city centres would still have been plague spots.

The squalor of working-class districts was increased by large numbers of lodging houses catering for trampers, drifters, casual labourers and Irish immigrants. In 1849 the pottery town of Hanley had 13 lodging houses five of which were believed to be brothels. Without ventilation, some of the rooms contained 9 or 10 beds, with 6 or 7 lodgers per bed, packed in head to feet.[15] In 1850, Derby had 57 lodging houses being inspected, and no doubt many more that were not.[16] Central Leeds had 222 of these crowded and filthy places.[17]

Besides overcrowding, a feature of rapid urbanisation which bred filth and squalor was the failure of sanitary provision to keep pace with the multiplication of houses and people. The science of sanitary engineers (like that of epidemiology) was immature, with rival schools of thought fighting for the supremacy of their own dogmas. It is a matter of hindsight that John Roe's system for disposing of sewage suspended in water flushed through small glazed brick pipes, so ardently championed by Chadwick, was to provide the eventual solution. Many contemporary engineers disagreed, while the local builders and plumbers were incapable of constructing impermeable sewers at the necessary slopes and levels to carry away waste. Sewers, or covered ditches and drains, were usually intended to drain streets of mud and rainwater rather than to dispose of human waste, which was provided for by bucket privies and dung carts. Hence the much criticised clause in various Improvement Acts, which forbade house owners, on pain of a fine, to connect their house drains with the public sewer. Yet many gentlemen's houses already had water closets connected by house drains with a sewer or cesspool. Apathy, the flight of the wealthy from town centres, the collapse of communal responsibility and communal administration, rather than lack of knowledge, were responsible for the spreading squalor. Overcrowding, filth and disease stole upon the nation like thieves in the night. The more spacious residential areas had local paving, drainage, lighting and highway boards, and few of their residents strayed into the neglected poorer parts of the towns. Other cities beside Manchester exhibited the pattern so graphically described by Engels, in which long streets passed gradually from a wealthy end to a poor end, but a continuous frontage of comparatively solid and well-decorated shop fronts concealed the chaos of mean alleys and courts behind.[18] Even when mortality figures became available they often concealed the realities, covering a whole town and hiding the high mortality in slum areas behind a small depression of the average.[19]

From this happy state of blindness and insouciance the well-to-do were periodically awoken by outbreaks of typhus, typhoid, smallpox, yellow and scarlet fever, tuberculosis, diarrhoea, and after 1831, cholera. Only for smallpox was a proved method of prevention known, and it took the best part of the century to enforce effective mass vaccination through the agency of the Poor Law medical services.[20] The most effective spur to public action was cholera, for it did not stop at the edge of the slums.[21]

The epidemic of 1831 evoked central and local Boards of Health, including doctors, magistrates and gentry. Although all this machinery was allowed to die as soon as the epidemic waned, it was undoubtedly the example for later occasions.[22] The cholera visitations of 1848–49, 1853–54 and 1866 resulted in flurries of legislative and administrative action which in their turn faded with the decline of the disease. But although the limited outbreak of 1853–54 failed to save the regime of Chadwick and Shaftesbury at the General Board of Health, cholera was still the sanitary reformer's most powerful ally.

Pollution and the water supply

The condition of the poor urban areas was described literally *ad nauseam* in evidence to select committees and commissions of inquiry. Since, with minor variations, the same causes produced the same effects in London, Manchester, Leeds, Birmingham and large cities everywhere, the accounts become monotonous. Industrial cities had special problems, partly because their population grew more rapidly than that of market or cathedral towns, partly because industry itself was a pollutant. Steam power entailed belching factory chimneys. Rivers, dammed or obstructed for the use of mills, also served as sewers for their industrial waste. It was even argued by interested parties that the effluent from the Leeds dye works disinfected the river.[23] Yet the most widespread sources of pollution were not new industry but the multiplication of traditional 'dirty trades' and the waste products of people. Greater demand increased the supply of small slaughterhouses, where animals were killed in the back room, or on the pavement, the blood and guts being washed into the street. In Leicester in 1859 there were 87 such slaughterhouses, and pigs were fed on the offal.[24] Horse stables and cow byres increased the muck. Poor families kept pigs in their back yards, surrounded by pails of rotting pig food; and official attempts to abolish this form of saving and self-help appeared to many 'a great hardship'.[25] Yet with all this, the greatest problem of Victorian Britain was the disposal of human waste, or as it was politely called, 'night soil'.

In the inner township of Leeds, Boot and Shoe Yard, surrounded by 34 houses with 57 rooms and 340 inhabitants, was neither paved nor sewered. During the 1832 cholera outbreak 75 cartloads of dung were removed from 32 of the houses, which had not been cleaned for 30 years.[26] York Road had drains under the houses, but they were choked up.[27] There was little improvement by 1840. What sewers there were ran into the river, which was cluttered with waste and rubbish.[28]

The problem was not confined to the industrial north. Merthyr Tydfil, the rapidly growing South Wales iron town, was reported in 1845 to have 37,000 inhabitants and a total absence of drainage. Its one sewer emptied into the River Taff.[29] The sanitation for Dowlais was provided by 1 privy per 50 or 100 people, and cesspools which drained back into the wells.[30] Similar conditions prevailed in the burgeoning suburbs of many large towns which were either outside the boundaries of their boroughs, or under the jurisdiction of committees set up by Local Acts for paving and lighting which contained no provisions for drainage.[31]

Whether or not drains and sewers had been built, the results could be equally disastrous. Privies were inadequate, and inadequately cleaned. Even in the 1860s a building regulation in Leeds that new blocks of houses were to have a 15-feet space between them resulted in the spaces being filled with privies, which were emptied into middens in the streets.[32] The better residential streets had middensteads, while the unpaved and undrained courts and alleys were filled with huge dung heaps. Since the manure was valuable for agricultural purposes it was allowed to accumulate before being carted away. Existing sewers were built of porous bricks which allowed moisture to soak through into house foundations. They had to be large enough to be broken into and cleaned by hand, but cleaning operations, when they did take place, often made matters worse, as the filth was piled in the street to await removal. Typical was the case of the new canal at Cardiff which was being used as an open sewer. When it was emptied for repairs the stench was intolerable, and it was reported that the neighbouring houses had fourteen deaths from fever.[33] Many sewers were laid in too shallow an incline so that, in heavy rain or spring tides (near tidal rivers), the water flooded back into the houses.

Lack of drainage accompanied unplanned building. Before the town council had awoken to the need for control, developers had filled the gardens in the ancient town centre of Leicester with mean courts and alleys. The houses built between 1830 and 1850 mouldered on into the 1880s, mostly without back doors or windows.[34] Even the philanthropic Leicester Freehold Land Society founded to purchase and distribute land for small householders was abused by speculators who bought up the plots and crowded houses on them.[35] Yet Leicester, at 33.2 persons per acre, had a far lower population density than Manchester at 82.2 persons per acre, or Liverpool at 98.0 per acre.[36] Liverpool abounded in cellar dwellings, mostly inhabited by poor Irish. Newcastle upon Tyne's problem was a medieval centre into which sanitary engineers had never penetrated, where privies leaned against the house walls and dung heaps filled the courtyards.[37] But recent design and construction were also at fault. Back-to-back houses were built in northern towns throughout the nineteenth century. Even a prohibitory Act of 1910 failed to stop them. Some houses were built on top of undried middens or cesspools, some were built of shoddy materials and odds and ends. In Leeds house-bricks were actually made of midden mire.[38]

Drainage is useless without water. But nineteenth-century towns rapidly outgrew their water supply. Clifton, the wealthy suburb of Bristol, had piped water. The rest of Bristol depended on public and private wells, many tainted by cesspools. In many places supply was in the hands of companies which took their water from the local rivers, and pumped it, unfiltered, to the houses of the wealthy and to standpipes and pumps for the poor. In a few places, notably Brecon, Halifax, Hull and Huddersfield, water was supplied by local commissioners, while in Leeds and Liverpool the Water Joint Stock Companies included corporation members on their boards.[39] But the public companies were no more efficient than those run for private profit. Leeds, which in its early reforming phase set up in 1823 a body of elected improvement commissioners to supervise the water supply, and in 1837 instituted a new water-works company with nine directors appointed by the town council, ran out of water in 1851. After endless quarrels and rival schemes its water problems were belatedly solved in the 1870s.[40]

Even in large houses whose owners had paid for lead pipes, the water was often supplied intermittently, and had to be stored in cisterns. Working-class householders had to collect their supply from standpipes, often several streets away. At Newcastle on Tyne it was sold at these standpipes at four times the cost of a house supply, one-third of the takings going to sales point attendants.[41] In some places it was turned on only two or three hours a week, and working people had to queue, or missed the sales hours and were greatly inconvenienced. When they got water they had to store it in buckets, in corners or under the beds, where it was easily contaminated. A water company with a local monopoly could afford to overcharge, or totally neglect the poor. Yet in Bath, with plenty of water and two companies, the competition between them led to wasteful duplication of works and pipes, and increased the cost still more.[42]

The consequence of this system, or lack of system, was that the poor who worked at dirty occupations and needed most water for washing had least. The scarcity, the cost and inconvenience of obtaining it, and doubtless the difficulty of heating it, bred dirty habits among the lower orders. The contrast between clean and dirty was one of the most conspicuous marks of class distinction in the nineteenth century.

The last main cause of pollution, distinct from drainage and water, but still intimately connected with the growth of urban population, was the overcrowding of graveyards. In the city burial grounds the dead were buried ten and twelve deep, and old bodies had to be dug out to make room for new ones. Chadwick, who conducted his own investigation, was worried about the effects of inadequate interments on the occupants of the surrounding houses. He wrote of bursting coffins, rotting corpses and graveyard smells, which endangered the living by their 'emanations'.[43]

Pollution and private interests

As more people awoke to the dangers from filth they began to realise the obstacles in the way of cleaning up. All attempts at public intervention ran into a hedge of private interests and public jealousies intertwined. Every aspect of nuisance prevention and every attempt at public provision was beset by private interests, from the Leeds millowners who would not curb the production of black smoke from their factory chimneys, to the London water companies who piped water from the polluted Thames although clean spring water was available in the Surrey sands. The liberal-minded vicar of Leeds, the Rev. Thomas Hook, after a new cemetery had been opened, insisted on burying his parishioners in the saturated churchyard, because they wanted to lie with their forefathers and he, presumably, wanted the fees. The funeral companies left the corpses of those whose relatives could not pay their extortionate charges lying in their homes, surrounded by their families, for days on end.[44] Night-soil men established dung heaps in public places, forever carted away and forever renewed. The 'speculating builders', most powerful of all interests, built slums.

Yet public bodies were little more conscientious or efficient than private ones. Local Commissioners of Sewers, whose nomination was authorised by a statute of Henry VIII, had long grown out of date, and many towns had their own Local Acts. The result was chaotic. Some towns had secured commissions for paving, lighting cleansing and watching (police) but not for draining. Some had Highway Acts which did cover draining, but empowered them to appoint a surveyor for one year at a time, without qualifications or security of tenure, and without providing for expert approval of costly public works before they were begun. Some had multiple or overlapping commissions. Birmingham, for instance, had different commissions under different Acts for lighting, paving and cleansing, and four boards of surveyors under a Highway Act, none of which co-operated with the others.[45] Liverpool had separate bodies for paving, for street draining, and for supervising the width and drainage of courts and alleys.[46] Manchester's drainage authorities had no supervision over the rivers.[47] Lancaster's drainage authority for the lower part of the town refused to let the drainage authority for the upper part of the town use its sewage outfalls.[48]

The Local Acts were rarely comprehensive in their powers or sufficiently extensive in their areas. Those covering drainage often omitted ground as yet unbuilt on, streets where fewer than half of the houses were complete, or streets which were not thoroughfares. The opportunity to plan and enforce the construction of proper drains at the start of a development was lost. Moreover, the alleys and closed courts which needed drains and sanitary provision most were regularly neglected. Liverpool's 2,398 courts housing 68,345 people went undrained.[49] The growing suburbs were also left out, and in the 1830s Liverpool's newest houses were being built beside stagnant pools full of rubbish, outside the jurisdiction of the municipality.[50]

Ultimately the neglect of public needs by private interests and the confusion of public or semi-public local bodies were connected. Improvement Commissions, Highway Boards, vestries and town councils attracted the members of water companies and building firms, who sat on them to protect their own commercial advantage. The champions of free enterprise and the champions of traditional local 'self government' made a marriage of convenience, the former loudly proclaiming their local patriotism, the latter their opposition to tyrannical centralisation.

Miasmatics and moralism

The impetus behind nineteenth-century sanitary reform was a growing awareness that dirt bred disease. In the absence of all knowledge of germs, how disease was generated and communicated was inevitably a matter of opinion based on guesswork. It was generally accepted that the earth in certain climates and seasons produced poisonous exhalations, which mingled with humours in the body to generate disease. The 'contagionists' believed that the poisons from diseased bodies were then spread by touch or other close association.[51] In the early nineteenth century, contagionism dominated the British medical profession, including the College of Physicians; and the leading precaution against epidemics was isolation at home and quarantine to prevent the import of sickness from abroad. The 'miasmatists', of whom Chadwick was a convinced, not to say pig-headed champion, discounted the communication of disease by contact, but believed it was engendered by exhalations from decaying matter and filth, although whether the noxious agent was a smell, or a gas causing the smell, is unclear. They thus considered isolation and quarantine a waste of time and money, and concentrated their efforts on the removal of dirt. There were, of course, 'contingent contagionists'[52] who tried to combine both theories, in the hope of removing faction fights and encouraging all possible methods of preventing disease.

Since the originating cause of disease was so un-specific, it was generally believed that one sickness could show different symptoms, or pass from one stage to another. Chadwick, a layman, was no more crass than the contemporary physicians when in the Factory Commission Report of 1833 he called bone malformations in child factory workers caused by repetitive movements 'incurable disease' and attributed them to general tiredness. The doctors lumped together diseases which spread as 'zymotic' diseases, sometimes called 'fever' or 'malaria', and failed to distinguish between typhus and typhoid, cholera and scurvy, while they believed summer diarrhoea, a comparatively mild bowel infection, to be the precursor, or early stage of Asiatic cholera.

In such a state of uneasy confusion, and in the absence, it would seem, of any attempt at systematic or even common-sense observation, sensational legends and old wives' tales flourished. Dr Southwood Smith, physician to the London fever hospital, and a strong miasmatist, maintained that poisonous exhalations could be condensed into a substance which, injected into a vein, caused rapid death. 'By varying the intensity and the dose of the poison thus obtained, it is possible to produce fever of almost any type, endowed with almost any degree of mortal power.'[53] Chadwick, presumably under his influence, retailed horror stories of bursting leaden coffins from which the escaping miasmata carried instant death to unwary grave-diggers.[54]

Little progress was made during the cholera epidemic of 1831–32, but by the late 1840s the whole atmosphere of medical investigation had changed. In 1848 Dr John Snow and Dr William Budd, working independently, discovered that cholera spread through a living organism carried in infected water. When cholera reappeared in Bristol in the outbreak of 1854, Budd was able to carry out a full programme of disinfecting sources of contamination.[55] The new views were not without influence, and by 1854 pathologists were investigating samples of local water and air, examining the lungs and viscera of cholera victims, and identifying bacteria in the atmosphere of cholera wards.[56] But by this time miasmatism, or the 'pythogenic' theory, had become the immovable orthodoxy. The Committee for Scientific Inquiries, appointed by the General Board of Health and therefore dominated by Chadwickians, discussing the case of a well in Broad Street, Soho, which was under suspicion of causing an intense local outbreak of cholera, could only conclude that the impure water might have 'participated in the atmospheric infection of the district'.[57] Meantime Chadwick had exerted all his great influence to have the sewers of London flushed into the Thames, whence still came most of London's drinking water. He had also hastened the demise of the quarantine precautions at the ports. It becomes increasingly clear that an unknown number of cholera deaths has to be weighed in the balance against the lives saved by the sanitary regulations promoted by his belief in miasmatism.[58]

If the doctors disagreed about the medical causes of disease, the experts also fought about the social causes. Inevitably the political radicals of the London Rotunda attributed the cholera fatalities of 1831–32 to poverty and hunger.[59] Middle-class sympathisers such as Thomas Wakley, the radical Westminster coroner and MP, and the influential medical teacher Dr Alison of Edinburgh, agreed. A commoner view attributed the high incidence of disease among the lower orders to ignorance and vice (especially intemperance). This suited the desire to do nothing, especially among the Malthusians, who suspected that disease was nature's way of controlling excessive population. The censorious attitudes which pervaded the Royal Commission report on the Poor Laws in 1834 were repeated in discussions on poverty and ill health. The surprising fact is that Chadwick did not share them. He would not admit that disease was the result of poverty and hunger. To do so would have forced him to recognise the existence of irresistible poverty among able-bodied adults, which would have rendered a deterrent Poor Law morally indefensible. He was therefore at pains to disprove that disease followed low pay and poor diet, and to prove instead that poverty was the consequence of disease. He was well aware that disease was caused by bad drainage and bad housing, and that such unhealthy living conditions were not the fault of the working-class tenants who had to endure them. He became an environmentalist, and showed that, in a town like London, the average age of death was governed by street drainage.[60] His actual arguments did not conflict with those in the Poor Law Commission report, but his tone and attitude towards sickness among the poor were not those exhibited in that document. There is an unexplained but genuine discontinuity between Chadwick on unemployment and Chadwick on disease, Chadwick on the idle poor, and Chadwick on the sick poor.

If Chadwick avoided the censoriousness of the moralists, he did not avoid moralism. He maintained that immorality did not cause disease, but was caused by it. He found that 43,000 widows and 112,000 destitute orphans on poor relief were mainly the result of diseases aggravated or propagated by atmospheric impurities from decomposing substances, damp and filth in close and overcrowded dwellings. These had attacked men under 45 years old; and good employment, wages and food had not protected them. The fatalities were always replaced by more births, and those of people inferior in health, less amenable to moral influence and education, short-lived, 'improvident, reckless, and intemperate, and with habitual avidity for sensual gratifications'.[61] The removal of men in their prime left behind a population of callow youth, easily influenced by demagoguery and sedition, 'always young, inexperienced, ignorant, credulous, passionate, violent, and proportionately dangerous, with a perpetual tendency to moral as well as physical deterioration'.[62]

This doctrine of the survival of the unfittest, in which responsibility for Chartism was attributed to dirt and bad housing, was stated in the condemnatory fashion always reserved by Chadwick for discussion of working-class discontents. But it was coupled with a defence of the lower orders against the common accusation that they preferred to be dirty. He did not subscribe to the 'most erroneous' view that they were incapable of appreciating the advantages and comfort of personal domestic cleanliness. Dirty habits were caused by dirt and overcrowding rather than vice versa.[63] Men had to live near their work and, perforce, in the accommodation provided for them. He thought that 'the great moral results consequent upon the increase in the means of cleanliness have not yet, we fear, received the attention which their importance merits'.[64]

Moralism of this kind was received in some quarters with derision. 'What had malaria to do with religion?' asked Henry Drummond, opposing the Public Health Bill of 1848 in the House of Commons.

> In that highly exaggerated and poetic book the Report of the Health of Towns Commission, he found it asserted that there was a direct connection between typhus and crime ... Mr Chadwick had, in that report, made a coincidence of crime with a low sanitary condition; and that was one of the grounds of this Bill. Could anything be more absurd?[65]

There was, however, a remarkable range of support for Chadwick's view, from R. A. Slaney's Select Committee of 1840 which emphasised the pernicious effects of dirt, damp and discomfort in encouraging drunkenness, to Charles Kingsley's moral tract, *The Water Babies*, in which Tom, the little chimney sweep, is painlessly drowned in the river while trying to make himself clean. Such moralism enabled disparate characters like Chadwick and Shaftesbury to work together with a common aim on the General Board of Health.

The Public Health Movement and the Public Health Act

The campaign for a comprehensive Public Health Act was started by Chadwick from the Poor Law Commission. It was a good opportunity, since Chadwick was being excluded from active participation in Poor Law affairs by George Cornewall Lewis,[66] but had the assistance of the Poor Law medical officers, as well as distinguished physicians such as Southwood Smith and Lyon Playfair. The first shots appeared in appendices to the Poor Law Commissioners' 4th Annual Report in 1838.[67] An outbreak of typhus inspired a request that the law should be amended to permit the expenditure of Poor Law funds to remove the causes of fever. It was illustrated by the answers of several Poor Law medical officers to a letter from Chadwick requesting information about contagion among the working classes, and reinforced by reports from the physicians Neil Arnott, J. Phillips Kay (at that time a Poor Law Assistant Commissioner), and Southwood Smith. In these reports can be seen all the leading ideas and preoccupations of the public-health reformers.

The agitation soon led to enquiries. They included Slaney's House of Commons Select Committee in 1840, Chadwick's semi-official inquiry through the Poor Law machinery from which came his *Report on the Sanitary Condition of the Labouring Population of Great Britain*, in 1842, with its *Supplementary Report on Interment*, and the great Health of Towns Commission which reported in 1844 and 1845. Three abortive government Bills in 1840 were castigated by Chadwick for their weakness and insufficiency. A Public Health Bill was defeated in 1847, and this overshadowed the real achievement of the Nuisances Prevention Act of 1846. But the final passage of the Public Health Act in 1848, boosted by Chadwick's Health of Towns Association and accompanied by his Town Improvement Company, was a Chadwickian triumph. Indeed Chadwick dominated the proceedings and wrote most of the reports. As a result it is possible that others have had less than their due share of credit.

The Select Committee of 1840, with its emphasis on the need to regulate the building of working-class houses, tried to tackle a vital problem which the Health of Towns Commission avoided. One of its main witnesses was Southwood Smith who (epidemiology apart) did not lack sense as well as zeal, but was subsequently overshadowed by Chadwick. As in the Poor Law, Chadwick drew most of his reforming ideas from selected local examples; and in this context progressive medical officers such as Duncan of Liverpool and Baker of Leeds, both indirectly through him and directly through their reports and evidence at the inquiries, were the pioneers of sanitary reform. The influence of politicians Slaney, Normanby, Morpeth and Palmerston was important in the sanitary movement; and the co-operation of Shaftesbury was vital, for he lent a respectability and attractiveness which partly counter-balanced the repellent effect which Chadwick seemed to exercise on so many of his contemporaries.

Yet there were contributions nobody but Chadwick could make. His genius for propaganda was assisted by his grasp of political realities. Realising that sanitary reform would be bitterly opposed on grounds of expense, he drew up balance sheets elaborating the social costs of urban squalor. These included the cost to the rates of widows and orphans, the cost of lost working days from sickness, and the national loss from a stunted and enfeebled population.[68] If the accounts were guesswork, they illustrated his point graphically. More concretely he could maintain that small-bore drains, flushed by water, cost less to run than flat-bottomed sewers cleaned by scavengers.

Chadwick contributed four main principles to the Public Health Movement. First, that drains should be small-bore and of glazed brick, and water-flushed; second that natural drainage areas should be treated as a whole, so that the overlapping and conflicting local boards, town councils and commissions should be rationalised; third, that improvement schemes should be comprehensive, unifying paving, drainage, sewerage, water supply and cleansing services under a single authority; fourth, that sanitary works should be financed by loans repayable in instalments over a long period and secured on the rates, so that the deterrent effect of compulsory repayment within three years would vanish.[69] These were applied in the Health of Towns Commission Report, especially in the review of Local Acts. Chadwick condemned those Acts under which the connection of house drains with public sewers were penalised, drainage surveys had not been made, and the poor parts of the town had been neglected. He praised the provisions at Leeds, Rochdale, Southampton and Manchester, where the courts were treated equally with the more public parts of the towns, and of the first three where houses could not be built until drains to a sewer or cesspool had been laid.[70] He wanted to make universal clauses giving local authorities the duty of removing rubbish from private premises, and allowing them to recover the cost from the owners.

Many clauses of the Public Health Act of 1848 empowered local authorities to coerce private occupiers in this way, by removing nuisances or carrying out sanitary works, and recovering the cost from them. This method had not originated with Chadwick, although he discussed it at length.[71] It was a spill-over from the Nuisances Prevention Act of 1846, and seems to have grown out of procedures authorised under the much older Law of Nuisance. On the whole Chadwick preferred prevention through a cautious measure of public provision. He recommended that house drains should be laid by the local authority, and paid for by a special rate.[72] This would ensure an economical uniformity in place of the differing shapes, sizes and materials supplied by private builders. Apart from this, his plans were mainly for regulation, including abatement of smoke, specification of the width of courts, and the size, sanitation and ventilation of cellar dwellings.[73] He would go as far as authorising the compulsory purchase of properties, so that they could be demolished for the better ventilation of blocked courts and alleys.[74]

As always, Chadwick was concerned with the provision of enforcement machinery. By now there were plenty of examples of inspectors, from those appointed by the local Boards of Health in 1831-32, to the Poor Law, prison, factory and school inspectors. The need in public health for properly trained and salaried surveyors, and medical officers, was obvious. It was more difficult to decide where ultimate responsibility for enforcement should lie. Chadwick, with the supineness of elected town councils and the pinch-penny meanness of Boards of Guardians elected by ratepayers before his eyes, favoured a committee of the Privy Council with himself as secretary supervising Crown-appointed local commissions which would carry out the local administration.[75] He really did desire the centralisation which his enemies professed so greatly to fear. But the plan was politically impossible; and the Royal Commission merely recommended a 'local administrative body' to direct all sanitary works, while the general power of supervision should belong to the Crown.[76] After another three years of discussion the Public Health Act created a Board of Health resembling the new Poor Law Board (not the old Poor Law Commission – its chairman was the Minister for Woods and Forests, and two out of its three members had seats in parliament). Local administration was committed to the councils of corporate towns and to elected Local Boards of Health elsewhere.[77] In this way the Act promoted the revival of local self-government by giving substantial powers to the town councils elected under the Municipal Corporations Act of 1835. It was an important development, but not promoted by Chadwick, who was disgusted with the arrangement.

The brilliance of Chadwick's official reports, and his incessant propaganda, tend to conceal the fact that his proposals were not as thorough-going as their language would suggest. He bitterly attacked the private water companies but (perhaps recognising their strength) proposed to leave supply in their hands, provided that they would accept contracts and specifications from the local authorities. The gas supply, regulated in several local Improvement Acts, was not even mentioned in the Health of Towns Commission Report. The housing sections were weak. The report proposed regulation in detail only of cellar dwellings, omitting to control room space, materials or strength of walls in the building of working-class houses. It did less in this direction than Liverpool's Local Act of 1846. It refused to condemn back-to-back houses. Its powers of compulsory purchase were for minimal use, and the problem of overcrowding, although discussed, was left without proposal for remedy.

Opposition and the passing of the Public Health Act of 1848

There was obstinate opposition to the Public Health Act in parliament from traditionalist Tories such as Sibthorpe, Urquhart, Newdegate and Lord George Bentinck. The philanthropic evangelical Tory, R. H. Inglis, who allied with Newdegate against political rights for Catholics and Jews, joined Shaftesbury and the factory reformer Brotherton in support of public health. Thus the government, backed by radicals and some philanthropic Tories, was facing the representatives of commercial interests backed by the serried ranks of landed gentry. The latter were reinforced in their defensive traditionalism by the recent repeal of the Corn Laws, as well as by the reaction against the Poor Law which followed the Andover case.

The opposition to the Public Health Act relied mainly on denunciations of continental despotism and centralisation as alien to the British Constitution.[78] Lord Morpeth, sponsoring the Bill in the Commons, not only spelled out the limitations placed on the powers of the Central Board, but emphasised that the powers of elected town councils would be greatly increased. The principle, he affirmed, was 'to leave all to local agency, advised and encouraged by central superintendence'.[79] Newdegate then defined centralisation to include the absorption of all the powers of the other local boards by the town council.[80] The opposition thus betrayed its concern not for local government but for the preservation of the existing administrative chaos.

Opposition speakers repeatedly expressed their apprehension that the elected town councils would extend their jurisdiction over the surrounding agricultural districts, and then force the rural property owners to pay the new rates.[81] This laid them open to Brotherton's riposte that he knew cases 'where landowners (in the suburbs) had their incomes advanced from £5,000 to £20,000 a year without doing a single thing to promote the welfare of the inhabitants by whom they were so much benefitted'.[82] Apprehension of interference with the remarkable profits produced by growing land values in the suburbs joined forces with the Tory gentlemen's jealousy of the new elected town councils, which they saw as a threat to their hegemony in local government. They stoutly maintained that the reformers' reports in general and those of the Health of Towns Commission in particular, were exaggerated. They sought to turn the tables on the Whig reformers by repeating that the real cause of sickness among the lower orders was bad and inadequate food.[83]

Tory politicians were sensitive to the very large amount of patronage the Bill would put in Whig government hands, and they were not mollified by the explanation that most of it would belong to the Local Boards.[84] They totted up the salaries to be paid to the Central Board, and hinted that the Bill was a 'job' by Chadwick for his own advantage. They believed the inspectors would act as government spies, and sneered at the moralistic connection seen by reformers between disease and crime. They succeeded in defeating the Bill in 1847 largely on the tactical point that London (which was to be the subject of a separate Bill) had been omitted from the general one. These were backbiting debates in which the force of the arguments bore little relation to the venom of the conflict. The anti-centralisation and anti-patronage cries were at least partly a front for those who cherished back-bench supremacy and the perpetuation of weak government.[85] But eventually a majority was found from the bulk of Whig members who, even if they disliked the Bill realised that the cholera known to be approaching necessitated action, and that, on the evidence of the petitions coming in, a considerable body of public opinion supported it.[86]

Sources and references

1. Cf p. 68.
2. **Jebb, John,** *Thoughts on the Construction and Polity of Prisons.* London, 1786.
3. Dissenting academies pioneered the teaching of science. Rational Dissent, science and sanitary engineering had logical connections.
4. For example, **Gauldie, Enid,** *Cruel Habitations.* George Allen and Unwin, 1974, *passim.* But Dr Gauldie points out that overcrowding and bad housing were often due to inability to pay an economic rent. *Ibid.,* p. 145.
5. Notes for a speech at Leicester, August 1843, p. 7. *Chadwick Papers,* 47. D. M. S. Watson Library, University College, London.
6. **Gosden, P. H. J. H.,** *Self-Help.* Batsford, 1973, pp. 143-53. Gosden makes the point that the eighteenth- and early nineteenth-century societies were savings groups to finance the actual building of subscribers' homes, while the later permanent building societies were mainly finance houses for borrowing and lending secured on real property.
7. **Flinn, M. W.** (ed.), *Report on the Sanitary Condition of the Labouring Population of Great Britain,* by Edwin Chadwick, 1842. Edinburgh U.P., 1965. Introduction, pp. 4-5.
8. *Ibid.,* pp. 13-15.
9. *Ibid.,* Report, p. 223.
10. *Ibid.,* Report, pp. 223-7.
11. Chadwick pointed out that many of the younger people left Rutland for work in the industrial areas, leaving a high average age population there. *Ibid.,* Report, p. 223.
    ort on the Sanitary Condition of the Labouring Population, etc. Supplementary Report on e Results of a Special Inquiry into the Practice of Interment in Towns. London, 1843, 2. PP 1843, XII.
    n Jones, Gareth, *Outcast London.* Clarendon Press, 1971. Part II, p. 159, *et*

14. **Allan, C. M.,** 'The genesis of British urban redevelopment with special reference to Glasgow', *Econ. Hist. Review*, 2nd series XVIII, 1965, pp. 600-2.

15. **Townley, W. E.,** 'Urban Administration and Health: a Case Study of Hanley in the mid Nineteenth Century'. Keele M.A., 1969, p. 89.

16. **Archer, Alan,** 'A Study of Local Sanitary Administration in Certain Selected Areas, 1848-75'. Wales (Bangor) M.A., 1967, p. 61.

17. **Toft, Jean,** 'Public Health in Leeds in the Nineteenth Century: a Study in the Growth of Local Government Responsibility, *c.*1815-1880'. Manchester M.A., 1966, p. 118.

18. **Engels, F.,** *The Condition of the Working Class in England.* W. O. Henderson and W. H. Chaloner (tr. and ed.), Basil Blackwell, 1958, pp. 54-6.

19. **Hennock, E. P.,** *Fit and Proper Persons: Ideal and Reality in Nineteenth Century Urban Government.* Edward Arnold, 1973, p. 113.

20. **Hodgkinson, Ruth,** *The Origins of the National Health Serivce.* The Wellcome Historical Medical Library, 1967, pp. 28-31, 125-8, 298-9.

21. However, it has been argued that the middle class generally believed cholera to be a disease largely confined to the poor, and that the well-fed and well-washed were exempt. See **Morris, R. J.,** *Cholera 1832.* Croom Helm, 1976, pp. 79-93.

22. Chadwick was Assistant Commissioner for London as well as Berkshire, investigating the state of the poor for the Poor Law Commission during the cholera epidemic of 1832.

23. Toft, Jean, *op. cit.*, pp. 167-8.

24. **Elliott, Malcolm,** 'The Leicester Board of Health, 1849-1872'. Nottingham M. Phil., 1971, pp. 29, 49.

25. *Ibid.*, p. 29.

26. Report of Dr Robert Baker to the Leeds Board of Health. Quoted in Toft, *op. cit.*, p. 13.

27. *Ibid.*, p. 13.

28. Evidence of Dr Williamson of the Leeds Statistical Committee. *Ibid.*, p. 30-1.

29. **Davies Jones, Tydfil,** 'Poor Law and Public Health Administration in the Area of Merthyr Tydfil Union, 1834-1894'. Wales (Cardiff) M.A., 1961, p. 160.

30. *Second Report of the Commissioners for Inquiring into the State of Large Towns and Populous Districts.* HMSO, 1845, pp. 317-21. (Hereafter called *Health of Towns Commission, Second Report.*)

31. *Health of Towns Commission, Second Report*, pp. 20-1.

32. Toft, *op. cit.*, p. 126.

33. The General Board of Health had to circularise the canal companies warning them not to lay dry the bottoms of their canals. *Report of the General Board of Health on the Measures adopted for the Execution of the Nuisances Removal and Diseases Prevention Act and the Public Health Act up to July 1849.* Wm Clowes for HMSO, 1849, p. 41.

34. Elliott, M., *op. cit.*, pp. 95-6.

35. *Ibid.*, pp. 118-21.

36. *Ibid.*, p. 97.

37. Newcastle caught the full force of the cholera outbreak of 1854. See Evidence of E. Charlton Esq., M.D., *Report of the Cholera Inquiry Commissioners, Newcastle on Tyne. PP* 1854, XXXV, pp. 135-41.

38. Toft, *op. cit.*, p. 149.

39. *Health of Towns Commission, Second Report*, pp. 85-6.

40. Toft, *op. cit.*, p. 265 *et seq.*

41. *Health of Towns Commission, Second Report*, p. 89.

42. *Ibid.*, pp. 92, 275.

43. *Sanitary Report: Supplementary Report on . . . Interment in Towns*, 1843, *passim.*

44. *Report on Interment in Towns*, pp. 32-42.

45. *Health of Towns Commission, Second Report*, p. 40-41.

46. *Ibid.*, p. 22.

47. *Ibid.*, p. 31.

48. *Ibid.*, p. 32.

49. *Ibid.*, p. 48.
50. *Ibid.*, p. 31.
51. For discussions of these theories, see **Lewis, R. A.,** *Edwin Chadwick and the Public Health Movement, 1832-1854.* Longman 1952, pp. 40-43. See also (and in more detail) **Durey, M. J.,** 'A Social History of the First Cholera Epidemic in Britain, 1831-33'. York D. Phil., 1975, p. 352 *et seq.*
52. Including Sir John Simon.
53. *Fourth Annual Report of the Poor Law Commission,* 1838. App. A, No. 1, p. 131.
54. *Report on Interment in Towns,* p. 15.
55. **Large, David** and **Round, Francis,** *Public Health in Mid-Victorian Bristol.* Bristol Branch of the Historical Association, 1974, pp. 11-13. For a recent discussion of the work of Budd and his Bristol friends, based on microscopic analysis, and of John Snow, based largely on mortality statistics, see Morris, R. J., *op. cit.,* pp. 206-10.
56. *Report of the Committee for Scientific Inquiries in relation to the Cholera Epidemic of 1854.* General Board of Health, 1855, p. 34 *et seq.* The Committee included Dr Neil Arnott, The Registrar-General William Farr and Sir John Simon.
57. *Ibid.*, p. 52. Morris, *op. cit.,* pp. 208-9. Snow got the Broad Street pump handle removed. A public house named 'The John Snow' now stands on the site.
58. Durey, M. J., *op. cit.,* pp. 152, 168-9. Opinion has been hardening against Chadwick since 1952 when R. A. Lewis wrote that in sanitary measures he did the right thing for the wrong reasons.
59. Durey, *op. cit.,* p. 336. Durey quotes from Hetherington in the *Poor Man's Guardian.*
60. Chadwick gave data from the parish of St Margaret's, London, that the average age of death among those who lived in a fully culverted street was 23, in a partly culverted street was 17, and in streets without any culvert was 13½. Notes for a speech at Leicester, August 1843, p. 4. *Chadwick Papers,* 47. These figures would not allow for alteration of average by infant deaths, etc.
61. Flinn (ed.), *op. cit.,* Report, p. 423.
62. *Report of the General Board of Health on the Administration of the Public Health Act, 1848-54,* p. 33. *PP* 1854, XXXV.
63. *Health of Towns Commission, Second Report,* p. 83-4.
64. *Ibid.*, p. 8. Chadwick even issued a dire warning against clearing streets and cellars without rehousing the occupants, the classic mistake of nineteenth-century slum clearance policies.
65. *Hansard,* 3rd series XCVIII, 5 May 1848, p. 727.
66. **Finer, S. E.,** *The Life and Times of Sir Edwin Chadwick.* Methuen, 1952, p. 154.
67. *Poor Law Commissioners' 4th Annual Report,* 1838. App. A, No. 1, pp. 93-153.
68. For example, Flinn (ed.), *op. cit.,* Report, pp. 422-5. This was copied by others. Cf. John Clay's report on Preston. *Health of Towns Commission, First Report.* App. pp. 33-55. *PP* 1844, XVII.
69. Flinn (ed.), *op. cit.,* Report, p. 424. *Health of Towns Commission, Second Report,* pp. 61-3.
70. *Ibid.*, pp. 49, 50.
71. *Ibid.*, p. 75 *et seq.*
72. *Ibid.*, pp. 52, 56.
73. *Ibid.*, pp. 109-10.
74. *Ibid.*, p. 107.
75. Lewis, R. A., *op. cit.,* p. 103.
76. *Health of Towns Commission, Second Report,* p. 11.
77. This was in substance a reversion to the proposals of Slaney's Select Committee of 1840.
78. Newdegate. *Hansard.* 3rd Series XCIII, 18 June 1847, p. 729. Urquhart, Banks, Drummond. *Hansard.* 3rd series XCVIII, 5 May 1848, pp. 711-22, 727-30.
79. Morpeth, *ibid.,* 1 July 1847, p. 1103.
80. Newdegate, *ibid.,* p. 1103.
81. Buck, *ibid.,* 18 June, pp. 716-17.

82. Brotherton, *ibid.*, p. 717.

83. Muntz, *ibid.*, p. 750. The radical Roebuck was unable to understand the newborn principle of popular feeling on the opposite side of the House. Thomas Wakley pointed out the inconsistency of those who had voted for the Poor Law Commission refusing to vote for the General Board of Health.

84. For example, Lord George Bentinck, *ibid.*, pp. 1110-11.

85. For example, Col. Sibthorpe was 'jealous of all governments, whether Whig or Tory'. *Ibid.*, p. 727.

86. The petitions were analysed by Morpeth on 18 June 1847. He found 220 petitions in favour of the Bill so far, and 22 against. *Ibid.*, p. 740. This does not suggest that the issue aroused much popular attention.

7 Public health: II

Enforcement: General and Local Boards of Health

Public health machinery set up in 1848 consisted in a General Board of three members chaired by the First Commissioner of Woods and Forests, (Morpeth) with a full-time paid member (Chadwick) and an unpaid member (Shaftesbury). Later Southwood Smith was appointed as medical commissioner. Its superintending inspectors, unlike the Poor Law inspectors, were part-time. They were professional engineers in private practice which the Board, subject to Treasury approval, hired at £3 3s a day.[1] They were to assist in the establishment of the Local Boards, which could be set up either following a petition from one-tenth or more of the local ratepayers, or where the annual registered deaths exceeded 23 per 1,000[2] Before the Local Board was established by Order in Council, there had to be an inspection, a public inquiry (after 14 days' notice) and a report to the General Board by the superintending inspector.[3] The whole process was complicated by the need to rationalise boundaries. If the health district proposed did not coincide exactly with that of a city or borough, there might be local representations and a further inspector's report.[4] Parts of boroughs incorporated in health districts consisting mainly in neighbouring boroughs had to give their consent. Such districts, together with those in which there was no corporate borough, had to be established by Provisional Order in Council, which required parliamentary ratification.[5]

In corporate towns the Local Board of Health would consist of the town council. In districts comprising two or more boroughs, or parts of them, the Board would include the mayor and council of the main borough, with councillors from the others, chosen by their councils. Local Boards in districts without a corporate borough would be directly elected by the ratepayers, and property owners with plural votes, up to six in number, one for up to every £50 rateable value.[6] Even villages of under 2,000 inhabitants, if not covered by a Local Board, would have some sanitary powers. Two-thirds of the ratepayers could call a public meeting which could instruct the churchwardens and parish overseers to drain a polluted pond, cover a stream, or construct a sewer.[7] Thus some parishes as well as boroughs were given more powers.

The Public Health Act laid down general regulations for sanitation. All new houses were to have w.c.s or privies, and ashpits. Older houses, if within 100 feet of a public sewer, were to have a drain connected with it, or otherwise provide a drain to a cesspool, at the house owner's cost.[8] No more cellars for living in could be built, and those already in occupation should have a ceiling at least 3 feet above ground, an open area at least 2½ feet in front, be drained, and provided with w.c. or privy, a window, a fireplace and approach steps.[9] The Act also laid down a long list of duties and powers for the local Boards of Health. They were made responsible for sewerage and drainage, for approving plans for new roads and for the sanitation of new houses, also for the water supply (for which they were to contract with the local water companies, subject to certain conditions being fulfilled). They could buy up premises, with owners' consent, for street widening.[10] They were to deal with all kinds of nuisance, including the prevention of dirty trades, the regulation (and if necessary provision) of slaughterhouses, the registration and inspection of common lodging houses.[11] For these they had the usual powers of entry, contracting and recovery. Moreover, they could provide various amenities, from public privies to parks, and cemeteries.[12] They could close graveyards considered dangerous to health, and prohibit burials in the latter.[13] They could pass by-laws carrying penalties up to £5.[14]

To carry out all these duties the Act prescribed a list of permanent officials for the Local Boards. They included a clerk, a treasurer, a surveyor, an inspector of nuisances, and, optionally, a medical officer who could be shared between several districts.[15] To finance their operations the Local Boards could levy rates of various kinds, including district, general, improvement, private and water rates. They could reduce or remit these in cases of poverty, or pay for some of the private house drains. With the consent of the General Board they could raise loans, repayable over a term of years and secured on the rates, for works of a permanent nature.[16]

The Public Health Act was, of course, a codification of former Acts, central and local. Yet despite its comprehensiveness and the considerable element of compulsion, it had gaps and inadequacies. It reproduced the omissions already noticed in the Health of Towns Commission Report, and it provided nothing like the nation-wide cover of the Poor Law. Even if towns with a death rate of over 23 per 1,000 could be forced to establish Boards of Health, large parts of the country would still be left unprovided for. Time showed that the General Board would rarely use its powers to set up Local Boards in districts of high mortality, so the spread of public health authorities was left to local initiative. The Poor Law Amendment Act had attempted to reform a universal, traditional and statutory service, whereas public health administration had hitherto been the province only of Local Acts and *ad hoc* activities. To give it the universality of the Poor Law was too much even for a Chadwick. But some of its weaknesses resembled those of the Poor Law, in acute form. While most of the compulsory powers were for Local Boards to use against local offenders, the General Board had few sanctions to force the Local Boards (many of them town councils not elected primarily for public health) to do their duty. The General Board's superintending inspectors made the initial inquiries and gave the initial advice, but there were no provisions for follow-up visits. The General Board's most useful means of control was the requirement that the Secretary of State should confirm Local Board by-laws, and that it should approve Local Board mortgages for public works (first seeing, and hence approving, the plans).[17] But it could not force the Local Boards to make the by-laws nor to undertake the works. In relation to the local authorities it was little more than an enabling Act, with few teeth.

Some of the Public Health Act's inadequacies were partly made up elsewhere. The Metropolitan Building Act of 1844, a harbinger of later building Acts, provided in London more specifically for space between and around houses, and for light, air and room heights than did the Public Health Act.[18] The omission of London, most disease-ridden of cities, from the general Act was partly rectified by that and by the City of London Sewers Act, which set up a Sewers Commission appointed by the Common Council with most of the powers of a Local Board of Health.[19] The lodging-houses clauses of the Public Health Act were soon supplemented by Shaftesbury's two Acts of 1851, one of which permitted the subsidising of municipal lodging houses from the rates. A Towns Improvement Clauses Act devised by Chadwick in 1847 provided a model for towns applying for their own Improvement Acts, conferring many of the same powers on their sanitary committees as those of the later Local Boards of Health, and offering the services of superintending engineers.[20] A short Act in 1846 had specified that plans for local Improvement Acts should be reported to the Commissioner for Woods and Forests (which minister was later to be chairman of the General Board of Health), who could send his surveyors to inquire and report.[21] Thus tentative steps were being taken towards extending the central supervision over the independent health authorities. Otherwise there was nothing except the higher cost of the legislation to prevent large towns from obtaining their own Improvement Acts, and running their own public health administration without reference to the central power.

Finally, the Nuisances Removal and Contagious Diseases Prevention Acts of 1846 and 1848, although intended primarily as emergency measures against cholera, afforded a further safety net of compulsive powers for the removal of pollution, especially in areas without any health authority.[22]

The Public Health Act of 1848 was, in fact, one measure among several which offered a choice of ways and means of tackling the sanitation problem. Local Authorities could do nothing, and continue to turn the blind eye to their overflowing sewers, dung heaps and slums. But they might be rudely awakened by a party of ratepayers petitioning for a Local Board of Health or by Poor Law Guardians and medical men issuing summonses for nuisance. They could themselves petition for a Local Board, or they could incorporate for that purpose. Alternatively, they could petition parliament for their own Improvement Act.

Cholera, 1848-49

As soon as it was constituted, the General Board was faced with the cholera epidemic of which the approach had forced parliament to accept the Public Health Act. The outbreak arrived from the Continent in November 1848, died away when the cold weather came after January, but returned in the following June, to reach its peak in September 1849.[23] At its onset the Nuisances Removal and Contagious Diseases Prevention Act was passed and activated. This put the General Board in charge of preventive measures, and was necessary because the organisation of Local Boards had not begun, and it had to work through existing local authorities and the Poor Law Guardians. But many of the former only wanted to put their heads in the sand. They detested being interfered with by a central department and they feared that public recognition of cholera in their district, not to mention the restrictions and regulations to follow, would damage trade.

The parochial board at Dumfries, where the plague struck early, did nothing for twenty days. 'Precious time was wasted in mere petty squabbles; the town has been clothed in mourning in consequence.'[24] In London where the outbreak was at its worst, the General Board was involved with chaotic and overlapping Paving Boards which refused to obey the Guardians. Under St. Pancras' 29 Local Acts, 16 boards had to be consulted before an opinion could be pronounced as to what could be done to cleanse the parish as a whole; and the Law Officers of the Crown said it would be illegal to overcome this obstacle by setting up joint Boards of Health on the 1831 model.[25] But the General Board also encountered the traditional hostility of Boards of Guardians to spending money. The Nuisances Removal Acts had given it no power to prosecute them itself, and it could do nothing unless a coroner pronounced an inquest verdict that their refusal to obey its orders had caused a death. The Whitechapel Board of Guardians resolved 'That it is the opinion of the Guardians that, at present, the order of the Board of Health, of the 18th November last, need not be acted on in this Union'. Then despite the expostulations of the coroner, it resolved that the Medical Officers be not called on to visit the places where disease was reported to have been prevalent.[26]

When cholera broke out in the overcrowded District Poor Law School at Tooting, two London Unions refused to withdraw their children, of whom 180 died.[27] The Unions were not only refusing to appoint the extra doctors ordered by the General Board for house-to-house visiting, but closing down dispensaries. The Board believed that cholera started with 'premonitary diarrhoea'. If caught in time by the removal of the patient to a less foetid atmosphere, and suitable dosing, it could be prevented from developing into the killing disease. Yet its attempts to organise rescue measures were so frustrated that it had to report people in many places dying without any medical attention. In Scotland the unpopular James Stuart did useful work in organising the inspection of large factories, yet many corpses were discovered in them. In the 1831–32 epidemic the Manchester factories had been a comparatively safe refuge from the infected slums.[28] The General Board's attempts to prevent the saturation of the London churchyards with cholera corpses met with the same obstructions. And the magistrates followed by the judges ruled that it had no right to compel the boroughs to close their graveyards.[29] Not until August 1849 did the Board obtain an amendment to their Nuisances Removal Act, giving it some of the powers it needed. Then it appointed a Principal Medical Inspector and four Assistants, and set about forcing the London Unions to organise house-to-house visiting and the removal of people from infected houses.

If the local authorities were callous and irresponsible there were other reasons for the lack of response to the Board's efforts. Its proposed remedies, opiate and peppermint water, brandy and water, chalk mixture, aromatic confection [?] and laudanum, did not cure cholera. But then nobody knew how to cure it.[30] Its preventive precautions were mostly common-sense measures. They included eating moderately, washing, wearing flannel next to the skin, burning infected bedding and clothing, and the immediate burial of cholera corpses with as little delay or assemblage as possible. Commands to eat moderately and wash frequently could only infuriate the poor, the loss of their clothes and bedding constituted disaster to those who could not replace them, while the orders for the disposal of the dead flouted the customs and superstitions of people (especially the Irish) to whom a proper wake was the most important thing in life – or death.[31] The Board's attempted precautions reinforced the existing working-class fear of doctors and hospitals, and public opinion could not be mobilised against the supine authorities. Eventually the epidemic wore itself out, presumably without help from the inadequate measures taken against it.

Local Boards and local government

The establishment of Local Boards of Health was a slow process. The General Board was overloaded, its part-time superintending inspectors often dilatory.[32] The compulsory powers of the Act were rarely used, the Commissioners preferring to await a petition, or at least strong evidence of local support.[33] By the end of 1848, 75 places had applied for inspection. By 1853, 284 towns had petitioned to adopt the Act, of which 182 had completed the procedure and obtained Local Boards covering some 2 million people. Of these towns, 70 had laid out plans for new works,

31 had had their plans for combined drainage and water supply approved by the Board, and loans worth over £1 million secured on local rates had been sanctioned. Only 13 towns had actually completed their works and were in process of connecting house drains with main sewers, but 35 more were expected to complete in less than a year.[34] This progress, if substantial, was hardly dramatic, although the General Board, by now fighting for its life, made the most of it. In fact the local adoption of the Public Health Acts continued piecemeal throughout the next half-century.

Any survey of the local adoption of public-health measures leaves an impression of the greatest variety in procedure and in progress. Leicester, for instance, noted for its high death rate, became committed to public health when its first election under the Municipal Corporations Act of 1835 displaced the rule of the Tory shopkeepers on the old corporation by that of Liberal Dissenters on the new Town Council. The Council then set up sanitary administration piecemeal. In 1845 the mayor unsuccessfully applied to the Home Department for an engineer to carry out a survey and suggest plans for drainage and sewerage. Proposals for an Improvement Act failed because of a dispute between two factions, one advocating the prestige project of a town hall and the other maintaining that the town hall was a waste of ratepayers' money and demanding sanitation. However, by 1848 Leicester had cemetery and water companies, an inspector of nuisances, two part-time Medical Officers, an Improvement Fund, an Improvement Committee and a Sanitary Committee of five. The latter was set up under the Nuisances Removal and Contagious Diseases Prevention Act of 1848. The town was divided into six districts, each with a police constable to report nuisances, which were to be severely dealt with by the magistrates. However, the death rate continued to exceed 23 per 1,000, and soon the Council petitioned the new General Board of Health for a superintending inspector. In due course the Council became a Local Board, delegating its duties to a Highways and Sewerage Committee. The Liberal majority which ran the Council had tried the Nuisances Removal procedures first, and finding them inadequate had adopted the Public Health Act.[35]

On the other hand, Leeds, starting the 1840s with a burst of reforming energy sufficient to obtain a Local Improvement Act in 1842, stagnated under that Act as its town council came to be dominated by ratepayers' associations and reactionary councillors.[36] The smaller Burton on Trent, fearing the tyranny of centralised control, also resorted to its own Improvement Act, in 1852. But its Board of twenty-seven Commissioners, with the best reforming intentions, then found that their powers were insufficient to overcome the obstruction of local property owners and other vested interests.[37] Birmingham obtained Improvement Acts in 1851 and 1861. But for more than two decades its municipal corporation failed to tackle its sanitation and housing problems, because it was dominated by a faction of 'economists' dedicated to the saving of ratepayers' money. Yet in the 1870s Birmingham under the influence of

Joseph Chamberlain and Dissenting moral enthusiasm was to emerge as the most progressive reforming municipality in the country.[38] Dr E. C. Midwinter has shown that in industrial Lancashire, medium-sized towns preferred to adopt the Public Health Act or, in some cases, to incorporate so that their town councils could enjoy the powers of a Local Board of Health. Great cities like Manchester and Liverpool shunned the General Board and proceeded under their own series of Local Acts; while the small townships clustered round them applied for directly elected Local Boards.[39] The great cities, rich enough to afford a series of Local Acts filling the gaps disclosed by experience, and to appoint well-qualified officials, could make progress with the help of their own resources. Medium and small towns needed the powers conferred by the Public Health Act and the advice of the General Board's superintending engineers. But the actual achievements in any of them varied enormously, depending as much on the will to use the powers taken as on which of the paths to sanitary reform the town chose to take.

Committees and local government services

All towns ran their sanitary administration by means of committees. Under its Improvement Act of 1842, Leeds Town Council set up a Street Committee and a Scavenging and Nuisance Committee. The latter was ineffective because its scavengers were paupers on relief scales, who would not work.[40] After its next Improvement Act in 1866 and the appointment of a Medical Officer, it instituted more committees, including a Sewerage Committee and sub-committees of the Scavenging and Nuisance Committee, one for night soil and one for cellar dwellings. These were also ineffective, and throughout the middle of the century such sanitary attempts as were made seem to have come from the Poor Law Guardians, exercising (not always legally) the powers of the Nuisances Prevention Acts.[41] Before the Potteries town of Hanley incorporated in 1857 it already possessed a wealthy, non-elective body of Watch and Lighting Commissioners, acting through sub-committees for rates, lighting, and the town hall.[42] On adopting the Public Health Act (of 1858) its elected town council set up committees for finance, general purposes, by-laws, burial, nuisance removal, lighting and rating, and later, a watch committee.[43] The committee system which prevailed after 1848 was merely a more systematic, and elective adaptation of a very old and traditional form of city government. Its models were to be found in Renaissance Europe, if not in ancient Greece. Inevitably there was a high degree of continuity between the more active of the old commissions and the new committees. As in the Poor Law, power tended to continue in the hands of those who knew how to get themselves appointed, or elected to important bodies and key posts, and were prepared to do the work.

The same continuity is evident in the development of the paid local government services. The officials specified in the 1848 Public Health Act were already known. The Inspector of Nuisances appeared in the 'Cholera Act' of 1831, a surveyor was stipulated in the Town Improvement Clauses Act of 1847, together with his oath of office, but was doubtless far older. Only the optional Medical Officer (following the famous Dr Duncan of Liverpool, and two part-time appointments at Leicester) was comparatively new. The clerk and treasurer were traditional municipal officials. Places adopting new sanitary powers increased their officials, to serve the new committees. Thus Derby, on becoming a Local Board of Health, appointed a surveyor, an inspector of nuisances, and also a rate collector, each with responsibility for specified services, to work with its committees.[44] Inevitably many of these new officials were survivals from the older regime.

The salaries and conditions of the local government officials varied with the size of the town and the generosity, or otherwise, of the Board of Health with the ratepayers' money. By far the highest provincial payer was Liverpool, target for emigrant ships full of starving and disease-ridden Irish. The city built up in the late 1840s a considerable local government service, with a medical officer receiving £750 and a surveyor £1,000 a year, borough engineer at £700, and a troop of cellar officers, lodging-house inspectors, midden clerks, cellar clerks, etc.[45] The medical officers at Edinburgh and Leeds had £500 a year, at Glasgow and Bristol only £200, while in smaller places such as Doncaster, Cardiff and Merthyr, they were part-time at less than £100.[46] But the offices tended to grow. Leicester started with a part-time borough surveyor at £150, who was overworked and unsatisfactory. By the 1870s it was paying a full-time surveyor £500–600 a year, with an assistant as well.[47]

The oldest sanitary office, and a key post in the attack on pollution, that of Inspector of Nuisances, was also the Cinderella of the local government service. It was often pushed onto the chief of police as an extra responsibility, or combined with other offices such as surveyor of highways or inspector of lodging houses or fire officer.[48] But the idea that the local constable ought to spot and report local nuisances was a practical and important link in the development of police and health administration.

Only by offering reasonable salaries could towns obtain fully trained and incorruptible officials. In this context dominant ratepayers' associations could hold up progress indefinitely, while the General Board had no direct control over appointments, dismissals or salaries. In Lancashire, and doubtless elsewhere, there were complaints of Local Board officials combining too many full-time jobs, being overworked, untrained, poorly paid, constantly changed, and inattentive to their duties.[49] Perhaps a more standardised and efficient service could have been built up if 'centralisation' had been more of a reality, and the General Board, like the Poor Law Commission, had at least been able to lay down rules and dismiss the unsatisfactory.

The decline and demise of the General Board of Health

The General Board of Health rapidly became unpopular. It was impossible to abolish nuisances or rationalise administration without damaging private interests; and every success for which the Board could be held responsible increased that unpopularity. The abatement of nuisances caused the most widespread irritation. For example, the Derby Local Board in its first three years (1850–53) issued 302 orders to house owners to remove foul privies and cesspools, 190 of which were fully complied with.[50] Its officials regularly inspected 62 slaughterhouses and 57 lodging houses.[51] With the help of police reports nearly 1,000 overflowing cesspools and drains were removed. 'Searchers of flesh' were appointed to confiscate bad food, and shops were ordered to remove signs which encroached on the pavements. The Derby Gas Co. was prosecuted for creating a nuisance; the local cement works, lead works and mills were ordered to abate their smoke. A local clergyman was sued for work carried out on his frontage, for £40 2s 3½d, and the General Board, on his appeal, upheld the Local Board's claim. But the owner of a tallow-melting works, prosecuted for emitting a noxious aroma, got the magistrates' conviction quashed on appeal, and the 'master stink' continued.[52]

Derby was not exceptional, nor its Council merely a new broom sweeping clean. Between 1855 and 1872 Leicester Board of Health issued orders to remove nuisances averaging between 300 and 500 a year, except in cholera years, when house-to-house visiting was organised, and they rose into the thousands.[53] The greatest number of orders were to remove offensive drains, then defective cesspools, then to cleanse dwellings, and then to remove pigsties. The number of actual prosecutions was small, the highest being fourteen in 1859. Apparently the threat was enough. There was also regular inspection of lodging houses, and the owners were made to wash them four times a year. But the unregistered ones remained filthy. The working-class pig-owners complained in vain about the attack on their home-bred meat supply, but the Local Board's campaign against belching factory chimneys was effectively resisted by the powerful chairman of its own Highways and Sewerage Committee, who owned one.[54] It was not merely that the rich could get away with nuisances while the poor were trampled on; many jobs depended on the large factories, and masters and workmen had a common interest in opposing expensive non-commercial improvements. In contrast with these towns, Leeds did nothing to abate nuisances. Indeed its municipal council was one of the worst creators of them.[55]

A subsidiary but influential reason for the General Board's unpopularity was Chadwick's doctrinaire insistence that all drains should be of the small-bore, glazed brick, water-flushed type, and the General Board's refusal to employ engineers who disagreed. Local Boards were also encouraged to employ the Board's part-time superintending inspectors on their own works,[56] and the engagement of eminent consultant engineers who favoured older methods was discouraged with all Chadwick's habitual tactlessness. When Leicester Local Board employed Thomas Wicksteed (engineer of the East London Waterworks Co. who had cast doubt on the possibility of keeping water at pressure in all mains simultaneously and had defended the old standpipe system before the Health of Towns Commission), the General Board opposed his plans, from flat-bottomed sewers to a company to sell sewage for agricultural manure. The Board sent a superintending inspector to Leicester without informing him, and after delaying three months, refused his plans and Leicester's application to raise a loan. The engineer Robert Stephenson, brought in from Liverpool to arbitrate, considered the remarks of the General Board, 'altogether undignified and unworthy' of a body 'especially appointed to encourage and forward, and not to thwart and delay, . . . or . . . stop improvements of a sanitary character, because they do not come quite up to their empirical standard, or are not to be carried out according to their particular system, which it is notorious does not in all cases meet with the approval of practical men'.[57]

Even if the Board was right about Wicksteed (whose sewers allowed storm water to flood back into the houses and whose sewerage works became progressively unable to save the rivers from pollution),[58] its rigid insistence on its own system could be disastrous. When the water supply failed, clogged drains were worse than a properly run pail-and-cartage system. And sewage schemes could fail for all kinds of reasons, from the refusal of landowners to have sewage piped across their land, as at Stratford on Avon,[59] to the control of water by greedy ironmasters to avoid paying rates and for use in their works, as at Merthyr Tydfil.[60] As late as 1867 the representatives of Burslem at a sewerage conference admitted that its w.c.s were a mistake.[61] Meantime the slighted engineers took refuge in the service of towns which operated their own Local Improvement Acts, and joined in the attack on the General Board of Health.

Unfortunately the General Board could not counterbalance its unpopularity with the professionals by gratitude from the general public, because the works it promoted were so costly. Chadwick argued truly but in vain that adopting the Public Health Act cost far less than procuring a Local Act through parliament,[62] and that self-cleansing sewers were less expensive to build and run than flat-bottomed deposit sewers.[63] He could not deny that money would have to be spent, and although he had encouraged the expedient of mortgaging the rates, loans being repaid over twenty or thirty years would have to be serviced from local taxation. Leicester Town Council became a Local Board of Health in 1849, and within a year its rates had risen from 9d to 2s 3d per head. After 1853 they were permanently above 2s 4d. The rise was accounted for by the Council's expenditure which between 1851 and 1875 rose from £6,351 to £37,702 a year.[64] The town grew rapidly, but costs outstripped the population. Labour costs were rising, partly no doubt because of the increasing demand for sanitary works. This would probably have happened anyway, but it was easy to blame the General Board of Health.

The clauses encouraging the voluntary adoption of the Public Health Act by local initiative, and especially the ratepayers' right to petition for a Superintending Inspector, inevitably involved the Local Boards in politics. Where a town council was dominated by liberal progressives who applied for a Local Board to strengthen its sanitary powers, as in Leicester, there might be comparatively little controversy. Elsewhere the attempt at reform could produce long-drawn-out struggles between rival political factions. The Hanley Local Board originated in a petition from the Stoke Poor Law Union, covering four Potteries towns, as a result of the 1848 cholera outbreak. It contracted into a scheme for the incorporation of Hanley, which ran into opposition from the existing exclusive and conservative co-opted Market Trust, and from the Watching and Lighting commissioners set up on a high rating qualification in 1825. In fact the reform was opposed, on the one hand by these traditional bodies which feared the loss of their privileges, and on the other by the Highways Boards and the Board of Guardians, which were elected by the small ratepayers. The pottery operatives and other ratepaying working men resisted the dissolution of the bodies by which they achieved their small share of local power. Later controversy focused on the level of the rating qualification proposed for seats on the new Board of Health. Even the local Liberal MPs were reluctantly drawn into the disputes; and when, in 1854, the reforming party had succeeded in obtaining a Provisional Order setting up a Board of Health, the Conservative member for the county managed to prevent it being confirmed in parliament. Hanley did not get its incorporation until three years later, nor its Board of Health until two years after that, on a modest rating qualification, by way of compromise.[65]

In the face of such factional fights the General Board could boast no very solid body of popular support. The extension of Local Boards depended on the ascendancy of small groups of well-to-do business and professional men, usually of the Rational Dissenting persuasion, and often from newly made or self-made families who had succeeded in breaking the power of older Tory families of much the same class and economic function. Palmerston thought that without the probing and prompting of the Health of Towns Commission followed by the work of the General Board of Health's Superintending Inspectors, not even the visitations of cholera would have aroused provincial leaders to more than a temporary awareness of the disgusting and dangerous state of their towns.[66] But the names of some of the enlightened provincial leaders are known: Dr Baker of Leeds, Dr Duncan of Liverpool, John Clay, prison chaplain, and Captain Veitch RE of Preston, and doubtless many others. The impression is that, once the propaganda of the government inquiries and of the new General Board had taken hold, extension depended almost entirely on local initiative. The fact that the dissolution of the General Board in 1858 did not stop this extension suggests that the roots of the

'Clean Party' were firmly established in the provinces. However, the reformers were thinly spread and extremely vulnerable. Dr Hennock has shown how closely the increase of shopkeepers and small businessmen on the town councils of Leeds and Birmingham and the consequent withdrawal of the big businessmen from municipal leadership coincided with reaction, penny-pinching stagnation, and refusal to tackle the sanitary problem.[67] Democracy did not spell enlightenment in sanitary matters, and the 'know-nothing' ratepayers of the 'Dirty Party' included artisans and the skilled élite of the working class. The Chartist leaders of Hanley, respectable pottery operatives, feared taxes more than filth. When trade was depressed they said: 'Good sewerage may increase our personal comforts and conveniences but if it tends to deprive us still more of our now scanty living, we fear the introduction of it.'[68] As against this, the threat of cholera at Newcastle on Tyne in 1847 produced two sanitary associations, one of medical men and town councillors, the other of working men. The latter was reported to be by far the most vigorous in advocating sanitary reform.[69] No generalisation is possible until a lot more work has been done on working-class participation in sanitary provision. But it does not appear that it was one of the 'causes' usually supported by working-class leaders. For this there were a number of reasons.

Firstly, the very worst sufferers from housing conditions, the cellar dwellers, lodging-house dwellers and slum families, included a mass of Irish immigrants, unemployed and casual workers too apathetic and inarticulate to join any party or demand any improvement. Secondly, the long-drawn-out hostility between capital and labour, operative and industrialist, precluded easy co-operation. Those who held Chadwick responsible for the new Poor Law would hardly credit him with benevolent motives in public health, and his persistent refusal to acknowledge that disease might be caused by poverty could only confirm their suspicions. Shaftesbury's association with him on the General Board merely weakened the prospect of a working-class–Tory philanthropist alliance against the small ratepayer in favour of public health. Thirdly, the advice and measures of the General Board in cholera epidemics tended to offend the poor, who could not enjoy a temperate diet, wash frequently, keep warm, nor replace the clothes and bedding which were ordered to be burned, and who, not without cause, dreaded the fever wards of public hospitals. The nuisance proceedings offended them as much as their wealthier neighbours, especially when directed against small workshops or slaughterhouses, or domestic pigsties. Finally, there was bitter hostility over the hasty disposal of cholera corpses in communal graves. The authorities had been insensitive over many generations towards the feelings and conventions of the poor about death and burial.[70] The 1820s were the era of the body snatchers or 'resurrectionists' when the private anatomy schools were not too particular about where the bodies for their teaching came from, and there were terrifying rumours, some of them well founded, of murder gangs to procure them.[71]

Medical progress depended upon dissection, but the gulf of incomprehension between utilitarians and fustian jackets was nowhere greater. The Anatomy Act of 1832 allowing unclaimed bodies from poorhouses and hospitals to be supplied to medical schools was seen as an attack on the poor in line with the Poor Law Amendment Act, and it helped to destroy the confidence between the lower orders and the medical profession.[72] It is difficult to know how far this alienation was important in depriving the sanitary reformers of popular support.[73] None the less, there seems to have been little organised working-class support for reforms from which, by and large, the working class would have benefited most.

By 1853 the General Board of Health was on the defensive. The following year Chadwick, Southwood Smith and Shaftesbury were forced by bitter parliamentary criticism to resign. The Board continued for four more years under the chairmanship of Sir Benjamin Hall, one of its most rabid critics, and was then disbanded.

The opposition had nothing new to say, merely repeating the accusations of centralising despotism and unconstitutional meddling, more bitterly than before. The core of the attack consisted of charges of self-seeking tyranny against Chadwick, Southwood Smith, and, by implication (for no one dared criticise him openly), Shaftesbury. The most vehement criticisms came from Lord Seymour, from 1850 to 1851 First Commissioner of Woods and Forests, and chairman of the General Board, in whom Chadwick had aroused the same kind of political and personal antagonism as he had in the Lewises, father and son, on the Poor Law Commission.[74] Shaftesbury in the Lords demonstrated that Seymour's attack was motivated by jealousy and vindicated by lies.[75] But the politicians failed to support him. The Earl of Carlisle (formerly Lord Morpeth) admitted that in Chadwick's make-up a certain degree of 'positiveness and precipitation' might be mixed up in any great question or idea.[76] And Palmerston, a consistent defender of the Board, commented that when more towns had organised themselves it might be no longer required.[77]

The spread of public health administration

The break-up of the General Board of Health was not the end of the story. But in view of its central position in the first phase of sanitary administration under the Public Health Act, it is worth trying to answer the question: How far had that Act been successful?

In 1854 the General Board claimed that nearly 27,000 houses in London (which was not under its jurisdiction) had been fitted with tubular drains, and admitted that only 13 towns had completed their drainage and water works.[78] The report's tone of agonised urgency revealed Chadwick's realisation that his sanitary schemes were in jeopardy. However, it would be grossly unfair to measure the success of the Act by the Board's achievements in 1854. There was an inevitable time lag between the establishment of a Local Board of Health and the completion of its works. Moreover, the decline of the central power did not kill the public-health movement. The General Board's duties were divided between the Privy Council, the Poor Law Board, and the Local Government Act Office, set up under the Home Office; and yet, in the decade 1858–68 towns continued to set up Local Boards of Health in increasing numbers, and that with little encouragement from the Local Government Act Office.[79] By 1871 there were some 700 Local Boards in England and Wales,[80] and the process had only to be completed by the Public Health Acts of 1872 and 1875, which established sanitary machinery for the whole country and codified the powers of the local authorities. This remarkable progress, Dr Lambert suggests, was due to the 'self-sustaining and self-generating impulse of administration itself'.[81] More profitably it might be attributed to the propaganda of Chadwick and his friends on the connection between disease and dirt, followed by the persistent endeavours of small groups of enlightened people in the provinces.

Yet if public-health administration continued to spread, it was neither quickly nor completely successful. Public sewerage ventures devised as self-financing frequently failed. Leicester failed to sell its night soil to farmers and its removal came back on the rates.[82] Water-flushed drains in the towns took water from the country and transferred pollution to the rivers. This increased the hostility of farmers and landowners, and Local Boards had no power to coerce outside their own boundaries. Thus Stratford on Avon's drainage area had to be reduced because its Board could get no land for a reservoir. Nor could it construct a drain to the river Avon, which the local landowners rightly feared would be polluted.[83] As with the Poor Law, some Local Authorities were set up specifically to thwart the intention of the Act. Birmingham's Improvement Acts of 1851 and 1861 were intentionally restrictive, forbidding the Town Council to raise loans for improvement without the prior consent of the ratepayers.[84] The Merthyr Tydfil Board of Health was established largely to facilitate the monopoly of the ironmasters over the water supply.[85] Planning committees inevitably attracted speculative builders who sat on them to protect themselves from building restrictions. Burial committees were apt to attract the managers of funeral parlours, and drainage committees the directors of waterworks companies. Big fish could nearly always protect themselves, and the Alkali Inspectors were to discover how difficult it was to make large millowners abate their pollution.[86] A City Council, whether dominated by ratepayers or factory owners was particularly hard to shift. The *Leeds Mercury*, organ of the more liberal millowners, denounced the Leeds Town Council; it had laid down

> a vast system of drains, and then finds the drains too small to carry off the refuse, and leaves the worst districts in the town as badly drained as before. . . . It gets bills to remove the refuse far

down the river, and leaves open becks to wind their polluting way through the densest portion of the town. It receives power to compell the consumption of smoke, and then wraps itself in smoke as in a garment, and becomes a proverb for its dirt and dinginess. It obtains powers to prevent houses being built on unhealthy principles, and forthwith runs up back-to-back cottages, the most unhealthy buildings which human perversity ever invented.[87]

The Royal Commission on the Housing of the Working Classes in 1885 denounced London's deficient water supply, its defective closet accommodation, its noxious trades such as rag-picking, rabbit-pulling and haddock-curing, and above all, its bad housing. And here, in housing, was the greatest failure of all. Not that this could be attributed to the 1848 Public Health Act, which had carefully omitted to deal with it. Housing had become imbued with the principles of self-help; to provide it, or subsidise it would pauperise the poor. It took the whole century to convince the governing classes that cellars could not be abolished nor slums cleared until there was somewhere for the evicted to live, at prices they could afford.[88] Meantime Shaftesbury, Chadwick and their friends resorted to charitable housing associations sponsoring model houses and flats, which nibbled at the problem, while denouncing the very suggestion of 'the mischief of state aid'.[89]

The criticisms of the Royal Commission on Housing in the 1880s were made by a generation for the most part without experience of the conditions Chadwick had witnessed in the 1840s. They do not prove that no progress had been made; only that progress was slow. The municipal provision of working-class housing awaited the working-class vote at the end of the century. Meantime it had to be measured against the continued growth of population and urbanisation, which ensured that pollution always threatened to overtake the measures devised to prevent it. The question is not only whether sanitary conditions improved, but whether they might not have deteriorated.

One criterion of the achievement in sanitary reform was the movement of the mortality rate. Mortality figures were sedulously collected, but continued to be misleading. In Birmingham the published rate in 1873-75 of 25.97 per 1,000 for the whole town was devised to conceal the appalling rate of 62.5 per 1,000 in the slums.[90] But over the whole country the mortality rate did decline. Cholera threatened a serious epidemic for the last time in 1872.[91] Cholera apart, the mortality rate decreased slowly in the 1850s, more rapidly by the 1870s. The improvement must be attributed to many factors; to the Public Health Acts, to the gradual solution of the technical difficulties of sewerage purification, and above all, to the piecemeal discoveries of the actual causes of the various diseases. Even these were slow and patchy. In the comparatively well-administered Leicestershire of the 1870s, when Pasteur's bacteriological discoveries were known, more babies died of summer diarrhoea than anywhere else in England. Nobody suspected infected milk.[92] By the very end of the nineteenth century the Public Health Movement had largely solved the two original problems; the control of epidemics and the drainage of the towns. In the twentieth century, sewage is ceasing to pollute the rivers (although industrial waste is not); instead it pollutes the sea. Because other kinds of rubbish, such as plastics and glass, are not seen as directly menacing the lives of the people, the effort to protect the environment is as weak in modern administration as it was in the government organs of the nineteenth century. *Si monumentum requiris, circumspice.*

Sources and references

1. 11 & 12 Vict., c. 63, Clauses IV-VII.
2. *Ibid.*, Clause VIII. This provision had not been suggested in the *Health of Towns Commission Report*, but appears in a draft Public Health Bill drawn up by Chadwick for the Duke of Buccleuch in 1844. At one time a petition by 1/50 of the ratepayers had been proposed. **Lewis, R. A.,** *Edwin Chadwick and the Public Health Movement, 1832–1854.* Longman 1952, p. 97. This, if carried out, would take the Act into the realm of local compulsion. The national average for England and Wales was 21 per 1,000 so the compulsion was not only intended for extreme cases. **Longmate, Norman,** *King Cholera.* Hamish Hamilton, 1966, p. 155.
3. 11 & 12 Vict., c. 63, Clauses VIII, IX.
4. *Ibid.*, Clause IX.
5. *Ibid.*, Clause X. This was a late concession to House of Commons criticism by Lord Morpeth. *Hansard.* 3rd series XCVIII, 5 May 1848, p. 874. No borough nor part of one could be put in the district of another borough without its consent except for main sewerage.
6. *Ibid.*, Clauses XII, XIII, XX-XXX. The vote was taken by ballot papers left at the voters' houses, as in the Poor Law.
7. *Ibid.*, Clause L.
8. *Ibid.*, Clause XLIX.
9. *Ibid.*, Clause LXVII.
10. *Ibid.*, Clauses LIV, LXXXV.
11. *Ibid.*, Clauses LVIII-LXVI.
12. *Ibid.*, Clauses LVII, LXXIV-LXXXI, LXXXV.
13. *Ibid.*, Clauses LXXXII-LXXXIII.
14. *Ibid.*, Clause CXV.
15. *Ibid.*, Clauses XXXVII-XL
16. *Ibid.*, Clause CVII.
17. *Ibid.*, Clauses CVII, CXV, CXIX.
18. 7 & 8 Vict., c. 84. The schedules included detailed specifications for width of streets and alleys, and construction of houses.
19. Local and Private, 11 & 12 Vict., c. 163. Cf. **Lambert, Royston,** *Sir John Simon, 1816–1904.* MacGibbon & Kee, 1963, pp. 88-95. A similar Act covered other parts of London. 11 & 12 Vict., c. 112.
20. 10 & 11 Vict., c. 34.
21. 9 & 10 Vict., c. 106.
22. 9 & 10 Vict., c. 96. 11 & 12 Vict., c. 123. The 1848 Act obtained by Chadwick to overcome the resistance of local authorities in face of the cholera epidemic, empowered the General Board to undertake, by Order in Council, sanitary

measures, acting through the Boards of Guardians. But it also encouraged the reporting of nuisances dangerous to health (in 1846 by corporations, commissions or Poor Law Guardians, in 1848 by two householders with the confirmation of two medical practitioners), followed by a summons of the owner or occupier before the magistrates, and an order to clear the nuisance. In default the complainer could enter the premises, carry out the work and recover the cost by an action for damages.

23. Longmate, *op. cit.*, pp. 158–80, pp. 345–7.
24. *Report of the General Board of Health on Measures adopted for the Execution of the Nuisances Removal and Diseases Prevention Act and the Public Health Act, up to July, 1849*, HMSO, p. 23.
25. *Ibid.*, pp. 24–5.
26. *Ibid.*, p. 28.
27. *Ibid.*, p. 30. **Finer, S. E.,** *The Life and Times of Sir Edwin Chadwick.* Methuen, 1952, p. 345. Longmate, *op. cit.*, p. 167.
28. Longmate, *op. cit.*, p. 105.
29. *Report of the General Board of Health on the Administration of the Public Health Act, and the Nuisances Removal and Diseases Prevention Acts, 1848–1854.* PP 1854, XXXV, p. 46.
30. All sorts of remedies were tried by various doctors, including electric shocks. Longmate, *op. cit.*, pp. 75–82.
31. For working-class fear of doctors and hospitals (too often associated with body-snatching for the anatomy schools), for suspicions that paupers were being murdered for their bodies, or alternatively, buried alive, in the earlier epidemic of 1832, see **Morris, R. J.,** *Cholera 1832.* Croom Helm, 1976, pp. 101–8.
32. **Midwinter, E. C.,** 'Social Administration in Lancashire, 1830–1860. Poor Law, Public Health and Police'. York D. Phil., 1966, pp. 167–8. Cf. Dr Midwinter's book of the same title. Manchester U.P., 1969, pp. 86–7.
33. Lewis, R. A., *op. cit.*, p. 291.
34. *Report of the General Board of Health on the Administration of the Public Health Act, 1848–54.* PP 1854, XXXV, p. 14.
35. **Elliott, Malcolm,** 'The Leicester Board of Health, 1849–1872', Nottingham M.Phil., 1971, pp. 8–40.
36. **Hennock, E. P.,** *Fit and Proper Persons.* Edward Arnold, 1973, pp. 187–92, 210–23.
37. **Archer, Alan,** 'A Study of Local Sanitary Administration in Certain Selected Areas, 1848–75'. Wales (Bangor) M.A., 1967, *passim.* Mr Archer compares three Midland towns, one with a Board of Health, one with a Local Act, and one with nothing.
38. Hennock, *op. cit.*, pp. 61–176.
39. Midwinter, *op. cit.*, p. 148 *et seq.* Midwinter, *op. cit.*, pp. 82–6.
40. **Toft, Jean,** 'Public Health in Leeds in the Nineteenth Century: a Study in the Growth of Local Government Responsibility, c. 1815–1880'. Manchester M.A., 1966, pp. 82–3.
41. *Ibid.*, pp. 82, 206.
42. **Townley, W. E.,** 'Urban Administration and Health: a Case Study of Hanley in the mid Nineteenth Century'. Keele M.A., 1967, pp. 114–20.
43. *Ibid.*, p. 267, footnote 44. For Committees of Lancashire Boards of Health, and Municipal Boards see Midwinter, *op. cit.*, pp. 89, 94–5.
44. Archer, *op. cit.*, pp. 47–8.
45. **Frazer, W. M.,** *Duncan of Liverpool.* Hamish Hamilton, 1947, pp. 46, 53–5.
46. Elliott, M., *op. cit.*, p. 189.
47. *Ibid.*, pp. 123–5.
48. Liverpool's Inspector of Nuisances in 1847 was full time at £170 a year. Frazer, *op. cit.*, p. 55. Leicester before it adopted the Public Health Act paid the head of its police force an extra £20 to inspect nuisances. Later it paid a police sergeant £75. By 1873 it had two Inspectors of Nuisances at £100 each. Townley, *op. cit.*, pp. 191–2. In Hanley, a smaller town, the same officer was in charge of

inspecting nuisances, lodging houses, conducting the police and the fire brigade. Townley, *op. cit.*, p. 121. Adam Smith mentioned inspection of nuisances in a list of police duties. Cf. **Radzinowicz, L.,** *History of Criminal Law.* Stevens & Sons, 1968, Vol. iv, p. 204.

49. Midwinter, *op. cit.*, pp. 173-4. For further comment on pluralism and inefficiency, see Midwinter, *op. cit.*, pp. 90-91.
50. Archer, *op. cit.*, p. 61.
51. *Ibid.*, Derby Local Health Board had adopted the provisions of Shaftesbury's Common Lodging Houses Act, 1851, as by-laws.
52. *Ibid.*, pp. 59-60.
53. In the cholera years 1866, 1871, 1872, they rose to 1,280, 2,241 and 2,085 respectively. Elliott, M., *op. cit.*, p. 68, Table V.
54. *Ibid.*, p. 56. Joseph Whetstone was an active and public-spirited councillor, but jibbed at the attack on his own interest.
55. Toft, J., *op. cit.*, p. 207 and *passim.*
56. Midwinter, *op. cit.*, p. 111.
57. Elliott, *op. cit.*, p. 85.
58. *Ibid.*, p. 88.
59. **Penny, R. I.,** 'The Board of Health in Victorian Stratford-upon-Avon. Aspects of environmental control', *Warwickshire History*, I, No. 6, 1971, p. 11.
60. **Davies Jones, Tydfil,** 'Poor Law and Public Health Administration in the Area of Merthyr Tydfil Union, 1834-1894'. Wales (Cardiff) M.A., 1961, pp. 200-29.
61. Townley, *op. cit.*, p. 315.
62. The average cost of an application for a Local Board of Health set up by Order in Council was £88, for one set up by Provisional Order confirmed by Act of Parliament was £136. (*Report of the General Board of Health*, p. 39. PP 1854, XXXV.) The average cost of a Local Act according to the General Board was £1,627 (*Ibid.*, p. 38).
63. Carlisle had obtained plans estimated at £70,000 for a deposit sewer under its Local Act: a self-cleansing sewer could be built for £23,000. *Report of General Board*, p. 39.
64. Elliott, *op. cit.*, p. 43, Tables II and III.
65. The compromise reached was a £15 rating assessment for a seat. Townley, *op. cit.*, *passim.*
66. *Hansard.* 3rd series CXXXIV, 6 July 1854, p. 1296. The names 'Clean' and 'Dirty' party, corresponding to Whig and Tory, seem to have been Palmerston's.
67. Hennock, *op. cit.*, *passim.*
68. Townley, *op cit.*, p. 188.
69. *Report of the Cholera Inquiry Commissioners, Newcastle on Tyne, 1854.* PP 1854, XXXV, pp. v, 118.
70. In the eighteenth century the bodies of hanged criminals were given to the doctors' agents for dissection, and this was looked on as a fate almost worse than the hanging. For this and for the battles over these corpses, see **Linebaugh, Peter,** 'The Tyburn Riot against the Surgeons', in Hay, Douglas, Linebaugh, Peter and Thompson, E. P., etc., *Albion's Fatal Tree.* Allen Lane, 1975, pp. 65-117.
71. **Durey, M. J.,** 'A Social History of the First Cholera Epidemic in Britain, 1831-3'. York D.Phil., 1975, p. 301 *et seq.*
72. *Ibid.*, p. 344. Cholera became involved in politics. Cobbett thought it was being used by the authorities to scare the poor into submission; Hetherington in the *Poor Man's Guardian* blamed it on the poverty promoted by the unreformed constitution. But it did not lead to wholesale rioting as in Russia.
73. The problem had been largely solved by the end of the 1840s, bodies for dissection being imported from Ireland, and the anatomy schools being absorbed by the hospitals. Durey, *op. cit.*, p. 346.
74. Lewis, R. A., *op. cit.*, pp. 244-5. Shaftesbury answered Seymour's complaint that his suggestions had been arbitrarily overridden by saying that they were impractical. He also said that Seymour had attended just 5 out of the Board's

183 meetings. *Hansard.* 3rd series CXXXIV, 6 July 1854, p. 1298. *Ibid.*, 3rd series CXXXV, 31 July 1854, p. 988. *Ibid.*, 14 July 1854, pp. 234-9.

75. *Hansard.* 3rd series CXXXV, 14 July 1854, p. 234-9.
76. *Ibid.*, p. 242.
77. *Ibid.*, CXXXIV, 6 July 1854, p. 1298.
78. *Report of the General Board of Health, etc. 1848-54*, pp. 15, 23. *PP* 1854, XXXV.
79. **Lambert, Royston,** 'Central and local relations in mid-Victorian England: the Local Government Act Office, 1858-71'. *Victorian Studies*, VI, No. 2, December 1962, pp. 121-50.
80. *Ibid.*, p. 138.
81. *Ibid.*, p. 149.
82. Elliott, *op. cit.*, pp. 50-2.
83. Penny, R. I., *op. cit.*, p. 11.
84. Hennock, *op. cit.*, p. 105.
85. Davies Jones, Tydfil, *op. cit.*, pp. 196 *et seq.*
86. **Parris, H.,** *Constitutional Bureaucracy.* George Allen and Unwin, 1969, pp. 240-7.
87. Quoted by Jean Toft, *op. cit.*, p. 202.
88. **Stedman Jones, Gareth,** Outcast London. Clarendon Press, 1971, *passim.*
89. By the 1880s the aged Shaftesbury was in alliance with the housing philanthropist Octavia Hill in opposing public provision of working-class housing. See **Hill, Octavia,** 'Improvements Now Practicable', and **Lord Shaftesbury,** 'The Mischief of State Aid', parts I and II of 'Commonsense and the Dwellings of the Poor'. *Nineteenth Century* Vol. 14, July-December 1883, pp. 925-33, 934-9.
90. Hennock, *op. cit.*, p. 113.
91. See the fascinating description of cholera in the ports in Lewis Carroll's *Sylvie and Bruno Concluded.*
92. Elliott, *op. cit.*, p. 155. A curious hybrid theory now supervened. In the late 1880s a Dr Bakard attributed summer diarrhoea to the 'zymotic power of a specific micro-organism which . . . under certain conditions . . . would . . . be capable of breeding in the superficial layers of the earth, and of spreading from there to infect the lower levels of the air.'. **Simon, Sir John,** *English Sanitary Institutions.* Cassell, 1890, pp. 411-2.

8 Prisons: I

Crime and crime prevention

Many people in the early nineteenth century were worried about an increase in crime. In 1832 a Select Committee of the House of Commons presented some alarming figures. From 1810 to 1815 the number of persons committed for trial at Assizes or Quarter Sessions in a year had increased from 5,146 to 7,818, while the number convicted had risen from 3,158 to 4,883. During the seven years ending on 31 December 1817, total committals for trial numbered 56,308 and convictions 35,259. In the seven years ending on 31 December 1824, total committals numbered 92,848 and convictions 62,412. In the seven years ending 31 December 1831, total committals numbered 121,518 and convictions 85,257.[1]

Admittedly nineteenth-century crime figures had, and have, to be regarded with the utmost caution. A steep rise in the figures did not necessarily reflect growing depravity in the nation. Apart from underlying economic or social causes, variations might result from some sudden change in procedure, such as the Act of 1827 which provided for the payment of expenses to those who brought proceedings for felony, or the Larceny Act of 1847[2] which increased the summary powers of magistrates to commit children under 14 to prison for periods of up to three months. It might be affected by the repeal of some draconian statute which had hindered prosecutions because the penalties were inordinately severe, or it might follow a police reform which increased the number of thieves caught. Moreover, the crime rate had to be related to the population, which rose between 1801 and 1831 from roughly 11,000,000 to 16,500,000 in the United Kingdom.[3] However, these statistical refinements were no consolation to frightened people who were more concerned about the safety of their lives and possessions than about abstract percentages.[4] In any case, the figures confirmed the impression that crime was growing, especially in urban and industrial areas.

The census of 1831 indicated that London and the urbanised county of Middlesex had by far the highest proportion of criminals per head of population: 1 per 400. Next came Hertfordshire with 1 per 520; then Edinburgh, 1 per 540; Gloucestershire (suffering from depression in the pin trade), 1 per 540; Lanark, 1 per 600; Cheshire, 1 per 630; Lancashire and

Essex, 1 per 650. These were the highest figures apart from exceptionally disturbed Ireland.[5] They reflected the aftermath of the 'Captain Swing' revolt in the Home Counties and the prevalence of crime in London and the industrial districts of England and Scotland.[6]

This impression of increasing danger to life, but still more to property (for the vast majority of offences were various kinds of thieving), continued to impart a sense of urgency to attempts to curb crime throughout the nineteenth century. But it was nothing new. The Law Lords and the landowners in the two Houses of Parliament had reacted to similar impressions in the eighteenth century by clapping capital sentences on ever more offences. They were still doing it in the first decade of the nineteenth century, when public opinion had turned against punishments which were seen to be self-defeating, and was beginning to demand a moderating of the severity of the criminal law.

Prison reform was, in fact, one aspect of a general revision of the methods of dealing with crime. The revision included a thorough overhaul of the criminal law including the repeal of the death penalty under Peel and the Whigs successively, on nearly 200 criminal offences, until only murder and treason were left as hanging crimes. It included reform of criminal procedure to allow defence counsel for those accused of felonies. It included the foundation of a professional police in the face of a Tory–Radical alliance in defence of the Englishman's liberty to be robbed without the intervention of a 'continental' force. All these aspects of crime prevention are dealt with in Radzinowicz's great multi-volume *History of English Criminal Law*. In this chapter it is proposed to deal only with the prisons.

The unreformed prisons

Theoretically there were two kinds of eighteenth-century prison; the gaol and the House of Correction. Gaols were intended for the safekeeping of criminals awaiting trial, and after conviction, awaiting removal to a place of punishment. Houses of Correction were intended to house those convicted of misdemeanours or other minor offences for which short sentences might be awarded, to keep 'sturdy beggars' and tramps awaiting removal, or putative fathers of illegitimate children in bastardy cases under the Poor Law. Gaols and Houses of Correction were often under the same roof, and tended to be used indiscriminately to house all classes of offenders. However, the distinction seems to have been more generally recognised than is sometimes maintained. The supervision of gaols lay with the magistrates in Quarter Sessions, and the Sheriff; of the Houses of Correction with the magistrates alone.[7] Newgate performed a different function from the Westminster and Middlesex Houses of Correction in Tothill Fields and Cold Bath Fields.[8]

Continued interest in prison reform was ensured by the decline of capital punishment in the second quarter of the nineteenth century, especially when this coincided with the piecemeal closure of the avenues of transportation. Even in the eighteenth century attempts to deal with serious crime simply by exterminating felons had been mitigated by transportation to slavery in the American colonies. When the dumping of criminals overseas was checked by the American revolt, the government looked for alternatives, and the first Penitentiary Act was passed in 1779.[9] This interest waned when transportation to Australia was started, but revived when the French wars made transportation more difficult. The Penitentiary movement first envisaged imprisonment as in itself a means of punishment for serious offenders, so that prison discipline focused the interest of reformers, and especially of those who wanted to promote prison as an alternative to capital punishment. Penal reform and prison reform were two aspects of one concern. An early Quaker-led pressure group was entitled 'The Society for the Diffusion of Knowledge relating to The Punishment of Death and the Improvement of Prison Discipline'.[10]

The demand for prison reform began well back in the eighteenth century, being stimulated by the exposures of the occasional middle- or upper-class victim of the criminal law. A fashionable London minister such as William Dodd or an erring nobleman such as Edward Gibbon Wakefield aroused the public conscience which the fate of scores of obscure and inarticulate individuals could not touch.[11] Moreover, there were occasional public scandals, when the endemic gaol fever (a kind of typhus) engendered by the filth and squalor of the prisons was carried into court and fatally infected judge, jury and witnesses.[12] The eighteenth-century collapse in administration was nowhere more apparent than in the management of prisons. The Webbs attributed this largely to the turning of gaols into private profit-making businesses; but the worst abuses seem to have been caused not by the hiring out of prisoners' labour but by the system of fees. The magistrates contracted the prisons to gaolers, who found it easier to make a profit by selling the necessaries of life to their (literally) captive customers than by making them work. In fact the prevalent complaint among reformers was not of overwork but of idleness.

In prisons money could buy everything, from private accommodation in the gaoler's house to a separate room on the master-side of the prison, with food, wine and women. Lack of money would mean imprisonment in the common-side, without food, fire, bedding, privacy, washing facilities or medical attention. In Newgate coals, candles, plates and cutlery all had to be paid for.[13] The fees for all these necessities (sanctioned by the magistrates) could be extorted by denying prisoners their letters and visitors, clapping them in heavy irons, or after they had been released by the courts, dragging them back to prison. The gaolers kept a tap for beer (water being lethal), and spirits. They allowed visits from wives and others, at a price, sold women, and encouraged the female prisoners to earn their keep by prostitution. In the unbridled search for profit, prisons were allowed to fall into disrepair and the inmates ironed to prevent them escaping. In Newgate they were ironed to distinguish them from the crowds of visitors. In the big London debtors' prisons where the regulations were less rigorous but even more permissive of extortion, prisoners could buy a licence to live 'in the rules', that is, in areas of varying size outside the prison walls. There was also a system of 'chummage' under which a prisoner could hire a private room, and then purchase the absence of whatever penniless and repulsive inmate was 'chummed' on him, i.e. thrust into the same room.[14]

In many county gaols there was a bread allowance worth $1d$ or $1\frac{1}{2}d$ a day. This did not extend to debtors kept in these gaols, who were supposed to be supported by their creditors. Poor prisoners sometimes shared endowments left by charitable persons, but to qualify for their share they might have to stand by the gate and beg from passers-by, which some of the poorest were too proud to do. John Howard, the prison reformer, complained that several Bridewells (Houses of Correction) had no food allowance and no work for the prisoners. The debtors had no bread, and their tools were taken from them lest the criminals used them to escape. There was also frequently a shortage of water. One gaol allowed only three pints a day per head for all purposes.[15]

Many prisons were filthy: Howard complained that the air was so corrupted that he could not travel by stage coach after visiting a prison because of the stench on his clothes. There was lack of light and air, because gaolers paid Pitt's window tax and therefore stopped up the windows. Dirty straw was laid on damp floors for bedding. Sleeping arrangements were always squalid. In 1817 the Newgate wards allocated to felons awaiting transport, which were built for twenty-four prisoners, had forty sleeping on the floor, including the children of the convicts awaiting transportation.[16] At Warwick gaol in 1812 the visitors from the Prison Discipline Society found an octagonal dungeon about 20 feet in diameter, at the bottom of 21 steps. Until 1797 this had been used as the night room for felons. A long heavy chain was passed through a link in the chain of each felon, the free end being carried up the steps and secured outside. There was a cesspit in the middle of the chamber, a stream at one side and an iron gate on top. Up to forty-five prisoners slept there. By 1815 this had been done away with and the prisoners had separate night rooms, but a similar dungeon was still in use in Bristol gaol.[17]

Where the prisoners wore their own rags and used the prison bedding (if any) the swarms of vermin must have at least matched those on the hulks, where washing hung out to dry was said to look as if it had been sprinkled with pepper.[18] The accumulation of filth was fostered by lack of sanitation. The King's Bench prison (mainly for debtors) was reported in 1815 to be overcrowded with men, women and children, and filled with smells from the sewers and from piles of dirt at the rear of the building, which the scavengers only took away when the quantity repaid the labour of removal. Urine was collected and stored in tubs for sale.[19]

By the 1830s such physical conditions were becoming less frequent in the larger prisons, although they lingered on in small borough or private-franchise prisons. As late as 1837 it was reported that Louth borough gaol was a dungeon 9 feet 6 inches square, with two straw-covered wooden beds and one pail. It held between ten and twenty prisoners, and 'when the door is opened, a stream of heat and effluvia pours forth which is insupportable'.[20] In all phases of prison administration, at least while the prisons were under local government control, up to 1877, the old existed side-by-side with the new. Although general trends in reform can be detected they were never uniformly realised.

Even more than by the filth and disease, prison reformers were disturbed by the moral effects of prison life. The plan on which most eighteenth-century prisons were built, in a succession of courtyards flanked by wards or open rooms, precluded separation or privacy. The only private accommodation for the majority was in punishment cells, tiny, dark, unventilated cupboards in which delinquents were immured on a diet of bread and water. In Newgate even those condemned to execution, except murderers, were kept in crowded rooms.[21] The murderers were kept in solitary cells and visited by the clergy by stealth, since they were not supposed to enjoy the offices of religion (presumably lest promises of consolation in the next life should weaken the deterrent effects of hanging). Other condemned convicts were kept in cells 8 feet by 6 feet three or four to a cell. Presumably most of these could expect to be reprieved and transported. Yet according to Gibbon Wakefield the condemned were kindly treated, regarded as important people, and even apparently envied by the other criminals.[22] The pre–execution-day Sunday service, when the condemned were exhibited and preached at in the pit of the chapel with a coffin in their midst, was an attraction to London sightseers.

In these crowded conditions old and young, male and female, hardened criminals and first offenders, debtors, thieves and murderers, convicted and untried, were mixed in indiscriminate association. The young and comparatively innocent were contaminated by those hardened in crime,[23] while new prisoners, especially those unknown to the members of the local criminal gangs who were the regular occupants, suffered from a double set of extortions, from the turnkeys and from their fellow prisoners.

As well as gaol fees newcomers in Newgate had to pay 'garnish' or drink money to the other inmates. Howard noted that the garnish was spent in riot and drunkennesss. Gaolers also extorted extra money, and those who did not pay were loaded with irons.[24] Newcomers could expect to be attacked and robbed by their companions. There was gambling of all kinds, with cards, dice, Mississipi and Portobello tables, billiards, fives, tennis, and the like. The latter sound innocent enough pastimes, and Howard hastened to add that he was no enemy to diverting exercise, but there was riot, brawling and profaneness.[25] Since Newgate was a collecting centre for the London criminal courts, prisoners were walked in from the provincial gaols, heavily ironed and chained together. Once there, men and women were shut up together in the same room for days and nights on end. Their shrieks and outcries could be heard outside the gaol.[26]

The Marshalsea debtors' prison was run largely by its inmates. Newcomers paid fees (men 8s, women 5s 6d) for entry to the common room, the right to boil water and cook their dinner on the fire, and to read the newspapers. A Society of Collegians with a chairman and committee of nine, nominating a secretary, a master of the ale room and a paid scavenger, met weekly to administer the funds thus collected.[27] But this civilised arrangement was only a constitutionalised reflection of the fact that all the large unreformed prisons were dominated by the stronger prisoners. These often occupied privileged positions as wardsmen or monitors. In Cold Bath Fields, the Middlesex House of Correction, such places were purchased from the turnkeys, and the yardsmen then obtained control of the food supply and made money by selling provisions. In Newgate unpopular prisoners or those who couldn't pay garnish were subjected to a mock trial before a jury and a judge wearing a knotted handkerchief on his head as a wig. Acquittal could be secured by a bribe, but the 'guilty' were punished by having their heads thrust through the legs of a chair and their arms tied to its back.[28] In Cold Bath Fields prisoners who complained of being attacked or robbed were compelled to run a gauntlet of knotted ropes. The example was set by the governor, Mr Aris, who was in the habit of walking about the prison with a knotted rope, and would seize some unlucky wight and beat him.[29]

The unreformed prison was a kind of inversion of the moral order, in which those who suffered most were the comparatively clean, honest, industrious and respectable. The thieves and prostitutes of the London gangs who belonged to the 'dangerous classes' might find in the prisons a kind of fellowship which bolstered their way of life and multiplied their kind. Reformers might pity the suffering but were affronted by the drunkenness, roistering and profanity. They thought prisons should be places of punishment, not of profane jollity. The committee inquiring into the London debtors' prisons found the Marshalsea rules ' indecorous and improper'. Some, no doubt, were 'fitted for festive meetings, in seasons of gaiety and opulence, but . . . little suited to the manners or necessities of a prison, where the property so wasted is not the debtor's but the creditor's, and where scenes of riot and dissipation are injurious and unwarrantable'.[30]

Bystanders who accused reformers of wanting to pamper criminals mistook their men. All reformers wanted to develop imprisonment as a suitable substitute for indiscriminate hanging, and wanted the prisons to be less physically damaging and morally corrupting but not easier nor pleasanter. George Holford writing in 1821 complained that the prisoner no longer feared disease, hunger, heavy irons and no bedding, but *proper* sufferings and privations had not been substituted.[31] Holford was a leader in his time of the penitentiary movement, which included many of the contemporary penal reformers. The attitude was common to all of them, although most marked in the Evangelicals and Quakers, those of a puritan outlook, who pioneered the early demands for separation and silence.

Early demands for reform: the classified prison

The demand for prison reform began effectively in the 1770s. Its most famous and respected exponent was the dissenting sheriff of Bedfordshire, John Howard. From 1773 Howard was touring the prisons, collecting the material for his survey which he published in 1777 as *The State of the Prisons*. In 1774 he had given evidence before a Committee of the House of Commons in favour of Sir John Popham's two Bills, for the relief of discharged prisoners, and for preserving the health of prisoners, which subsequently became law.[32] Howard, who eventually sacrificed his life to gaol fever on a tour of foreign prisons, was the hero of early prison reform, and immensely influential. But his expression of views was practical and vigorous rather than consistent, so that, later on, his authority was claimed by rival advocates of the controversy over the silent and separate systems of prison discipline. He certainly favoured solitude (at least at night) and prison conditions designed to promote reflection and repentance, but not with the single-mindedness of his contemporary, Jonas Hanway.

Hanway, a well-known philanthropist, was inspired by the dedication of the 'unfortunate' Dr Dodd's *Thoughts in Prison*, and by his exhortation 'as a *Christian* and a *Man*' to pursue the improvement of the gaols with zeal. In 1776 and 1781 he published two pamphlets setting out his ideas for solitary confinement as a means of reforming criminals.[33] These works contained all the essential features of what was later to be called the separate system, including seclusion, cell labour, and religious exhortation.

It is perhaps significant that these early critics of the prison system were Dissenters, who were not inured to the running of decayed institutions as were so many Anglican gentry, and of an evangelical outlook or moralistic piety which rendered them more sensitive to abuses than most of their fellow countrymen. They tended to look upon crime as sin and the purpose of punishment as the conversion and reformation of the sinner.

Another school of prison reformers, greatly influenced by Beccaria's *Dei Delitti e delle Pene*, was led by Beccaria's English disciple, Jeremy Bentham. Bentham added a detailed criterion of the efficacy of punishment, according to its certainty, immediacy, propinquity, severity, duration, etc, basing it on his psychology of motivation by pleasure and pain. To him the main purpose of punishment was deterrence through nicely graduated apprehension, acting through public example.[34] He wanted to reduce, or even to abolish the death penalty, and to substitute penal imprisonment; and at first he subscribed to the Hanway gospel of solitary confinement and religious exhortation.[35] But given the hope of actually running a penitentiary, he started advocating a regime geared to industrial production by prisoners working in groups. To Utilitarians crime was not sin but incivism, to be cured primarily by deterrent example and also by inculcating habits of industry in the prisoner, rather than by inducing a religion-inspired moral conversion.

At the end of the eighteenth century these two main schools comprised most of the thought on penal reform. In both there was an effort to reconcile reformation and deterrence, but with differing priorities and emphasis. Overt retributive theories (there was retributive *tone* in some of the upholders of the existing system as well as among the more puritanical reformers)[36] as well as theories of atonement, were absent from the British scene. To a considerable extent early prison reform may be seen as a product of the reaction and interaction of the Evangelical and utilitarian schools of thought.

The Penitentiary Act of 1779, drafted by the jurist William Blackstone and the social commentator Frederick Eden, included a clause which was to become famous:

> ... and whereas, if many Offenders, convicted of Crimes for which Transportation hath been usually inflicted, were ordered to solitary Imprisonment, accompanied by well-regulated Labour and Religious Instruction, it might be the Means, under Providence, not only of deterring others from The Commission of the like Crimes, but also of reforming the Individuals, and inuring them to Habits of Industry, be it further enacted. ...[37]

This passage smacked of Hanway, but the substance of the Act which prescribed solitary confinement at night, associated silent labour and exercise by day, hard and servile drudgery with a profit-sharing scheme, coarse food, prison clothing, cleanliness and religious instruction – the maximum health and the minimum pleasure – reflected the more moderate ideas of Howard. Although the penitentiary was not built, the Act served as a model for Local Acts and building schemes. In the 1780s the Houses of Correction were becoming crowded, and counties began programmes which resulted in forty-two new prisons being built, many with a proportion of separate cells. By 1791, when a General Prisons Act invited all prison committees to adopt the penitentiary rules, many had already changed from the fee system to salaried gaolers, and many had set up committees of Visiting Justices to supervise the running of the local prisons.

Thus the first phase of prison reform was not dominated by the ideas of Hanway. It was managed by reforming local magistrates, and it owed much to the Maison de Force at Ghent, popularised by Howard. It was also probably influenced by the contemporary movement for Houses of

Industry. The upshot was not a series of local penitentiaries but classified industrial prisons.

The schemes for classifying prisoners which became widespread between about 1780 and 1823, were described in the evidence to the Select Committee of the House of Commons on Crime and Punishment in 1819. Cold Bath Fields, the Middlesex House of Correction with 2,500 inmates, mostly rogues and vagabonds, offered a full classification table. The prisoners were divided into male and female, apprentices, conspirators, the disorderly, debtors, felons, misdemeanours, assaults, riot and bastardy cases, reputed thieves, rogues and vagabonds, and perpetrators of unnatural crimes (presumably homosexuals). The main prison occupation was picking oakum, but a treadmill for grinding corn was proposed. What this haphazard list really meant, apart from a tribute of lip service to the principle of classification, is difficult to say; the appointment of the reforming governor, Chesterton, was still ten years away, and there were insufficient courtyards to do more than separate men from women.[38] A more genuine example was Bury gaol, at this time something of a model prison. It had ten separate classes: (1) male debtors; (2) female juvenile offenders; (3) King's evidences (who had to be separated from those against whom they had testified); (4) male transports and felons; (5) male misdemeanours; (6) males on trial for felonies; (7) male juvenile offenders; (8) males on trial for misdemeanours; (9) female debtors; (10) females on trial for felonies. There was also some attempt at sub-classification according to conduct and character, since the preservation of the comparatively innocent from contamination by hardened criminals was the stated purpose of classification. For those sentenced to hard labour there was a corn-grinding treadmill. The women did spinning and washing. Some prisoners worked at their own trades, while others could learn weaving or straw plaiting. The untried could keep what they earned, and there was a shop for display of the goods made. The profits from the corn mill were divided, 2s 3d to the county, 1s 5d to the governor, 2s 5d to the prisoners. The governor reported with some pride that two poachers had learned basket making, and went out with new suits and £6 or £7 each. Bury paid much attention to cleanliness, employed a prisoner as schoolmaster, and had plans to extend its buildings on the radial model of Ghent. Indeed, the influence of the Maison de Force was evident in that silence was already being enforced. The governor said that it induced reflection and the desire to work and to read.[39]

Less of a model but perhaps more typical was Preston House of Correction, which employed its inmates in picking cotton for the nearby mills, and in weaving. On discharge they received one-half of their earnings. There was some classification but, as yet, no enforced silence.[40] It was said to be 'a scene of active and much too cheerful industry',[41] with very lax discipline; yet it claimed a low recommittal rate.

By modern standards this first phase of prison reform, which produced the classified industrial prison with elementary handicraft training, profit-sharing schemes, supplementary payments by the magistrates to discharged prisoners who could prove they had held employment and pursued honest courses a year after their release, attention to hygiene, and rudimentary efforts at education, was a not unenlightened nor unhopeful era. Very little research attention has been given to it, and it would be interesting to know how many prisons were affected and how many were genuinely reformed. It received government accolade in 1823, when Peel's Prison Act summarised its philosophy as: 'Due Classification, Inspection, Regular Labour and Employment, and Religious and Moral Instruction'.[42] The Act ordered that men and women were to be confined separately, each in five different classes in every gaol and House of Correction. Those sentenced to hard labour were to work ten hours a day, excluding meals. There were to be prayers every morning, and instruction in reading and writing. Regulations were laid down for diet, prison dress, exercise, the suppression of alcohol, gaming and garnish. The duties of chaplains (salaried at up to £250 in prisons with more than 200 inmates) and surgeons were specified. Prisoners were to have a share of the net profits of their earnings or an allowance, as well as a sufficient grant to get them home on release.

The Prison Act was evidently intended to generalise the industrial reformed prison in the face of much evidence of continuing abuses in places still untouched by reform. Yet there were many factors working against the success of this kind of reformed regime. There were the protests of local craftsmen who felt their livelihood was threatened by prison competition. Largely for this reason the industrial prison tended to die out, except where there was a ready market for its products, as in the northern spinning mills. There was the growing uselessness of many kinds of semi-skilled handwork with which machines could compete, together with the strong public feeling that criminals ought not to be put in a more eligible position than honest persons by being educated or taught a skilled trade. And this, encouraged by dismay at the growing incidence of crime, fostered the reaction towards the deterrent view of imprisonment that it should constitute an example of punishment, and not a scene of 'cheerful industry'.[43] Indeed, this view was already being enforced with the growing imposition of silence.

Unfortunately, eighteenth-century reforms were usually counter-balanced by the growth of abuses. The prison hulks, established in 1779 as a purely temporary expedient, to house convicts who could not be sent to America, and employ them in dredging and cleansing the Thames, multiplied and became permanent. In these cramped and decaying vessels proper supervision, classification and hygiene were all impossible. Administered by the Capper family, uncle and nephew, who fed their superiors on optimistic reports and neglected their charge, every abuse of the unreformed prisons from vermin to prison 'bosses' perpetuated itself.[44] The hulks, denounced by successive Select Committees, yet outside the main stream of reform, were untouched by Peel's Act of 1823.

Panopticon frustrated

In the era of the classified industrial prison, the penitentiary idea was never quite forgotten. The sheriff of Gloucester, Sir George Onesiphorus Paul, inspired and helped to manage a borough gaol, opened in 1791 especially to realise the system of discipline proposed by the Penitentiary Act of 1779. The regime was based on separation at night (in night cells) and separate cell labour by day (in day cells), at occupations which could be carried out alone. There was prison diet, no earnings, limited education for the reading of tracts, and frequent religious services, in a partitioned chapel.[45] The prison became a terror to the neighbourhood. It had been preceded by Horsham and Petworth prisons on the estates of the Duke of Richmond, under Howard's advice. Gloucester was opened at about the same time that Bentham stepped in with his offer to carry out the Penitentiary Act by building and managing a prison under government contract.

The story of Bentham's frustrated attempt to build Panopticon Prison has been told in detail by Gertrude Himmelfarb in an essay entitled 'The Haunted House of Jeremy Bentham'.[46] Dr Himmelfarb has made the case that Bentham's high-sounding plans for prison reform were little more than a cover-up for a penal establishment of convict labour from which he expected to derive a handsome profit. It is impossible to disagree with this interpretation of Bentham's motives and with the disagreeable light it throws on his character. Bentham undoubtedly intended the building – for which it took him over five years to find a site – to house large stone- and wood-polishing machines invented by his brother Samuel, to be operated by the inmates. The whining tones in which he criticised George III who failed to sign the contract, and other ministers – such as Pitt – who failed to support him, suggest frustrated hopes of a fortune far more than disappointed public spirit. On the other hand, the Panopticon plan must be seen as an example of the contemporary industrial prison. If Bentham intended to make a profit, it was done by other prison keepers, and forced labour was less likely to be abusive than a system of fees. The idea of permitting – or persuading – discharged prisoners to continue in employment at the prison factory was enthusiastically endorsed by Colquhoun, the London police reformer and ally of Bentham, who supported Panopticon before the Select Committee of 1798.[47] The final defeat of Panopticon was not due to George III nor the hesitations of ministers, but to the planned opposition of what may be called the Penitentiary Party. At the Select Committee of 1811 Bentham was faced by George Holford in the chair and Sir George Paul and the Rev. John Becher as leading witnesses; a combination which lends some substance to his complaint that the Committee had been got together to defeat Panopticon.[48] The Committee fully realised that Bentham planned an industrial prison for his own profit, and did not consider that this met the intentions of the Penitentiary Act.[49] They dismissed his proposed safeguards with contempt. The promises to pay fines for escapes, reconvictions, and deaths above the existing average in the London area were too flimsy to deserve consideration. The safeguard of 'inspection' by the curious public was rightly pointed out as an old-fashioned remedy already tried and found useless.[50] Instead, Holford proposed government inspectors – reporting to the Home Office – several years before Bentham took up the idea in his *Constitutional Code*.[51] But the fundamental objection was to any prison depending on industrial profit. The group industry (and possibly night work) proposed by Bentham would destroy both the solitude required for reflection and the priority which ought to be given to religious exhortation and instruction. Sir George Paul was the fatal witness; it is more difficult to understand the reasons for the virulent tone of the criticism voiced by Becher, whose regime at Southwell of prisoners working in small groups was not unlike that proposed for Panopticon. Perhaps jealousy of Bentham's known hostility to the established church was at work.[52] In any case, not only was Bentham defeated; his site and his project (subject to £20,000 compensation) were taken over by the inheritors of Howard and Hanway. Millbank, with Holford and Becher on the committee, signified that the future of prison reform lay not in classified or group industry but with separation and religious instruction.

Early penitentiaries: Millbank

A curious feature of the drive for solitary confinement with religious instruction was the way in which, even when a new prison was to be built, practical planning lagged behind the harshly formulated doctrine. Millbank, opened in 1816 as a Penitentiary House for London and Middlesex under a voluntary committee of management, adopted a two-stage discipline, of which the first stage represented the ideas of Sir George Onesiphorus Paul, and the second stage those of the Rev. John Becher. The prisoner would spend the first half of his sentence in solitude, with cell labour and frequent religious instruction. The second half he would spend in some kind of associated productive labour.[53] Yet the regime never contemplated a period of complete solitary confinement. Four times a day in summer, and twice in winter, each prisoner would spend half an hour on the treadwheel, grinding corn or pumping water, followed by a quarter of an hour's exercise, during which he would be allowed to converse with a walking partner.[54] Millbank offered a classification system in its six pentagons, surrounded by an octagonal wall. The second-stage prisoners were occupied as in an industrial prison. Millbank was a kind of transitional hybrid. The pentagons, built with ranges of cells facing a warder's tower in the centre, obviously resembled *Panopticon*. Partly because of its marshy and unhealthy site, and partly because of this inconclusive planning, it was an expensive failure. It cost £400,000 to build, and when Fowell Buxton visited it in 1818 the foundations had sunk and the walls had large fissures.[55] The warders could not control indiscriminate communication between the prisoners in the infirmary, the chapel and the laundry, and as the cells were not properly ventilated the wooden outer cell doors had to be kept open while the prisoners were at work, and they conversed through the gratings when the warders were out of the way.[56] When this was stopped the prisoners communicated through the pipes and ventilators. During the second stage of imprisonment associated labour was hindered by the difficulties of finding suitable work. Fowell Buxton feared the prisoners were serving 'an apprenticeship to idleness'.[57]

Millbank had a bad health record. In 1822 there was an outbreak of scurvy attributed to unwise experiments in reducing diet, followed by diarrhoea attributed to the miasma of the marshes, but probably due to tainted water. The inmates had to be transferred to the hulks or released. When the building reopened in 1824 there were disciplinary problems and an outbreak of suicides, real and feined, followed by escape attempts and rioting. A late nineteenth-century historian of the prison, Arthur Griffiths, attributed all these troubles to the meddling of the Millbank Committee, and to over-tenderness towards the felons.[58] Flogging, originally prohibited, was re-introduced in 1826 to punish the rioters.[59]

After the House of Commons Select Committee on Secondary Punishments in 1832, the Millbank Committee set up a Committee of Inquiry, which reported that prisoners were instructing each other in schemes of vice and depravity, and recommended stricter separation.[60] The result was a tightening of measures to prevent communication (followed by cases of insanity) and abolition of the stage of associated labour. Millbank was now promoting the transition of penal practice towards actual separate confinement. A member of its committee, William Crawford, went to America, and on return reported enthusiastically in favour of this system. By 1836 suitable cells were being constructed in the prison.

Meantime an enthusiastic prison chaplain was taking seriously the Millbank Committee's intention of reforming criminals by means of religious instruction. The Rev. Whitworth Russell proposed three-hour classes in chapel each morning with the chaplain, followed by three-hour classes each afternoon with the schoolmaster, as well as cell visits from both. Fanatical, overbearing and insensitive, Russell had neither the character nor the judgement to succeed in such an experiment. He used his powers to punish whose who resisted him, and achieved mockery and disorder. When he appeared in the pulpit, prayer books were thrown at his head. When he said 'Let us pray' a voice replied, 'No, we have had praying enough.' When his monitors, who had to take morning and evening services, referred to Balaam they were greeted with shouts of 'Ba-a Lamb!' At catechism time the question 'What is your name' received the reply 'George Ward; and you know it as well as I do.' Joseph Wells wrote on his pint pot:

> Your order is   but mine is
> for me to go   that I'll go to
> to chapel   Hell first[61]

When Russell was appointed a prison inspector in 1836, his successor, the Rev. Daniel Nihil, carried on his work with equal zeal. In 1837 Nihil was appointed prison governor as well as chaplain, in the face of Lord John Russell's strong doubts as to the wisdom of combining the two offices.[62]

Nihil tightened up the administration and discipline of Millbank, achieved something approaching real solitary confinement, and imparted a religious flavour to the whole organisation. Warders (mostly old soldiers) were required to 'cultivate the feeling and demeanour of true Christians – not only for the sake of the prisoners under their charge, but for their own.'[63] They were rebuked in front of their charges, and dismissed for unbelief or swearing.[64] In self-defence the unfortunate warders conformed to the prevailing fashion and walked about with bibles under their arms. The prison was full of mock-biblical jargon, and the monitors became over-familiar and insubordinate.

However, the enemies of Millbank criticised it not for humbug but for cruelty. In 1838 it was alleged in the Lords that two young men had been kept in solitary confinement, contrary to the Act of 1837, until they had become imbeciles. Three little girls, aged 10, 8 and 7, had been kept in solitary cells, where they twisted their bedclothes into the form of dolls.[65] An inquiry set up by Lord Melbourne refuted these charges. The little girls, all at least 10 years old, and very depraved characters, had been in separate, not solitary confinement. They had had exercise twice a day, school, chapel and visits from the Ladies' Visiting Committee. Their stay in prison had done them good. The regime continued with increasing rigidity, although separation had to be limited to the first three months of each sentence. But by 1842 Millbank as a reforming penitentiary was overshadowed by the opening of Pentonville. Soon after it became a depot for convicts awaiting transportation or allocation to other prisons.

In view of Millbank's high cost and poor record, the appointment of Crawford and Whitworth Russell as Prison Inspectors for the Home District after 1835, in a good position to propagate their ideas, shows how strongly the evangelical tide of prison reform was running. By now silence and separation, the twin and almost undifferentiated aims of the Howard–Hanway generation, were attracting rival supporters. Both seemed better ways of preventing prison contamination than classification, which was felt to have failed. But the American reformers were trying them out as rival methods of prison discipline. The Quakers of Philadelphia had inaugurated at Cherry Hill prison a horrific system of total solitary confinement, while the reformers of New York had introduced in Auburn prison a silent system of equal harshness. Englishmen visited and admired most of them, returned and took sides. But if the American experiments converted a sufficient body of opinion to enable serious attempts at the new methods of prison discipline to be made in Britain, the ideas did not originate in America. As we have seen, the blueprint for separate confinement was British, while the silent system seems to have come first from Belgium.

The Select Committees and the silent system

Concern about the rising crime rate resulted in the appointment of two Select Committees, one in the Commons, which reported in 1832, and one in the Lords, which reported in 1835. The Select Committee of the House of Commons on Secondary Punishments, while demonstrating statistically the increase in crime, recommended greater severity, greater uniformity of conditions, central inspection, and greater summary powers for the magistrates, so that they could inflict deterrent short sentences which might be served in separate confinement.[66] The Committee envisaged total silence, which would render classification superfluous. Prisoners could be housed in separate cells at night (which would have to be built) and work in silent association by day. The Committee commended Millbank, but called for the completion of its separate accommodation, and the abolition of gratuities for good conduct.[67] It added a scorching report on the hulks, which was ignored.

The Lords' Committee was interesting chiefly for the evidence given by Whitworth Russell of the growing imposition of silence in prisons. His list of silent prisons included eight Houses of Correction and nine county gaols.[68] It was plain from both these Committees that a tide was running strongly for greater severity. Hard labour on the treadwheel (adapted for gaol use by the engineer Cubitt at Millbank in the 1820s) was advocated in place of industry and profit-sharing. Training which might make the lot of the criminal more eligible than that of the honest labourer was deprecated. The Prison Discipline Society wanted more solitude, no remission for good conduct, and a uniform stint of 12,000 feet a day on the treadwheel (regardless of the injury such exertion could do to the weak or ailing).[69] The attitude had been promoted by commentators such as that famous Whiggish wit, the Rev. Sydney Smith, who thought that the only work done by felons should be hard, dull and uninteresting.

> We should banish all the looms of Preston jail, and substitute nothing but the treadwheel, or the capstan, or some species of labour where the labourer could not see the results of his toil – where it was as monotonous, irksome, and dull as possible, – pulling and pushing instead of reading and writing, – no share of the profits – not a single shilling. There should be no tea and sugar, – no assemblage of female felons round the washing-tub, – nothing but beating hemp, and pulling oakum, and pounding bricks, – no work but what was tedious, unusual, and unfeminine.[70]

Only Elizabeth Fry (who had tamed the women awaiting transportation in Newgate by sympathy, prayer, self-government and light industry) and her cousin Thomas Fowell Buxton disagreed. Mrs Fry protested against the treadwheel, silence, and long periods of separation, especially for women. 'In some respects', she told the Lords' Committee, 'I think there is more cruelty in our Gaols than I have ever before seen.'[71] But she was ignored.

Both Committees called for greater uniformity in the treatment of criminals, and for that purpose suggested the establishment of government-appointed prison inspectors. As we have seen, the idea was not new, but it was much easier to realise now that the precedent of factory inspectors and permanent Poor Law Assistant Commissioners had been established. The immediate upshot was the Prison Act of 1835, under which two inspectors were appointed in the Home District (Southern England), one each in two other large districts in England, and one each in Scotland and Ireland, reporting to the Home Department. The inspectors appointed to the Home District (which included London) by the Home Secretary, Lord John Russell, were William Crawford and the Rev. Whitworth Russell.

From the early 1830s until the Act of 1877 under which the central government took over the administration of all prisons, the development of prison administration may be seen as a long, slow struggle to achieve uniformity of treatment and standards by means of centralisation.[72] This is a valid view, which does not conflict with the wider treatment preferred here, of examining the successive phases in the purpose and administration of prison discipline during the earlier part of the nineteenth century.

The separate system: Pentonville

The conversion of official policy to the separate system of prison discipline has been described more than once, and there is no need to repeat it in detail.[73] Crawford and Whitworth Russell, by means of a magnificent series of propaganda reports reinforced by letters to the Home Secretary, managed to convince the government that they could reform criminals as well as deter others from crime. This would entail a massive programme of prison building, and they succeeded in coaxing large sums out of the Treasury for a 'model' prison. Their plans for 'cellular' prisons designed for separate confinement were set out in their second and third reports, in 1837 and 1838.[74] The cells were to be built to a specification of 12 feet by 8 feet by 10 feet, large enough for each inmate to work as well as to sleep in. They were to be 'light', i.e. to have a small window at the top of the wall, and each would have its own tap, basin and water closet. To prevent communication, the walls would be built double, to a total width of 29 inches with a space between.[75] Unlike the

Millbank pentagons, the wings would be designed on Blackburn's radial plan, in a kind of cartwheel of corridors radiating out from a central point, with rows of cells facing each other across each corridor. Thus the warder from his central point could see right down each wing, but not into the cells which (apart from a peephole in the door) were secluded as befitted solitary confinement. There was really no need for the prisoner ever to leave his cell. But caution had to be exercised, since news of the dreadful effects of solitary imprisonment at Cherry Hill had leaked across the Atlantic, and resulted in an Act of 1837 forbidding solitary confinement in English prisons for more than one month at a time or three months in one year. So the Model Prison, Pentonville, was designed with partitioned airing grounds for exercise, and a chapel filled with steeply banked rows of stalls, partitioned so that the occupants could see the preacher but not each other. And the term 'solitary confinement' was abjured in favour of 'separate confinement' which (as was reiterated) was quite different in that the prisoner would work in his cell, would learn to read the Bible, have religious instruction, and constant visits from governor, taskmaster and chaplain. In fact the criminals would be separated from each other, but not from the improving influence of their betters.

Pentonville, opened in 1842 as a government penitentiary supervised by a government-appointed honorary committee (including the two Home District inspectors), was the first, and in many ways the most complete expression of the separate system. It was designed for 500 separated prisoners and lacked communal workrooms since there was to be no second-stage imprisonment here. Those consigned to it were to be young, fit, first offenders convicted of serious crimes. They would be kept in separate confinement for eighteen months, allowed to work as a favour, taught to read, bombarded with religious exhortation and finally shipped off to Australia, as free men on ticket of leave, or under restrictions, or to a 'probation', i.e. chain gang, according to the report on their character given by one of the chaplains to the committee.[76] Thus embodied, the separate system had become a carefully thought out and sophisticated means of reforming the prisoner by conditions designed to induce a moral or religious conversion. Crude punishments such as the treadwheel, crank or starvation diet were deprecated; productive labour was presented as a mitigation of solitude rather than a forced inducement to habits of industry; and by integration with the transportation system, exile to Australia was presented as a reward for good conduct, as the hope-giving prospect of a new life when solitude, repentance and religion had done their work.

Although the separate system had been propagated by the penitentiary party and was exemplified in Pentonville, it was never intended only for application to government, long-sentence prisons. While Holford had seen solitude as suitable for a penitentiary and hard labour as suitable for short sentences in local Houses of Correction, Crawford and Russell claimed that separation was equally appropriate to both; as an agent of moral conversion in long sentences and as a sharp deterrent in short ones. The inspectors had submitted cellular plans for various sizes of prison, and continued, on tours of inspection, to encourage the local building of cells. Moreover, it had been taken up by the authorities in some borough gaols such as Wakefield, Glasgow (an industrial prison with some cell accommodation) and Preston. Preston opened 150 cells for separate confinement in 1843, at the persistent persuasion of the chaplain John Clay, who however, soon found that the inmates had to be taken out for periods of silent associated labour in the open air.[77] These local prisons in fact had mixed accommodation. When transportation to Van Diemen's Land ended in 1846 the government was forced to look elsewhere for convict quarters. The careful selection of suitable subjects for the separate system experiment in Pentonville gave way to the indiscriminate allocation of criminals to the penitentiary without regard to their suitability for separate confinement. The government also began renting cells in local authority prisons for the confinement of convicts. By 1854 it was paying for some 818 cells in county and borough gaols all over the country.[78] But the very extension of the system undermined its force. There were already signs that the intentions of its pioneers were being misunderstood or perverted.[79] After the deaths of Crawford and Whitworth Russell, both in 1847, and at the insistence of Palmerston, the period of separate confinement at Pentonville was reduced first to one year and then to nine months.

The first, or missionary phase of the separate system did not last long. The piecemeal closure of the Australian colonies to convict settlement removed the element of hope which had been so important psychologically. The system failed to produce the many conversions expected of it, and those intimate with day-to-day administration reported that chaplain and governor had no time for constant cell visiting, and separate was in fact not different from solitary confinement.[80] Most serious of all were the alarming symptoms of mental instability which occurred among the Pentonville prisoners on the convict ships and the signs of mental apathy and degeneration among separated prisoners in general.[81] By the 1850s it was nearly over, even though its legacy of cell building was only beginning.

The advocates of separate confinement had always been a minority. The Prison Discipline Society was initially against it, probably because its Quaker and Nonconformist members disliked the growing influence of the Anglican chaplains whose power and position it exalted. The two other inspectors of English prisons, Dr Bissett Hawkins and Captain John Williams, opposed it.[82] G. L. Chesterton, the reforming governor of Cold Bath Fields, hardened against it. The layout of his huge House of Correction, with its open wards and constantly changing inmates, made separation impossible. Chesterton had introduced silence in 1834 and was now prepared to defend it, not merely as a second best, but as a positive method of instilling order, discipline and self-control into villains. He claimed that it was less unnatural than total separation, and equally effective in preventing communication and contamination.[83] Like other defenders of the silent system, he was sceptical of the exalted claims and the costly building programmes of the 'separate party'. He was not impressed by the counter-claims that silence in association was at least as unnatural as solitude, that its enforcement necessitated endless irritating punishments which embittered the prisoner and thwarted all hopes of a penitent state of mind; that the intensive supervision required perpetuated the abuse of monitors or wardsmen; and that it did not, in fact, stop communication.[84] Meantime, the outside public voiced a different criticism. Convinced by the propaganda of Crawford and Russell on the cosiness of separate confinement, they assumed that criminals were being pampered, and called for greater severity.[85]

The triumph of separate confinement as a government policy coincided with the ascendancy of the prison chaplain. Chaplains' salaries had steadily improved. At Millbank and Pentonville the senior chaplains were the only prison officials given direct access to the supervising committees without having to go through the governor. Also the fate of the convict in Pentonville and other prisons depended largely on the chaplain's report of his character. Inevitably there was friction between chaplains and governors.[86] Meantime, the success of the evangelical element in separate confinement depended on the enthusiasm and abilities of the chaplains; and this varied enormously. There were the rare conscientious and sensitive enthusiasts such as John Clay of Preston, several naïve fundamentalists such as J. C. Field of Reading, who had his prisoners learning chapters of the Bible all day long in their cells,[87] and mere authoritarians such as J. T. Burt of Pentonville. The clergy as well as the lay advocates of separation were divided as to its ultimate purpose. Many of them saw it as an efficient method of breaking the criminals' spirit, or will to resist the law. This smoothed its transition into a uniform means of repression in the second half of the nineteenth century.[88]

Sources and references

1. *Report from the Select Committee on Secondary Punishments. PP* 1832, VII, pp. 3, 4.
2. 7 Geo. IV, c. 64.
3. **Ashton, T. S.,** *The Industrial Revolution 1760–1830.* O.U.P., 1948, p. 3.
4. For a consideration of the difficulties of using these figures and an estimate of some long-term nineteenth-century trends, see **Gatrell, V. A. C.** and **Hadden, T. B.,** 'Criminal Statistics and their Interpretation', in *Nineteenth Century Society. Essays in the Use of Quantitative Methods for the Study of Social Data.* Wrigley, E. A., (ed.), C.U.P., 1972, pp. 336–386.
5. Evidence of Mr G. T. Bullar, Secretary of the Society for the Improvement of Prison Discipline, *Report from the Select Committee of the House of Lords on Secondary Punishments. PP* 1835, XI, p. 30.
6. Cf. Gatrell and Hadden, *op. cit.* They make the point that drunkenness was higher in Lancashire than anywhere else in England and Scotland, and resulted in violence which rose when trade and wages were good and declined in times of

recession. They maintain that offences against property rose to a peak in the first half of the nineteenth century and then declined as the country became fully policed. Theft resulted from real want and was at its height in times of unemployment, in contradistinction to the present day when crime is greatest during booms.

7. **Holford, George,** *Thoughts on the Criminal Prisons of this Country, etc.* London, 1821, pp. 12–15.

8. Newgate contained mostly prisoners awaiting trial for serious crimes, and convicted prisoners awaiting transportation. This may be one reason why it resisted reform for so long. Public opinion was always uneasy about the separate confinement of those awaiting trial.

9. 19 Geo. III, c. 74.

10. Founded in 1801 on the example of an American Quaker society for prison reform. It was later known as The Prison Discipline Society. See 'An account of the origin and object of the Society for the Diffusion of Knowledge upon the Punishment of Death, and the Improvement of Prison Discipline'. London, 1812. *Montagu Tracts,* 2149.

11. William Dodd was executed in 1777 for forging a bond in the name of his pupil, Lord Chesterfield, despite frantic efforts to get the sentence commuted. He was a friend of Dr Johnson and of Jonas Hanway, whose attempts at prison reform he encouraged in his last letters. He wrote a clumsy but moving poem about Newgate while awaiting execution. Edward Gibbon Wakefield was also in Newgate on trial for bigamy. He published a pamphlet, *Facts Relating to the Punishment of Death in the Metropolis,* strongly criticising the uncertainties associated with the many death sentences, in 1831.

12. **Howard, John,** *The State of the Prisons,* 1777. Everyman edition, p. 7.

13. **Griffiths, Arthur,** *Chronicles of Newgate.* Chapman and Hall, 1884, p. 358.

14. *Report from the House of Commons Select Committee on the King's Bench, Fleet and Marshalsea Prisons.* PP 1814–15, IV, pp. 5, 18. Is this the origin of the word 'chum'?

15. Howard, *op. cit.,* pp. 1–4.

16. Griffiths, *op. cit.,* p. 356.

17. *Third Report of the Society for the Diffusion of Knowledge relating to the Punishment of Death and the Improvement of Prison Discipline.* Section entitled 'A Visit to Warwick Gaol'. London 1816, pp. 3–5. *Montagu Tracts,* 2149.

18. **Branch Johnson, W.,** *The English Prison Hulks.* 2nd ed., Phillimore, 1970, p. 139.

19. *Report from the Committee on the King's Bench, Fleet and Marshalsea Prisons, etc.* p. 14.

20. Letter from Inspector Williams, 5 September 1837. PRO HO 20, Box 6.

21. Newgate had been burned down in the Gordon Riots of 1780 and rebuilt on the same plan as before.

22. Wakefield, *op. cit.,* (see Note 11), pp. 87, 93–4.

23. Note William Dodd's early warnings of this contamination:
> View the *young Wretch,* as yet unfledg'd in vice,
> Just shackled here, and by the veteran Throng,
> In every infamy and every crime
> Grey and insulting, quickly taught to dare.
> Harden'd like them in Guilt's opprobrious School . . .

Thoughts in Prison. London, 1781, pp. 51–2.

24. Howard, *op. cit.,* pp. 11–12.

25. *Ibid.,* p. 12.

26. *Ibid.,* p. 13.

27. *Report of Committee on the King's Bench, Fleet and Marshalsea Prisons, etc.* pp. 25–6.

28. Griffiths, *op. cit.,* p. 357.

29. **Chesterton, G. L.,** *Revelations of Prison Life.* 2nd ed. Vol. 1, London, 1856, pp. 18–19.

30. *Report from the Committee on the King's Bench Fleet and Marshalsea Prisons, etc.* p. 25.

31. **Holford, George,** *Thoughts on the Criminal Prisons of this Country.* 1821, p. 78.

32. The first, 14 Geo. III, c. 20 laid down that the prisoners should be freed in court after acquittal, and that gaolers should be forbidden to demand fees, being compensated from a county rate. Howard had been aroused by the sight of innocent prisoners hauled back to prison. The second, 14 Geo. III, c. 59. provided for the elementary precaution of periodical limewashing of buildings, and the maintenance of separate sick rooms and a prison doctor. But it was believed not to apply to Borough Gaols.

33. *Solitude in Imprisonment with Profitable Labour and a Spare Diet.* London, 1776.
   Distributive Justice and Mercy; showing that a temporary real Solitary Imprisonment of Convicts, supported by Religious Instruction, is essential to their Wellbeing and the Safety, Honour and Reputation of the People. London 1781.

34. **Bentham, J.,** *Works,* John Bowring (ed.), Vol. I. Edinburgh, 1859 or 1843. pp. 397–406. (NB. Some copies have 1859 in place of 1843 on the flyleaf.)
   Radzinowicz, L., *A History of English Criminal Law.* Stevens and Sons, 1948, Vol. 1, pp. 371–96.

35. In *Principles of Penal Law*, Bentham argued that solitude, darkness and hard diet were conducive to penitence, solitude encouraging reflection and being peculiarly fitted 'to dispose a man to listen with attention and humility to the admonitions and exhortations of religion'. *Works*, Vol. I, p. 426. In *Panopticon*, written in 1787, he proposed that prisoners should be secluded from all communication with each other by partitions. By 1791 (when a government contract for Panopticon penitentiary was on the cards) he had changed his mind, quoting Howard's authority for opposition to solitary confinement for more than a short time. Solitude was productive of 'gloomy despondency or sullen insensibility', and with darkness and a low diet was 'torture in effect, without being obnoxious to the name'. *Works*, Vol. 4, p. 74. Bentham now wanted to run an industrial prison.

36. For example, William Paley, another Utilitarian, defended the existing system of capital punishment mitigated by pardons and held *in terrorem* over offenders' heads. Since hanging for so many crimes against property left little extra sanction against murder, he recommended that in aggravated cases the criminal should be devoured by wild beasts.

37. 19 Geo. III, c. 74, Clause V.

38. *Select Committee on Crime and Punishment.* Evidence of William Adkins. *PP* 1819, VII, pp. 279–80.

39. *Ibid.*, Evidence of John Orridge, pp. 322–34.

40. *Ibid.*, Evidence of J. J. Gurney, p. 319.

41. **Clay, W. L.,** *The Prison Chaplain: a Memoir of the Rev. John Clay B. D.* MacMillan, 1861, p. 105.

42. 4 Geo. IV, c. 64, preamble.

43. Holford, *op. cit.*, p. 79. The objection to 'cheerful industry' was voiced by the evangelical reformers who favoured separation, and did not believe inculcating habits of industry to be a primary object of prison discipline. Holford emphasised the punitive and deterrent purpose of the gaol.

44. Branch Johnson, W., *op. cit.*, pp. 89–97.

45. *First Report from the Committee on the laws relating to Penitentiary Houses.* PP 1810–11, III. Evidence of Sir G. O. Paul. App. 1, pp. 23–32.
   See also **Whiting, G. R. S.,** 'Sir G. O. Paul's Reform of Gloucestershire Prisons, 1776–1820'. Geneva College, Indiana, D. Litt., 1973, *passim*. Sir George Paul was a considerable, and much more kindly reformer in the care of lunatics.

46. **Himmelfarb, Gertrude,** *Victorian Minds.* Weidenfeld and Nicolson, 1968, pp. 32–81. Bentham's correspondence and comments on the Panopticon Prison project was published in his *Works*, Vol. 11, Appendix.

47. Evidence of Patrick Colquhoun. *28th Report from the Select Committee on Finance, Police and Convict Establishments.* PP 1810, IV, I. App. D, p. 53. Nothing was done for discharged convicts, and the suggested further employment may be interpreted as forced labour (Dr Himmelfarb) or as a useful provision for their

livelihood (Colquhoun). Colquhoun stressed that, in any case, Panopticon was likely to be less harmful than the hulks.

48. *Works*, Vol. 11, p. 106.

49. The Select Committee asked what would happen when control of the penitentiary passed from Mr Bentham to the hands of some less respectable individual. It attacked the concentration of power to govern, supply and exploit the prisoners' labour in the hands of one person. *First Report from the Committee relating to Penitentiary Houses. PP* 1810-11, III, pp. 12-14.
See further criticism of Panopticon in Holford's *An Account of the Penitentiary at Millbank*. London 1828, pp. 13-16, especially footnote. Holford pointed out that Bentham would never operate the clause in the Penitentiary Act permitting the penitentiary committee to release early prisoners who exhibited extraordinary industry and merit – he would not want to lose his best workmen.

50. Inspection by curious sightseers already existed in the hulks and in Bethlehem Hospital and provided no safeguard whatever against abuses.

51. Holford, *op. cit.*, p. 22.

52. Becher commented on the impossibility of building a properly equipped prison for the estimate Bentham had offered – £18,000 with £12 a year for each convict up to £1,000 and £18 each in excess of that number. Becher accused him of planning a watch tower surrounded by cages, 'nearly similar to those used for the restraining wild beasts'. *First Report from Committee re Penitentiary Houses. PP* 1810-11, III, pp. 40-2.

53. **Holford, George,** *An Account of the Penitentiary at Millbank. passim.*

54. *Ibid.*, pp. 69-70.

55. **Buxton, T. Fowell,** *An Inquiry whether Crime and Misery are produced or prevented by our present System of Prison Discipline*. London, 1818, p. 103. Buxton represented the Prison Discipline Society, which did not approve of Millbank and its experiments.

56. Holford admitted this in his *Account of the Penitentiary at Millbank*, (p. 47) which tried to answer Fowell Buxton's criticisms, and was a general apology for the costs and administration of the penitentiary. See also *First Report from the Select Committee of the House of Lords on Gaols and Houses of Correction. PP* 1835, XI. Evidence of Rev. W. Russell, pp. 35-6. Joseph Adshead, *Prisons and prisoners*, London, 1845, pp. 221-4.

57. **Buxton, T. Fowell,** *op. cit.*, p. 111.

58. **Griffiths, Arthur,** *Memorials of Millbank*. Chapman and Hall, 1884, pp. 45-6. Griffiths was a prison governor under the Du Cane regime, when disillusionment with reforming experiments was at its height. He was also a writer of stories for boys. His accounts of Millbank and Newgate lost nothing in the telling.

59. Holford, *op. cit.*, pp. 239-41. Griffiths, *op. cit.*, pp. 129-132.

60. Griffiths, *op. cit.*, p. 138.

61. Griffiths, *op. cit.*, pp. 150-4.

62. Lord John Russell thought, 'the strict enforcement of discipline in a prison is a duty hardly to be reconciled with the consoling and charitable offices of a minister of religion'. *Ibid.*, p. 157.

63. *Ibid.*, p. 160.

64. One was dismissed after a prisoner had reported him for saying that St Paul took up several chapters in telling women what sort of ribbons to put in their hair; one for referring to a prisoner as a 'rascal'; a third for swearing and saying he considered it all humbug taking the prisoners to chapel. *Ibid.*, pp. 162-4.

65. For this controversy see *ibid.*, pp. 225-9.

66. *Report from the Select Committee on Secondary Punishments. PP* 1831-32, VII, pp. 7-10. Holford in 1828 had envisaged solitary confinement as suitable only for penitentiaries. Deterrent short sentences in county Houses of Correction would be more suitably spent in hard labour. By 1832 the idea of separation was becoming generalised.

67. *Report from the Select Committee on Secondary Punishments*, pp. 10–11, 12–14.

68. The Houses of Correction were Abingdon, Cold Bath Fields (Middlesex), Wilton (Wiltshire), West Riding, Brixton, Lewes, Horsham and Westmorland. The county gaols were Devon, Dorset, Hertfordshire, Lancaster, Northamptonshire, Bury (Suffolk), Nottinghamshire and Wakefield (Yorkshire), also Petworth (Sussex). The list was probably incomplete – but so was the silence. . . .

69. Chesterton, G. L., *op. cit.*, p. 155. Chesterton wrote that the task had to be reduced by 4,500 steps.

70. **Smith, Sydney,** 'Prisons', *Edinburgh Review*, 1822, XXXVI, p. 359. Smith was a forerunner of this trend. Quoted in **Collins, Philip,** *Dickens and Crime.* Indiana University Press, *PP*, 1968, p. 79.

71. **Henriques, U.,** 'The rise and decline of the separate system of prison discipline', *Past and Present*, **54**, February 1972, p. 72.

72. See **Tomlinson, Margaret Heather,** 'Victorian Prisons: Administration and Architecture, 1835–1877'. London Ph.D., 1975, *passim*.

73. See Collins, Philip, *op. cit.*, pp. 142–55. Henriques, *op. cit.*, pp. 61–93. I differ from Professor Collins only in taking rather more seriously the intentions of at least some of those who claimed to be able to reform criminals in this way.

74. *Second Report of Inspectors of the Home District – General Principles of the Arrangement and Construction of Prisons*, p. 21, *et seq. PP* 1837, XXXII. *Third Report, Plans for a gaol for 208 prisoners* drawn up by Crawford, Whitworth Russell and Jebb, p. 113, *et seq. PP* 1838, XXX. The *Fourth Report, PP* 1839, XXI, contains the plans for Pentonville.

75. For an account of the various experiments in preventing communication between cells, see Tomlinson, M. H., *op. cit.*, pp. 110–12.

76. Sir James Graham's official letter to the Pentonville Commissioners explaining this procedure and its reforming intentions was published in the pamphlet by **Burt, J. T.,** *Pentonville Prison.* London, 1852, pp. 264–8; also in **Mayhew, Henry** and **Binny, John,** *The Criminal Prisons of London, and Scenes of Prison Life.* London, Griffin, Bohn & Co., 1862, p. 114.

77. Clay, W. L., *op. cit.*, p. 282.

78. **Jebb, Col. C. B.,** *Report on the Discipline of the Convict Prisons and the Operation of the Act 16 & 17 Victoria c. 99*, 1854–55, HMSO, 1856, p. 1.

79. Some over-enthusiastic justices built or used cells smaller than those stipulated for separate confinement, without Home Office approval, e.g. Worcester county and Huntingdon, which the inspectors advised should not be sanctioned, as they were much too small. Crawford and Russell to I Mark Phillips, 3 January 1838. Bisset Hawkins to Ld John Russell, 29 December 1838. PRO HO 20/6. There were complaints of overcrowding and complaints that the larger cells were too expensive to build. *Ibid.*

80. In 1838 the Millbank Committee had informed Lord John Russell that if the chaplain were to visit daily the prisoners confined in the 76 cells, his round would take up six hours and incapacitate him from doing his other duties. The same was true of the schoolmaster and the governor. PRO HO 21/4.

81. It was reported that in the convict ship *Stratheden* 20 per cent of the Pentonville prisoners suffered from convulsions. Cf. Kingsmill, Joseph, *Chapters on Prisons and Prisoners, etc.* App. II. *Report of the Chaplain of Pentonville Prison etc.* 1853, p. 500.

82. Evidence of Captain John Williams to the Select Committee of the House of Lords on the execution of the Criminal Law, 1847. *PP* 1847, VII, pp. 281–8. Williams maintained that there was in essence no difference between separate and solitary confinement.

83. Chesterton, *op. cit.*, II, pp. 1–36.

84. For these counter-claims, see *Second Report of the Inspectors for the Home District*, pp. 2–8. *PP* 1837, XXXII.

85. **Carlyle, Thomas,** *Model Prisons.* London, 1850, *passim*.

86. Burt was made to resign from Pentonville by the governor following his pamphlet criticising the shortening of separate confinement and the changes in discipline

there. Tomlinson, *op. cit.*, p. 75, Footnote 1.

87. **Field, J. C.,** *Prison Discipline: The Advantages of the Separate System of Prison Discipline, as Established in the New County Gaol of Reading, etc.* London, 1846, *passim.*

88. Tomlinson, *op. cit.*, pp. 67–85. My differences with Dr Tomlinson are largely semantic. I have used the term 'separate system' to denote separate or solitary confinement for the purpose of religious or moral conversion. Of course the building and use of separate cells continued and even intensified in the second half of the century.

9 Prisons: II

Joshua Jebb and the public works prisons

The real architect of the nineteenth-century prison system was Joshua Jebb. This officer, after twenty-five years' service in the Royal Engineers, was appointed initially for six months to assist the inspectors in prison building. By 1839 he was established under the Home Office at £500 a year (to the £800 of the Inspectors for the Home District), and in 1844 he was appointed Surveyor General of Prisons to approve building and alteration plans submitted by the local magistrates, and also Director General of Military Prisons, to remove military prisoners from the civilian prisons to new military gaols. When Crawford and Whitworth Russell died in 1847 he inherited their influence as the senior government official in prison administration.

Although there was jealousy between Jebb and the inspectors, especially Crawford and Russell, because he wanted the salary and status of a full inspector and they resented his competition, Jebb was always an ardent supporter of separate confinement.[1] He contributed to the propaganda for the separate system, planned cellular prisons, and designed Pentonville down to the details of ventilation, door locks, plumbing and the compartmented prison vans which transported the convicts to the Model Prison. When the Australian colonies closed themselves piecemeal to the dumping of British convicts, he designed the public works prisons which took their place. He supervised the transition from the first to the second phase of separate confinement, or from the experimental and missionary to the routine system of the cellular prison.

Jebb in all probability never believed in the evangelical conversion of criminals, although he did believe in the virtues of enforced 'reflection' in solitude. He certainly considered separation a means of breaking the will to resist, and rendering the criminal more malleable to moral and social suasion. His view of prison discipline as a whole was more military than evangelical. In 1855, a period of some disillusion, he remarked that the number of criminals reformed in the strict meaning of the word might be limited,

> but years of steady and persevering efforts to instil moral and
> religious principles - to inculcate and enforce obedience,

> cleanliness and industry – together with the regular attendance at morning and evening prayers, and the Sunday spent in the service of God and in peace and quietness, must and do produce an impression on the character and feelings, and create habits which will not be easily obliterated.

He compared the discharged convict with the soldier, who was generally found to be more trustworthy and intelligent than the average man of the class from whom he was recruited.[2] These views must have been endorsed by many army and navy officers who in increasing numbers were entering the prison service. Jebb was not narrow in understanding, nor particularly harsh and unyielding. He discussed the social causes of crime, wrote compassionately about delinquent children, urged the need for better care of discharged prisoners, and defended the ticket-of-leave system against an angry and panicky public outcry. None the less, his rise marked the ascendancy of military attitudes and unimaginative common sense over the religious fanaticism which had tinged the preceding phase of prison discipline.

Jebb had to deal with the long-drawn-out crisis which accompanied the piecemeal abandonment of transportation. After the Molesworth Committee had criticised the practice, the government in 1840 had ended the old system of assigning convicts as slave labour to free settlers, and New South Wales thereupon refused to take further prisoners.[3] By 1848 most convicts were being sent out on tickets of leave, although Van Diemen's Land remained a penal colony. The Australians were furiously divided, the British government uncertain, and an alternative to transportation was obviously needed. The alternative, developed by Jebb, was the public works prison, to which convicts could be assigned after nine months or a year in separation, followed either by a ticket of leave to Australia, or a completion of sentence before release at home.

Under the Home Secretary's scheme of 1847 long-sentence convicts were serving their terms in three phases: separation, followed by a term in a public works prison, followed by transportation on ticket of leave.[4] But in 1853 Van Diemen's Land, which had failed to find work for many of the exiles, refused to take any more.[5] A system of equivalents was worked out and imposed under the Penal Servitude Act of 1853. A sentence of 7 years' transportation would now mean 4 years' penal servitude; 7–10 years' transportation would carry 4–6 years' penal servitude; 10–15 years' transportation would carry 6–8 years' penal servitude, and 15 years or over would carry 6–10 years' penal servitude. But life transportation would carry penal servitude for life.[6]

The months of uncertainty when exile in freedom to Australia ended but no alternative existed had led to serious riots and disturbances in some of the public works prisons, which Jebb minimised in his official reports so far as he could.[7] After a Select Committee, an amending Act was passed in 1857, under which convicts could earn a remission of sentence, but it did not apply to those sentenced to penal servitude under the Act of 1853. This unfair omission, which seems to have arisen largely out of confusion due to hostility between Jebb and Horatio Waddington, the Permanent Secretary at the Home Office, produced more outbreaks.[8] Meantime, a number of convict prisons had been built or adapted, starting with Portland which opened in 1849, followed by Dartmoor, 1850, Portsmouth, 1852, Brixton adapted for 720 females in 1853, and Chatham, 1856.[9] The main public works prisons were at ports where the convicts could be employed in harbour building or dock labour. Jebb designed them with mixed dormitory and cell accommodation, in wood and corrugated iron.[10] For the associated stage of a long sentence they were convenient (and removable) but hardly salubrious or secure. But perhaps the greatest advantage of the public works prisons was that between 1853 and 1856 they facilitated the piecemeal abolition of the hulks, whose inmates destroyed their old 'homes' with gusto.[11]

Local prisons in the mid-nineteenth century

The substitution of penal servitude for transportation was forced on the government rather than planned by it, but some positive rationale for punishment by imprisonment had to be found. The building of new local gaols on the Pentonville model, and the reconstruction of old ones, went on inexorably in the 1850s. Between 1842 and 1850, over 50 prisons were rebuilt or remodelled, while further alterations from 1850 to 1877 numbered 90 – some of them to the same prisons.[12] In almost all cases the work was to establish or refurbish large county gaols with a portion of cells certified for separate confinement, while the small borough and franchise prisons were closed. Why then, with the steam gone out of its religious element, did the drive to separate confinement continue?

Building is a long-term activity, and the impetus to build for the separate system, started in the early 1840s, although adopted slowly, was not easily exhausted. Nor could it be reversed until some strongly motivated alternative system of prison discipline came in which required a different arrangement of buildings. But this had not happened. There were alternative proposals, such as Maconochie's 'marks' scheme, under which the convict by hard work and good conduct would earn himself remission, and would be taught the virtues of foresight and self-denial, since prison luxuries could be earned in direct competition with measurable periods of earlier release.[13] But although Maconochie had some influence (especially in Ireland) no British government was prepared to legislate for indeterminate sentences to be worked out in terms of labour units. The idea dwindled into a mere reinforcement of the growing 'stages' system of earning prison privileges and qualifying for permitted remissions of sentence. The scheme of the City Solicitor, Charles Pearson, for a network of convict prisons deterring and reforming criminals through spade labour in the surrounding fields would have retained separate cells, and was in tune with the general call for harder conditions.[14] The punitive force of separate confinement had become recognised. Some of its frills or excesses such as the masks worn whenever the prisoner left his cell, and the separate airing yards, for which rope walks or spaced-out tramping round the prison square were substituted, were abandoned. The hand crank facilitated the combination of solitary confinement with hard labour, and prisoners could be forced to earn their meals by impossible tasks on it, as in Leicester prison. The mid-century mood was one of disillusion and repression rather than enthusiasm and reforming zeal. A period of separate confinement became an accepted 'short sharp shock' for short sentences and a harsh introduction to long ones.

A less publicised but probably more cogent reason for the continuation of cellular prisons was the fact that prisoners were far easier to control in separate cells, less dangerous, and not in need of constant supervision. Such an arrangement suited the governor and the warders, required less staff, and once the prisons were built, reduced their running costs.[15] So the rebuilding of local prisons on the Pentonville model continued, and what at first undoubtedly increased the differences between one prison and another, was to become after 1877 the uniform pattern for all county gaols.

What emerged from the ruins of the Evangelicals' hopes of reformation in solitude was a development of the old idea of a stages system. This had been the basis of organisation at Millbank in the 1820s and was now perforce restored in convict discipline by the need to keep serious offenders at home and employ them on public works. It owed something to the theorising of reformers such as Maconochie, Pearson, and Matthew Davenport Hill, the Recorder of Birmingham, who outlined to the Lords' Committee of 1847 the scheme of a special prison for reprieved murderers and violent criminals serving life sentences.[16] There they would endure a regime of restricted sleep on plank beds, and be loaded with heavy irons. Incorrigible thieves would be treated in the same way, but without the irons. Good conduct would earn shorter working hours, longer rest, better beds, and opportunities for education, although not to a level which the humblest member of society would esteem one of even tolerable welfare.[17] Hill had some liberal ideas; he favoured abolishing capital punishment, and proposed that the length of the prison term should depend on proof (unspecified) of reformation. But his sales talk of prisons as 'moral hospitals' did not disguise a harshness of tone which was common in the mid-century. This may have been connected with the peaking of crime in the late 1840s,[18] and was kept alive by outbreaks of 'garroting', i.e. robbery with violence, in the early 1860s when the total crime figures were declining. So advocates of a stages system proposed reversion to heavy irons or to repeated floggings, or to plank beds, penal diets, treadwheels and shot-drill in the early stages of a sentence.[19] The upshot of this general encouragement to severity was the institution of rigorous regimes in some of the local prisons, which, under the administration of a few sadistic officers and callous magistrates, produced scandalous cases of cruelty. The scandal uncovered at Birmingham, when a boy of 16 hanged himself after having been confined for days on end in a crushing strait-jacket for failing to perform a task on a hand crank which was beyond his strength, was only the tip of an iceberg. Birmingham – and Manchester City Gaol – had copied Leicester. There were cases of cruelty at Hull, Newcastle and Leeds.[20] The prison inspectors, now reduced to two, were quite unable to keep up with their task, and more such cases may have remained undiscovered.

The stages system

The practical architect of the late nineteenth-century stages system was Joshua Jebb, who introduced it first at Parkhurst and in the convict prisons. He described it in an appendix to his *Report* of 1854–55.[21] The new convict would be subjected to separate confinement, presumably in Pentonville or one of the cells rented by the government in other prisons. After six months' good conduct he would receive a badge entitling him to a visit from a friend, if he had any. After nine months he could have another visit. On transfer to a public works prison he would be immediately classified in the first, second or third class of the lowest of four stages. In the second stage he would be entitled to write and receive letters and to a visit every two months; and he would have an extra 6*d* a week added to a gratuities account already opened for him. In the third stage he would be entitled to monthly visits, another 3*d* gratuity, a better Sunday dinner with a half pint of beer, and tea instead of gruel for supper. In the fourth stage there was a further 3*d* gratuity, more variety in diet, and lights were allowed on in the cell for an additional hour. Each stage was marked by badges, but the fourth-stage prisoners also had a different dress. Bad conduct would mean instant demotion to a lower stage. A similar system was applied to women, who started their sentence, not in separation, but in silence, in Millbank. They moved on to Brixton, where a large part of the rewards offered consisted in permission to talk.

A rather more liberal stages system existed in Ireland under the direction of Sir Walter Crofton, the Director of Irish Convict Prisons. It differed from the English system mainly in the existence of an intermediate convict prison, where the regime was directed towards accustoming the man who had nearly served his term to living in the world again.[22] The two systems probably aroused more controversy than their differences warranted.[23] The real need was for a proper system of employment and aftercare for the discharged convict; which Jebb called for, but could do little to bring about.

The best that mid-nineteenth-century prison administration had been able to substitute for moral conversion through solitude and religion was a series of minor inducements to be good by means of punishment and reward, in which criminals were treated as erring children. Yet Jebb had tried hard to keep moral endeavour alive. The progressive stages system was nearly complete when he died suddenly in 1863. In 1864 the minimum sentence of penal servitude was increased to five years, but by Home Office circular marks were introduced, which could be earned by industry and good conduct to secure remission of part of the sentence. By 1877 when all prisons were placed under Home Office control, the progressive stages system had grown into an elaborate ladder.[24] The first stage entailed six or eight hours' daily solitary and useless labour on crank or treadwheel, a plank bed, no visits and no education. The last gave the prisoner a mattress on his bed every night (in intermediate stages it was allowed only certain nights per week), visits, letters and gratuities, instruction and library books. Somehow, classification, industry and earnings had crept back into prison life. It only remained for Jebb's successor, Sir Edmund Du Cane, known later for the secrecy and rigidity of his prison regime, to condemn separate confinement as an artificial state of existence, 'so absolutely opposed to that which nature points out as the condition of mental, moral and physical health, and so absolutely unlike that which he is prepared to follow on his discharge from prison, that it cannot be expected to fulfil the required object'.[25] When reform did come, the separate system would be seen as an obstacle to its realisation, and the prison cells (often now crowded with three inmates) as a hindrance inherited from the past.

The treatment of young criminals

Nineteenth-century criminologists were acutely aware of the problem of juvenile delinquency. They confused the issue and possibly exaggerated the numbers by failing to separate returns of children from those of young persons up to the age of 16, or 17, or even 21. Thus when in 1818 the Prison Discipline Society carried out an inquiry on young criminals, its secretary, Samuel Hoare, reported that 624 juveniles under 21 were convicted of serious crimes at the Old Bailey, and other courts, out of a total of 1,430.[26] A reason for this concern was the known existence of gangs of young thieves in the big cities, organised territorially by receivers of stolen goods. London had up to thirty of these, at Paddington, Covent Garden, Gray's Inn Lane, Spitalfields, and elsewhere. They met in public houses, the Spitalfields gang haunting the *Virginia Planters*.[27] William Crawford, in the 1820s a philanthropist on the Committee of the Refuge for the Destitute, estimated that there were some 200 'flash houses' or criminal public houses in London and Westminster. He distinguished three classes of juvenile depredators: boy servants; shoplifters and pickpockets, who haunted the shops in gangs of three, lifting handkerchiefs and watches; and older boys who assisted adult robbers and burglars. The pickpockets attended public executions, where they carried out their trade while the crowd's attention was riveted on the hanging. Most were orphans, sleeping out of doors, ignorant and wretched.[28]

Since there was no special public provision for these children, who were legally responsible for their crime from the age of 7, they went to prison. In 1813 the Prison Discipline Society found 123 boys of 17 or under in Newgate. In 1816 there were 247, and in 1817, 315.[29] Some of those under 15 were segregated from the adults in a 'school', but all were filthy and unclothed.[30] In Tothill Fields, the Westminster Bridewell (House of Correction), there were 10 or 12 boys under 21 confined with the adult felons, as was not unusual in prisons.[31] Crawford stressed that the newcomers were always contaminated, soon becoming reconciled to prison company, learning to gamble and to pick pockets. Although the proportion of juveniles was not, in fact, very high,[32] the evils were obvious, and hardly needed over-dramatising in Dickens' *Oliver Twist*.

Fully classified prisons had separate classes for juveniles, but in many gaols the boys were classified with the men, and the small number of girls with the women, mostly prostitutes. Possibly on the theory that they should be deterred early, they were, in some ways, more harshly treated than adults. In place of two years, boys might be sentenced to three or six months in gaol with periodical whippings.[33] Magistrates who believed in nipping crime in the bud would inflict a short sentence with a whipping to remember at the beginning and end; a practice officially sanctioned by the Larceny Act of 1847.

Severity failed to stop the numbers of young criminals growing. In 1847 the Governor of Newgate reported some 400 boys under 16 there out of a prisoner total of 3,000 in the year. In the same year Cold Bath Fields contained 83 boys and 2 girls under 16, some as young as 8. The boys slept in a long dormitory and spent their days in silence, making mats or picking oakum.[34] Before the 1850s when the adult prison figures began to decline, those of juveniles continued to rise.[35] This may well have been due to the Larceny Act of 1847 which gave summary jurisdiction to magistrates over children under 14 in cases of simple theft, and its extension in 1850 over young persons under 16. But the problem was not simply one of numbers, since reformers recognised early that keeping children in adult prisons was ineffective, and an abuse.

One of the earliest attempts to treat children differently from adults was made in Warwick Gaol, where, in 1819 the boys, both before and after trial, had a special regime. They spent six hours a day heading pins, two hours reading and writing on the monitorial system with a felon or debtor as schoolmaster, and they also did prison chores, such as sweeping and carrying coals. They had prayers or recreation – walking in a circle round a paved courtyard – for half an hour each morning and evening, and three-quarters of an hour at midday. Their work could earn them enough to supplement the basic bread-and-water diet with potatoes and other food. They slept two or three in a bed in wards of twenty beds. This regime, it was claimed, had a reforming effect.[36]

More promising, perhaps, were the attempts, dating from the eighteenth century, to provide institutions by voluntary agency in which delinquent children, and the children of delinquents, could be cared for with a view to reform rather than deterrence. Jonas Hanway, who formulated the principles of separate confinement, was also a founder of rescue institutions for delinquent and destitute children. He was connected with the Marine Society, which trained boys for sea, the Female Orphan Society, and the Magdalen Hospital. His contemporary Robert Young founded the Philanthropic Society, which in 1788 ran industrial schools at Hackney and Southwark, and a more prison-like Reform Institution for young offenders at Bermondsey. In 1821 it opened a farm school at Redhill, Surrey.[37]

The Prison Discipline Society supported a Refuge for the Destitute at Hoxton, which admitted male prisoners under 21, taught them a trade, and apprenticed them. According to Samuel Hoare, they were kindly treated and there was a rush to get in. In 1830 two more institutions were founded; Captain Brenton's Asylum for Boys at Hackney Wick, and the Royal Victoria Asylum for Girls at Chiswick. Brenton's sponsoring body was the Society for the Suppression of Juvenile Vagrancy (a name reminiscent of the repressive evangelical Society for the Suppression of Vice) which soon changed its name to the Childrens' Friend Society. These institutions resembled each other in their emphasis on early rising, close supervision (called 'inspection'), industrial training and labour, and book education sufficient to enable the children to read the Bible and profit by religious instruction. Since no government would contribute to this work from public funds, most of the societies were chronically short of means, and compelled to economise on the children's food and clothes. They never developed on a large scale. In 1834 the Children's Friend Society, the biggest of them, received 276 boys and 39 girls. It sent 213 boys and 37 girls trained in agriculture, handicrafts or (the girls) domestic service to be apprenticed in the colonies.[38]

The institutions had other difficulties as well as shortage of cash. In 1834, thirty-four children absconded from Brenton's asylum, four were expelled, and some of the older boys refused to be apprenticed in South Africa.[39] Moreover, the children could not legally be forced to stay in the 'refuges', although some magistrates gave them prison sentences suspended on condition they went into one of them. At Stretton on Dunsmore, an asylum run by the Warwickshire Magistrates, this last difficulty was overcome by apprenticing the children to the master. If they were caught behaving badly or absconding they were sent to prison with a recommendation for solitary confinement. Stretton, although well known, was small. In 1831 it held only thirty boys, mainly occupied in husbandry.[40] Other privately run institutions included Elizabeth Fry's House of Discipline for vicious and neglected girls at Chelsea, and Henry Wilson's School of Industry for young thieves at Woolwich.

These somewhat forbidding early refuges for destitute and criminal children (undifferentiated) were important as pioneer and experimental institutions, but they made little impression on the numbers of children in prison. In 1849 Jebb reported (quoting from a pamphlet of the School Inspector, Joseph Fletcher) that there were 12,955 prisoners under 17 years of age in the United Kingdom, including 1,431 under 12, and 2,912 between 12 and 14.[41] But the refuges were forerunners of the much more extensive reformatory movement which began about 1846 with the help of Charles Pearson, Matthew Davenport Hill and Mary Carpenter. By 1856 Jebb could list (in extracts from a pamphlet by Adshead) 19 reformatories in England and 15 ragged and industrial schools serving the same purpose in Scotland.[42]

Children were not always badly treated in prison. Dr Tomlinson gives the example of Major William Fulford, governor of Stafford County Prison, who told the Select Committee of 1863 that he had one boy so young that he gave him a little kitten to play with, and kept the children's gas lamps on at night, and their cell doors open because they were afraid of the dark.[43] But this was hardly the Victorian idea of penal discipline, especially in the mood of 1863. The state juvenile prisons, as they developed, did not err on the side of mildness. Moreover, magistrates insisted on sending convicted children to serve a term in gaol before they could go to a reformatory which, the reformatory party maintained, diminished the chance of reforming them.

Among the more sinister penal institutions, for children as for adults, were the hulks. In 1815 there were only 12 boys under 16 on them, but the numbers rapidly increased.[44] In 1823, 320 boys were separated from the men and sent on board Nelson's old flagship, the *Bellerephon* at Sheerness, where they learned verses of scripture under the direction of the Rev. Edward Edwards, a forerunner, it would seem, of the Rev. J. C. Field of Reading. When *Bellerephon* decayed the boys were moved to the smaller and more cramped frigate *Euryalus*, where many, considered too young to be transported, were kept sewing prison clothes and awaiting a ship to Australia when they reached 15 years.[45]

Euryalus became notorious for overcrowding, squalor, disease, bullying and moral contamination. The boys were locked up unsupervised all night. By 1835 there was a rough system of classification, with first offenders on the upper deck, second offenders on the middle deck, and the 'worst characters' on the lower deck. There were two daily periods for silent exercise: from 12.30 to 1.30, and after supper between 5.30 and 6.30. There were three hours in chapel learning reading and writing for each boy twice a week. According to Capper, each hulk had a garden on shore for the convicts to work in. Punishments were mainly deprivation of food, and flogging.[46] As stated by Capper these were much the same as the punishments in the more severe reformatories. But *Euryalus* had an evil reputation. Thomas Dexter, a shoemaker-convict, in evidence to the Duke of Richmond's Committee said he would rather see a child of his dead at his feet than sent to that place. The hulk was ruled by the 'Nobs', a set of older boys who terrorised the younger ones, stole their food, and took vengeance on any who 'peached' to the authorities. Efforts to get sent away to a hospital ship were numerous, including even attempted suicide and self-mutilation. Children put their arms on the edge of a table and got others to break them by dropping weights on them; or burned themselves with hot buttons and rubbed the place with soap and rum to make it fester. The reforming achievement was such that eight out of ten of those released returned to crime.[47] The hulk was evacuated in 1844.

The first serious attempt at a state penal institution for children was Parkhurst prison on the Isle of Wight. Holford had called for a special prison for boys, as early as 1821;[48] but nothing had been done until the Duke of Richmond's Lords' Committee took up the idea in 1835, and persuaded Lord John Russell to pursue it. Parkhurst opened in December 1838, with 102 boys transferred from the hulks and the London gaols, under sentences varying between two years' imprisonment and fifteen years' transportation. By 1849 the entry qualifications had narrowed to male convicts of 14 years and over, at least 4 feet 6 inches tall, and 'of a character so depraved that he would be sentenced by the Court to transportation if Parkhurst prison did not exist.'[49] Between 1844 and 1846 some 1,271 young persons under 17 had been sentenced to transportation (one-eighth of the total thus sentenced) mainly in order that they should be sent to Parkhurst. In 1844 Parkhurst held 31 of these under 12 years old, 75 between 12 and 14, and 233 between 14 and 17.[50] After 1846 the policy had to be changed because the numbers were becoming too great. When Mary Carpenter wrote, presumably in 1850, there were 622 inmates of Parkhurst, but after another change in policy more than half were 18 years old or over. They were all convicted of serious crimes, and considered to be a collection of desperate characters. Even so, those found incorrigible were sent back to Millbank or transported.

For the first two years after its opening, Parkhurst prisoners wore leg irons, existed on a 'low diet' which stunted their growth, and were compelled to observe silence when out of their cells. Even after the irons were discontinued and the food improved they were allowed no play except an occasional game at leapfrog which (as Sergeant Adams observed to the Lords' Committee of 1847), because it was permitted, they did not want to do.[51] It was too much to expect that in an institution founded when the tide of opinion for separate confinement was running so strongly it would not be applied to the young. All Parkhurst inmates were confined on the 'general ward' in cells for at least their first four months. If refractory they remained there for six or twelve months. They had two hours out in the day, for chapel and for exercise, walking round the prison yard. Otherwise they were locked up with knitting and a good book, alone apart from an occasional visit from the chaplain or schoolmaster. If considered of good behaviour (Baron Alderson asked how good behaviour in a cell was identified) they went on to learn a trade or perform industrial labour in association, were allowed leapfrog and gymnastics, while the juniors under 14 could play in the yard.[52] Much time was spent in school where, on paper at least, a curriculum comparable with that in a good National or British and Foreign Society school was available. However, it was felt that the boys, many of whom had drifted into crime by way of truancy from schools outside, did not profit. In 1849 education was reduced in favour of outdoor agricultural labour, which the prison chaplain thought was 'The best thing that was ever done for our institution'.[53] In 1853 the boys were still having nine hours' schooling a week, and if the chaplain's figures can be believed, making good progress in the three Rs and scripture information.[54] They were allowed a new library book each week, to read at meals and in spare time. There was a variety of industrial work, including the operation of a 93-acre farm cultivated by spade labour, with a farmyard and animals to be fed, and carts and implements to be repaired. All prison clothes as well as outfits for those released or sent abroad were made on the spot. A flax dresser was engaged to teach the dressing of flax grown on the prison land, and there was cooking, baking and washing. But the principal heavy labour was brick- and tile-making. In 1853 300,000 bricks and 85,900 tiles were produced, and 270 yards of lime burnt.[55] Again if Jebb is to be believed, the later stages of a term in Parkhurst provided a very reasonable combined agricultural or industrial and literacy training by contemporary working-class standards. But Jebb was good at making things sound cosy when it suited him.

Inevitably the prison authorities and the upholders of the reformatory movement clashed. It has been observed that Mary Carpenter did not scruple to attack Parkhurst in an unfair and partial manner.[56] She disliked all large impersonal institutions for children, being sure that there is 'no reformation without home, or love to touch the heart'. Parkhurst, with its walls and cells, was run like a regiment, with mechanical and military discipline. Mary Carpenter preferred the Mettrai system, where the large unit was broken up into 'families'. She also complained that religious instruction at Parkhurst was formal and mechanical. It was vain to look for reformation 'where the heart is not touched'.[57] Instruction was also too intellectual, and Miss Carpenter, like the Parkhurst chaplain, apprehended danger from too much intellectual training for the members of the dangerous classes. She proved to her own satisfaction that the boys' prison was a failure from the number of boys sent back to Millbank for transportation,[58] but she made no allowance for the fact that it contained the toughest young delinquents in the country. Jebb, of course, defended Parkhurst stoutly; but he occasionally expressed some doubts about its regime. He questioned whether boys between 9 and 14 or 15 ought to be so severely dealt with as they were in the prison, or to be branded as convicts when they had never had a chance in life. On the other hand he wondered whether they ought to have a better training than honest and well-conducted boys of the poorer classes.[59] But although he would have preferred a system of district prisons for boys under 15 run by unions of counties and boroughs (presumably on the lines of a district Poor Law school) he believed that Parkhurst provided a harmonious system for the real welfare of the young persons in its care.

Parkhurst invited criticism by its initial four months of separate confinement. Reformers had already questioned the suitability of this treatment for children. Mary Carpenter recalled that at Wakefield (second only to Pentonville in its enthusiasm for separation) 70–80 boys, some of them 10–11 years old, had been put in separate cells. They had soon suffered from physical debility and the premonitory sluggishness and feeble-mindedness which herald insanity. At Millbank where adolescents of 13–16 were immured in separate cells, the insanity rate was 4 per 1,000, compared with the adult rate of 1 per 1,000. There the boys whiled away the time writing their names on the cell walls, boring holes in the doors, and damaging the gas pipes and thermometers. Miss Carpenter found that separate confinement, like flogging, had a hardening effect on young criminals, who emerged from their cells bold, strutting and defiant.[60]

Others agreed with Mary Carpenter that separate confinement did children no good. The young had no experience to reflect on, nor capability of reflection. Even Whitworth Russell thought separation bad for children except as a short, sharp deterrent lesson for first offenders.[61] Some magistrates who preferred whipping to separation, would have the offender whipped and returned to his parents to keep him out of prison.[62] Matthew Davenport Hill made a practice of returning delinquent children to their masters or parents, under surety that they would be properly supervised and taken care of.[63] Jebb and the reformatory party were already both well aware of the effect of a bad home in creating young criminals, and they wanted children to be removed from the care of bad parents and exposed for long periods to a reforming regime – the parents or parish, or both, being compelled to pay towards their upkeep and training.[64] They both stressed the importance of aftercare. In fact, before the 1850s great concern was being expressed for the fate of delinquent children, and an inquest was proceeding on the causes of juvenile crime. Blame was cast on drink, bad housing, bad education, and bad literature, i.e. penny romances and cheap theatres.[65] But even allowing for Parkhurst it was the mid-1860s before special institutions for children began to make any real dent in the numbers consigned to prisons.[66] As in other aspects of life, good intentions for protecting children outstripped the practical reality. Sometimes the intentions have been misunderstood, as when the Liverpool magistrates sentenced a child of 7 to the borough gaol, 'doubtless in the hope of placing him in the contemplated Penal Reformatory School'.[67] Many of the savage sentences passed on children were probably intended to get them away from the bad influence of their homes and into what was believed to be the better one of a public institution. But the authorities had not solved the problem of juvenile delinquency. Nor have we.

The prison service

Prison reform required, first and foremost, reform of prison staffs. No regime of any kind could succeed with the venal and often hereditary dynasties of corrupt gaolers exemplified in Governor Aris of Cold Bath Fields. As in all public institutions inherited from the eighteenth century, reform was slow and piecemeal. Prison administration differed from that of the Poor Law in that it was not apparently reformed at a stroke by a revolutionary Act such as that of 1834. No large field of administration was ever suddenly reformed, because new regimes inevitably inherited the personnel of the old. But if the prison service reformed itself more gradually than that of the Poor Law, the change was probably more thorough.

The influence of government prison inspectors on the administration of local prisons was a passing phase. After the deaths of Crawford and Whitworth Russell in 1847 the prison inspectors were reduced to three, one of whom (Captain John Kincaid) was a factory inspector as well, and after 1863 there were only two. The convict and government establishments were directed by Joshua Jebb. After 1877 all prisons were centralised under government administration. Meantime the inspectors had been entirely inadequate to exercise supervision over the local prisons, which, apart from the tenuous and sporadic control arising from government inspection and approval of their building plans, had been left to go their own way.

The piecemeal change in the public conception of what a prison governor ought to be is shown in the history of Cold Bath Fields House of Correction. Here a reforming Justices' Committee as early as 1829 appointed George Laval Chesterton, a retired Artillery Officer reading for Holy Orders, as Governor. Combining to some extent the military and clerical character, Chesterton fulfilled George Holford's demand that the governor 'should belong to that rank of society, which will command the respect of his prisoners, and procure for his orders or admonitions that consideration which can never be created by the mere power to punish'.[68] Succeeding a line of corrupt and brutal thief-takers, Chesterton revolutionised the prison. Turnkeys, nurses, passagemen, all of whom had purchased their posts and were in cahoots with the privileged prisoners or 'yardsmen' to live in comfort by trading with and fleecing the other prisoners, were sacked. An ex-sergeant was installed as chief warder, the prison was reduced to order, and in 1834 silence was imposed.[69]

A similar process but at a later date has been traced at the New Bailey prison, Salford. Here a father and two sons had mis-run the prison from 1794 until 1841. By 1848 an army captain who had risen from the ranks into a commission was administering the prison efficiently.[70] The rise of the officer-governor was masked by the temporary ascendancy of the chaplains. But at Millbank the reign of the chaplain-governor the Rev. Daniel Nihil was an unsuccessful experiment. His successor was Captain John Groves, an unpopular martinet, who, however, smartened up the warders, had the prisoners' hair cut, and came out of an enquiry promoted by disgruntled prison staff with reasonable credit.[71] The new race of prison governors came from the officer ranks of the army and navy; not perhaps from the top ranks nor from the crack regiments, but from a cadre of reasonably efficient men, more or less gentlemen, devoted to the military discipline which succeeded the original evangelical ideals of the separate system. They gradually replaced the old turnkeys (later warders, and later again prison officers) with salaried and uniformed NCOs and military other ranks. How far this invasion of the prison service by the military went, and how long it took has not yet been worked out. But it is obviously connected with the developing character of nineteenth-century prison administration and discipline.

The prison service grew with the numbers of prisoners. At Salford New Bailey the staff rose from 16 in 1823 to 48 in 1864. In 1840–41 there were 38 staff to 774 prisoners, a ratio of 1 to 20. In 1850–51 there were 42 staff to 416 prisoners, a ratio of 1 to 10.[72] This improvement may reflect the temporary decline in the adult crime rate and adult prisoners in the late 1840s noticed by Mary Carpenter. Only a lot more studies of individual prisons would show whether Salford New Bailey was exceptional, or whether it reflected a regional or a national trend. As each prison was reformed and abolished its monitors and wardsmen, it demanded more warders, and this was so whether it was silent, separate, or mixed. The Act of 1839[73] forbidding the employment of prisoners as turnkeys, wardsmen and monitors doubtless promoted the demand for paid officers, even though the employment of prisoners as trade-instructors, schoolmasters and in other 'trusty' positions could not cease entirely. However, the smaller prisons were being demolished or absorbed by county and large borough gaols, and these 'economies of scale' necessarily restricted the growth of the service.

In the first phase of separate confinement, profitable industry became less of an object,[74] profit-sharing was discouraged, the governors lost their entitlement to the proceeds of the prisoners' labour, and staffs were wholly salaried. As in other branches of civil and local government services, salaries became important. In the 1830s the normal salary of the governor of a large prison seems to have been £600, of a smaller one from £200 to £400.[75] At Salford New Bailey the governor's salary was fixed in 1826 at £500, with a house and some minor perquisites, but with the appointment of Captain Mitchell in 1848 it rose to £750.[76] The governor of Millbank received £600 a year, as did his chaplain. The governor of Cold Bath Fields also got £600, but in 1835 the governor of Lancaster Castle was paid £1,000, his chaplain £350, the surgeon and taskmaster £120 each, and the matron and schoolmaster £60 each.[77] Despite the variations, salaries being controlled by the prison committees and local committees of visiting justices (as were senior appointments), they were roughly comparable with those of the government inspectorates. If the Poor Law Unions had paid similar salaries to the masters of the big workhouses, mid-Victorian Poor Law administration might at least have been more efficient. Curiously, the half-pay military gentleman could be attracted by something much less than his predecessor. In 1815 the Marshal of the King's Bench Prison (largely for debtors who may have been easier to squeeze than the common thief) had obtained – earned is hardly the word – the astonishing average net income of £3,590 a year.[78] The standing of this profession rose as its profits declined. There were still some perquisites, such as the utilisation of prisoners as servants. Whether the occasional gentleman prisoner could still buy or was afforded privileged treatment in some prisons requires investigation. The more murky aspects of prison life were less public after reform than before.

The payment of the warders or Prison Officers also varied. From 1834 right up to 1859 the warders at Salford New Bailey received 25s a week (£65 a year), less than a skilled artisan, although eight of them also had family accommodation within the prison.[79] In 1835 the warders (still called turnkeys) at Cold Bath Fields received 30s a week (£78 a year).[80] Dr Tomlinson makes the point that the pay and conditions of prison officers varied enormously, only gradually becoming more uniform as the century wore on. That the quality varied as much having regard both to the piecemeal character of prison reform and the generally low pay, is not surprising.[81] If there was corruption and cruelty among senior officers, how could it be different among the lower ones? The estimation – and the social class – aimed at seems to have been that of the NCO or the elementary school teacher, with whose pay the prison officer's salary was comparable. There were also growing staffs of salaried and sometimes pensioned deputy governors, chaplains, matrons, clerks and instructors. A detailed study of the development of the prison service still has to be made. Many prisons also had a voluntary ladies' visiting committee, a legacy from the days of Elizabeth Fry and her lesser-known contemporary, Sarah Martin of Yarmouth. These were tolerated with reluctance as meddling amateurs who made pets of the worst characters and neglected the better ones, and interfered with the running of the prison. On the whole the direction of development of the prison service was away from the corrupt private-enterprise gaoler of the eighteenth century and towards the hidebound public-service official of the later nineteenth century.

Conclusion

During the central period of the nineteenth century, prison conditions had become on the whole less sensationally abusive, harsher and more inflexible. Not until the Herbert Gladstone Committee of 1894–95 did a glimmer of liberalisation penetrate the thick walls of the system. In the course of the twentieth century it was to be transformed. Unfortunately the treatment of the convicted criminal has not proved to be the key to preventing crime; and as criminals persist, so phases of liberalisation and harshness tend to recur. The spectre of solitary confinement has not been exorcised.[82] The conflict between deterrence and reformation which ran like a refrain through nineteenth-century schemes of discipline has not been resolved. Imprisonment as punishment continues to be what it was originally, a *faute de mieux* in the fight against crime.

Sources and references

1. **Tomlinson, M. H.,** 'Victorian Prisons: Administration and Architecture, 1835-1877'. London Ph.D., 1975, pp. 237-44. Cf. Jebb's many reports and writings. I am indebted to Dr Tomlinson for interesting details of Jebb's career, including information about some of his architectural and building mistakes. His biography has yet to be written.
2. **Jebb, J.** *Report on the Discipline of the Convict Prisons, etc.* 1853. Eyre and Spottiswoode, for HMSO 1854, p. 23. Jebb supported the power of the prison governor against the claims of the chaplains to decide the fate of the prisoners.
3. **Shaw, A. G. L.,** *Convicts and the Colonies.* Faber and Faber, 1966. p. 312 *et seq.*
4. Shaw, *op. cit.*, pp. 320-1.
5. *Ibid.*, pp. 311, 321. There were also convict settlements at Gibraltar and Bermuda.
6. Jebb, *Report, etc.* 1854-55, pp. 11-12.
7. There were disturbances at Parkhurst, Portland and among the women at Brixton. Order had to be restored at Portland by flogging. Jebb, *Report, etc.* 1854-55, pp. 37-8, 61, 278.
8. This has been discussed in detail in Tomlinson, *op. cit.*, pp. 34-8. Exactly what happened is still unclear.
9. Dartmoor was an old prisoner-of-war camp, converted inadequately into a prison for invalid convicts. Brixton was built in 1819-21 and adapted for women prisoners in 1853. Cf. note 12.
10. Tomlinson, *op. cit.*, pp. 307-8.
11. **Branch Johnson, W.,** *The English Prison Hulks.* 2nd ed. Phillimore, 1970, pp. 194 *et seq.*
12. Tomlinson, *op. cit.*, p. 99. Cf. Dr Tomlinson's long and detailed table of the construction and alteration of prisons all over England and Wales. Apps. C and D, p. 431 *et seq.*
13. **Barry, J. V.,** *Alexander Maconochie of Norfolk Island.* O.U.P., Melbourne, 1958, pp. 69-79. **Maconochie, A.** *Report on the State of Prison Discipline in Van Diemen's Land, 1837,* published as an appendix to Barry's biography; and **Captain Maconochie,** *Crime and Punishment: the Mark System.* London, 1846; and Maconochie's evidence before the House of Lords' (Brougham's) *Select Committee on the Execution of the Criminal Law.* PP 1847, VII, pp. 91-119 *et seq.*
14. Mr Pearson's Report. *Report from the House of Commons Select Committee on Prison Discipline.* PP 1850, XVII, pp. xx-xxxvi.
15. For the Prison Officer's point of view, see **Thomas, J. E.,** *The English Prison Officer Since 1850: a Study in Conflict.* Routledge, 1972, *passim.*
16. **Hill, M. D.,** Draft Report on Principles of Punishment. Appendix continued from *First Report of Select Committee of the House of Lords.* PP 1847, VII, pp. 222-8.
17. *The Recorder of Birmingham. A Memoir of Matthew Davenport Hill, with selections from his correspondence by his daughters Rosamund and Florence Hill.* Macmillan, 1878, pp. 214-6. For further information on Hill's career, see **Bartrip, P. W. J.,** 'The Career of M. D. Hill'. Wales (Cardiff) Ph.D., 1975.
18. **Gatrell, V. A. C.** and **Hadden, T. B.** 'Criminal Statistics and their Interpretation,' in *Nineteenth Century Society. Essays in the use of Quantitative Methods for the Study of Social Data,* Wrigley, E. A. ed. C.U.P., 1972, p. 373, fig. 4.
19. See the Lords' hearty endorsement of separate confinement combined with useless hard labour, low diet and restricted sleep. *Report from Select Committee of the House of Lords on Discipline in Gaols and Houses of Correction.* PP 1863, IX, pp. iii-xvii.

20. Tomlinson, *op. cit.*, pp. 167-71. Cruelties included starvation, dark cells, and handcuffing women to their beds. The Birmingham suicide became a *cause célèbre* which was celebrated (and slightly embroidered) in Charles Read's novel *It's Never too Late to Mend*. **Henriques, U.,** 'The rise and decline of the separate system of prison discipline', *Past and Present*, **54,** February 1972, p. 85.

21. Jebb, *Report on the Discipline of the Convict Prisons etc.* 1854-55. 1856. p. 103 *et seq.*

22. The Irish System was described by Mary Carpenter (who clearly didn't like Jebb) in *Our Convicts*, Vol. II, Longman, 1864, p. 31 *et seq.*

23. Jebb was in controversy with Crofton.

24. **Hinde, R. S. E.,** *The British Penal System 1773-1950.* Duckworth, 1951, pp. 131-3. A pale reflection of Maconochie here.

25. **Griffiths, A.,** *Memorials of Millbank*, p. 465.

26. *Report from the Select Committee on Gaols and other Places of Confinement, etc. PP* 1819. Evidence of Samuel Hoare Jnr, p. 158.

27. Evidence of Dr Stephen Lushington, a lawyer of the Court of Arches, and a well-known liberal before the same committee. Lushington reckoned there were some 8,000 young criminals in and around London. *Ibid.*, pp. 162-3.

28. *Ibid.*, p. 169-70.

29. *Ibid.*, Evidence of Samuel Hoare, p. 159.

30. *Ibid.*, Evidence of S. Lushington, pp. 165-6.

31. *Ibid.*, Evidence of Rawlinson Barclay, pp. 167-8.

32. Gatrell and Hadden estimate that juveniles accounted for about one-tenth of the serious offences, adolescents about a quarter. *Op. cit.*, p. 384. There was some contemporary inconsistency in counting criminals of 20 as juveniles and factory workers of 18 as adults.

33. This was advocated by G. L. Chesterton, reforming governor of Cold Bath Fields. *First Report from the Select Committee of the House of Lords on Gaols and Houses of Correction. PP* 1835, XI, p. 96.

34. *House of Lords Select Committee on the Execution of the Criminal Law, 1847.* Evidence of G. L. Chesterton. *PP* 1847, VII, pp. 288-97. It is not clear from the text whether these were reconvicted. Chesterton also reported he had at least 100 prisoners under 16.

35. See arguments in **Mayhew** and **Binny,** *Criminal Prisons of London, etc.* London, 1863, pp. 384-97. According to Mary Carpenter, between 1847 and 1850 the numbers of adult criminals on the whole declined, but the number of juvenile thieves increased by 7 per cent. **Carpenter, Mary,** *Reformatory Schools for the Children of the Perishing and Dangerous classes, and for Juvenile Offenders.* London, C. Gilpin, 1851, p. 10. But Gatrell and Hadden state that juvenile deliquency declined markedly from 1841. Gatrell and Hadden, *op. cit.*, p. 384.

36. *Report from the Select Committee on Gaols, etc. PP* 1819, pp. 301-4.

37. **Pinchbeck, I.** and **Hewett, M.,** *Children in English Society.* Routledge, 1973, Vol. II, p. 419 *et seq.*

38. *Fourth Annual Report of the Children's Friend Society.* Printed in App. No. 3 of Part IV to the Minutes of Evidence taken before the *Select Committee of the House of Lords on Gaols and Houses of Correction,* 1835. *PP* 1835, XII, p. 397.

39. *Ibid.*, p. 397.

40. Pinchbeck and Hewett, *op. cit.*, p. 466-7.

41. Jebb, *Report on the Discipline and Management of Convict Prisons,* 1853. HMSO, 1854, p. 84.

42. Jebb, *Report on the Discipline of the Convict Prisons, etc.* 1854-55. HMSO, 1856. App. pp. 347-8.

43. Tomlinson, *op. cit.*, p. 215.

44. Branch Johnson, W., *op. cit.*, pp. 147-8.

45. *Ibid.*, pp. 148-50.

46. *Report from Select Committee of the House of Lords on Gaols and Houses of Correction.* Evidence of J. H. Capper. *PP* 1835, XL App. Part II pp. 258-9.

47. *Ibid.*, p. 318. Branch Johnson, *op. cit.*, pp. 150-6.

48. **Holford, G.,** *Account of the Penitentiary at Millbank.* London, 1828, pp. 310-39.
49. Sergeant Adams, quoted in Carpenter, Mary, *op. cit.,* p. 28.
50. Carpenter, *op. cit.,* pp. 293-4.
51. *Ibid.,* p. 318.
52. Evidence of Captain Hall, Governor of Parkhurst. *Select Committee of the House of Lords on the Execution of the Criminal Law.* PP 1847, VII, pp. 241-6.
53. Jebb, *Report on the Discipline and Management of Convict Prisons,* 1853. HMSO, 1854, p. 65. The chaplain thought 'that an industrial education, combined with Religious Instruction and training, and accompanied with a mild and firm discipline, is that which is best adapted, by God's blessing, to correct the vicious and to prepare them to gain an honest livelihood', i.e. he did not believe in a literary education for the youth of the Perishing and Dangerous Classes.
54. *Ibid.,* p. 65.
55. *Ibid.,* p. 67.
56. Pinchbeck and Hewett, *op. cit.,* p. 465.
57. Carpenter, *op. cit.,* p. 322.
58. She found that 79 boys were sent back to Millbank for transportation in 1846. *Ibid.,* p. 319.
59. Jebb, *Report, etc.* 1853 HMSO, 1854, p. 72.
60. Carpenter, *op. cit.,* pp. 299-300.
61. *Ibid.,* pp. 296-7.
62. Peter Laurie, barrister and magistrate of Middlesex and Westminster, thought a whipping post at every police court would have a most beneficial effect. *Select Committee of the House of Lords on the Execution of the Criminal Law.* PP 1847, VII, p. 369.
63. Rosamund and Florence Hill, *op. cit.,* (see note 17), p. 155. No probation officers were proposed; and this was not really as has been suggested, a foreshadowing of the probation system.
64. Jebb, *Report, etc.* 1853. HMSO, 1854, pp. 83-7.
65. See **Symons, Jelinger,** *Tactics for the Times as regards the Condition and Treatment of the Dangerous Classes.* London, 1849, p. 3.
66. Tomlinson, *op. cit.,* p. 214.
67. Carpenter, *op. cit.,* p. 266.
68. Holford, *op. cit.,* p. 132.
69. **Chesterton, G. L.,** *Revelations of Prison Life.* Vol. 1, London 1856, *passim.*
70. **Bell, E. P.,** 'A Social History of Salford New Bailey Prison'. Salford M.Sc., 1972, pp. 82-3.
71. Griffiths, *op. cit.,* pp. 328-32.
72. Bell, *op. cit.,* p. 88. In 1836, four out of the fourteen warders had a military background. Unfortunately the background of subsequent appointees is not given.
73. 2 and 3 Vict., c. LVI, Clause VI.
74. Some large prisons remained industrial right up to 1877, earning large sums to save the rates. Glasgow combined industrial labour with separation. Efficient industrial prisons included Wakefield, Bedford and Holloway, and prisoners were allowed to earn. See Tomlinson, *op. cit.,* pp. 178-84.
75. Return of Establishment of Officers and Servants, *2nd Report of Select Committee of House of Lords on Gaols and Houses of Correction.* PP 1835, XII, App. 22, p. 593 *et seq.*
76. Bell, *op. cit.,* pp. 81-2.
77. Return of Establishment, etc., pp. 604, 607.
78. *Report from Committee on the King's Bench, Fleet and Marshalsea Prisons.* PP 1814-15, IV, p. 3. The Keeper of Newgate at this time, with a salary of £450 minus the expenses of running the prison, but plus fees, reckoned to clear between £600 and £1,000 a year. *Report from the Committee on the State of the Gaols of the City of London, etc.* Evidence of Mr J. A. Newman, p. 15. PP 1813-14, IV.
79. Bell, *op. cit.,* p. 88.

80. Return of Establishment, etc., p. 607.
81. Dr Tomlinson makes the point that the quality of prison officers improved as more skilled trade instructors and specialists were required. For further discussion of their pay and conditions of work see Tomlinson, *op. cit.*, pp. 204-10.
82. See the recent publicity concerning 'Control Units' for refractory prisoners, which seem to reproduce the harshest conditions of separate confinement. Few prison governors seem to have read any history, or even to realise that they have 'been here before'.

Education and social aims

'Every philosophical investigator of human nature is compelled to admit that the sole aim of education is the harmonious development of faculties and dispositions which, under God's grace, make up a personality.'[1] Thus wrote the famous Swiss educator, Pestalozzi. The aim is as valid today as it was in the eighteenth century, and nearly as far from realisation. In practice education is a social activity. Schools train children for their future role in life. Where society is hierarchical this includes their station in the hierarchy. Education is both product and buttress of the social order, and its aim becomes diluted accordingly. Baldwin Francis Duppa, Secretary of the Central Society of Education, defined the objects of that liberal and secular group of influential people in 1837: 'For schools to be efficient, it is necessary that they should be so ordered as to supply the wants peculiar to the class intended to be educated at them; that they should have a regard to existing evils, and that they should have reference, not to one class of faculties alone, but to all.'[2]

To some extent the English education system supplied these wants through the un-selfconscious pressure of parents seeking a suitable preparation for the status and career they envisaged for their children. But education is also, or is believed to be, the most easily controlled instrument for moulding public morals and social attitudes. Governments and politicians cannot leave it alone. This was as true in the early nineteenth century as it is today. Indeed, education invited manipulation even more than it does now because of the prevalence of the Hartleian or Associationist psychology, according to which a child's character and opinions were created entirely by his early training.

A crude example of this popular psychology can be found in the writings of the industrialist, educationist and later socialist, Robert Owen.

> For every day will make it more and more evident *that the character of man is without a single exception, always formed for him; that it may be, and is, chiefly created by his predecessors; that they give him, or may give him, his ideas and habits, which are the powers that*

govern and direct his conduct. Man, therefore, never did, nor is it possible he ever can, form his own character.[3]

Holding such convictions, no socially conscious person of influence could leave education to chance. So it became enmeshed in conflicting social and political aims. When economic conflict gave rise to class consciousness, men of one class saw a means of controlling other classes by offering them education on their own terms. When there was religious or sectarian conflict, education became involved in that too. While class and religion were related (the different forms of Christianity having a close affinity with the economic position and social status of those who adhered to them), the cross-currents generated by these conflicts influenced, and possibly distorted the development of English education.

The eighteenth-century educational hierarchy

The educational hierarchy did not originate in the Industrial Revolution. In eighteenth-century England the young nobleman enjoyed his private tutors, his leisurely sojourn at Oxford or Cambridge, and his continental Grand Tour. The farmer's, trader's or craftsman's son got his education in an endowed but fee-paying grammar school, or where that did not exist or had decayed, in a 'private adventure' school. The child of a small farmer, artisan or labourer, if he did not have to work as soon as he could walk, learned his letters in a dame school and continued into the lower forms of a village school kept by the local clergyman, or even into those of the endowed school. The child of very poor parents was lucky if he could find a charity or industrial school to take him free. Although the system (if such it could be called) was hierarchical, the dividing lines were not clearly drawn, just as there was no absolute distinction between literacy and illiteracy. There were, however, some distinguishing marks. One was the learning of Latin as a main school subject, and this dividing line seems to have come about the middle of the grammar schools, or sometimes between the town and village school.[4] A classical education denoted the gentleman, the potential undergraduate of Oxford or Cambridge, and (since the only two English universities defended themselves against the incursion of Dissenters by demanding subscription to the Thirty-nine Articles of the Church of England) the Anglican, especially the Anglican clergyman. This dividing line, with all it entailed in social opportunity, seems to have produced little rancour in a comparatively stable society. It was reinforced by parents demanding that their sons should learn, in their mother tongue, the subjects most suitable for a farming or commercial career.

The dividing line at the bottom of the scale was between the primarily academic and the primarily industrial school. Some industrial schools gave a sound training in agricultural or craft skills, while others were really sweated labour manufactories; but all smacked of the Poor

Law or of charity. This division was to reinforce the association of manual labour with the lowest ranks in society, and set up an obstacle to the inclusion of agricultural and industrial training in elementary education.

Between the upper and lower dividing lines the professional, commercial and nascent industrial middle classes evolved their own private educational hierarchy, from the Dissenting academies such as Warrington, which led the nation in the teaching of science, history and politics, down to Dickensian establishments advertising in copperplate their ability to teach neat handwriting and the casting of accounts. Modern languages and drawing (at a mechanical and superficial level) were largely the province of the few and despised girls' schools. The public boarding schools, the main growth point in upper-middle-class education during the first two-thirds of the nineteenth century, adopted and cherished the distinguishing mark of the dead languages. Thus education reinforced the social divisions, with schools distinguished from each other in management, teaching, games and curriculum. And in addition, class divisions were marked by the length of time the child remained in a school of any kind.

Hostility to popular education

English public elementary education grew in the face of constant fear and opposition from sections of the upper and middle classes. An illustration often quoted is the speech of Davies Giddy in the House of Commons against Whitbread's bill for the instruction of poor children, in 1807.[5] Education, thought Giddy, would teach the lower orders to despise their lot in life, enable them to read seditious pamphlets, and render them insolent to their superiors. This attitude persisted, notably among rural farmers and gentry, throughout the nineteenth century. After 1839 school inspectors not infrequently reported that opposition to the education of the lower orders was now dying out, a sure indication that it was still alive. In 1847, the Rev. John Allen, Inspector for Bedfordshire, Cambridgeshire and Huntingdonshire was pained by the avowal of persons 'blessed with every advantage of early training and the soundest education of the opinion that schools were but of doubtful good'. *He added*, 'If it should be distinctly professed by any, "*We cannot help having a school, but we think it adviseable that as little as possible be taught therein!*" it seems to me that every-one who has a voice to be heard should raise it in protest against such a miserable policy'[6] Not long ago the retired headmistress of a Herefordshire primary school described to the writer of this book how disgusted her farmer uncle had been when she took up the useless career of elementary school teacher.

If overt hostility to any education for the lower orders gradually retreated into the backblocks of rural England, it was followed more slowly by the attitude of those who wished to give them just so much education as would enable them to read the Bible, learn their duty to God and Man, and the place in life to which Providence had been pleased to assign them. Hannah More, founder of the Cheddar Sunday schools in the 1780s and friend of William Wilberforce, taught reading, writing and sewing to the local farmers' children; but she would 'allow of no writing'[7] for the poor. The Wesleyan Methodist Conference forbade the teaching of writing in their Sunday schools in 1819, amid protests from the parents of their scholars.[8] William Lovett, the 'moral force' Chartist leader, denounced these educationists as 'hawks and owls of society', seeking to perpetuate that state of mental darkness most favourable to the securing of their prey. From caste selfishness they considered education as their own prerogative; a boon to be sparingly conferred on the multitude instead of a right belonging to all.[9]

In time this attitude also weakened, partly under the blows of Lord Ashley, who, although an enemy of secular state schools, was an enthusiastic champion of working-class education. But its successor was the 'Morals before Intellect' line of those who demanded that working-class education should be primarily religious, because its primary purpose was to inculcate good morals and obedience. This was often to be found among High Churchmen, such as the Rev. Alexander Watson, curate of St John's, Cheltenham, who believed that 'no secular knowledge really desirable for the bulk of the population could be fitly taught apart from a constant reference to religion'.[10] And it was typical of the conservative landed gentry. As Sir Charles H. I. Anderson, Bart., of Lea, near Gainsborough, Lincolnshire, put it to the Newcastle Commission, 'I consider those schools to be the most promising where The Commandments and the Duty to God and Man are regularly taught, because without moral and practical religious training there can be no real education.'[11]

The secular educationists, a small, if noisy group, advocated moral without religious training. Inspector the Rev. John Allen was exceptional in insisting that an intellectual education, although misused, was better than entire mental darkness.[12]

Education as 'rescue'

Modern Labour historians are wont to hold that the purpose of early Victorian educationists was the social control of one class by another, or, as Harold Silver put it, 'Rescuing the poor for religion and a concomitant stable society'.[13] A scrutiny of early nineteenth-century justifications for educating the poor makes it difficult to disagree. But like most such dicta, it is an oversimplification. In the first place, while the 'rescue' theme was extremely common, it meant different things to different men. Among middle- and upper-class philanthropists it was an argument for enlightened self-preservation. Educational reformers, from Robert Raikes, founder of the first Sunday school for the children from the Gloucester pin factories who ran wild in the streets, damaging the property of respectable citizens, to Brougham, Ashley, and the great Kay-Shuttleworth; all believed education would rescue the lower orders from crime and sedition. The means varied. While churchmen sought to inculcate religion and morals to buttress duty and obedience, liberals like Brougham and Whately attacked sedition and socialism by inculcating popularised versions of classical political economy.[14] They did this rather more intelligently than the churchmen with their cheap Bibles and endless catechisms, but they were prepared to use the religious sanction also, provided it was not made a means of proselytising Nonconformists by the High Church party. Brougham the sceptical Scottish Whig even conceded the management of a national system of education to the churchmen, rather than have none, though his attempt to put education before religion foundered on his bad political judgement. On the other hand, Robert Owen's New Lanark Institute for Moral Regeneration, i.e. his day and evening schools, was intended to rescue mankind from the hypocrisies of supernatural religion and enslavement to clerical influence. Lovett sought to rescue the working classes from their dependence on an oppressive upper class and a self-seeking and greedy middle class. But the middle class also was to be rescued from spending 'careworn lives in pursuing wealth or rank through the soul-debasing avenues of wrong',[15] i.e. from the evils of competitive materialism and the capitalist ethic. The aristocratic and influential Central Society of Education also denounced the heaping up of capital 'without regard to the pain that is reflected in its acquisition, or to its legitimate application when acquired'; and attacking the exploitation of children in factories, looked to non-sectarian, universal and eventually compulsory education as the remedy.[16] Rescue meant conversion to the moral and social imperatives of the rescuers, who represented the spectrum of attitudes and motives in contemporary society.

Moreover, there was a good deal of common ground among all educationists. Lovett and Owen no less than Ashley and Brougham looked to education to rescue the lower orders from their propensity to vice and crime. They agreed with those who abstracted and compared figures from the literacy enquiries and the judicial or prison returns to demonstrate the connection between ignorance and criminality. There was no ethic of revolution or social violence for its own sake to separate the aims of upper- and working-class educational reformers. They all wanted a stable society, though Lovett wanted more social equality (and looked to equal education to procure it), while Owen's educational views were essentially classless.[17] 'Rescue' could denote the general feeling that education was failing to keep pace with the growth of population and the needs of contemporary civilisation, and that it ought to 'elevate the views and refine the character of the mass of mankind'.[18]

One reason why education in the early nineteenth century appeared to be merely an instrument of class control was the decline in its parallel conception as a means of social mobility. This had been uppermost in the demands of eighteenth-century Rational Dissenters for equal educational opportunity, but it declined as the professional and industrial middle class, fortified with new economic power, turned to defensive measures against the classes forming below them. Remnants of it were found to be in Brougham's vision of the Mechanics' Institutes as providers of opportunity for clever workmen to contribute to the technical improvement of their own industries, and so rise in the world.[19] Indeed the association of working-class further education with scientific and technical training was in part such a survival;[20] for Chrestomathic (Benthamite for useful) education was intended by the reformers for the curricula of their own schools, not merely as a packet handed down to the lower orders. Only the propensity of middle-class parents to social climbing weaned them from science to the dead languages.[21]

When all this is said, education did become involved in the class struggle. The Pestalozzian definition of educational aim as the harmonious development of the faculties and dispositions found occasional expression, as in Lovett's view that 'education means the developing and training of all the faculties of mind and body'[22] (a claim stated in opposition to the concept of limited education for the lower orders). But for Lovett, too, education was politicised. He looked on it, rightly, as a source of power. In the 1830s there was a danger that the control of popular education would be contested by class-based politico-religious parties, all trying to rescue the lower orders according to their own ideas. There were Church schools teaching the Anglican catechism, Dissenting schools ludicrously teaching private morality from unanno-tated extracts from the Bible, and public morality from readers in political economy, and Owenite schools propagating socialism from Minter Morgan's *Fable of the Bees*.[23] At least the dominance of the rescue motif as interpreted by middle-class enthusiasts prevented education from being permanently divided into forms of propaganda serving conflicting social and political aims. Moreover, their enthusiasm for knowledge as an instrument of improvement, embodied in the idea of the 'march of mind', with its roots in a very ancient liberal tradition, provided a counter-force to the Low and High Churchmen's preoccu-pation with faith, duty and obedience.

The monitorial system and the sectarian divide

The origins of nineteenth-century elementary education are sometimes seen in the Sunday-school movement of the 1780s and 1790s, sometimes in the day schools of Andrew Bell and Joseph Lancaster. The Sunday-school movement, started by Robert Raikes in a small way, and publicised in the *Gloucester Journal* on 3 November 1783, spread with extraordinary speed. By 1784 Stockport had 7 Sunday schools, one with nearly 1,000 pupils, and by 1806 it had some 3,000 children on its

Sunday-school books. In September 1784, Manchester already had nearly 1,800 children on the books of 25 Sunday schools, or school rooms, and by 1797 it had 5,171 children enrolled in 42 schools (16 of them in Salford).[24] Such figures suggest an explosive demand for education in industrial towns where school provision was inadequate and children both in factories and domestic labour were working hours which prevented them attending day schools. But the movement also spread in the country. Hannah More's Cheddar Sunday schools, founded in 1789 at Wilberforce's suggestion, by 1800 numbered 12, with 3,000 children and parents participating.[25] In Wales the movement of Griffith Jones, revived by the Rev. Thomas Charles in the 1780s, was even more popular, for the teaching was in Welsh, the schools were closely associated with Nonconformist chapels, of which they sometimes formed the nucleus, and in some the curriculum developed far beyond the Bible reading which formed the main fare of the majority of English ones.[26] In 1818 there were some 500,000 children going to Sunday schools in England and Wales; by 1833, 1,500,000; by 1898, 7,500,000.[27] The schools merely changed in character, becoming more sectarian as the Anglicans reacted against the Nonconformists' interdenominational initiative, and more theological as day schools took over secular education.

The monitorial system was devised (or revived) towards the end of the 1790s by Andrew Bell, Anglican chaplain in India, who observed Indian children teaching each other by writing on sand, and the Quaker Joseph Lancaster who founded his Borough Road school with the children using slates.[28] For a time the two elaborated each others' ideas. Then in 1805 the officious Mrs Trimmer, organiser of Church Sunday schools, wrote to Bell that Lancaster was 'building on your foundation',[29] and compounded the mischief with a pamphlet, *A Comparative View of the New Plan of Education promulgated by Mr Joseph Lancaster*.[30] The ensuing quarrel soon widened into a split between the Anglican and Nonconformist promoters of Sunday schools. The interdenominational Sunday School Society fell apart in 1800, and regional committees of the Established Church began to run their own schools in rivalry with those of their former colleagues. Anglicans and Nonconformists would never again be able to combine in the common cause of popular education.

Whether, as is traditionally held, sectarian rivalry delayed an adequate system of state schools for generations,[31] or whether, as Mary Sturt has suggested, it saved English education from state-dominated uniformity, and encouraged a useful competition in school building,[32] is a matter of opinion. But even without Mrs Trimmer, the division could hardly have been long delayed. Church and Chapel quarrelled, not through conflicting educational aims, but as the result of a power struggle. Methodism of various brands and allied branches of the Trinitarian revival were swelling the Nonconformist congregations, while enclosures were augmenting the lands and wealth of many beneficed Anglican clergymen.[33] When local or national depressions weakened the ability of Dissenting businessmen to finance local schools, these were apt to fall under clerical control.[34] The revival of dogmatic faith and Trinitarian zeal was making both Church and Dissent more intolerant. The Nonconformists, themselves split into different denominations, were more or less compelled to continue the old Rational Dissenters' non-sectarian policies, but the Churchmen, once they realised the need for or inevitability of working-class literacy, perceived an opportunity for asserting the Church's social domination. In particular, the High Church party believed strongly in the divine mission of the established sacramental Church to teach the nation. Greater prosperity merely enabled the parish clergyman who had long kept the parish school, to hire a paid teacher, while still maintaining control. The Society for Promoting Christian Knowledge, which in the early eighteenth century had founded many charity schools, insisted that the children should be taught the catechism and taken to Church twice on Sunday.[35] In the nineteenth century High Church zealots reasserted these precepts with increasing vigour. They were alarmed both by the rapid growth of Nonconformity and by the 'infidelity' which spread among the politically aware élite of the lower orders in the wake of the French Revolution, with which they mistakenly associated the Methodist revolt. A Church–Chapel conflict was simmering; and Mrs Trimmer was but the occasion of its eruption.

After the quarrel, elementary education was promoted by rival sectarian associations. In 1810 the British and Foreign School Society, having pushed out Lancaster who had become a financial liability, was organised by a committee including Brougham, Whitbread, Romilly, James Mill, and (temporarily) Wilberforce. The National Society for the Education of the Poor in the Principles of the Established Church was supported by Southey and Coleridge, both now socially conscious Tory sages. Starting in 1811, it was incorporated by Royal Charter in 1817, and by 1823 had obtained a royal letter sanctioning parish collections for it – the equivalent of a guarantee for some £10,000 a year.[36] Joshua Watson of the 'Hackney Phalanx' on its committee ensured High Church influence. The evangelical churchmen who from their stronghold, the Society for Bettering the Condition of the Poor, had, since 1804, advocated limited education (reading only) for the lower orders, hesitated between their Nonconformist and sometimes sceptical allies, and their High Church enemies. Finally Wilberforce led them into the National Society. They were to suffer similar hesitancies in the founding of London University a decade later.

First attempts at legislation

Under Bell and Lancaster's monitorial system, the master instructed a group of older or quicker children, each of whom passed on what he had learned to groups of younger children. It was a powerful instrument for the dissemination of bare literacy and numeracy, for a hundred or more could be taught at a time, without equipment more costly than some slates and teaching cards. With a limited form of mass education apparently brought within easy reach, there was a wave of enthusiasm among middle-class educationists. The mildly radical Whitbread (following Tom Paine fifteen years before) believed the Poor Law could be made almost obsolete by education. His Parochial Schools Bill of 1807 would empower magistrates to set up village schools with help from the rates. But this was unacceptable to a country gentry-dominated wartime parliament. MPs feared that education would lend power to sedition, and the reactionary evangelical Tory prime minister Spencer Perceval voiced another perennial apprehension; that public provision would destroy voluntary effort. He proposed instead an inquiry into the possibility of financing popular education through existing endowments.[37] In the prevailing political climate this was probably the most hopeful means of getting a sizeable capital for elementary education; and after Whitbread's death in 1815 it was vigorously pursued by the Scottish Whig, Henry Brougham.[38]

In May, 1816, on Brougham's motion, a House of Commons Select Committee was set up to inquire into the education of the lower orders in the Metropolis. Brougham was hoping to use London as an experimental field for elementary education under state sanction. The Committee included a number of liberal educationists such as Romilly, Mackintosh and Francis Horner (editor of the *Edinburgh Review*), along with the radical Sir Francis Burdett, and the evangelical Tory Wilberforce. Sending out questionnaires and examining witnesses including the headmasters of Charterhouse, Westminster and Christ's Hospital, the committee obtained information on the one hand about educational destitution among the poor, and on the other about the abuse of charitable funds in educating the rich. Brougham hoped to obtain vast charitable and educational endowments, estimated vaguely at between £1,500,000 and £3,000,000, for a network of popular day schools.[39] He considered that the large sums spent on boarding, feeding and clothing the favoured few could be redistributed to provide a basic education for the many, without either rendering them dependent on charity for their subsistence, or encouraging the growth of population.[40] To get his hands on these endowments Brougham obtained what he called a 'Parliamentary Commission' appointed by the government. But it was too early, and Brougham was no Chadwick. The post-war economic troubles, the seditious writings of Cobbett and others, the working-class unrest and the inflated fears fomented by government spies were ill-calculated to persuade a reactionary government of the advantages of popular education. Then Brougham attacked the privileged institutions such as Eton and Winchester and the great public schools of the politicians he should have been conciliating. When the endowments proved out of reach he wavered between plans for central grants and rate support. Finally he fell foul of the conflict between Church and Chapel. Trying to conciliate the bishops, he proposed the appointment of schoolmasters by parish vestries with the approval of the incumbent, subject to episcopal visitation and dismissal and under the requirement of a sacramental test.[41] This last provision, reflecting the terms of the hated Test and Corporation Acts, ensured a furious reaction from the Nonconformists. They refused to be placated by a conscience clause permitting them to withdraw their children from religious instruction, and organised a Committee for the Protection of Religious Liberty against the Bill, until it was withdrawn.[42] During the committee stage the proposed Commission was whittled down in size and scope. It became a restraint on the Select Committee it was supposed to reinforce. Brougham's efforts to extend elementary education between 1816 and 1819 were a failure. If the Select Committee had been able to produce an acceptable plan for the conversion of local endowments, their diversion to the founding of boarding schools for the rich might have been checked at an early stage,[43] and the spread of elementary education accelerated. As it was, effective state intervention was delayed for a generation.

The first state grant

After the defeat of Brougham's Bill, educationists concentrated their efforts largely on adult education. In 1824 Mechanics' Institutes were started in London and Leeds. In 1825 Brougham published his *Practical Observations upon the Education of the People*, and the following year he founded the Society for the Diffusion of Useful Knowledge, with Lord John Russell as vice-chairman. The society was to provide cheap copies of good scientific and literary works, and to inculcate correct views of political economy, and self-help among the poor. Its publishers, Charles Knight and later Cradock and Baldwin, produced in instalments a Library of Entertaining Knowledge, a Library of Useful Knowledge (mainly scientific), a Penny Magazine, a Penny Cyclopaedia, farmers' booklets, and almanacks and maps. In 1828–29 nearly 30,000 of the scientific works were sold, although by 1832 the numbers had fallen to between 6,000 and 9,000.[44] Plainly the SDUK could only succeed on the basis of a reading public. The same was true of the Mechanics' Institutes, where the progress of some of the working-class students was held up by lack of basic literacy.

In the 1820s much educational effort went into provision for middle-class education, such as the foundation of University College, London, and London University (an examining body) on undenominational lines. But in Ireland, where social experiments could be carried out without too much interference from the natives or the British parliament, up to £60,000 of public money was already being spent, largely by the evangelical Kildare Street Society in building Protestant schools to which the Catholics would not go. When the Whigs came into power in

1830 educational reformers had some reason to hope their demands for a national system of elementary education would at last be met.

Under the Whigs, Brougham went to the Lords as Lord Chancellor, leaving education to be promoted in the Commons by the 'Benthamite' J. A. Roebuck, Thomas Wyse of the Central Society of Education, and Lord John Russell. On 30 July 1833, Roebuck moved that the House should acknowledge education as a matter of national concern, and proposed a scheme of compulsory schooling between the ages of 6 and 12, at parish infant schools, and Schools of Industry. These would be run by district committees elected by heads of families or contributors to the school funds. School fees would be charged, but those of the poorest would be paid by the state from a general fund. A Ministry of Public Instruction would apportion the state grant, advise on teaching methods, and supply school books. Religious instruction would be undenominational, but sectarian teaching could be provided if demanded. Normal schools entered by examination and providing education from 14 to 20, with a certificate on completion of the course, would train the teachers.[45] This scheme was far too sweeping for the Whig grandees, Grey, Althorp and Melbourne, who were nearly as mistrustful of popular education (especially after the Labourers' Revolt) as their Tory counterparts. It was too undenominational for the Church Party, and too committed to public funds for many of the Whigs. The motion was withdrawn, but at Brougham's suggestion the Committee of Supply proposed a grant of £20,000 in aid of school building, to be channelled through the two religious voluntary school societies.

The voluntary societies: state aid versus the bishops

Thus public provision for elementary education began not with a bang but a whimper. In 1819 parliament had voted £1,000,000 to build new Anglican churches; in 1833 it provided £70,000 to build new stables for the King's horses.[46] The grant of £20,000 was little more than a token gesture. But it meant that as between the alternatives of financing education by the conversion of endowments, or rate aid, or central exchequer grant on the Irish pattern, the latter had won. But this was not to say that caution, or jealousy of pauperisation had been entirely lost. To ensure that the poor were not spoiled by free schooling nor the sources of charity dried up, the grant was to be distributed only on the recommendation of the religious societies, after approval of the school building plans, and only to committees which could first raise one-half of the estimated cost. Preference was to be given to large towns, where the need was considered greatest.[47] Thus the voluntary principle was honoured, while sectarian jealousy was kept at bay.

But the tide for education was running strongly, and the miserable

£20,000 (renewed annually until 1839) proved to be but a beginning. 1833 saw an apparently spontaneous outbreak of statistical societies, which concerned themselves largely with research into educational provision. The report of House of Commons enquiry into working-class literacy (popularly known as 'Lord Kerry's Returns') was answered by the Manchester Statistical Society with figures showing gross educational deficiencies in Manchester and Liverpool, and then in other northern towns.[48] The influential Central Society of Education, with Thomas Wyse as Chairman, Lord John Russell as a life member, and eighteen MPs on its council, was founded in 1836. As evidence of the need of more public expenditure on education built up, Roebuck and Brougham (who had lost office in 1835) continued to pester the government with demands and abortive motions based on the simple theme that 'infant schools were better than Newgate school'[49] until Althorp moved for a House of Commons Select Committee on the state of education in England and Wales and the application of the grant. Meantime Brougham continued to flit from one scheme to another; for a state Normal (Teachers' Training) College; for a Central Board of Commissioners, or of Commissioners and Ministers; for grant aid to municipal councils and elected rural school boards, which could also be helped from the rates.[50] Although Brougham's initiatives were persistently resisted by Melbourne's government, it had become obvious that the £20,000 a year was not being used satisfactorily. There was no auditing machinery on expenditure, many of the new buildings had proved unsuitable, and the teachers were untrained, ill paid, and inadequate. The Anglican gentry were wealthier than all but a very few Nonconformist industrialists, and the local churches found it easier to raise subscriptions than did the chapels. So by 1839 the National Society had taken three-quarters of the grant.[51] The bulk of public money was going to the richer places where money could be raised, and the poorest areas, where there was educational destitution, got nothing. There was an obvious need of inspectors to report on school provision and check on expenditure; and the National Society was already experimenting with unpaid volunteer inspection. So was the British and Foreign School Society, which in 1830 appointed a paid 'travelling agent' and a part-time inspector for its London schools. School inspectors had been appointed in Ireland since 1820.[52] School inspectors, of a kind, predated those of the Poor Law Amendment and Factory Acts.

In 1839 Lord John Russell, as Home Secretary, launched his elementary-education scheme. The Central Grant would rise to £30,000 a year, payable through a range of agencies, and directed especially to the poorer districts. Distribution would be supervised by school inspectors answerable to a Committee of Education of the Privy Council of up to five members. Teacher training would be encouraged by a state Normal School on non-sectarian lines.[53] To by-pass the bishops in the Lords, the Committee of the Privy Council on Education was set up by Order in Council in April 1839. But the Church Party bitterly attacked the government, already in political decline. Petitions against the secular state training college poured in. Archbishop Howlett of Canterbury threatened an address to the Queen craving revocation of the Order in Council. The bishops encouraged the National Society school committees to refuse the grant. Brougham, on the other side, was pounding the government for paring down what ought to have been a universal measure for the education of the people into a single training college and a government supervising committee.[54] The government yielded to the ecclesiastical outcry. The Normal School was dropped in favour of a grant of £10,000 to the religious school societies to help them found their own training colleges. When the National Society was discovered to be accepting little more than a quarter of the school building grant offered it, Lord Lansdowne, President of the Council and of the new Education Committee, together with Russell, approached Archbishop Howlett for a compromise. The result was the celebrated 'Concordat' of 1840 under which the Church authorities secured control of the appointment of the inspectors of state-aided schools, together with the right (as well as the Privy Council) to receive their reports. The instructions for religious education were to be framed by the Archbishop of Canterbury.[55] These powers were not extended over non-Anglican schools, which received a lay inspector. However, what Kay-Shuttleworth called the 'Medieval Party' claimed a great victory, and there were subsequent complaints of clerical gentlemen visiting British and Foreign School Society schools, and reporting on their religious teaching.[56] The early school inspectorate became a mainly clerical preserve, the Church swung over to supporting state provision for education, and the Nonconformists, suspicious of the new Education Committee, which they felt was dictated to by the bishops, swung into opposition. The bishops insisted that money should continue to be given only to local committees which could raise a subscription, thus continuing to secure the lion's share. The most positive result of the Concordat was the appointment as secretary to the new Committee of Education of James Kay-Shuttleworth.

Poor Law education

The resistance to state elementary education and the sectarian conflict made it impossible to start a national system according to the Chadwickian technique of a Royal Commission followed by a governing statute. Educationists were forced to adopt a step-by-step approach, from the small grant of 1833 to the Privy Council Minutes of 1846 which governed the mid-century expansion. By 1839 the Committee of Education of the Privy Council, virtually a small Education Department administering a body of inspectors, was in existence. But in the 1830s and 1840s there were at least two other roots from which a national system of primary education might have grown: the new Poor Law, and the

Factory Acts.

Chadwick and Senior as Poor Law Commissioners always had education on their agenda as a depauperising influence, sharing the facile assumption of Paine and other radicals (not to mention Robert Owen) that universal education would in some unexplained way cure unemployment and render poor relief largely unnecessary. Their enthusiasm was shared by several of the Poor Law Assistant Commissioners, who believed that pauperism as well as crime could be eradicated by early training. Poor Law Commission writings and reports on education always exhibited a completely different tone from those contemplating the treatment of adult paupers. Thus, Assistant Commissioner Edward Twistleton, criticising a Norfolk Guardian who wanted to dismiss the local workhouse schoolmaster to make the workhouse less eligible, insisted that the workhouse child needed a better education than the child of an independent labourer. There should be no stint and niggardliness, but, 'their opening minds should be richly furnished with all that is useful and exalted'.[57] He met the objection that pauper parents would fail to provide for their children if these had received a good education, by pointing out that most pauper children were orphans or bastards (without the proper complement of parents) and the most important consideration was the beneficial influence on this majority. The children must be rescued from 'the contagion of moral pestilence' which pervaded the workhouse, and dwell in the pure atmosphere of a well-regulated school. The Assistant Commissioners had ambitious plans for combining Unions into School Districts large enough to draw 400–500 children out of the Union workhouses. Economies of scale would permit new buildings or radical conversion of old ones, the cost of trained teachers and of proper equipment. The children could be rescued from the tainted atmosphere and contacts of the workhouse and educated not only in religion and morals but in industry or farm work suitable to their prospects in life.

The architect of Poor Law education (as later of state elementary education) was James Phillips Kay. He was the son of a Rochdale cotton manufacturer, trained as a physician in Edinburgh, and experienced in treating and observing the poor in Edinburgh and Manchester dispensaries.[58] Already known as a founder-member of the Manchester Statistical Society and a pamphleteer on social questions, who supported Malthus and criticised indiscriminate medical charity, he was recruited (following a breakdown in health) by Nassau Senior as Poor Law Assistant Commissioner for Norfolk and Suffolk in 1835.[59] Kay-Shuttleworth (as he called himself after his marriage) was an administrator comparable in stature with Chadwick, to whom he was not dissimilar in character – apart from being more pious in a Broad Church way. He described in his autobiography how he found some 3,000 children (reduced under new Poor Law reorganisation to about 1,900 in 35 Unions) living in the East Anglian workhouses. They were kept apart from the adult paupers in schools of 40–50, or 20 each when boys and girls were separated, but taught by paupers, since the schools were too small to justify qualified teachers, and the guardians were also reluctant to vote teachers' salaries. Rendered unfit to train, the children were apprenticed to masters who didn't want them and treated them harshly, or to urban tradesmen who took them for the premium and then turned them out.[60] Some of these children were sent to local schools, but always to the cheapest and the worst. No industrial training was available, and the parents of children at the better schools objected to them associating with the workhouse juveniles.

Kay began by inducing the more intelligent guardians to employ young trainee teachers from two famous Scottish academies as organising masters.[61] In this way he had (so he claimed) improved the workhouse schools up to a point at which the Guardians would be persuaded to take more interest in pauper education, and perhaps consent to the creation of school districts. He hoped, by a sound industrial training, to avoid the need for apprenticeship and its abuses in future. But he admitted that some guardians thought educating pauper children was 'like putting the torch of knowledge into the hands of the rick-burners'.[62]

When Kay was appointed Secretary to the new Committee of Council on Education, he toured the schools of the Children's Friend Society and Lady Byron's school at Ealing Grove.[63] On the outskirts of London he came across the relics of Jonas Hanway's scheme for boarding and apprenticing London pauper children in the country. The single nurses (in modern parlance foster homes) had grown into contract establishments of 40 to 1,100 children. Pallid, underfed, scantily clothed and often harshly punished, they were occupied sorting bristles or making hooks and eyes.[64] In the London workhouses he found slum children, half-starved, diseased, and accustomed to alternate neglect and capricious cruelty, to whom their arrival in the workhouse was 'the climax of their misfortune'.[65] They sorted bristles and picked oakum under pauper supervision. The boys were broken-spirited, cringing and deceitful; the girls refractory, obstinate, boisterous and insolent.[66] Kay's indictment was borne out by Chesterton, who as Governor of Cold Bath Fields House of Correction obtained many of its younger inmates from the London workhouses.

Kay selected the best of the large contract establishments, Aubin's of Norwood, for his experiment in pauper education. He persuaded Frankland Lewis to obtain from Lord John Russell a grant of £500. He imported teachers from Wood's school in Edinburgh, and obtained from the Admiralty the deck and rigging of a brig which was set up in the playground along with two guns from HMS *Excellent*. The girls did all the cleaning, washing and cooking for the establishment, learned plain cooking suitable for domestic service in a middle-class family and frugal cooking for the economical use of the earnings of a labourer against their own marriages.[67] The boys were trained mainly for the sea service. The cleverest children were selected as pupil-teachers and rewarded with special food and separate bedrooms. According to Kay the discipline was mild, resting on the children's co-operation. Their interest was maintained by alternating workshop labour with religious instruction, school work and play; and they were taken on excursions to a nearby heath. The only amenity lacking was a garden and farm for horticultural and agricultural training.[68]

During his three years' superintendence of Norwood, Kay turned it into a model for the district-school movement, and a nursery of pupil teachers for elementary schools. He recruited pupil teachers from it to start his new foundation at Battersea; and when Battersea Training College was donated to the National Society in 1843 its students moved into the main stream of elementary education.

Kay-Shuttleworth's autobiography gives an impression of victorious single-handed endeavour. In fact he was closely assisted and partly financed by his friend Carleton Tuffnell, the son of a wealthy MP, who was secretary of the London Statistical Society and later a Poor Law School Inspector. He was supported by Assistant Commissioners Day and Mott, followers of Chadwick (although he personally favoured Cornewall Lewis in the power struggle on the Poor Law Central Commission). Cornewall Lewis and Edmund Head on the Commission promoted the plans for district schools. Russell fostered them and Peel's government after 1842 slowed but did not abandon them.[69] But the politicians were not prepared to coerce the Unions; and only a few enlightened Boards of Guardians would co-operate with each other in setting up school districts, or indeed improve the education of their pauper children by establishing separate schools and buying lands for training in 'spade husbandry'.

The failure of the district school movement, and the later substitution of 'separate' and 'detached' schools (separate and detached from the adult workhouse), together with the cottage and scattered homes of late-Victorian England have recently been described by Francis Duke.[70] Despite the helpful measures of Russell's government of 1846 which confirmed Peel's Poor Law teachers' salary grant, appointed five Inspectors of Poor Law Schools and helped to establish Kneller Hall as a Poor Law Teachers' Training College, the movement never achieved more than three Metropolitan School Districts and six small rural ones. It fell victim to the reluctance and jealousies of guardians, the apathy of governments and its own unforeseen practical difficulties. The large establishments were not economical. Assistant teachers, supervisory and maintenance staffs had to be engaged. The target of 400 children to a school was soon abandoned. Existing workhouse buildings proved unsuitable, and the Treasury refused to sanction building grants. Many London Boards preferred to establish their own separate schools, and provincial Guardians feared that district schools would fall under the control of Anglican gentry and clergymen. It was more expensive to keep a child in a district school than in a workhouse, so backward Guardians would not send them. For this reason, and because the pauper indoor population fluctuated continually and rapidly, there were always children left behind in the workhouses.

The failure of the district-school movement was partly compensated by the growth of separate schools in the wealthier and more enlightened Unions. By 1857, fifty-seven of these could be listed in a parliamentary return.[71] Two large and famous separate schools at Kirkdale and Swinton in Lancashire on the Norwood model, offered a range of industrial (really craft) instruction. As well as the basic school subjects, they taught such trades as shoemaking, tailoring, carpentry, gardening, baking and blacksmithing. Kirkdale had a military band. Privately founded Quatt School, Shropshire (later a district school), was known for its farm training and spade husbandry, as well as its proficiency in intellectual subjects.[72] Some smaller workhouses had detached schools on the workhouse site. When, after 1846, a system of graded teaching certificates was established and inspection started, the use of untrained pauper teachers slowly diminished, while the school standards greatly improved.[73]

Despite these developments, Poor Law education never aspired to becoming a basis or a model for state elementary education. It was on too small a scale even to fulfil its own task. It was intended for workhouse children, numbered in 1855 at 50,279, of whom 37,813 were in Poor Law schools of some sort, including 2,732 in the district schools. But there were also some 277,000 children of families on outdoor relief, unprovided with any education except in refuges or mission and 'ragged' schools.[74] Then the district and other workhouse schools were necessarily boarding establishments, and far too costly to be substituted for elementary day schools. Moreover, their residential nature contributed to the perpetual difficulty of finding and keeping suitable staff. The teachers constantly complained of low pay, poor accommodation, insufficient holidays, lack of privacy, hours of supervisory and menial duties, and subordination to uneducated and despotic workhouse masters. In 1860 the resident schoolmistress at Great Boughton resigned because the matron insisted on calling the girls out of class to make the workhouse beds.[75]

Mr Duke has dealt with most of these complaints, pointing out that conditions improved; the pay, including board and lodging did not compare unfavourably with that of the elementary day schools, and there were objects of ambition in the highly paid headships of Norwood, Kirkdale and Swinton.[76] In fact by 1857 the schools, enormously improved, were reasonable, provided comparisons include the private elementary day schools, and not merely the élite of the state-inspected and subsidised primaries. One might add that the extra duties are incidental to all indifferently staffed boarding schools. And yet the permanent barrier to a contented and efficient Poor Law education service was lack of status. If some of the Poor Law teachers were pupil teachers who had been unable to complete their training college courses, they may have been a 'marked improvement' on most of their predecessors[77] but they could only have reinforced the inferior position of the generality of Poor Law schools. The graded certificates were of lower standard than those obtainable at teacher training colleges. Industrial training, however useful – and it was generally aimed at the more menial and lowly-paid occupations, the lower decks of the sea service, and domestic service – tended to limit the time given to school subjects, especially those beyond the three Rs and religious instruction. Moreover, the industrial element was shared with prison schools and reformatories. Pauper schools were a separate and unequal system, isolating pauper children; from which the best were selected as pupil teachers, only to be channelled back into Poor Law teaching. It was not surprising that the most able of them either abandoned teaching for the better-paid posts of workhouse master or Relieving Officer, or shook the Poor Law dust from their feet.[78] Kneller Hall collapsed in 1855 because the pupil-teachers would not go there.

The problem of the illiterate children on outdoor relief was partly met by the Ragged School movement, started by a Portsmouth shoemaker in the 1840s and enthusiastically patronised by Lord Shaftesbury. The Ragged School Union was formed in 1854, and by 1861 it had 192 schools with over 20,000 children and 14 evening schools.[79] But this voluntary and charitable undertaking disquieted philanthropists, since its schools were non-industrial, and taught the rudiments free of charge to dirty and ragged street children (hence its name). Mary Carpenter, while praising the rescue of 'an almost destitute section of the population' argued that the bulk of the children of outdoor paupers ought to be in industrial schools, and the better-off ones in fee-paying schools.[80] Educationists feared that the ragged schools would draw children away from the day schools, thus lowering the general standard of working-class education. The Newcastle Commission refused to recommend them for a government grant.

Poor Law schools were the top grade of a hierarchy catering for the very lowest layers of society. A few enlightened spirits wanted to educate paupers and 'free' children together; but in view of the working classes' carefully fostered fear of pauperism it must be doubted whether mixed schools could have developed harmoniously. The pauper education problem had to wait for a solution until primary education became both compulsory and free, and the children of the indigent, whether outdoor or indoor, could be sent to state-aided and inspected elementary schools, along with their contemporaries.[81]

Factory schools

The factory school was not new in 1833. Dr Michael Sanderson in an interesting article has pointed out that a few of the larger millowners ran schoolrooms with teachers for their young hands as early as the 1780s. This was not pure altruism, but a way of disciplining and improving the work force.[82] Peel's Health and Morals of Apprentices Act of 1802 laid down that the millowner was to provide schoolroom and paid teacher, and that the apprentices were to be taught during some part of every working day, for their first four years in the mill. They could hardly have learned much at the end of a twelve-hour working day, and the Act did not apply to 'free', i.e. non-apprentice, labour. None the less, contrary to what is usually said, it seems to have exercised some influence in promoting factory schools between 1802 and 1833. Sanderson lists a number of mill schools, including several belonging to the Peel family. Other well-known firms, including Pooley's of Manchester, Thomas Welsh of Horwich, the Gregs at Caton, and Henry Ashton at Turton Mill, tried to educate their mill children. They organised Sunday schools, evening schools and infant schools for children below working age. Robert Owen's infant and evening institutes at New Lanark differed from others mainly in their early date and in their experimental curricula and teaching methods. Inevitably millowners sought to avoid interfering with the working day, and young children were taught in the daytime, child workers and adults in the evening. Owen conformed to this pattern, differing only in his anxiety to raise the age at which the young ones left school and entered the factory. Most owners, as the complacent reports of Andrew Ure indicate, were unwilling to admit that long working hours and education were incompatible. Indeed it has been suggested that some foremost opponents of factory legislation for a shorter day salved their consciences by professing an interest in working-class education, and joining the statistical societies to promote it.

A master was traditionally responsible for the education of his apprentices, in theory if not in practice. The Factory Act of 1833 infuriated millowners by making them responsible for the education of children who were not their apprentices but lived with their own parents. It picked on cotton, wool and flax mills, partly exempting silk and wholly exempting lace factories, and it left all other industries untouched. The Act did not require the employer to provide the education himself, but only to obtain a certificate of school attendance for the previous week; but it was accompanied by irritating liabilities. As Dr Sanderson has pointed out, owners could be punished for the truancy of children outside their premises, and even be compelled to send them home and disrupt their own workforce.[83] Many progressive millowners were alienated by the education clauses. W. R. Greg, enthusiastic organiser of factory schools, and an associate of Kay in the Manchester Statistical Society which campaigned for nation-wide elementary education, became a leading opponent of the Factory Act. A few owners had sought to solve the education problem by organising a voluntary relay system. Dr Sanderson cites Howarth, Hardnum Norris & Co. of Bury as employing twenty-three apprentices in the 1820s and having them taught in groups of three or four during brief periods throughout the day.[84] But for reasons already explored, relays were unpopular and coercion to use them was resented. After 1833 much enthusiasm for the voluntary provision of factory schooling was lost.

Despite this resentment, compounded by the loss of rate-assistance for factory-school building from the 1833 Bill in the Lords, a number of schools were initiated under its promptings. Messrs McConnell and Kennedy, acquainted in the past both with New Lanark and with the Gregs' school at Caton, on Leonard Horner's advice, built a school at their Manchester fine-spinning factory. The costs (as was usual at works schools) were met by deductions from wages as well as contributions from the firm. The children were taught in batches, from 10 till 12 in the morning and 2 till 6 in the afternoon, with classes for those over 13 held in the evening.[85] Belper mill had a school with 143 children, each taught for two hours a day between 2.0 and 11.30 a.m. or 1.0 and 6.30 p.m. in a complicated system of classes and relays.[86]

Millowners unable or unwilling to provide their own schools tried to obey the Act by sending their children out to the local day schools. But such arrangements were not often successful. The children arrived at impossible hours, dirty and dishevelled. Their faces and hands were stained with dye, their dress and hair soaked in oil or covered in cotton fluff. 'They seem to take their places in the School as if they didn't belong to it, and had no business there', reported the Rev. Frederick Watkins, National School Inspector for the Northern District, in 1845.[87] At Trinity School, Bolton, the factory children were huddled in a large class near the door, in the coldest and most comfortless part of the room. The master said he could not include them in the ordinary classes without injury to the progress of other children.[88] Although Watkins changed his mind, next year reporting that many factory children were not to be distinguished from the others, whether in neatness of dress or progress in instruction,[89] the Rev. Alexander Thirkell, Inspector for the North West, disagreed. 'The contrast in the looks of the factory children with those of the other scholars, amongst whom they were found, was often quite painful; and it was equally striking and painful in respect to their comparative culture. They stood usually a head and shoulders above the children of equal attainments, amongst whom they mixed – dirty, ignorant, and dull.'[90]

The section on factory education in the Newcastle Commission Report was largely an indictment of the factory schools. Leonard Horner, whose reports were quoted, still believed in 1857 that the half-time system was 'eminently successful' if only the young workers attended a really good school.[91] But he stressed that the defects in the 1833 Act had never been remedied. Rate aid had never been restored, the quality of the education for which attendance certificates were exacted was never checked, and the factory schools had failed to develop. There were a few good schools, but in numerous cases the education of the children was 'another mockery'.[92] Education under the later printworks regulations was no better. The Factory Inspectors' joint report of October 1855 declared they permitted 'nominal school attendance',[93] and in 1857 Inspector Redgrave thought the Print Works Acts nearly useless because the children were 'buffeted from school to work, from work to school, until the tale of 150 hours was told'.[94]

Factory education might have been improved, at least in the small mills, if the millowners had co-operated in setting up shared schools. In 1834 Rochdale Dissenting manufacturers were supporting a British and Foreign School which opened at special hours for the factory children.[95] But they seem to have been exceptional. This lack of provision, together with the low proportion of mills adopting the relay system – never more than one-third in Manchester – suggests large-scale evasion of the education clauses.[96] In 1837, Horner, newly arrived in Lancashire, tried to enforce the law. That year 148 out of 694 convictions in his area were for educational offences, the proceeds of the fines going to schools attended by factory children. But Horner's prosecutions of Greg and Ashworth can have done little to win the co-operation of the millowners.[97] In 1843 Horner listed 117 factory schools, categorising only 16 as 'good'.[98]

Despite these discouragements the factory inspectors clung to their faith in the part-time system, and in the early 1840s tried to make a reality of it. Unfortunately, the scheme, devised by R. J. Saunders, the Tory Anglican Inspector, and put before Peel's government by the Home Secretary Sir James Graham, plunged factory education into the sectarian quarrel.[99]

Graham's Bill of 1843 proposed to reduce the hours of children to six and a half per day, worked either morning or afternoon, with three hours in school. Up to one-third of the cost of school buildings would be obtainable by exchequer loans, repayable from the Poor Rate. The schools would be run by management trusts of seven members, including the vicar, his two church wardens, and four members chosen by the magistrates from mill and property owners. They would be inspected by the clerical trustee. The teachers would be appointed by the trustees, subject to the diocesan's approval. The pupils would have daily lessons in the Scriptures and the Church catechism, and go to church on Sunday, subject only to a conscience clause allowing Nonconformists to withdraw their children from catechism and church.[100]

When the Bill reached its second reading the opposition under Russell, supported by Mark Phillips of the millowners' lobby, Cobden, Ewart and Milner Gibson, rallied against it. Public meetings were held to petition against what was dubbed the 'Tractarian Plot'.[101] Despite government offers to modify the Bill, opposition was not appeased.[102] In face of the growing clamour the government withdrew it, and the Factory Act of 1844 was passed without education clauses. A repetition of Brougham's mistakes in the 1820s destroyed the chance that the factory schools might lead the movement for a rate-assisted system of elementary education. In 1857 Horner classified only 76 schools out of 427 attended by factory children as 'good', 26 as 'tolerably good', 146 as 'inferior', 112 as worse than indifferent, and 66 as positively mischievous, as deceptions and 'a fraud upon the poor ignorant parents who pay the school fees'.[103]

The Print Works Act of 1846 introduced a new principle, in that children were required to produce a certificate of full-time school attendance for the six months preceding their employment. Thereafter they were to attend school for at least thirty days in each six months of work.[104] But the irregular attendance permitted, along with parents' complaints that they could not afford to send their children to school before they were earning, marked dissatisfaction with the arrangement. Reformers soon began to demand that certificates not only of attendance but of educational proficiency should be made the condition of employment. The idea of the literacy test for leaving school and starting work caught on, and was later embodied in Cross's Education Bill of 1874 and the Elementary Education Act of 1876.[105] It was a vicious principle, tending to terminate the full-time education of the cleverest children soonest, and only partly redeemed by the evening schools.

There was another system of factory schools, less well known to historians – the heavy-industry works schools. Those in Wales have recently been explored by Dr Leslie Wynne Evans.[106] Foreign communities of miners and metal workers, especially the Swedes, had brought the tradition of works schools with them into Cumberland, Durham, the Midlands and Cornwall in the sixteenth and seventeenth centuries.[107] Run by the employers and financed by poundage from the parents' wages, they preceded the Industrial Revolution. They formed part of isolated mining, iron- or copper-smelting village communities, where the workers were housed, supervised and educated by the owners, and they were the product of a stronger paternalism than was common in the textile industry. One wonders if Robert Owen knew of Humphrey Mackworth's Works Chantry Schools in Neath and Cardiganshire, or had read his *Familiar Discourse Concerning the Mine Adventure*.[108]

The development of heavy industry in the late eighteenth century, sucking numbers of migrant workers into the industrial areas, resulted in pockets of educational destitution. As a result, some enlightened employers founded schools, sometimes in rivalry with each other. The most important were not single schools but hierarchies, from infant to secondary schools and evening classes, forming a progressive educational ladder. Admittedly, these did not develop much before the middle of the nineteenth century. The most famous example was Sir John Guest's Merthyr Tydfil Schools, which started in a small way in 1814. Guest got help with his building costs from the National Society, and took 1*d* a week from the pupils, contributing company money where needed. His wife, Lady Charlotte, helped with the organisation and teaching. In 1844 new schools were built, and a comprehensive group of institutions appeared, including four infants' schools, a girls' day school, boys' lower and upper schools, male lower and upper evening schools for works employees, and a female evening school for their relatives. The highest actual attendance recorded in these schools in the first half of the century (on 15 October 1850), was 1,041.[109] Guest's scheme was far larger than Owen's earlier Institute; and there were others not far short of it, such as Vivian's copperworks Hafod Schools at Swansea. It would be interesting to know whether educational ventures on this scale appeared in English or Scottish heavy industry areas.[110]

The schools reached an advanced standard in the top classes, especially in science. The 'rescue' operation of the three Rs and religious instruction, which sufficed the ordinary factory school, formed the basis of the curriculum, but at the top promising boys could learn chemistry, mathematics and physics. There were even sandwich courses for young operatives. Brougham's vision of the opportunity for talent to make its way through technical discoveries was being made practical, although no doubt the basic factor was the need of the metal industries to train their own skilled supervisors, and draftsmen. Presumably by the 1840s the textile mills relied on the machine-tool industry for their technical advances, so there was less requirement for a basic scientific or technical education for their overlookers.[111]

However, works schools were not suitable models for a national system. Those which advanced into secondary education were few. The colliery schools were smaller and lower in standard; indeed the mining areas (Sunday schools apart) were often reported as destitute of educational facilities. And most technical education was undertaken not by works schools, but by the Mechanics' Institutes, of which the survivors became, in due course, Technical Colleges, or even the ancestors of provincial universities.[112]

The failures of factory education, especially through its involvement in the sectarian disputes, certainly delayed the spread of elementary education. Disgusted Nonconformists turned to the voluntarist movement, led by Edward Baines of the *Leeds Chronicle*. The Churchmen, making no doubt valiant individual contributions, too patently preferred the perpetuation of ignorance to giving up their own control of education. So now a section of the Nonconformists, inspired by the Congregational Board, set out to convince themselves and others that an efficient elementary school system could be created without external aid, from the Treasury, the rates, or even the factory owners as such. Faced with such attitudes, the government contribution to the development of education in the mid-nineteenth century had to be made largely by stealth.

Sources and references

1. Quoted in **Sturt, M.,** *The Education of the People*. Routledge, 1967, p. 19.
2. **Duppa, Baldwin Francis,** 'Central Society of Education – Objects of the Society', *Central Society of Education*. First Publication of 1837. Woburn Press, 1968, p. 13. The Society's President was Thomas Wyse and it included Lord John Russell among its life members.
3. **Owen, Robert,** *A New View of Society*, 1812. Everyman Edition, p. 45.
4. **Simon, Joan,** 'Post-Restoration development: schools in the county 1660–1700', in *Education in Leicestershire 1540–1940*, Brian Simon (ed.). Leicester U. P., 1968, pp. 32–3.

5. **Smith, Frank,** *A History of English Elementary Education, 1760-1902.* University of London Press, 1931, p. 79. **Simon, Brian,** *Studies in the History of Education.* 1969 ed. Lawrence and Wishart, Vol. I, p. 132.

6. *Minutes of the Committee of the Privy Council on Education,* 1843-44, London HMSO, 1945, pp. 4, 5.

7. Sturt, M., *op. cit.,* p. 13.

8. **Ward, R. G.,** *Religion and Society in England 1790-1850.* Batsford, 1972, pp. 96, 137-40. A. P. Wadsworth gives the date as 1814. See 'The First Manchester Sunday Schools' in Flinn, M. W. and Smout, T. C. (eds.), *Essays in Social History.* Clarendon Press, 1974, p. 111.

9. **Lovett, William,** *Address from the Working Men's Association to the Working Classes on the Subject of National Education.* London, p. 3.

10. **Watson, Alexander, Rev.,** *A Letter to Henry Lord Bishop of Exeter occasioned by a letter from W. F. Hook, etc.* London, 1846, p. 10.

11. Submission of Sir Charles Anderson, 28 June 1859. *Newcastle Commission Report, Answers to the Circular Questions.* Eyre and Spottiswoode, 1861, Vol. V, p. 9. Anderson harped on the theme of Morals before Intellect for the lower orders.

12. Report of Rev. J. Allen, *Minutes,* 1843-44. London, 1845, p. 4.

13. **Silver, Harold,** *The Concept of Popular Education.* MacGibbon and Kee, 1965, p. 26. The discussion of motives in his more recent book, *English Education and the Radicals, 1780-1850.* Routledge, 1975, is more subtle and better balanced.

14. Brougham commissioned Harriet Martineau to write popular stories with free-trade and self-help morals for cottage reading, and Whately wrote economic textbooks for Irish schools, which found their way back into English ones. **Webb, R. K.,** *The British Working Class Reader, 1790-1848.* George Allen and Unwin, 1955, p. 98 *et seq.* For the cheap publications of the Society for the Diffusion of Useful Knowledge, see *Ibid.,* pp. 66-82. Cf. **Goldstrom, J. M.,** 'Richard Whately and Political Economy in school books, 1833-80', *Irish Historical Studies,* XV, No. 58, September, 1966, pp. 131-46.

15. **Lovett, W.** and **Collins, J.,** *Chartism; a New Organisation of the People* (1840). Leicester U. P., 1969. p. 70.

16. Duppa, Baldwin Francis, *op. cit.,* p. 2.

17. The unusual feature of Owen's New Lanark Infant school was not the experimental nature of its methods and curriculum but the fact that the teaching was applied to working-class children.

18. **Brougham, Henry,** *Practical Observations on the Education of the People, Addressed to the Working Classes and their Employers.* London, 1825, p. 10.

19. *Ibid.,* p. 10.

20. It was also in part a response to the need for technical expertise so surprisingly lacking in much early nineteenth-century justification of popular education. For an interesting discussion of the involvement of scientific with working-class education, see **Stephens, M. D.** and **Roderick, G. W.,** 'National attitudes towards scientific education in early nineteenth century England', *The Vocational Aspect of Secondary and Further Education,* XXVI, No. 65, December 1974, pp. 115-20. See also other articles in the same journal.

21. The famous experimental schools of the Hill family, Hazelwood and Bruce Castle, were forced to abandon their teaching of science, languages and political economy in favour of the classics as their fame attracted a more aspiring class of pupil. See **Bartrip, Peter,** 'The Career of Matthew Davenport Hill'. Wales (Cardiff) Ph. D., 1975, pp. 31-40.

22. Lovett and Collins, *op. cit.,* p. 64.

23. Some Labour historians seem unable to realise that education was as much politicised by working-class as by middle-class spokesmen - presumably because they agree with the formers' moral and social views. For example, Simon, Brian, *op. cit.,* p. 177 *et seq.*

24. Smith, Frank, *op. cit.,* pp. 48-61. **Wadsworth, A. P.,** 'The first Manchester Sunday Schools', in *Essays in Social History,* Flinn, M. W. and Smout, T. C. (eds),

pp. 106-119. The latter figure was before the division between Anglicans and Dissenters which produced a temporary decline in numbers.

25. Smith, Frank, *op. cit.*, p. 56.

26. **Evans, L. Wynne,** *Education in Industrial Wales, 1700-1900.* Cardiff, Avalon Press, 1971, pp. 233-9.

27. Smith, Frank, *op. cit.*, p. 60.

28. *Ibid.*, pp. 71-6. Sturt, M., *op. cit.*, pp. 20-1.

29. Sturt, M., *op. cit.*, p. 23.

30. Smith, F., *op. cit.*, p. 78.

31. For example, **Adams, Francis,** *History of the Elementary School Contest in England,* Chapman and Hall, 1873, p. 64.

32. Sturt, M., *op. cit.*, p. 23.

33. **Simon, Joan,** 'Was there a Charity School Movement? The Leicestershire evidence', *Education in Leicestershire, 1840-1940,* Brian Simon (ed.), pp. 90-6.

34. *Ibid.*, pp. 89-96.

35. The extent of the charity-school movement is debated. Joan Simon (*ibid.*) minimises its influence in Leicestershire. **Johnson, Marion,** *Derbyshire Village Schools in the Nineteenth Century.* David and Charles, Newton Abbot, 1970, p. 15. Here it is claimed that in 1800 Derbyshire had 74 charity village schools. For compulsory church attendances, see Johnson, M., *ibid.*, p. 22.

36. Adams, *op. cit.*, p. 63.

37. Adams, *op. cit.*, pp. 65-7.

38. **New, Chester,** *The Life of Henry Brougham to 1830.* Clarendon Press, 1961 p. 211 *et seq.* **Gilbert, Amy Margaret,** 'The Work of Lord Brougham for Education in England'. Univ. of Pennsylvania Ph. D., 1922, pp. 14-49. Franklin Repository. A copy is in University College, Swansea, Library.

39. **Hurt, John,** *Education in Evolution,* Hart-Davis, 1971, p. 19.

40. Gilbert, A. M., *op. cit.*, pp. 45-6.

41. *Ibid.*, p. 44.

42. *Ibid.*, p. 47-9.

43. See **Simon, Brian,** *op. cit.*, pp. 312-17.

44. For the SDUK see Webb, *op. cit.*, pp. 66-74.

45. Smith, Frank, *op. cit.*, pp. 138-9. Sturt, M., *op. cit.*, pp. 67-8.

46. The grant for the royal stables became a stock reproach by educationists and historians. In 1811 the Army had received £120,000 for the elementary instruction of private soldiers. (I am indebted for this information to Mr David Allsobrook of University College, Cardiff.)

47. **Gosden, P. H. J. H.,** *The Development of Educational Administration in England and Wales.* Blackwell, 1966, p. 1.

48. Adams, *op. cit.*, pp. 93-5.

49. Gilbert, *op. cit.*, p. 92.

50. *Ibid.*, pp. 90-101.

51. Adams, *op. cit.*, p. 89-90.

52. **Ball, Nancy,** *Her Majesty's Inspectorate.* Oliver and Boyd, 1963, pp. 8-21.

53. Adams, *op. cit.*, pp. 107-15. Sturt, M., *op. cit.*, pp. 77-85.

54. Gilbert, *op. cit.*, p. 106-7.

55. Adams, *op. cit.*, pp. 13-14. Sturt, M., *op. cit.*, pp. 96-7.

56. Adams, *op. cit.*, p. 115.

57. **Twistleton, E.,** *Report from the Poor Law Commissioners on the Training of Pauper Children. Poor Law Commission Report,* 1841, p. 374.

58. **Smith, Frank,** *The Life and Work of Sir James Kay-Shuttleworth.* John Murray, 1923, pp. 1-34.

59. *Ibid.*, pp. 30-1.

60. **Bloomfield, B. C.** (ed.), 'The autobiography of Sir James Kay-Shuttleworth', *Education Libraries Bulletin,* Supplement 7, 1964, pp. 26-8. Workhouse schools continued to be taught by paupers until Russell, adopting a proposal of Peel, provided £30,000 in the Poor Law estimates of 1846 for workhouse teachers' pay.

61. These were Stow's Glasgow Normal Seminary and Wood's Edinburgh Sessional School.
62. *Autobiography*, p. 28.
63. Lady Noel Byron had been an amanuensis of the famous Swiss educationist de Fellenberg, who ran a school for the sons of gentry and a school for the poor at Hofwyl. English liberals sent their sons to the former and copied the latter for their industrial schools and institutions for the children of the poor.
64. *Autobiography*, pp. 38-9.
65. *Ibid.*, pp. 32-4.
66. *Ibid.*, p. 33.
67. *Ibid.*, pp. 40-2.
68. *Ibid.*, pp. 43-5.
69. **Duke, Francis,** 'The Education of Pauper Children: Policy and Administration, 1834-55'. Manchester M.A., 1968, p. 62 *et seq.* Kay-Shuttleworth also had the backing of Hickson of the Central Society of Education.
70. **Duke, Francis,** 'Pauper education', in Fraser, Derek (ed.), *The New Poor Law in the Nineteenth Century.* Macmillan, 1976, Ch. 3. pp. 67-86. See also his more ample thesis above, on which much of this section is based.
71. *PP* 1857, XXXII, quoted in Duke, Francis, 'The Education of Pauper Children', pp. 183-4.
72. *Ibid.*, pp. 183-5.
73. *Ibid.*, App. 1, pp. 272-3. The grades were Efficiency, Competency, Probation and Permission, each of the first three in three classes.
74. *Ibid.*, pp. 15-21, Footnote 2. In 1855 pauper education facilities were extended to those on outdoor relief, i.e. their school fees could be paid.
75. **Handley, M. D.,** 'Local Administration of the Poor Law in Great Boughton and Wirral Unions and the Chester Local Act Incorporation, 1834-71'. Wales (Bangor), M.A., 1969, p. 241.
76. These headships at £120 a year plus emoluments, were well above those of the average day school. Duke, 'The Education of Pauper Children', pp. 203-70.
77. Duke, 'Pauper education', p. 76.
78. Duke, 'The Education of Pauper Children', pp. 254-5.
79. *Report of the Commissioners Appointed to Inquire into the State of Popular Education in England*, 1861 (hereafter called the *Newcastle Commission Report*), p. 388.
80. *Ibid.*, pp. 392-5.
81. This also allowed the separation of institutions where the children lived from where they were formally educated, and facilitated the reaction against 'barrack schools'.
82. **Sanderson, Michael,** 'Education and the factory in industrial Lancashire', *Econ. Hist. Review*, 2nd series XX, 1967, pp. 266-79.
83. *Ibid.*, p. 271. Cf p. 96 above.
84. *Ibid.*, p. 268.
85. *Ibid.*, p. 273.
86. Johnson, Marion, *op. cit.*, p. 71.
87. *Minutes of the Committee of Council on Education*, 1843-4, London, 1845, p. 134.
88. *Ibid.*, p. 134.
89. *Minutes*, 1846. London, 1847, I, p. 439.
90. *Minutes*, 1847. London, 1847-48, p. 150.
91. *Newcastle Commission Report*, pp. 204-6. Horner, who retired in 1857, became very disillusioned and pessimistic in his last years.
92. *Ibid.*, p. 208.
93. *Ibid.*, p. 212.
94. *Ibid.*, p. 211.
95. Sanderson, Michael, *op. cit.*, p. 274.
96. *Ibid.*, p. 274.
97. *Ibid.*, pp. 275-7.
98. **Robson, A.,** *The Education of Children Engaged in Industry in England 1833-1876.*

Kegan Paul, 1931, p. 71.

99. *Report of Mr R. J. Saunders, upon The Establishment of Schools in the Factory Districts*, in February, 1842. Presented to the House of Commons in pursuance of an Address dated 2 August 1843. W. Clowes and Sons.

100. Robson, *op. cit.*, pp. 73-5.

101. **Symons, Jelinger,** *Light and Life for the People*. London, 1843, pp. 11-16. Symons attacked the whole plan of inspection. Adams, *op. cit.*, p. 120.

102. Adams, *op. cit.*, p. 122.

103. *Newcastle Commission Report*, p. 206.

104. Robson, *op. cit.*, pp. 117-9.

105. *Ibid.*, pp. 207-13.

106. Evans, L. W., *op. cit.*, *passim*.

107. *Ibid.*, pp. iv-v.

108. *Ibid.*, pp. 5-9.

109. For the Dowlais Schools, *ibid.*, pp. 95-120. By 1865 the total attendances reached 2,156. *Ibid.*, pp. 101-2.

110. Miss Hope, a Scottish headmistress, described some colliery and ironworks schools to the Newcastle Commission, but they do not seem to have offered technical or scientific education. The top class of the evening school was reading Greek Testament. *Newcastle Commission Report, Answers to Questions*, 1861, Vol. V, pp. 224-6.

111. Note Howard and Bullough's Works School, Accrington, attached to a firm of textile machinery manufacturers, one of three institutions which merged into Accrington Technical College. But the school was not founded until the 1870s. **Stones, E.,** 'The growth of technical education in nineteenth century Accrington', *Vocational Aspects*, No. 18, Spring 1957, pp. 26-37.

112. See Note 111; and cf. **Roderick, G. W.** and **Stephens, M. D.,** 'Approaches to technical education in nineteenth century England. Pt. IV, The Liverpool Mechanics' Institution.' *Vocational Aspects*, XXV, No. 61, August 1973, pp. 99-104.

11 Elementary education: II

Nineteenth-century controversies about elementary education were conducted with the help of arsenals of statistics. The first of these were collected by Brougham's Select Committee of 1818. In 1833 Lord Kerry's Returns were classified under Infant Schools, Daily Schools and Sunday Schools; and re-classified as schools financed by endowment, by subscription, by fees, and by subscription with fees. In 1834 the Manchester Statistical Society started its attempts to dispel the unfavourable results of Lord Kerry in the industrial towns; and other statistical societies showed special interest in education. Their results were co-ordinated with those from reports of the National and the British and Foreign School Societies by the House of Commons Select Committee on the Education of the Poorer Classes in England and Wales, in 1838.[1] School inspectors continued with a liberal supply of educational statistics in the 1840s, and from 1851 school enrolments and attendances were included in the ten-yearly population census figures. The statistics gave a spurious air of solidity to the conclusions of their various collectors; but the statisticians failed to agree.

The Kerry report of 1833 concluded that about 1,200,000, or roughly one-third of the children in England and Wales between the ages of 4 and 14, were attending day schools; 1,548,890, or under one-half, were attending Sunday schools, of whom one-third went to day schools as well.[2] The Manchester Statistical Society discovered that of some 50,000 children in Manchester between the ages of 5 and 15, two-thirds, or about 33,000, attended schools of some kind, but of these only about one-fifth, or some 10,000, were in day or evening schools, the other 23,000 going to Sunday school only. In Liverpool over half the children attended no school at all. The unsatisfactory nature of educational provision thus revealed was compounded by the Rev. B. Noel, a National Society School Inspector, who had visited Birmingham and found the schools half-empty. Far fewer children were actually in school than appeared on the school books and in the returns.[3] Moreover, the Kerry Report – and Edward Baines – had made the figures more favourable than they really were by counting many children who went both to day and Sunday schools twice over. All these figures were surveyed in a masterly article in the *British Quarterly Review* in 1846 by the Rev. Robert Vaughan,

Principal of the Lancashire Independent College, an anti-voluntarist, who was busy attacking Edward Baines and was anxious to demonstrate the need for more state help to education. Vaughan concluded that less than one-third of the nation's children went to day schools, one-third to Sunday schools, and one-third had no schooling at all. If the average school life was reckoned at 5 years (and for working-class children it was not more than 3 years 4 months) some 1,250,000 children never went to school and must be considered illiterate.[4] Moreover, few of those who only attended Sunday school learned to read, and many day schools were worthless, so the illiteracy figures must be still higher.[5]

Conclusions of this sort were unpopular with the voluntarists who wanted to show that all the education necessary could be supplied without state aid. In 1846 the liberal High Church Vicar of Leeds, Walter Hook, produced a plan for national elementary education organised in school districts established by the county Justices of the Peace and financed by a combination of school pence, government grants and a county rate. Secular lessons would be taught by trained lay teachers, and religious instruction would be provided by ministers of different denominations at special hours twice a week.[6] This careful attempt to deprive a gentry-run state education of its Anglican bias was promptly attacked by Edward Baines, who sought to show that state aid was superfluous as well as productive of Anglican domination and political tyranny. But Baines' position was weak. He had to repudiate Hook's proposal that school places should be provided for one in six of school-age children, and demand only one in nine. He proposed to abandon the children of the city slums, where 'squalid poverty, heathenish ignorance, and brutal sensuality are found in dreadful combination' to the police and missionaries.[7] In fact he appeared as a half-hearted educationist; his figures were shown to be partial and his plan for voluntary schools run by the various religious societies to be an encouragement of sectarian domination and religious controversy.[8]

One reason for the disagreements about literacy figures in the 1830s and 1840s was that the basis on which they were calculated varied continually. School age was reckoned at 5-15, 4-14, 5-13, 3-13, etc.[9] In 1844 Inspector the Rev. John Allen counted parishes without effective schools in his district, and came up with 65 in Bedfordshire, 57 in Cambridgeshire, and 49 in Huntingdonshire. Vaughan concluded that only about one-quarter of the children went to school in rural areas, compared with one-third in towns.[10] The Select Committee on the Education of the Poorer Classes in 1837 used yet another basis, calculating that in any large town, school education ought to be provided for one-eighth of the total population. It then concluded that, on average, only one-twelfth of the population had any kind of daily instruction. Allowing for the worthlessness of most dame schools and many day schools, only 1 person in 24 was enjoying an education likely to be useful. In London the proportion was more like 1 in 27, in Manchester 1 in 35, in Birmingham 1 in 38, and in Leeds 1 in 45.[11]

The statistics thus convey only a rough and inaccurate idea of the proportion of the totally uneducated in the 1830s and 1840s.[12] The impression abides that over one-third of the children had no effective schooling, and it was recognised at the time that the mushrooming industrial towns had the least educational provision. However, by the time of the Newcastle Commission, which drew much of its information from records of 1858, more optimism prevailed. The Assistant Commissioner for the Western District, the Rev. J. Fraser, estimated that two-thirds of the school-age children were actually in school. Of those not in school two-thirds were at work and one-third idling, playing or begging in the streets.[13] Despite this continuation of the 'one-third' impression, the Commissioners, who saw a great improvement since the 1840s, 'Failed to discover any considerable number of children who did not attend school for some time, at some period of their lives'.[14] They later estimated that the number of children on the books of all kinds of weekday schools was 1 in 7.7 of the whole population, the proportion in public (non-profit-making) schools being 1 in 11.65. Actual attendance was, of course, lower, being about 76.1 per cent of those on the books in the public schools, and 84.8 per cent of those on the books of private schools. This record compared favourably with that of other European countries, France's figures of weekday scholars to population being 1 in 9, Holland's 1 in 8.11. In Prussia, where education was compulsory, the proportion was 1 in 6.27.[15]

As well as numbers, educationists were concerned with the length and regularity of school life. This was shortest and most spasmodic at the bottom of the social scale. Baines pointed out that, while controversialists had reckoned school life at roughly 10 years, it was generally nearer 5.[16] Inspector Rev. F. C. Cook reported that in 1845 the average stay of children in west London schools was $1\frac{1}{2}$ years, in east London schools under 12 months; while the average age of children in the top class was below $10\frac{1}{4}$ years. It was as bad in rural eastern England, where boys aged 6 to 8 were kept out in the fields scaring crows for 6 to 7 weeks together. When they returned to school their eyes had 'a furtive wild and startled glance', and they seemed almost to have forgotten how to speak.[17] In Norfolk all the boys between 8 and 10 and some of the girls were kept away from school by their parents at least 4 months in the year, and most left at 10. The reasons given for irregular attendance and early leaving included bad schools, lack of interest in their children's education by some working-class parents, and above all, the need of parents, farmers and other employers for the children's labour. As we have seen, irregular attendance was facilitated by the factory laws in some trades, while conservative opinion – including that of the Newcastle Commissioners – considered the financial independence of the family more important than the education of the individual child.[18]

The results of education could not be estimated simply by the average figures for a more or less brief sojourn in a day school. It was too easy to forget what little had been learned. Mid-nineteenth-century educationists were still concerned with bare literacy. Joseph Fletcher, Committee of Council Inspector for the British and Foreign Society schools, commented in 1846 that half the men in Bedfordshire could not write their names.[19] The usual test, favoured by Horace Mann, the Registrar General in the census of 1851, was whether people signed the marriage register by name or by mark. This was admittedly imperfect. No doubt people learned to write their names for the occasion of their wedding. Moreover, even in 1870 there was still an average 17 years' gap between leaving school and marrying, which meant that the marriage register as a test of school efficiency was always out of date. However, by this test, in 1840 one-third of the men and one-half of the women were illiterate. By 1870, 20 per cent of the men and 27 per cent of the women were illiterate. By 1891 only 6.4 per cent of the men and 7.3 per cent of the women were signing the marriage register by mark.[20] These figures do suggest a rapid and sustained rise in literacy.

A final indication of the need for educational provision could be afforded by a surge in the number of school places, once the 1870 Education Act had enabled the gaps to be filled through school boards and rate subsidies. An example can be found in Derbyshire, where the 1870 enquiry found a deficiency of 8,288 school places in 8 of its Poor Law Unions. Within five years 12 school boards were operating in the county; by 1882 there were 42 Boards and 89 per cent of the school-age population were on the Board School books.[21] Perhaps Derbyshire was untypical, since its efforts brought it up from the bottom to fourth place in the list of average county school attendances. In less enterprising rural Devon, 116 village school boards were established during the 1870s in addition to 10 town-based boards running village schools.[22] But again these figures have to be used with caution. Some 119 of the schools eventually run by Devon's new boards were former voluntary schools taken over. By 1875 Devon had 47 new rural schools, while 70 of the old ones had new buildings. But as Professor West has pointed out, even these were not necessarily additional places. The school board schools, backed by the rates, were driving out of existence a number of the old private and voluntary day schools, and absorbing their pupils.[23] Doubtless this varied in extent. Apart from a few great city boards such as Birmingham, or the Metropolitan School Board, which attracted liberal notabilities and educational enthusiasts, most boards reflected the outlook of the ratepayers who, as we have seen, were not noted for their social generosity.

Controversies about the extent and progress of provision for elementary education in the nineteenth century will doubtless continue; the use of statistics, contemporary and subsequent, being, as always, influenced by disagreements of purpose and attitude among the statisticians. Many have wished to emphasise the importance of state provision in general and the 1870 Act in particular in the achievement of a literate populace. Professor West seems to prefer the thesis that parent demand and private provision, i.e. market forces, were solving the elementary-school problem without the drastic state intervention of 1870, which he considers retarded rather than assisted popular education. Social historians have axes to grind. The available figures, however imperfect, do suggest a steady and marked improvement from the late 1840s onward, and these are reinforced by the steadily increasing percentage of those attending school between 1851 and 1871 drawn from the census occupational lists and enumerators' books by Dr Coleman.[24] Whether the improvement was as great as it could, or should, have been is a matter for the politicians to argue.

Kay-Shuttleworth

By the 1830s educational reformers realised that quality as well as quantity of educational provision was important, even for the poor. The man who sought to give practical expression to this realisation was James Kay-Shuttleworth. This was hardly to be expected, since Kay-Shuttleworth, like Chadwick, frequently expressed fear of and contempt for the people on whom he spent his time and labour, seen as a class.

> The festering mass of crime and debauchery in our towns – the poisonings of our secluded hamlets – the bloody conspiracies of our trade unions – the fanaticism of superstition – the hired assassins of ribandism – the incendiarism of the rural districts – the blank solitude of separate imprisonment – the living hell of a convict ship and the lower depth of a convict gang – these are in the dark background of England's security and wealth.

He saw 'no system of prevention so merciful as that which would elevate these classes to the capacity to fulfil their duties as Christians and citizens'.[25]

Such essays on the 'rescue' theme – and they are frequent in Kay-Shuttleworth's writings – suggest defensive and class-interested motives which could have resulted in very restricted objectives in working-class education. But he was an enthusiast for education seen as the teaching of children, and in this his tone was altogether different and his attitudes enlightened. He deplored the prevalence of beating in schools which, he said, merely made learning repulsive. He criticised the spirit of emulation (encouraged by coloured counters hung around the children's necks, after the fashion of Owen's 'silent monitors') which he found at Lady Noel Byron's school; for he wanted both moral and intellectual learning made attractive for their own sake.[26] Like Owen, he thought children should be encouraged to reason and synthesise, not merely memorise. He recommended plenty of recreation, variety and cheerful activity. He included the singing of secular songs in his curriculum, and stressed the importance of secular learning.[27] He detested both sectarian rivalries and pious jealousy of working-class education, lashing out at the 'medieval party' for trying to establish Anglican domination of the schools, and at the Nonconformist voluntarists who rated the evils of ignorance as 'naught in comparison of the disasters which would occur' if a rate were assessed on the population to finance a national system of education.[28] While he would not curtail intellectual education nor sacrifice it to the inculcation of religious dogma, he would keep it on a Christian and moral basis. He considered the secularists' attempts to separate education from religion contrary to the whole trend of English tradition; so there must be intelligent, not parrot religious teaching in the schools, subject to full safeguards for Nonconformist scruples. This may have been 'rescue' through Christianising the poor; it also resembled Dr Arnold's views on civilising middle-class children.

The quality of education

The abysmal state of infant and day schools may have been exaggerated by early nineteenth-century reformers, but the unanimity of early school inspectors and select committee witnesses is persuasive. Modern defenders of 'the much maligned dame schools' need to prove their thesis in the face of the testimony of contemporary investigators. J. R. Wood, who examined dame schools for a committee of Friends of Education in Birmingham, concluded that only 20 out of some 1,000 in that city were 'of a very superior description'.[29] Wood was not biased, disapproving of the infant schools of the Home and Colonial School Society as much too large and impersonal, and their teaching as too mechanical for small children. In fact, he considered a good dame school 'the most natural and the most proper for children'.[30] But he found that in the majority of them the pupils sat on forms, often unoccupied, and were punished if they made a noise, like the children in a silent-system prison. In one he had visited the mistress had said, 'Hold your tongues, you little devils', and burst into a violent fit of passion, striking the child nearest to her.[31]

The dame schools charged 2d to 7d or 8d a week for children from 2 to 7 years, as did the private common day schools. In the dame schools 26.05 per cent of the pupils learned reading only, and 73.95 per cent learned reading and sewing. In the day schools 42.62 per cent learned reading only, 21.38 per cent learned reading and writing, and 36.00 per cent learned reading, writing and arithmetic.[32] These figures for the Birmingham area, despite their particularity must have been approximate. A few of the more expensive day schools taught grammar and geography.[33]

Wood found many of the dame schools little more than child-minding establishments run as a second line by people pursuing humble occupations such as laundering. They were often kept by women of 'very sour tempers'.[34] One mistress, asked how many pupils she had, thought it unlucky to count them. '"No no", said she, "you shan't catch me counting; see what a pretty mess David made of it when he counted the children of Israel."'[35] Another said 'It is not much they pay me, and it is not much I teach them'.[36] While dame schools were often in damp cellars, Wood described his visit to a common day school with forty children in a garret. 'On a perch, forming a triangle with the corner of the room, sat a cock and two hens; under a stump bed, immediately beneath, was a dog-kennel in the occupation of three black terriers, whose barking, added to the noise of the children, and the cackling of the fowls on the approach of a stranger, were almost deafening; there was only one small window, at which sat the master obstructing three fourths of the light it was capable of admitting.'[37]

The Select Committee, which included W. E. Gladstone, expressed concern for religious and moral training; but in this the schools had little to offer. Henry Althans, London Inspector for the British and Foreign School Society, thought the dame schools could teach children little more than to repeat the Lord's Prayer and the Ten Commandments without explanation.[38] To a question on morals one day-schoolmaster replied, 'That question does not belong to my school, it belongs more to girls' schools.' 'Morals!', said another, 'How am I to teach morals to the like of these?'[39] One dame school mistress replied simply, 'I cannot afford to teach morals at 2d a week.'[40]

Witnesses agreed that the infant schools of the Home and Colonial School Society and the elementary schools of the National and British and Foreign Societies were greatly superior to the dame and day schools, as well as cheaper (at 1d a week). But this was not saying much. In the religious societies' schools, where the monitorial system prevailed, one master struggled with 100 or more children, assisted only by monitors of any age between 7 and 13. Bare literacy and numeracy could be taught by monitorial 'draft', but the instruction was purely repetitive and mechanical, and moral training was obviously impossible. In both National and British and Foreign Society schools, reading lessons were given from the Bible, simply because Bibles were cheap and plentiful and no other books were available. One boy said, 'Yes, I learned to read the Bible at school, but I dinna like to read it now.'[41] The alphabet was learned from the Bible 'amid much flagellation and many tears'.[42] Children were compelled to learn portions of the scriptures as school punishments. It gave them a lasting disgust of Holy Writ.

The early reports of the Committee of Council Inspectors confirmed those of the Select Committee witnesses, and they were reporting on schools which had received government building grants, and might be expected to be the best and most up to date of their kind. The Rev. John Allen, in 1844 complained of lessons devised to occupy the scholars' time with as small demand on the pains and attention of the teacher as possible. The children were learning columns of the English dictionary or pages of grammar textbooks by heart. The schools, he said, put on a show of drilled discipline, while the stronger boys were furtively engaged in tormenting their weaker neighbours.[43]

The Inspectors agreed that in most schools the children were not taught (in the words of Robert Owen) to read and to understand what they read. Up to 300 children supervised by one teacher assisted only by young and often reluctant monitors repeated their lessons in 'stations' round the walls of a large, echoing hall, amid deafening hubbub. It was hardly surprising that children repeated the Lord's Prayer as 'Our Father charter Heaven'.[44] The Rev. F. C. Cook of the Metropolitan area reported that of 3,022 boys he had examined, 1,244 could read only monosyllables, 1,168 read very simple narratives, 611 could read with ease, and some few with intelligence and correct intonation. The proportions among girls were much the same. The standard was generally lower, but 'in some schools, however, they read much better than the boys'.[45] Most London schools taught writing, simple arithmetic, scripture and geography in varying amounts.

There were occasional exceptions to this dismal standard. One such was King's Somborne School, Stockbridge, much praised by the Inspectors.[46] The local rector, the Rev. Richard Dawes, a former Fellow of Downing College, Cambridge, had the children of small farmers and farm labourers taught together. They studied natural science from familiar examples, such as physics from boiling kettles. They read from interesting if pious books such as the *Pilgrim's Progress*, which were in the lending library so that children could take them home to read to their parents. They also had some secular school books from Ireland, presumably Archbishop Whately's. The boys learned geometry, the girls learned to cut out and make up their own clothes. The school ran singing classes and gave concerts. The children were required to come to school clean. There were suggestions that the most able of them should be encouraged by the offer of posts in the lower ranks of the civil service (an anticipation of educational arguments for competitive entry to the service put forward by promoters of the Northcote–Trevelyan reforms in 1851). But such an enlightened administration, which depended on the personal interest of a cultivated clergyman, was not often described in the Inspectors' reports.

The Minutes of 1846

Kay-Shuttleworth believed the key to better standards was better-paid and trained teachers. He set out to change the monitorial system into a sound preliminary to a professional training, and to attract teachers of the right class and calibre by raising salaries.

By Committee of Council Minutes of August and December 1846, selected pupils would be apprenticed at the age of 13 to their teachers. They would receive a grant of £10, increasing annually by £2 10s to £20 when they were 18. They must be taught by the master for 1½ hours each day, and pass the annual Inspector's examination. They were to assist the master in teaching and he would train them in class management and routine duties. He would be paid for this work, provided they passed their examinations.[47]

The pupil-teacher system was not new. Kay-Shuttleworth had seen it in Dutch schools and had introduced it at Norwood.[48] It also formed part of Bishop Blomfield's plan to improve Church schools in London. It was designed to recruit the best of the elementary school pupils, from parents sufficiently prosperous to allow their children to stay at school up to 13 and then continue at a wage lower than they might have earned elsewhere. Although the first pupil-teachers came from the pauper school, Kay-Shuttleworth intended that the bulk of them, without aiming too high in income or social status, should form a link between the children of labourers in elementary schools and the school managers, who were clergy and gentry. They would therefore be mostly from the upper working and lower middle classes. The top section of this ladder of recruitment and training was formed by the teacher training colleges. In 1839 four day training colleges with model schools already existed in the United Kingdom. The best known was Stow's Glasgow Seminary. The other three, all in London, were the Home and Colonial Infant School Society's Training School in the Gray's Inn Road, the National Society's School in Westminster, and the British and Foreign Society's schools in the Borough Road.[49] They took students for very inadequate practical courses of six weeks to three or four months. Thwarted of the state Normal College, Kay-Shuttleworth with Tufnell's help founded Battersea Training College in 1840. Intended at first for Poor Law school teachers, it was handed over to the National Society in 1843. It soon had a High Church rival in St Mark's, Chelsea. Then came St John's College, York, and Chester Training College. The Established Church, having shed its reservations about state grants, took up the challenge; the multiplying Teachers' Training Colleges were mostly diocesan foundations, except for a few such as Homerton, Cambridge, run by the Congregational Board. By 1858 there were thirty-four colleges, and the normal course had extended from one year to two.[50] They were partly financed by the Education Department (as the Committee of Council was often called), through Queen's Scholarships. Free places were awarded to pupil teachers who could produce suitable testimonials from their masters and school managers, and pass the Inspectors' examination.[51] The trained teacher obtained his certificate after two years' probation in a teaching post, in the first, second or third grade according to his final college year examination result. He could then claim a supplement to his salary of between £15 and £30, from the school managers, out of their state grant. Later, with the Inspector's approval he could employ and train his own pupil teachers, receiving a further grant of £5 for one, £9 for two, £12 for three, and £3 each for more. Thus, without interfering with the varieties of basic salary, the Committee of Council supplemented them in such a way as to supply incentives for the qualified and to raise the general level of income and standing of teachers.

The Minutes of 1846 had brought to birth the trained elementary schoolteacher. Did they really improve the standard of teaching? Inevitably there were compromises. The fully certificated teacher long remained only a portion of the teaching force. Teachers in service were allowed to sit the examinations from 1847, although after 1851 they had to have been in a Training College for a year, or in an inspected school for three.[52] By 1852 there was a second rung of assistant teacherships for candidates who had failed to win a Queen's scholarship to a training college. Private and non-grant-aided schools continued to employ whom they pleased, although there was a College of Preceptors offering examinations from 1850. But, in any case, was a certificate holder a better teacher than the others? Professor West has suggested that the colleges were 'pedant factories whose machinery efficiently removed whatever traces of interest in human culture the scholars had somehow picked up earlier in their careers', and that their products were victims of the Victorian obsession with rote learning.[53] To some extent the Newcastle Commissioners agreed, although they failed to propose any changes which would encourage a more humane approach. The early school Inspectors had also protested about the mechanical nature of school teaching, attributing it mainly to the monitorial system for which none of them (except rather surprisingly Joseph Fletcher of the British and Foreign Society) had a good word to say. But it must be doubted whether many of the failed shopkeepers, artisans, labourers or pensioned-off employees appointed by local patrons without qualification, or who set up little schools of their own, made more inspiring teachers, or indeed taught anything at all. Educationists did not entirely fail to notice natural teaching talent, as J. R. Wood showed when he described to the 1837 Select Committee an infant school kept in a cellar by a blind man, 'who hears his scholars their lessons, and explains them with great simplicity', although interrupted by having to turn his wife's mangle.[54] But they did want children to be taught the basic literate skills for further learning, which untrained teachers, whatever the 'colourful variety' of their experience,[55] failed to teach. It seems hardly fair to blame the training colleges for succumbing to mechanical methods which were almost universal. In reasonably efficient private schools lessons were overloaded with 'facts' for memorisation. Children learned the multiplication tables and the names of principal towns and rivers in chorus. But was this much less inspiring than the upper-class boarding schools' constant 'construing' of Latin and Greek prose into English, and the composing by children who were not poets and never would be, of Greek verse? The Teacher Training Colleges may have ruined a number of moderately promising candidates (real talent can usually survive bad training), but they did provide a little teaching material, method and possibly much-needed self-confidence; and they gave the general run of grant-aided schools some sort of safety net or basic standard of informed instruction. The colleges' failing was not so much mechanical learning as the long hours, vast syllabuses, addiction to textbooks, and the pretentious and superficial nature of the courses (features by no means dead in all present-day Colleges of Education). These were severely criticised by the Newcastle Commissioners who, however, did not seem to have decided whether less should be learned more thoroughly and intelligently to improve teachers' education, or whether elementary schoolteachers did not need to know so much, anyway.[56]

A more inspiring Training College course might have followed from Kay-Shuttleworth's judicious mixture of academic with agricultural and industrial training at Battersea. But although a few colleges such as Chester (as well as the eternal plain sewing for girls) had industrial courses, they tended to die out. College staffs, students, teachers and parents tacitly turned their backs on educational schemes resembling those designed to inculcate 'habits of industry' in the refuse of society. Instead, Training College students learned Latin, which they could never teach, because their Oxford- and Cambridge-educated principals could teach it to them. They learned English and imperial history, the former to encourage patriotism, the latter, it was said, to encourage emigration, in a factual way. They learned the rules of English grammar, and worked out complicated and arid mathematical problems. The Inspectors themselves discouraged both analytical thinking and imagination by their examinations which (as examinations do) conditioned the syllabus and nature of the teaching. Compulsory questions were scattered thinly over enormous tracts of political history and English literature. The questions were always of the 'recount' or 'describe' kind, requiring no attempt at explanation or critical understanding.[57] The spread of superficial knowledge thus demanded amounted to an education in bits and bobs. If serious scholarship was out of the question, it was a pity that nothing more inspiring could be found at the apex of this lower grade of higher education. The gap in standing opened between training college and university tended to perpetuate itself when vocational aim and intellectual proficiency began to take over from social class as the guiding influence in young people's choice of further education.

The teachers

The main cause of poor teaching in elementary schools was generally considered to be the low wages of teachers and the low esteem which they reflected. The Minutes of 1846, which attempted to solve the problem by state grants, left the basic variations and inequities untouched. Salaries varied from area to area and from school to school, depending on endowments, contributions and school fees. In some cases, school pence, collected by the teacher, increased according to the number of subjects taken by the pupil. Inspector Rev. Henry Moseley found the average salary of a schoolmaster in the Midlands, calculated from 55 boys' schools, was £51 15s 3d, that of mistresses calculated over 46 girls' schools was £28 19s and that of infant-school mistresses, calculated over 18 schools was £18 6s 1d. In 30 out of 54 schools a rent-free teacher's house was provided. Of 47 teachers examined 28 had received a few days' or weeks' training at a model school.[58] This was, of course, before the Minutes. A salary of £51 was less than an adult male operative could earn in a spinning mill, even adding a low-rent cottage or living room over the school. Women got one-third to one-half less, which continued despite their tendency to be from a superior social background, since work openings for young middle-class women were so few. By 1855 the average earnings of a certificated schoolmaster were assessed by the Education Department at about £90.[59] The Newcastle Commissioners referred casually and disparagingly to boys educated at the public expense who could be sure of average earnings of £100 for a five-day week with six or seven weeks' vacation.[60] Salaries had risen with the multiplication of state grants, culminating in the big capitation grants calculated on the number of school attendances, which spread from rural to urban schools in 1853–56. They were still far short of Inspectors' salary levels, despite the reduction of the latter from £600 to £450 (and Assistant Inspectors at £250) designed to attract impecunious graduate curates.

Higher pay would have removed elementary schoolteachers too far from the class of their pupils, and weakened the sympathy and understanding supposed to be felt between them. The teacher stereotype developed by Kay-Shuttleworth and the early Inspectors was of a devoted, unambitious, unenterprising, self-sacrificing individual. Kay-Shuttleworth told Inspectors of Training Colleges to ascertain whether the diet was so simple, the household arrangements so divested of luxury, the domestic duties so formed as to prepare them (the students) for the humble position and probable privations of a schoolmaster's life.

Henry Moseley, the most distinguished of the early Inspectors, described the rewards of the good teacher:

> In the enjoyment of the friendly regard of his clergyman, the esteem of his neighbours, and the grateful affection of the children entrusted to his charge, I have seen this man surrounded by many of the amenities of a station in life superior to his own, without its factitious wants; and reflecting on the allotment of happiness to different orders of men, and upon the degree in which they severally minister to the glory of God and the public welfare, I have thought that of the elementary schoolmaster, whilst it was surpassed by no other in value or importance, to yield to no other in its proper sources of enjoyment.[61]

The struggle of Kay-Shuttleworth and his Inspectors for more education, better schools and higher salaries and status was entirely compatible with their conception of the humble position of the elementary schoolteacher. The gulf between the institutions of the lower orders and the public boarding schools and ancient universities of the upper ones was so wide, and the substance so different, that no encroachments need be feared. Even the poor clergyman's son who earned his bread as an Oxford scholar acting as servant to a young nobleman sporting a gold tassel on his mortar board, had his foot on an entirely different educational ladder from that of the elementary schoolteacher.[62] The latter had only to keep his place, and refrain from 'an indiscreet display of information' on Latin which . . . 'is very apt to alarm or disgust the bystander at public examinations'.[63] Etymology, a curious subject in which children were taught the linguistic roots of English words, seems to have been considered as close to Latin as the elementary schoolchild should be permitted to aspire.

Yet however often this humble ideal was presented for emulation, the reality was often different. Elementary schoolmasters were educated above their station. In the 1850s they began to demand promotion to the Inspectorate, to leave the schools for better jobs, or to climb into the Church.[64] The Newcastle Commissioners, ever blending common sense with snobbery, refuted charges that teachers were conceited and bad-mannered in a manner suggesting that they agreed with them. They rejected the teachers' demand for promotion to the Inspectorate on the grounds that their complaint of not being recognised as social equals by school managers and clergy was a conclusive argument against it.[65] In 1861 a new grade of Assistant to the Inspectors for routine examining under the Revised Code started the process of bridging the gap, and the Newcastle Commissioners' verdict was repudiated by the Cross Commissioners in 1888. But the consciousness of being treated as inferior had sunk deep. In the 1850s and 1860s the rescue operation designed to reconcile the classes at a time of bitter social conflict was exciting social jealousy at a time of comparative harmony. Frederick Temple, a much-quoted witness to the Newcastle Commission, envisaged an educational ladder for clever boys, from elementary to middle-class schools, and thence, through a modern education in literature, languages, mathematics and science, to the universities.[66]

Grants and Inspectors

If educational progress can be measured by expenditure, there was remarkable progress in the mid-nineteenth century. The original £20,000 grant for school building of 1833 had become by 1850 grants totalling £189,000 in the year, and by 1860, £724,000. They covered pupil-teachers' stipends, teachers' augmentation grants, Training Colleges, school apparatus, maps and books, and most expensive, the capitation grants originally designed to compensate for the weaknesses of voluntary fund-raising in poor areas. From 1856 the Committee of Council on Education had a Vice-President to represent it in parliament. It supervised the School of Design, and ran a staff of 127, including clerks, examiners, and some 46 travelling Inspectors and Assistant Inspectors. Education, advocated as so much cheaper than crime, was costing nearly £1,000,000 compared with the £460,029 of prisons and convict establishments.[67] Yet the 1850s were considered a period of comparative educational stagnation. This was partly because all reformers (except the voluntarists) were now convinced that a national school system could not be completed without support from the rates, while the continuing sectarian jealousies defeated all attempts to secure rate support. Resolutions by Lord John Russell in 1846, Bills in 1850, 1852, 1853, the recommendations of the Newcastle Commission in 1861 and a further Bill by Sir John Pakington in 1862, all failed.[68] Most of the schemes included school districts, rate support, and elected school committees with a proportion of ratepayer representation. Pressure for them came largely from secular groups such as the National Public Schools Association.[69] Their failure ensured that government bounty continued to be channelled through the voluntary religious societies, now increased to cover most of the sects.[70] Dissatisfied reformers procured the capitation grants to provide some of the money for education lost with the Bills. Only the occasional enthusiast betrayed misgivings as to the actual effects of rate aid and its concomitant, ratepayers' control. Temple, worried about the proposals for parish school districts, warned that districts should not be too small. The school guardians would be 'too near the poor to be wisely trusted with their interests. . . . Such vestries would be much more likely to regard with jealous fear any improvement in the labourer's condition which raised him nearer to themselves'.[71] Moseley conceived that local support would consign many schools to the care of the classes most suspicious of working-class education. It was well known that rural schools were poor because the farmers and landowners refused to contribute, leaving all the fund-raising to the more enlightened parish clergy and their women folk.[72]

The continuation of central grants ensured the survival and increase of the Inspectorate. The Inspectors had multiplied rapidly. From 2 in 1840, they had become 23 with 2 Assistant Inspectors in 1852, 36 with 25 Assistant Inspectors in 1861, and 62 with 14 Inspectors' Assistants (the new examination aides chosen from the teachers) in 1864.[73] The early appointments of mature men of experience and distinction had gradually given way to those of younger Oxford and Cambridge graduates seeking a secure if dull berth. The process was probably speeded by the uninspiring presence of Lingen, who succeeded Kay-Shuttleworth in the Secretary-ship in 1849, and the drop in salary. The early Inspectors had generally been welcomed as allies of the struggling teachers. The later ones, having lost the enthusiasm which compensated for differences of class and education from those they inspected, were looked on increasingly as aliens. After 1861 the Revised Code tempted some of them to become petty tyrants. The reports of such pioneers as John Allen, F. C. Cook, Joseph Fletcher and Henry Moseley, leave an impression of zeal for education regardless of the sectarian jealousies which plagued the voluntary societies. In the very eye of the sectarian storm this religiously divided body of men seems to have been freer from disagreements than the Factory or the Prison Inspectors. The rows between the travelling Inspectors and Lingen in the 1850s over the editing of the Inspectors' reports cannot have helped morale, while the enormous task of examining annually all the children in the inspected schools after 1861 could not but exercise a bad influence on Inspectors' manners. A wearing routine combined with too much power over individuals is bad for anyone.

The growth of education, and the Newcastle Committee

Despite its many deficiencies, the notable feature of elementary education between 1833 and 1861 was its comparatively rapid and solid development. Possibly it was fortunate that it was not handed over to local government in the 1850s. Even after 1870 few of the school boards attracted the distinguished talents and enthusiasm of the London School Board or those of a few other cities. Many rural boards inclined to a pinching economy. Despite the battle of figures, historians on the whole seem to agree with contemporaries that a substantial improvement in literacy took place in the 1850s, while the Newcastle Commissioners assumed that the rescue mission had been accomplished. The Inspectors reported that discipline was excellent, good or fair in 94.3 per cent of the grant-aided schools, and in 75.7 per cent of the others.[74] The result, as illustrated by Kidsgrove School, Burslem (a colliery school established in 1839 and rebuilt in 1853), was a local respect for the Church, absence of drunkenness, improvement in female morals, general orderliness and lack of crime.[75] The Dean of Bristol was quoted as remarking on a fundamental improvement in the candour, intelligence and civility of the inhabitants of the back streets, which the Inspector attributed largely to education.[76] The Newcastle Commissioners concluded that 'the religious and moral influence of the public schools appears to be very great, to be greater than even their intellectual influence. A set of good schools civilises a whole neighbourhood. The most important function of the schools is that which they best perform'.[77] The Commissioners forgot they were reporting in a time of prosperity, which might, equally with education, account for the quiescence of the lower orders.

The Commissioners did not attribute this improvement to religious education, which they believed to be usually mechanical and useless. They relied on the moral influence of non-sectarian religion and secular learning. They were impatient of sectarian rivalries, and their recommendation for county and borough school boards financed from taxes and rates was a milestone in the adoption of secular policies in public education.[78]

A vital indication of the condition of elementary education lies in the subjects taught and the expectations of educationists as to what a school should be able to achieve. In 1846 Joseph Fletcher, inspecting the British and Foreign Society schools found that the majority of children did not get beyond the three Rs. Much of the girls' time was taken up with plain needlework. The monitors, however, were being taught some geography ('learning maps'), music, drawing, mensuration (mental arithmetic), and 'etymological exercises'.[79] H. W. Bellairs from the Western District regretted the absence of geography and history in many schools.[80] In 1847 Henry Moseley from the Southern District reported that 1 in $2\frac{3}{4}$ of the children was writing on paper – presumably more advanced than on slates – 1 in 5 learning geography, 1 in $10\frac{3}{5}$ learning grammar, 1 in $11\frac{1}{5}$ learning English History, and 1 in $5\frac{7}{9}$ learning 'vocal music'.[81] Only a small minority reached the academic heights, and since in some schools the 'extra' subjects still depended on extra fees, the tendency of the better-off to be better educated tended to reconstitute itself, even at this humble level. Yet by the end of the 1840s it seems that something more than bare literacy was expected in the top pupils of elementary schools; while the training of monitors, and after 1846, of pupil-teachers, was promoting some expansion into the secondary-school level. By 1853, Kay-Shuttleworth could claim that, where formerly a vast number had left school unable to read, write or cipher, a fair proportion could now 'write neatly and not incorrectly from dictation, read the Holy Scriptures and common secular books with tolerable ease, work elementary rules in arithmetic with facility, and have some acquaintance with geography, the history of their own country, and . . . the rudiments of natural history'.[82] It was a far cry from Hannah More allowing 'of no writing for the poor'.

Eight years later the Newcastle Commission pitched its expectations no higher. Concluding that the pupil-teacher and Training College system was encouraging teachers to neglect the basic education of the lower standards and poorer children who left early, for the instruction of the older and brighter children in fancy subjects, it reversed the trend towards secondary education. It should be left to the evening schools 'to give full cultivation to those who even in the humbler classes are found endowed with superior mental powers, and with the legitimate desire to raise themselves by their improvement'.[83] The teachers should be made to carry out their proper function of drilling the three Rs into the younger children who formed the bulk of the elementary school population. It gave official blessing to the goal formulated by Assistant Commissioner the Rev. J. Fraser for the child leaving school in an agricultural district:

> If he has been properly looked after in the lower classes, he shall be able to spell correctly the words that he will ordinarily have to use; he shall read a common narrative – the paragraph in the newspaper that he cares to read – with sufficient ease to be a pleasure to himself and to convey information to listeners; if

gone to live at a distance from home, he shall write his mother a letter that shall be both legible and intelligible; he knows enough of ciphering to make out, or test, the correctness of a common shop bill; if he hears talk of foreign countries, he has some notion of the part of the habitable globe in which they lie; and underlying all and not without its influence I trust, upon his life and conversation, he has acquaintance enough with the Holy Scriptures to follow the allusions and arguments of a good plain Saxon sermon, and a sufficient recollection of the truth taught him in his Catechism to know what are the duties required of him towards his Maker and his fellow man.[84]

This, they thought, was the plain education demanded by working-class parents for their children, who patronised the schools which gave it, and had, provided they were not forced into church on Sundays, little regard to their religious complexion. The grants system should be recast to ensure that it was available. In future there would be two grants – one from the Treasury to schools with a certificated teacher, at 5s 6d to 6s 0d per pupil for schools of fewer than 60 children and 4s 6d to 5s 0d for larger schools, another from a county rate of between 22s 6d and 21s 0d for each child over 7 who had attended at least 140 days in the preceding year and passed the Inspector's examination.[85] This was the inspiration for the famous Revised Code which instituted 'payment by results' on the basis of examinations in reading, writing and arithmetic. The Commissioners' recommendation could be interpreted equally as an attempt by that conservative and class-ridden body to keep working-class education in its place, or as the first of those swings towards safeguarding the education of the 'average' child at the cost of the intellectual élite, with which we are all familiar. Under Lowe it became an economy measure which retarded the development of working-class schools and the teaching profession until the 1870s.

Compulsory education and free education were still to come. The need for compulsion had long been apparent to the Inspectors. The failure of many of the poorer classes to educate their children, wrote the Rev. Frederick Watkins from the Northern District in 1845, 'arises, I believe, not so frequently from abject poverty as from utter carelessness, and an almost inconceivable indifference to everything beyond the concerns of the merely animal life'.[86] Compulsion came late because it marked acceptance of the principle that the state should interfere for the child against its parent.[87] It also established education as the barrier to, instead of the accompaniment of, child labour. This was facilitated by the fact that the demand for child labour was at last beginning to wane. Free education ended the invidious distinction between those who came with their school pence and those who did not, within the schools. It marked a very small step towards the demand for equal educational opportunity.

Elementary education in the 1860s entered a period of some regression. The low intellectual target set by the Newcastle Commissioners for the education of the poor can be compared with the hardening in Poor Law attitudes in the 1870s. Although slightly out of phase with each other, several aspects of social administration went through these periods of regression in the third quarter of the nineteenth century. Despite the reforms of the Gladstone and Disraeli ministries, social attitudes towards the lower orders remained fairly constant until the 1880s. In that decade came signs of a serious movement towards building educational ladders through the elementary school to middle-class schools and universities. Once again education was coming to resume its role as a means of social mobility. But by that time English education had become so deeply entrenched in the class structure that the education of children was doomed to fall victim to the social and political struggles of the twentieth century.

Sources and references

1. *Report from the Select Committee to consider the means of providing useful education for the poorer classes in large towns throughout England and Wales. PP* 1837–38, VII. The figures were taken from the reports of the National and the British and Foreign School Societies, and from the Statistical Societies of Manchester, Birmingham, Bristol and London. School age was given as between 3 and 13, calculated as being about one-quarter of the total population. The early inquiries are briefly discussed in **Coleman, B. I.,** 'The Incidence of Education in mid-century', in Wrigley, E. A. (ed.), *Nineteenth Century Society*, C.U.P., 1972, p. 398.
2. The figures were quoted in **Vaughan, Robert, D. D.,** 'Popular education in England', *British Quarterly Review*, VIII, 1846, pp. 444–508.
3. *Ibid.*, p. 454.
4. *Ibid.*, pp. 456–60.
5. On the other hand, it has been more recently suggested that a number of the smaller day schools in the larger towns eluded these early inquiries, so that the figures were unduly pessimistic. Coleman, *op. cit.*, p. 398. The number of school children omitted is unascertainable.
6. **Hook, Walter Farquhar, D. D.,** *A Letter to the Lord Bishop of St Davids, on the Means of Rendering More Efficient the Education of the People*, 9th ed. London, Murray 1846, *passim.*
7. **Baines, Edward, Jnr.,** *A Letter to the Rt. Hon. Lord John Russell on ... State Education*, London, 1846, pp. 20–1, 22–3.
8. **Temple, Frederick,** 'National Education', in *Oxford Essays*. London, 1856, pp. 218–70, *passim.*
9. The proportion was, of course, affected by the length of the period designated 'school age', the peak attendances being generally between 5 and 10. **West, E. G.,** *Education and the State*, Inst. of Economic Affairs, 1965, pp. 144–5. Professor West suggests that at the time of the Newcastle Commission, 5–11 would have been a more realistic calculation than that of Forster's officials in 1869, who gave it as 5–13, and this would have given a higher proportion in school.
10. Quoted in Vaughan, *op. cit.*, pp. 461–2.
11. *Report from the Select Committee on the Education of the Poorer Classes in England and Wales*, 1838, pp. iv–viii.
12. *Ibid.* Coleman shows that after 1851 these figures can be compared with the children listed as 'scholars' in the occupational sections of the census surveys, which yield rather higher numbers of those being educated. Coleman, *op. cit.*, pp. 398–410.

13. *Newcastle Commission Report*, p. 85.

14. *Ibid.*, p. 85.

15. *Ibid.*, p. 573. The Commission calculated that out of a possible 2,655,767 children (estimated by counting all the children between the ages of 3 and 15 and halving them to produce an assumed school life of 6 years) 35,000 were on the books of collegiate and superior endowed schools, 286,768 in private schools for the upper and middle classes, and 2,213,694 in schools for the poorer classes. These, including ragged, reformatory and prison schools, left only an estimated 120,305 who had never been on any weekday school register at all. This included those educated at home (presumably quite a lot of upper-class girls) and the unknown number of physically and mentally disabled. It was, on any reckoning, a small minority.

16. Obviously a rough guess. Baines, *op. cit.*, pp. 29-31.

17. *Minutes*, 1845. London, 1846, I, pp. 153-8.

18. *Newcastle Commission Report*, pp. 170-92. The commissioners estimated the average school life in their town at 5-7 years.

19. *Minutes*, 1846. London, 1847, II, p. 26.

20. West, E. G., *op. cit.*, pp. 132-3. Professor West discusses the whole question of literacy tests in the nineteenth century in Chapter 9 of his book.

21. **Johnson, Marion,** *Derbyshire Village Schools in the Nineteenth Century.* David and Charles, 1970, pp. 118-21.

22. **Sellman, Roger,** *Devon Village Schools in the Nineteenth Century.* David and Charles, 1967, p. 55.

23. West, E. G., *op cit.*, pp. 151-6.

24. See the figures for Warwickshire. Coleman, *op. cit.*, p. 404.

25. **Kay-Shuttleworth, Sir James,** *Public Education as affected by the Minutes of the Committee of the Privy Council from 1846-1852.* London, 1853, p. 46. He was arguing against the voluntarists for government support for education.

26. Evidence to the *Select Committee on the Education of the Poorer Classes in England and Wales*, 1838, pp. 18-20.

27. Evidence of Kay-Shuttleworth, *Select Committee on the Education of the Poorer Classes*, 1838, p. 20. See also Twistleton's report on the Training of Pauper Children and on District Schools. *Report from the Poor Law Commissioners on the Training of Pauper Children.* London, 1841, p. 365.

28. Kay-Shuttleworth, *op. cit.*, p. 27.

29. *Report from the Select Committee on the Education of the Poorer Classes*, 1838, p. 117.

30. *Ibid.*, p. 117.

31. *Ibid.*, p. 116.

32. *ibid.*, p. 120.

33. *Ibid.*, p. 137. Evidence of Henry Althans. The distinction between 'private' and 'common' day schools is not clear.

34. Evidence of J. R. Wood, *ibid.*, p. 116. Evidence of Henry Althans, *ibid.*, p. 136.

35. Evidence of J. R. Wood, *ibid.*, p. 104.

36. *Ibid.*, p. 104.

37. *Ibid.*, p. 103.

38. Evidence of Henry Althans, *ibid.*, p. 136.

39. Evidence of J. R. Wood, *ibid.*, p. 106.

40. *Ibid.*, p. 120.

41. *Ibid.*, p. 125.

42. *Ibid.*, p. 112.

43. *Minutes*, 1843-44. London, 1845, p. 6.

44. *Ibid.*, p. 69.

45. *Ibid.*, p. 66.

46. For reports on King's Somborne School see *Minutes*, 1843-44, pp. 48-51; *Minutes*, 1845, pp. 103-6; *Minutes*, 1847-48. London, 1848, pp. 4-14. Inspector Allen also described and praised some of the works schools in Pembrokeshire.

47. **Ball, N.,** *Her Majesty's Inspectorate, 1839-1849.* Oliver and Boyd, 1963, pp. 124-5.

48. **Bloomfield, B. C.** (ed.), 'The autobiography of Sir James Kay-Shuttleworth', *Education Libraries Bulletin*, Supplement 7, pp. 49, 57, 64. Kay-Shuttleworth, *op. cit.*, pp. 58–61.

49. Ball, N., *op. cit.*, p. 149.

50. *The Newcastle Commission Report*, pp. 114–5, gave a list of these training colleges in 1858. There were 13 C. of E. Colleges for men, 11 for women, and 2 co-educational. There was a Roman Catholic College for men at Hammersmith and a British and Foreign non-denominational men's college at Bangor, North Wales. There were also 2 Roman Catholic colleges for women, 4 British and Foreign non-denominational mixed colleges, and a Wesleyan college in Westminster. Homerton was voluntarist, and refused the state grant.

51. Ball, N., *op. cit.*, p. 125. According to the Newcastle Commission Report some three-year courses had been found unsatisfactory and reduced to two years by Archbishop Temple.

52. **Hurt, J.,** *Education in Evolution.* Hart-Davis, 1971, pp. 95–7.

53. West, E. G., *op. cit.*, p. 168, quoting from Altick, R. D., *The English Common Reader*.

54. *Select Committee on the Education of the Poorer Classes in England and Wales*, 1838, p. 105.

55. West, *op. cit.*, p. 167.

56. *Newcastle Commission Report*, pp. 132–7.

57. For examination papers, see *Minutes*, 1847–48. London, 1848, pp. lv–lxi.

58. *Minutes*, 1845. London, 1846, I, p. 241.

59. **Duke, F.,** 'The Education of Pauper Children: Policy and Administration, 1834–1855'. Manchester M.A., 1968, p. 234. Hurt gives the average salary in 1854 as £85 15s 6½d, ranging from £132 in London to £65 in Somerset, and £60 in Roman Catholic schools, which paid the lowest salaries. Hurt, J., *op. cit.*, p. 143.

60. *Newcastle Commission Report*, p. 160.

61. *Minutes*, 1843–44. London, 1845, p. 244. Moseley was a mathematician, and had been Professor of Natural Philosophy and Astronomy at King's College, London. His promotion to the inspectorate (and Leonard Horner's) says something about the high standing of these early public servants.

62. Cf. **Hughes, Thomas,** *Tom Brown at Oxford*.

63. Cook's Report on the Eastern District. *Minutes*, 1845. London, 1846, p. 144.

64. Hurt, J., *op. cit.*, p. 135 *et seq.*

65. *Newcastle Commission Report*, pp. 157–60.

66. Temple, Frederick, *op. cit.*, p. 267. Temple was Principal of Kneller Hall, an essayist in the controversial *Essays and Reviews*, and later Archbishop of Canterbury. The Chief Rabbi, Herman Adler, also suggested a scholarship ladder in his evidence to the Newcastle Commission.

67. £893,118 at Lord President of the Council's disposal, but police and justice cost £2,565,301. Hurt, J., *op. cit.*, pp. 186–7.

68. **Gordon, Peter,** 'The Elementary School Manager and the Management of Education, 1800–1902'. London Ph. D., 1970, pp. 178–201.

69. Founded in 1851 as the Lancashire Public Schools Association.

70. These now included the original National and British and Foreign Schools Societies, the Wesleyan Education Committee (1837), the Congregational Board (1843), the Catholic Poor School Committee (1847) and the London Committee of British Jews.

71. Temple criticising Russell's Bill of 1856. Temple, *op. cit.*, pp. 255–6. Gordon, P., *op. cit.*, pp. 251–8.

72. *Minutes*, 1845. London, 1846, I, p. 226. Cf. Table of Annual Subscriptions paid by Landowners, Occupiers and Clergy, in *Newcastle Commission Report*, p. 77.

73. Hurt, *op. cit.*, p. 42, Table 1.

74. *Newcastle Commission Report*, p. 267.

75. *Ibid.*, pp. 267–9.

76. Report of Mr Cumin, Assistant Commissioner for Bristol. *Ibid.*, p. 272.
77. *Ibid.*, p. 273.
78. *Ibid.*, pp. 328–31.
79. *Minutes*, 1846. London, 1847, II, pp. 86–107.
80. *Minutes*, 1846. London, 1847, I, p. 476.
81. *Minutes*, 1847–48. London, 1848, p. 3.
82. Kay-Shuttleworth, *op. cit.*, p. 94.
83. *Newcastle Commission Report*, p. 266.
84. *Newcastle Commission Report*, p. 243.
85. *Ibid.*, pp. 329–30.
86. *Minutes*, 1843–44. London, 1845, p. 129. Complaints about the indifference of parents to their children's education abound in the Inspectors' reports. It is difficult to agree with Professor West that good schools would, without compulsion, have produced universal education.
87. This was, of course, a subsidiary and unpublicised aim of the 1833 Factory Act and its successors.

12 The machinery of reform

Pressure groups

The reform of nineteenth-century social administration displayed at least five common features. Firstly, reforms were usually promoted by one or more pressure groups, some representing the victory of one pressure group over its rivals or opponents. Secondly, reforming measures were often preceded by government enquiries in the shape of parliamentary Select Committees, or government-appointed Royal Commissions, or both. Thirdly, such measures were usually enforced with the help of government inspectors, responsible either to a new commission or embryonic government department, or to a new branch of an existing department. The Poor Law Commission is a classic example of the former, the prisons section of the Home Office of the latter. The Committee of the Privy Council on Education was a compromise or hybrid. Fourthly, the inspectors were one example of a growing professionalism associated with administrative reforms. Many of the measures involved a continuous effort to turn fee-taking officials such as gaolers, or the employees (often under contract) of decayed local institutions, such as workhouse-masters and local constables, into professional, salaried, sometimes uniformed and more-or-less uniformly-paid state or local government servants. This usually took a very long time, and was not always successful. Finally, the reforms nearly always necessitated new regional or local organisations. These varied from the huge, uneven and unstable districts of the factory inspectors to the Poor Law Union, which formed a potentially strong unit of local government.

Almost all legislation had to be forced on the government by pressure groups of one kind or another.[1] Their pressure was often applied by means of mass petitioning campaigns, particularly effective in the period 1780–1833 when petitions were regularly introduced and debated in the two Houses of Parliament. This technique was particularly useful in promoting 'once-for-all' measures such as the repeal of the property tax in 1816, and Roman Catholic emancipation in 1829.[2] It was occasionally used in the context of administrative reforms, notably in efforts to get them modified or abolished, as in the attack on the Poor Law Amendment Act in 1837. But mass petitioning was less suitable for laws which needed long-term enforcement, at least on its own. Where a law had not only to be formulated, promoted and passed but continually enforced against slackness or opposition, there was need of a watchdog or vigilante society, acting through friends in high places. Such societies might enforce the law themselves, as did the Proclamation Society, its successor, the Society for the Suppression of Vice, and the later Sabbath Day Observance Society (all run by the Evangelicals), inspiring the laws and then prosecuting those who broke them in the courts. But most long-term pressure groups, such as the Prison Discipline Society or the Health of Large Towns Association, had to operate by pressure on government administrative agencies.

Pressure groups so numerous, varied and pervasive are easier to detect than to classify.[3] However, it is possible to distinguish at least two main types of early nineteenth-century pressure group for social reform. One is the large, multi-branched group, barely if at all distinguishable from a mass movement. Such were the short-time committees, distinguished from the trade unions on which they were based largely by the presence of a few philanthropic factory masters, which enabled them to acquire a parliamentary lobby. The millowners formed a rival pressure group, also acting through a parliamentary lobby. The Factory Act of 1833 was the fruit of Chadwick's neat insertion of his own solutions between those of the warring factions. Other such groups were the anti-Poor Law Associations, containing many of the same local leaders, and doubtless with a trade-club basis, which, however, did not achieve a significant parliamentary lobby. They may be compared with the anti-Corn Law League and with the Chartists; but the restricted franchise made it more difficult for working-class movements to gain the advantage of a lobby at the centre of politics.

More typical were the Quaker-led Prison Discipline Society, or the Evangelical Labourer's Friend Society, which began in 1830 as an association for providing labourers with allotments and was later reconstituted as the Society for Improving the Condition of the Labouring Classes, focusing on working-class housing.[4] These small groups, which exercised their influence largely through the wealth or nobility of their leading members, were primarily philanthropic associations. Their prison visiting, or their attempts to provide allotments or model housing schemes, made them into experts. From this, by way of evidence before inquiries and detailed advice to any minister who would listen, they became pressure groups. Nor was their pressure only 'from without'. Chadwick was able to promote his own public-health policies by founding the Health of Large Towns Association. The Association supported the government servant, who had organised it largely to put pressure on his political superiors.

Education was beset by rival pressure groups, because of its involvement in sectarian rivalry. In the 1840s the Central Society of Education pressed in vain for secular state-financed elementary schools, against the voluntarists led by the Congregational Union. But the bishops, acting as a pressure group of the Established Church on behalf of the National School Society, were too strong for them both.

While each branch of social administration attracted its own pressure groups, there was a borderland where the pressure group is hard to identify. Could it be said, for instance, that the managers of Swallowfield, Southwell, Cookham, Hatfield, and other 'reformed' workhouses before 1834 constituted a pressure group? Probably not, at least until Senior and Chadwick marshalled their evidence on the Poor Law Commission. Curiously, the most notorious of all the reforms, the Poor Law Amendment Act, was passed almost without the assistance of organised pressure groups, although some of the anti-mendicity societies propagated its principles in the 1820s.[5] Perhaps this was due to the inability of the country gentry to make up their minds what ought to be done, until Senior and Chadwick did it for them. The Justices, mainly conservative but producing a small minority of pioneer reformers, were too divided to form a united pressure group for anything, except the maintenance of their own powers.

Some multi-interest associations acted as pressure groups on several branches of social administration simultaneously. Such were the statistical societies of London, Manchester, Birmingham and other large towns, which appeared suddenly (along with the Statistical Department of the Board of Trade) round about 1833. They conducted their own investigations, and campaigned for public health, education, the maintenance of a reformed Poor Law and other causes, supplying statistical evidence for their recommendations.[6] They were particularly important in that, like the older literary and philosophical societies, they provided a means by which local and provincial middle-class élites could influence public policies. At the same time, individual members of these élites could multiply their reforming influence by operating through several of these pressure groups or other instruments of reform. Thus Joseph Fletcher, barrister, who had been Secretary to the Commissions of Inquiry on the handloom weavers and on children's employment, was editor of the Statistical Journal and became Government Inspector of the British and Foreign Society (Nonconformist) schools. In this office he gave powerful encouragement to Mary Carpenter at the start of her pioneering work in ragged and reformatory schools.[7]

Among the agents of pressure for reform, it is usual to include the newspapers and periodicals which proliferated in the early nineteenth century. The *Edinburgh*, *Quarterly* and *Westminster* Reviews; the *Examiner*, *Chambers'*, *Blackwood's*, and (unstamped) Cobbett's *Political Register*; Carlile's *Republican*, Doherty's *Voice of the People*, Hetherington's *Poor Man's Guardian*, together with the *Black Dwarf*, the *Yellow Dwarf*, the *Cap of Liberty* and other ephemeral radical publications gave sporadic attention to administrative as well as political reform. Important survivals from the eighteenth century such as the *Gentleman's Magazine* commented on social as well as literary and antiquarian happenings. National dailies such as *The Times* and the Whig *Morning Chronicle* took part in reform controversies from the point of view of their respective editors. Many of the larger provincial towns had rival papers on party lines, taking opposing sides, as, for example, the *Leeds Chronicle* and the *Leeds Intelligencer* over factory reform. In fact the role of the press was mainly to publicise and intensify controversy. As agents of pressure the papers tended to cancel each other out. Social controversies had been adequately conducted in the eighteenth century through pamphlets, as any reader of the literature accompanying the campaigns for the repeal of the Test and Corporations Acts or even the campaign for the repeal of the Jew Bill of 1753 will know. The political pamphlet continued to flourish in the nineteenth century (*vide* the sectarian war over education), and many articles in the quarterlies were written as reviews of a group of pamphlets on the topic concerned. Although published in magazines they were really pamphlets themselves.[8]

Select Committees and Royal Commissions

The main instruments for the formulation and control of innovative legislation were parliamentary Select Committees and Royal Commissions.[9] The Select Committees of the House of Lords and the House of Commons, the investigative weapons of parliament, had a continuous history from the seventeenth century. Their members were selected by the chairman (normally the member who had carried a resolution for the committee) with regard to party balance in the House. They had powers to send for papers and examine witnesses on oath, which they did not use. But they could only sit during the parliamentary term, being abruptly suspended when parliament adjourned, and broken up when parliament dissolved. They were tied to Westminster, and their witnesses had to come to London. They could be 'packed' by an experienced politician, or influenced by the selection and coaching of witnesses, as occurred in the Select Committee on the Combinations Acts in 1824, and Sadler's Factory Committee in 1832.[10]

In contrast, the Royal Commission, its members appointed and often paid by the Crown, i.e. the government of the day, was still associated in the public mind with seventeenth-century Stuart tyranny.[11] It had been rescued from limbo in 1780 during the American revolt by the appointment of the Commission on Public Accounts. Between 1800 and 1831 some 60 Commissions of Inquiry were appointed, and between 1830 and 1890, some 388 more. Some of these were Special Commissions to investigate cases of bribery, and others were on minor matters. But the Royal Commission was the most effective single instrument in securing the great reforms in the Poor Law, Factory Act, public health, and police. Independent of MPs and of parliamentary terms, it could send investigating commissioners armed with questionnaires to the provinces, operate uninterrupted (except by angry mobs or impatient cabinet ministers) until its business was completed. Except where Assistant Commissionerships were utilised by politicians as government 'jobs', it could persuade ministers to appoint the most appropriate investigators. Royal Commissions had no powers to demand papers nor examine witnesses on oath (unless statutorily conferred) but they did these things notwithstanding. Some naïve historians have believed that their special virtue was their 'scientific' and impartial dedication to the discovery of truth; but in fact they were easier to manipulate than the Select Committees. The massive evidence published as appendices to their reports was beyond the capacity of the public to read, and could be used selectively to justify the preconceived recommendations of the Commissioners. The Central Commissions were often dominated by a small group of determined policy makers. In fact the utilisation of a Royal Commission to secure evidence in favour of legislation on lines already decided before the Commission had reported – or sometimes even met – was the trade mark of Edwin Chadwick. But this was sometimes copied in other Whig reforms, as in the Commission preceding the Municipal Corporations Act of 1835.

Once the law had been passed, a Royal Commission could be turned into a permanent enforcement Commission. This was assisted by some continuity of personnel. The Poor Law Commission of 1834 had new Central Commissioners, but several of the Assistant Commissioners of Inquiry became Assistant Commissioners carrying out the Poor Law Amendment Act, while Chadwick, part-author of the Report, became secretary of the permanent Commission.

Some reforms, notably where Chadwick's influence was muted or lacking, took a step-by-step path, following a series of parliamentary Select Committees, but without a Royal Commission. Select Committees on crime, prisons or transportation sat in 1798, 1811, 1823, 1835, 1847, 1850 and 1863; and various developments in penal policy followed them. Inspection of lunatic asylums and protection of pauper lunatics followed the parliamentary Select Committees of 1808, 1827 and 1845, each brought about by some revelation of cruelty or mistreatment of the helpless insane. After the failure of Brougham's 'Parliamentary Commission'[12] there was no Royal Commission on elementary education until the Newcastle Commission of 1858–61. The central machinery of inquiry was used according to the politics and circumstances of each case, and education was such a controversial topic that a public enquiry was likely only to stir up strife.

Inspectors and public administrators

The new enforcement agent of the nineteenth century was the government inspector. The importance of the inspectorate has been well recognised, but its origins present an intriguing puzzle.[13] Even in the eighteenth century inspection was no new idea; but it was in the hands of local Justices or (in the early nineteenth century) private or corporate bodies such as the College of Physicians or the religious school societies or the government-appointed but unpaid Charity Commissioners.[14] The movement towards professional centrally directed inspection seems to date from the 1820s. Ireland then already had government inspectors of schools and prisons,[15] while England had hybrids, such as the government-appointed Commissioners (11 unpaid laymen and 5 physicians at £1 an hour) who inspected and licensed private madhouses in the Metropolitan area. By 1830 the voluntary school societies were employing their own inspectors to supervise the expenditure of the subscribers' money, and ensure that their own religious tenets were taught in the schools. The idea of central inspection was not new. George Holford was advocating prison inspectors in 1821 when Bentham (to whom the idea is generally ascribed) was proposing 'inspection' by the curious public or by the nominees of the King's Bench.

The reasons for the sudden growth of inspectorates after 1832 remain obscure. Bentham had come round to the idea of central inspection as part of his own brand of Utopian government, and publicised it in the *Constitutional Code.* To some extent it grew out of the Commissions of Inquiry which recruited and trained new government servants accustomed to investigating in local circuits. The prime mover was Chadwick, who proposed inspectors in the Factory Commission Report of 1833, the Poor Law Report of 1834, and the Public Health Reports. Thereafter the convenient device was copied.

Inspection was devised for four main purposes: (1) for protecting helpless individuals, as under the lunacy laws, the Passenger Acts, and to some extent in public health and prisons, factories and mines; (2) for uniformity of treatment as in prisons and workhouses; (3) for safeguarding the use of grants of public money, as in schools; and (4) (including all these) for enforcement. Accordingly, the inspectors had varying powers and conditions of work. The unpopular factory inspectors were endowed with the powers of justices, but found it better to enforce the laws through prosecutions despite the unfriendliness of the courts. The Poor Law Assistant Commissioners had the negative power of surcharging Guardians but it was insufficient to enforce uniformity. The prison inspectors had some power to enforce minimum standards through recommendation for building grants. The Public Health inspectors could institute proceedings for nuisance, and approve plans for building and drainage works. None of the powers was adequate for full enforcement, and all represented an element of education or exhortation. Differences in origin soon became unimportant as aims and methods of enforcement were mixed. Probably the most constructive use of inspectors was in education, where Kay-Shuttleworth deliberately used inspectors in conjunction with a grants system to raise the standards of schools and teachers.

The Inspectorate was a new career for the well-educated, and generally speaking the sons of gentlemen.[16] Salaries varied between the £1,000 a year of the factory inspectors and the £450 a year of the school inspectors, the average being around £600.[17] There was often a second rank of assistants, drawn from a slightly lower social class at about half the salary. Assistant Commissionerships and inspectorships rapidly formed a career, and men (like, for instance, Tremenheere, a school and then a mines inspector) moved from one inspectorate to another. One, Captain Kincaid was simultaneously a factory and a prison inspector.

Government Inspectorates formed a new career more or less open to talent. Admittedly appointment was by patronage, and there were some scandalous 'jobs'.[18] But there were also some distinguished appointments among the early inspectors. Their work was worthwhile, for they were pioneers, with influence on the growth of social policies. Later the inspectorates would either fade away, as in prisons, or settle into a mechanical routine. The Public Health Inspectors, already a special case in that they were professional engineers, were exceptional in giving rise to a new class of local-government officers. Among the early inspectors most of the 'zealots' were to be found.[19] They formed the prime growth point of the nineteenth-century civil service.

The staffing of new or reformed public services with trained and uniformed police and prison officers, with suitably qualified relieving officers and workhouse masters, or with educated and trained teachers was essential if the reforms were to last. But it was continually held up, by survivals from the old order, by lack of suitable applicants, and, above all, by the parsimony of ratepayers and Treasury, which ensured that conditions and salaries were never adequate to attract the right people. Kay-Shuttleworth's complicated system for supplementing teachers' salaries was probably the most successful experiment in overcoming this difficulty. The professionalisation of public services, where achieved, was also part of the general movement towards standardisation and professional qualification in such professions as medicine, nursing, engineering and public-school teaching. It did not always represent progress. There were corrupt and sadistic prison officers just as there had been corrupt and brutal turnkeys.

Centralisation and local government

The outcry against centralising despotism by enemies of the new commissions was unconvincing to the disinterested. The ardent defenders of 'local self-government' were in fact merely propping up the traditional units of the parish and the unpaid justices. Some spoke for the JPs who saw their power reduced by the new Poor Law in favour of ratepayers socially beneath them. Others spoke for private interests, such as millowners, water companies, speculative builders, and others who feared the effects of state competition on their profits. Indeed, some reforms, such as the Poor Law, public health and police, produced a renaissance in local government. This was not the intention of Chadwick, who at first failed to realise the obstructive power he was putting in the hands of the elective Boards of Guardians, and later would have preferred government-appointed agencies for public health, emancipated from the stinginess of ratepayers. However, this was the outcome of the reforms as they emerged from the political process.

The influence of county Justices could not be weakened while the landowners remained prosperous, even in the nineteenth century. Ousted from control of some of the more urban Unions, prison acts and lunacy laws gave them more powers as Visiting Justices. But an additional unit of local government intermediate between parish and county had arrived (sometimes mentioned as though it were a revival of the old hundred) – the Poor Law Union. The Unions soon attracted other functions, as local registration districts after 1837, local health areas after 1848, vaccination districts, etc. They tended to subdivide into medical districts or relieving officers' districts, and more occasionally to combine, as into school districts. They were so important that their gradual disappearance when County, Rural and Urban District Councils took over their duties at the end of the century must be attributed to the continuing hatred of the Poor Law itself. Moreover, the Public Health Act under which borough councils became Local Boards of Health while cities obtained health powers through Local Acts, produced substantial programmes of reforming activities for the new town councils set up after the Municipal Corporations Act of 1835. This Act enabled progressive groups in some towns to oust the old Tory oligarchies and begin the arduous task of cleaning up the town.

The county JPs were not weakened but strengthened by the responsibilities of county asylums, reformed prisons and county police. The central agencies had little control either over the counties or the elected Boards, while in education the Committee of the Privy Council tried to run a kind of partnership with the voluntary-school societies and their school committees through financial assistance and expert advice. Centralisation was a myth, for the Commissions and departments were never strong enough to enforce the unformity in whose name they were justified. While diversity continued in workhouses, prisons and schools, greater centralisation was almost always matched by greater local powers. The real grievance of those who attacked the 'Bashaws of Somerset House' and broke up the General Board of Health was not centralisation but the increasing intervention of both central and local government.[20] So opponents of reforms who relied on *laisser faire* and the unfettered play of market forces joined with those who, holding the traditional suspicion of government activity, appealed to old institutions and Anglo-Saxon liberties. In public health there was an unlikely alliance between reactionary squires and the 'wide boys' from the water companies and property developers.

The concern thus manifested with the creeping extension of public authority was reflected in the preoccupation of political philosophers such as Walter Bagehot and John Stuart Mill with the spheres of public and private activity and the limits of state action. The effects of the Industrial Revolution and of growing population were forcing a reconsideration of older theories of liberty. The philosophers, in the face of the obviously growing requirement for state intervention, were trying to make up their minds where liberty lay and how it could best be preserved.

Sources and references

1. The investigation of early nineteenth-century pressure groups is in its infancy. **Hollis, Patricia** (ed.), *Pressure from Without in Early Victorian England.* Edward Arnold, 1974. This book goes some way to fill the gap. But the essays in it concentrate on the 'once-for-all' type of legislation, such as the reform of the parliamentary franchise, the abolition of slavery, and the anti-Corn Law League, which dissolved on achievement of their object. But there were other groups of a more permanent nature, based on sectional interests; e.g. The Protestant Dissenting Deputies, a body of the lay heads of congregations, which after a long campaign helped to obtain the repeal of the Test and Corporation Acts in 1828, but remained in being to demand further benefits for Nonconformists.

2. **Fraser, Peter,** 'Public petitioning and parliament before 1832', *History*, LXVI, 1961, pp. 195–211.

3. Dr Hollis's classification into parliamentary reformers, Manchester Free Traders, and Dissent is unsatisfactory. The first two are categorised by their aims, the last by its members. They all overlapped. Moreover, Dissent did not form a united pressure group except where its leaders campaigned for religious and civil equality for Dissenters with members of the Established Church; and even that hardly applied to the Wesleyan Methodists. Dissent was split between the Rational Dissenters who, with their intellectual descendants the Unitarians, Deists and Philosophical Radicals, pursued liberal aims, and the Trinitarian Dissenters who often shared the social attitudes and aims of the conservative Church of England Evangelicals. Hollis, *op. cit., passim.*

4. This society may be instructively compared with the present-day influential 'Shelter'.

5. For anti-mendicity societies at Cheltenham, Bristol, Gloucester and Stroud, see **Christmas, E. A.,** '*The Administration of the Poor Law in some Gloucestershire Unions, 1815–1847*'. Bristol M. Litt., 1973, pp. 40–43. Their work seems to have anticipated that of the Charity Organisation Society.

6. **Cullen, M. J.,** *The Statistical Movement in Early Victorian Britain.* Harvester Press, 1975, fails to give any explanation for the sudden appearance of the statistical societies in 1833, and fails to explore their connection with the literary and philosophical societies which performed some of the same social and political functions in the previous generation.

7. **Manton, Jo,** *Mary Carpenter and the Children of the Streets.* Heinemann, 1976, p. 94.

8. Obviously much more could be said about the role of the press in social reform. Much has already been written about the explosion of early nineteenth-century journals (stamped and unstamped), but more remains to be done, e.g. about the attitudes of the various working-class papers to reforms such as the sanitary laws and the Factory Acts.

9. **Clokie, H. M.** and **Robinson, J. W.,** *Royal Commissions of Inquiry.* Stanford University, 1937, *passim.*

10. For a fuller discussion of the constitution and use of Select Committees and Royal Commissions see **Henriques, U.,** 'Jeremy Bentham and the Machinery of Social Reform', in Hearder, H. and Loyn, H. R. (eds), *British Government and Administration.* Univ. of Wales Press, 1974, pp. 169–86.
11. Especially conservative minds, including both Toulmin Smith, the leading Tory opponent of 'centralisation', and Jeremy Bentham.
12. A kind of hybrid, but with most of the powers and procedures of a Royal Commission.
13. Two major books on the nineteenth-century inspectors are **Roberts, David,** *Victorian Origins of the British Welfare State*, Yale U. P. 1960; and **Ball, Nancy,** *Her Majesty's Inspectorate.* Oliver and Boyd, 1963.
14. The Charity Commissioners later became merged with the Assistant Poor Law Commissioners. Cf. Note 17.
15. Ireland had a national Inspector-General of Prisons as early as 1786. **MacDonagh, Oliver,** *Early Victorian Government 1830–1870.* Weidenfeld and Nicolson, 1977, p. 188. For Irish administrative centralisation, cf. MacDonagh's interesting chapter on Ireland, pp. 178-196.
16. **Roberts, D.,** *Victorian Origins of the British Welfare State.* pp. 152-5.
17. The Central Commissions were divided between highly-paid professionals and unpaid honorary aristocrats who still gave their services free, like Lord Shaftesbury. In 1835 there were 20 stipendiary Charity Commissioners and 12 honorary Commissioners, of whom 3 were the Poor Law Commissioners and 1 an Assistant Poor Law Commissioner (paid in the latter role). By 1836 all the Poor Law Commissioners and Assistant Commissioners were also Charity Commissioners, and the two had presumably amalgamated. For these Commissioners and their Inspectorates with salaries, see *Return on Commissions to House of Commons*, 4 August 1836, pp. 1-25. *PP* 1836, XXXVII. *Return to House of Commons* of 7 March 1837, *Commissions not included in last session*, pp. 1-7. *PP* 1837, XXXIX. *Return to House of Commons*, 8 February 1842, 1-7. *PP* 1842, XXVI.
18. For example, James Stuart, the Scottish factory inspector.
19. **Parris, Henry,** *Constitutional Bureaucracy.* Allen and Unwin, 1969, pp. 200-203.
20. This could be called a reaction of 'individualism' against increasing 'collectivism', rather than a reaction of localism against 'centralisation'. (It is difficult to see how the strengthening of local government can be called centralisation.) On the other hand, the intervention of local government (as of the Treasury) was often negative – designed to save the ratepayer and thus to encourage 'individualism'.

13 Conclusion

Further topics: police and lunacy reform

In this book I have attempted to trace the foundation or the transformation of five of the most important departments of social administration in early industrial Britain. Many more could be found. For instance, prison reform was only one aspect of the war against crime. The long battle for the reduction of the number of capital offences, as well as actual executions, conducted mostly by the prison reformers, bore fruit in the governments of Peel and Grey, as did the reform of criminal law and appeal procedures. Above all there was the foundation of the modern police. The transformation of the old Watch into the modern police forces was arguably the most difficult of all the nineteenth-century administrative achievements. It forms one of the grand themes, in range and complexity very similar to the development of public health administration and the Poor Law, with which (through the duties of the humble local constable in reporting nuisances and arresting vagrants, as well as the presence of the same people on all the different local government committees) it was closely connected. Those who would reform the police had much to contend with. They were opposed not only by the professional thief-takers but by almost all the political writers and the Whig and Radical politicians of the day. Adam Smith as well as Blackstone and Paley were hostile to police reform, fearing 'continental despotism', 'standing armies', and any increase in the physical power of government more than they feared public disorder and crime.[1] Popular writers such as Paine and Robert Owen harked back to various versions of the old ideal of a 'people's militia' in place of army and police alike.[2] Early advocates of police reform such as Bentham and his ally Patrick Colquhoun failed to get Radical backing, and formed an isolated minority. They also had to contend with the jealousy of many vigilante groups and local volunteer self-protection forces which had grown up for lack of the very public forces they opposed.[3] Then there were the many untrained special constables enrolled in times of civil unrest, as well as the part-time yeomanry whose failures in crowd control were so strikingly exhibited at Peterloo. These opponents were middle class, but later in the 1830s and 1840s the police (who could be despatched by train to the scene of Luddite, anti-Poor Law and Chartist rioting) incurred the suspicion and hatred of the various working-class movements.

The idea of a civilian police force developed piecemeal. In the eighteenth century the term 'police' had a very wide meaning, covering almost any kind of civic regulation. To Adam Smith it meant 'the regulation of the inferior parts of government, viz: cleanliness, security and cheapness or plenty.' He added, 'Carrying dirt from the streets, and the execution of justice, so far as it regards regulations for preventing crimes or the method of keeping a city guard, though useful, are too mean to be considered in a general discourse of this kind.'[4] Eighteenth-century Evangelicals thought in terms of a 'moral police', repressing vice rather than crime, a sort of adjunct of their Proclamation Society and its successor, the Society for the Suppression of Vice.[5] This was supplemented or superseded by the proposals of the London magistrate, Patrick Colquhoun, for a 'supervisory' or 'preventive' police, endowed with wide powers of licensing and censorship. These included the control of coffee- as well as ale-houses; a 'pauper police' to supervise, search and detain tramps and vagrants, wandering Jews and Gypsies; the registration of servants, and the registration of at least seventeen dangerous trades. The latter included pawnbrokers, night hackney coachmen, and milkmen who sold dirty milk.[6] All-embracing and efficiently applied, they might indeed be considered to raise a prospect of the police state which Whigs and Radicals feared. Moreover, there was the question of plain-clothes police, who in the early nineteenth century were hardly to be distinguished from the spies and informers employed by successive governments, from hired *agents provocateur* to factory inspectors ordered to report on Chartist meetings.[7] The idea of a detective police whose main function was to identify and catch law-breakers and bring them to justice before the courts had a slow growth.

The evolution of a modern police – except in so far as it was pioneered by the Fielding brothers in mid-eighteenth-century London and developed from the example of the Metropolis – was largely a Benthamite achievement. Bentham's concept of police was as diffuse and all-embracing as that of other contemporary writers[8], but his special emphasis on a crime-prevention force grew out of his insistence that certain and immediate punishment was a better way of deterring criminals than ferocious penalties.[9] But he was also at his most practical in his promotion of the London river patrol to check smuggling in the Thames. Chadwick, who attracted Bentham's patronage by his article on 'Preventive Police' in the *Westminster Review* in 1829, had given evidence to Peel's Committee on the Police of the Metropolis in the preceding year. He was responsible for the sections on the Ministers of Health and Police in Bentham's *Constitutional Code*, and later wrote the *Report* of the Constabulary Force Commission in 1839. Radzinowicz makes the point that he was more directly Bentham's heir in this than in any other subject.[10] But while Bentham and Chadwick envisaged a centralised, government-controlled police force, Chadwick was in the end content to hand over much of the administration and three-quarters of the pay of the forces to the county magistrates.[11]

Claims have been made that the real founders of the modern police came from the armed forces, especially Charles Rowan, a young officer from the 52nd Light Infantry who, with the barrister Richard Mayne, organised the London force for Peel;[12] but these have been contested.[13] Eventually the uniformed and disciplined police bodies were established piecemeal under the Municipal Corporations Act of 1835 and the County Police Act of 1839, and made compulsory as well as subject to inspection under the Police Act of 1856. Their supervision was shared uneasily by the borough Watch Committees in the towns and the JPs in the counties, and albeit minimally the Home Office. Their administration was thus a vital part of reformed local government, but it was not made easier by the fact that they owed obedience to two masters.[14] They suffered from all the troubles of low pay, corrupt officials and the survival of unsuitable personnel from the older forces which were also found in the Poor Law.[15] They could be the sport of political power struggles on local committees, and they might be torn between the role of hunting criminals and maintaining order, a dualism which continues to the present day and has facilitated claims that the police were (and are) primarily a means of social control and hence of class oppression.[16]

Another important subject of reform was the care of the mentally deficient (in modern jargon 'handicapped') and the mentally ill. Lunacy reform included the piecemeal provision of county asylums.[17] It also included the inspection of private madhouses, particularly for the protection of the pauper lunatics too dangerous or troublesome to be retained in workhouses, and so cheaply disposed of by Justices and Poor Law authorities to the tender mercies of private keepers.[18] The care of the insane did not present the constitutional difficulties of police reform. But reformers were few, partly because madness was a painful and furtive subject, cocooned with ancient superstitions and fears of satanic possession, while at the same time rationalised as a deserved punishment for sin.[19] Moreover it was a depressing subject in view of the persistent medical helplessness and inability to cure what could not be understood.[20] Inevitably, madhouses were primarily places of detention, their powerless inmates even more subject to mistreatment than convicted prisoners.[21] Early attempts at reform were largely in the hands of small groups of Evangelicals and Quakers, including the Welsh magnate, Charles Williams Wynn, Sir Robert Seymour, and the young Lord Ashley.[22] The development of inspection and control resulted from the investigations of parliamentary Select Committees rather than Royal Commissions. There was little Benthamite interest or contribution, and Chadwick's concern, through the Poor Law Assistant Commissioner Gulson, was to get the asylums placed under Poor Law control and economise on them.[23] In the face of the persistent exploitation, cruelty and neglect of private madhouse keepers, inspection grew slowly, remaining for long on a part-time, *ad hoc* and often unpaid basis.[24]

Historically the development of lunacy reforms is interesting at least partly because it was largely untouched by the social attitudes and constitutional techniques of Chadwick.

All these reforms could be analysed into various elements. The new police entailed public provision on a large scale. Lunacy reforms entailed new public provision in the county asylums, financed, like the police, from the rates and therefore largely under local government. But they also entailed public inspection of institutions run by private enterprise. Education entailed grant-aid, or subsidisation of private charitable bodies from central funds, with inspection. If nineteenth-century governments were reluctant to increase the range of public provision, as in their flat refusal to provide housing, or were inclined to attach penal conditions where possible, as in the Poor Law, they were prepared to undertake many kinds of experiment in extending public control.[25] Perhaps the least complicated were those forms of regulation intended to protect the more helpless members of society from the grosser forms of exploitation by private enterprise. These would include the Factory Acts, the Passenger Acts which sought to prevent the cheating and abuse of poor emigrants by shipowners and laid down minimum standards of food and accommodation at sea,[26] and the regulation of the railways, especially to prevent the horrific accidents which multiplied as trains became faster and more frequent.[27] But in some spheres public provision could not be avoided. Social administration was growing on all sides and in all ways. Many more instances could be found; and to treat them all adequately would be a task without end.

The inspiration of social reform

Historians have long occupied themselves with the fascinating conundrum, how were these reforms inspired or originated? This preoccupation has produced one of the most celebrated and superfluous of historical controversies.[28] This many-branched controversy goes back to A. V. Dicey's misunderstanding of Bentham, whom he regarded as the apostle of individualism, or *laisser faire*. It developed through a series of dichotomies; individualism versus collectivism, *laisser faire* versus state intervention, Benthamism versus Evangelicalism, Benthamite or planned reform versus reform through 'inner dynamism', and (the most recent) traditionalism versus 'incrementalism'.[29] Occasionally the dichotomy becomes co-operation. Halevy in *Philosophical Radicalism* observed that Benthamites and Evangelicals both contributed to social reform. He also attempted an elaborate academic explanation of how the Philosophical Radicals sought to reconcile theories of *laisser faire* and the free labour market with their penchant for state intervention and social engineering, by using the latter to produce an artificial identity of public with private interests. The dualism was there, in contemporary thought and action.

Henry Parris has pointed out that aspirations towards *laisser faire* and its moral reflection, self-help, proceeded *pari passu* with increasing state intervention, not only to regulate (as with water supply) but in the provision of or help with goods and services, as in education.[30] Yet to perpetuate this dualism in the historiography of the period limits the view. Dr Kitson Clark got away from it in pointing out how, as well as Benthamites and Evangelicals, professional groups such as doctors and engineers had contributed to the development of social administration.[31] However, it tends to persist in the war of models and counter-models. Models can be useful as a tentative framework for an account of events, but as a form of historical explanation they are dangerous. There is always the possibility that by a kind of circular process, generalisations induced from events will be used to interpret those same events; and there is a probability, when models are used, that historical selection will take into account evidence which accords with them and omit that which does not.

While there was some basis in contemporary thought for these dualistic explanations they have undoubtedly been prolonged by present-day battles between left- and right-wing historians, who tend to argue everything directly or indirectly in terms of whether the working class was or was not oppressed. This, again, has some historical validity in the undeniable class conflicts of the early nineteenth century, but it has reinforced the artificiality and oversimplification which have beset these arguments, and limited their value as means of historical explanation.[32]

One of the least sensible disputes is between those who attribute the early nineteenth-century reforms to Benthamism, or planned reform, and those who explain it by internal dynamism, or incrementalism, or groping. The argument was unnecessary, as the two explanations do not conflict. If Chadwick was a Benthamite, the new Poor Law, the 1833 Factory Act, the county police and the General Board of Health were Benthamite or planned reforms. But the development of Poor Law educational services and medical services, the extension of factory regulation, lunacy reforms, the spread of by-laws on sanitation, as well as the regulation of conditions on emigrant ships and the prevention of railway accidents, were at least partly due to internal dynamism. But internal dynamism was not an impersonal force of history. A closer knowledge of the people concerned: of Horner and Saunders in the Factory Inspectorate, of Whitworth Russell and Joshua Jebb in prisons, of Rowan in the police and Moseley in the Education Inspectorate, soon helps to indicate why administration took the course it did.

A curious explanation of reform (already noticed in Mrs Hart's percipient article 'Nineteenth Century Social Reform: a Tory Inter-pretation of History')[33] is that the abuse concerned was 'intolerable'. This is not as unhelpful as it seems, provided it is coupled with the question, why did it seem intolerable? Mrs Hart points out that those who gained by exploitation did not find its social results intolerable. The owners of unregulated textile mills, coal mines, truck shops, emigrant ships, jerry-built houses and inefficient water works did not find them intolerable; nor did West Indian planters find slavery intolerable. The question may highlight the blinding effects of self-interest on human opinions and attitudes; but a leftward response about the evils of unbridled capitalism does not seem to be the complete answer. As has been suggested, the unrestrained greed for profit distinguished the conduct of gaolers and overseers of the pre-industrial period more than the paid professionals of the nineteenth-century reformed public services. Indeed, the idea of the salaried public servant, properly attributable to Chadwick and Kay-Shuttleworth at least as much as to Bentham, was a concomitant if not a product of capitalist society. Yet even Labour historians have not contended that the paid and qualified public servant *per se* is merely a tool of class oppression, however much the early examples may have been caught up in the climate of class conflict. Moreover, one may ask why conditions in Newgate were borne with equanimity in the eighteenth century and regarded with horror in the nineteenth. Why was the negative attitude of farmers to the education of their labourers seen as natural and respectable in the eighteenth century and increasingly retrograde and selfish in the nineteenth? Self-interest, of course, accounts largely for it; and when there is class conflict self-interest tends to coincide with class interest. But there are other reasons, psychological as well as sociological. People are often incurious about what they don't see, even while they tend to avoid revelations which may disturb them or make them feel guilty. On the other hand, they are normally apathetic or acquiescent towards evils which are familiar, but do not affect them personally. Such attitudes are at their strongest in times and among types of people conditioned to a traditional rather than a forward-looking outlook. They facilitated the justification of the poverty of the many as necessary for the civilisation of the few, reflecting a state of society which had, after all, existed since time immemorial. To rouse them from apathy required special circumstances; either personal suffering resulting from the system, or some violent shock to the consciousness, or participation in some sub-culture in conflict with the system and views supported by the majority, or finally, contact with some group left behind when the climate of opinion had changed.

Wealthy and respectable people tolerated Newgate until the voice of Dr Dodd, with whom they identified themselves as they could not with a common thief, penetrated their armour. Interest in criminal law and punishment was kept alive in people by fear for their own safety and that of their property, fortified by the publication of crime figures. So when the judges' severity was seen to have failed the reformers (men in touch with European Enlightenment thinking) got a chance to introduce alternative methods. The threat of pauperism was brought home by rising rates and driven home by the labourers' revolt. People were awoken to the dangers of filth by cholera, and other epidemic diseases, although to drive that lesson home Chadwick had to conduct politicians around the undrained slums. Of the reformers themselves, most belonged to some special religious or intellectual or cultural minority. They were middle-class Dissenters, more sensitive than others to abuses of government because they had long felt themselves excluded and oppressed on grounds of religion and class; or Evangelicals, whose religion conferred on its converts not only a censorious and repressive outlook, but also a sensitivity to the grosser forms of suffering; or medical men of the Dissenting intelligentsia whose training rendered them abnormally observant of disease and degradation. Once these pioneers had induced a change in the climate of opinion, the older views began to seem retrograde. Thus response to social evils came from different groups and different individuals, for different reasons. And it is remarkable that, in social as in political administration, the blueprints or programmes of reform were often formulated (sometimes with the help of foreign examples) generations before rapid social change had generated sufficient discontent to overcome the obstacles to their realisation.[34]

Originators of social reforms

It is worth considering briefly one or two of the main groups responsible for reform. Pride of place is usually conceded to the Benthamites, or in Halevy's slightly broader view, the Philosophical Radicals. Since, according to Halevy, James Mill was the decisive influence in radicalising Bentham's political thought, it is apparent that Philosophical Radicalism included at least two elements, a Scottish as well as an English. In fact Scotland was producing reforming groups, such as the Whig journalists who founded the *Edinburgh Review*, distinct from the London Benthamites. But where are we to put Henry Brougham, the Malthusian partisan of Poor Law reform and the unsuccessful proponent of national elementary education? Brougham is an important if ambivalent figure in early nineteenth-century social reform, and his use of his great influence on patronage in building up the early inspectorates awaits investigation. Where are we to put Kay-Shuttleworth, recruited by Nassau Senior for the Poor Law, but trained in Scotland under W. P. Alison, and closely connected with the enlightened industrialists of the Manchester Literary and Philosophical Society? These pioneers were not the followers of one man, nor even of one school of philosophy. But generally they were the most prominent among many leaders thrown up by the small provincial élites of successful manufacturers and their educated friends from the professions (usually Dissenters), who in the 1780s had joined the Birmingham Lunar Society and similar associations. Benthamites must share their place with wider circles and independent sources of reforming inspiration.

But the doctrinal inspiration of reform, it is said, was the Utilitarian or Greatest Happiness principle, defined and popularised in England by Jeremy Bentham. It is true that Bentham preached and developed the

Enlightenment philosophy of the greatest happiness of the greatest number, which he claimed to have discovered in a treatise of the Rational Dissenting sage, Joseph Priestley. This formula had many uses. It provided a secular morality alternative to the religious morality preached by Christians who denied the possibility that a man could be moral unless he believed in a supernatural or saving Christ. Moreover, this secular morality was free from the Evangelical preoccupation with sin. The formula was useful to later secularists such as Bradlaugh; but it had little direct connection with the inspiration for social reform. As a political ideal it could be used to support aristocratic and conservative political systems, as in David Hume's justification of the balanced constitution, as well as the democratic franchise (aimed at overcoming the 'sinister interests' of monarchy, aristocracy and Established Church) proposed by James Mill.[35] As a legal or social ideal it could be used, as by Paley, for a reactionary defence of the eighteenth-century criminal law; but in radical hands it could become a powerful solvent of mere traditionalism. It was used as such by Bentham in his attacks on civil and criminal law, as well as on the Church. Like many philosophical formulae, its practical effects depended on how it was applied.

Bentham contended that all his political and social proposals were inspired by the Greatest Happiness principle. But a closer study soon reveals that in some cases the principle was irrelevant, or was dragged in to justify some traditional argument or attitude dressed up as philosophy. The logical key to Bentham's retreat from a thorough-going social and economic radicalism was that he found security (especially security of property) more important than equality.[36] His attitude was a class attitude; and he soon found a way of avoiding the demand for redistribution of property in which the pursuit of the Greatest Happiness principle seemed to be involving him. But the Utilitarian Utopian Robert Owen, preferring equality to security, could advance his communitarian plans on the same principle. The 'principles of 1834' could be justified on Greatest Happiness grounds, provided a free labour market was accepted as the essential instrument of the general prosperity. Otherwise they might be considered as a means of oppression. Bentham's attack on Pitt's Poor Bill of 1794 smells of personal dislike and class prejudice rather than concern for the greatest happiness of the greatest number.

If Bentham played a more ambiguous role in social reform than was once believed, how are we to rate his achievements? His canonisation (like that of other saints) is currently under review, and a lasting verdict has yet to be arrived at. His motives as a prison reformer have been attacked.[37] His plans were a failure and his influence was largely destroyed by the advocates of the separate system. As Poor Law reformer he was probably influential in two ways; in rejecting Malthusianism and in devising middle-of-the-road formulae pursued by Senior and Chadwick, the real architects of 1834. But how far Chadwick really was influenced by Bentham in the path he took is, as we have seen, disputable. Of Bentham's two important Poor Law formulae one was that of 'less eligibility', which in fact sloganised a well-known and traditional principle of severe administration, going back to Defoe. The other was the guiding distinction between poverty and 'indigence' which did not last. By the third quarter of the nineteenth century it had almost vanished from Poor Law administration in favour of the distinction between the deserving and undeserving poor. Bentham's gobbledegook continued to be used (who knows that 'juvenile delinquency' is a Benthamite expression?), but the adoption of a publicist's peculiar phraseology is not necessarily a proof of his substantial influence.[38]

In the reform of social administration, not the ideas (mostly old and obvious) but the machinery made realisation possible. Here Chadwick, not Bentham, was the pioneer. Bentham was too out of touch with reality, and by the end of his long life he was in many ways a reactionary. His demand for central inspection, late in the day, was harnessed to an unreadable and unrealisable constitutional Utopia. He had not advanced to the realisation that politics and administration were becoming separated. He had no understanding of the possible role of Royal Commissions of Inquiry in securing reforms, and he had never known how to use a Select Committee to secure his own ends.[39] Although a pioneer in advocating entry to the public service by academic examination (but he would, impossibly, have applied it to the political members of government as well), he had no conception of the need to pay proper salaries in order to secure efficient and uncorrupt service. Bentham was a protean figure, touching many sides of public life; but while a de-bunking exercise is perhaps too facile, a more balanced assessment will be helped rather than hindered by not being undertaken as a hagiography.

Of other groups from which reforms originated, the Evangelicals (and in education the High Churchmen) were scarcely less influential than the Benthamites and other liberal circles. In prison policy some of the time and in education most of the time, Christian influence was greater than that of Utilitarianism, or political economy. In the Ten Hour Movement and the unsuccessful fight against the new Poor Law the Tory–Radical alliance held, because some Evangelical Christians rejected Malthusianism and the social corollaries of classical political economy. They were therefore able to ally with trade unionists and local leaders of working-class movements to an extent impossible to the most well-meaning Whig Radical. Some historians have decried their achievements and sneered at their efforts as paternalistic. To this it can only be said that Sadler and Shaftesbury in central politics achieved more for the welfare of the oppressed poor than did Robert Owen, or William Cobbett. Evangelicals and High Church together formed the only effective parliamentary opposition to the Poor Law Amendment Act against the united ranks of Tory country squires, Peelites and Whigs. Evangelicals, with the small lobby of paternalistic millowners, forced the Whig government at least to adopt Chadwick's scheme to protect the mill children. But here one sees that the interrelationship of Benthamites and

Evangelicals was extremely complex. In the Poor Law and Factory struggles Shaftesbury and Chadwick were on opposite sides. (In factory regulation Chadwick and Senior were also opponents.) By 1840 Horner and Shaftesbury were nearing a tacit alliance to extend the protection of working children. Chadwick and Shaftesbury worked together on the General Board of Health. Admittedly, this was made easier because Shaftesbury moved slowly towards Whig positions, succumbing to the self-help morality which reflected the assumptions he repudiated, of political economy and the free labour market, but which chimed in with Evangelical puritanism. In the 1880s Shaftesbury with Octavia Hill was fighting a rearguard action against the provision of publicly subsidised housing.

The importance of professional groups, of men who were neither Benthamite nor Evangelical, has already been explored. Engineers and medical scientists contributed to, and fought over, sanitary systems in public health. Army and navy officers were largely responsible for prison discipline in the mid-century, and contributed greatly to the police. The role of the military engineers such as Sir Joshua Jebb is now appreciated; but the people invariably left out are the politicians. These are dismissed as uninterested weaklings, or at best, tools of the backroom boys. There is an element of truth in this. Some, such as Sir George Grey, were weak. Some such as, perhaps, Sir James Graham were reactionary. Some were too easily influenced by determined advisers. One wonders why Lord John Russell, a sceptical Whig if ever there was one, succumbed to the specious promises of Crawford and Whitworth Russell that criminals could be reformed *en masse* by solitude and religious indoctrination. Nevertheless, the amount of time, care and labour devoted by some of the great as well as the lesser politicians to social problems, in parliamentary debates, select committees, administrative correspondence and the patronage of voluntary societies, was enormous. If the biographers of Lord John Russell and Palmerston gave as much attention to Home Office papers, draft bills and official business as has been lavished on political and family correspondence, a juster estimate of the role of these politicians in social reform might be made. The same might be said of the writings and precepts, if not the practice, of that Tory Radical, Benjamin Disraeli.[40] The persistence of such second-rank politicians as George Holford, R.A. Slaney and Sir John Pakington created the background of a reasonably well-informed opinion without which Chadwick and Kay-Shuttleworth would have got nowhere.

Social reform and class

The diversity and complexity of the influences which fashioned social administration in the early nineteenth century was increased rather than diminished by the effects of social class. Most reforms were preempted by middle-class activists and riddled with class attitudes. Class-inspired repression dominated reform of the Poor Law, both in so far as it was and was not carried out, e.g. in the failure to end settlement. Class-inspired 'rescue' dominated elementary education, and to a large extent public health. The measures were imposed, and the voteless were not consulted. Meantime the élite of the nascent working classes propagated their own developing institutions: Friendly Societies (approved by the higher orders), trade unions (disapproved by the higher orders),[41] building societies, savings banks and experimental co-operatives of various kinds. Here was a mingling of collectivist and individualist attitudes, of group co-operation, public support and self-help. Friendly Societies approved by the local Justices, or after 1834 by the Registrar of Friendly Societies, were given by law the privileged status of corporations which could sue individuals in order to protect their funds.[42] The Rochdale Pioneers availed themselves of this facility.[43] Yet the bridges were narrow, and over the general field of social administration there was little working-class contribution. This was precluded firstly by continuing class antagonism. Working-class groups which founded Sunday schools and mechanics' institutes tended to lose control of them to middle-class educationists.[44] Dr Leslie Wynne Evans gives three instances of Welsh workmen refusing to send their children to the Anglican schools provided by their employers, and joining to provide their own.[45] There must have been other examples, but the impression remains that, with the exception of the ephemeral Chartist and Owenite schools, and the little private-enterprise dame and day schools, education was promoted *de haute en bas* by people of the higher classes for the lower. Even in public health, where the fundamental interests of the upper and lower classes were identical (for in the long run disease knows no boundaries), the climate of suspicion and class conflict, augmented by contempt for working-class custom and feeling, and by insensitive regulations, precluded co-operation.[46] A second reason for the lack of working-class contribution was that initiatives for reform were beyond the capacity of the casual labourers, the slum dwellers, the farm workers, the factory children, the aged and infirm, the orphans and illegitimate children who were the objects of most social administration. The working-class élite were often as remote from them as they were from the classes above them. Working-class attitudes towards some social reforms need further investigation; but sanitary reform, for instance, was not a well-publicised working-class cause, while building societies were content with mutual self-help.[47] In poor relief, there were initiatives from Robert Owen and from the Chartists. But Owenite rural communities were never organised as a serious alternative to the Poor Law, being taken up with communitarian-utopian purposes as a means of changing society. Chartist small-holding schemes never did more than scratch the surface of rural poverty. In an era of increasing capitalisation of farming it seems doubtful whether, in any case, they could have survived.

The poor, therefore, were subjected to a package deal from those above them; inspired principally by members of middle-class minority groups, with occasional noble or gentry participation. The deal was inspired by very mixed motives. Landowners and industrialists, although driven by their own jealousies and class antagonisms frequently displayed a common fear of the growing numbers and alienation of the lower orders. The attitudes of reformers were therefore often tinged with apprehension and contempt – hence the prevalence of 'mock reforms' [48] as in the central workhouse clauses of the Poor Law Amendment Act. All reforms contained humane elements – most obvious in the lunacy laws, the Passenger Acts, the Coalmines Regulation Acts, the improvement of prisons and of criminal-law procedures, the provision of elementary and industrial schools, and in all measures specifically devised to protect children. There were also other elements – of fear and callousness in the Poor Law, of sexual jealousy in its bastardy clauses, of vengefulness and puritanism in prison reform, of snobbery and repression in education, of capitalist partisanship in the 1833 Factory Act. These attitudes persisted in great measure all through the nineteenth century. The slack period of the 1850s and 1860s did little to undermine them. Nor did the great reforms of the 1870s, which might be considered as a completion of the administrative revolution of the 1830s and 1840s. [49] In public health, central direction was restored and re-unified, although unfortunately under the domination of Poor Law attitudes, under the new Local Government Board. The many sanitary and housing Acts which had accumulated in the previous decades were codified and strengthened, while the principles of compulsion and compulsory purchase were increasingly used, especially in slum clearance. The factory laws were also strengthened and codified. Elementary education at last rate-aided, was made universal and compulsory by stages from Forster's Act of 1870 onwards, until provision by locally-elected school boards (later elected local government councils) gradually overtook the older system of central government grants to voluntary religious school societies. By means of persistent lobbying, protection at sea was extended from passengers to crew, under the Merchant Shipping Acts. The Poor Law jettisoned Bentham's principle of the workhouse as the only means of testing indigence, in favour of co-operation with the vast resources of Victorian private charity channelled through the Charity Organisation Society on the assumption that it *was* possible to distinguish between the deserving and undeserving poor. But in other respects it reverted to the 'principles of 1834'. The division between contempt for the 'able-bodied pauper' and compassion for the unprotected child reopened with test workhouses for the one, and with reformatories, cottage homes, and other incomplete realisations of Mary Carpenter's insights into the special needs of children, for the other. In some areas of social administration the effort at uniformity which had started with the inspectorates of the 1830s was continued more successfully by other means. Inspection of prisons was abandoned in favour of a rigidly centralised prison administration. Much more was done, but by and large the principles were those (sometimes a little extended) of the earlier phase of reform. They formed the underlying unity of the Victorian era. Only in the 1880s accents of uncertainty and signs of class-conscious guilt began to appear among some middle-class intellectuals.[50] Real change in social policies awaited the advent of the working-class vote, the new welfare liberalism of Chamberlain, Lloyd George and Churchill, and the rise of the Labour Party.

Conclusion

The social problems which accompanied early industrialisation were met with the adaptation or creation of many branches of public administration, some on their own, some in partnership with voluntary effort. They were neither complete, coherent, nor always successful; and they bore all the marks of piecemeal, *ad hoc* development. But they were based on a reluctant admission of the need for central and local government intervention, the expenditure of public money on that intervention, and the creation of bodies of salaried, uncorrupt government servants to make good that intervention. Yet there is a profound disjunction between the aims and policies of nineteenth-century social administration and those of the present day. Indeed, it is difficult to see how measures of which the Poor Law Amendment Act was the centrepiece can be termed 'Victorian origins of the British welfare state'.[51] A distinction has been made between the 'social service state' in which minimum standards are provided for the poor, and the 'welfare state' in which services are provided at optimum standards for the whole population.[52] The liberal reforms of the early twentieth century were largely of the former type. Built not on the Poor Law, but on pensions and social insurances, the very proposals defeated in 1834, they embodied, despite the inclusion of plans for the coercion of the workshy,[53] arrangements for more comprehensive and non-penal provision for the genuinely poor and helpless than had been known before. The residue of the Poor Law lingered on in public assistance for the destitute, in which the means test replaced the workhouse test. The old principles have survived in corners, such as the wages stop on supplementary benefit, (the latest name for poor relief, or public assistance). But the Welfare State represents, at least in theory, the total reversal of nineteenth-century attitudes. The men of 1834 saw that it was necessary to feed the starving, but were preoccupied with preventing the poor from becoming pauperised, i.e. depending on the public purse instead of earning their bread by productive labour. This they justified by insisting that extreme poverty was the fault of the poor, which entailed a concealed preference that some of the innocent should suffer rather than that parasitism should flourish, and the motive for productive labour be weakened. The Welfare State, product of an underlying drive for social equality, prefers the chance of occasionally subsidising imprudence, idleness and vice (the existence of which its more extreme exponents, as did Robert Owen, attribute to the influence of an unjust society rather than to any inherent defects in human nature) to the danger of victimising the helpless. This argument, together with the question of whether we can afford the full Welfare State, has by no means been terminated. The contenders relapse, once more, into a dualism which bids fair to continue until the nation falls under a one-class tyranny, or learns to harmonise its social endeavours, and live at peace with itself.

Sources and references

1. **Radzinowicz, L.,** *History of Criminal Law*. Vol. 3, *The Reform of the Police*, Stevens & Sons, 1956, pp. 417-26. The Italian Liberal, Beccaria, with more experience of continental despotisms, was also hostile. *Ibid.*, pp. 426-8.
2. Radicals feared, with some justification, that police would be used to quell popular demonstrations. Owen proposed military drill as part of the school curriculum, presumably as training for the People's Militia. See his *New View of Society* (1814). Everyman Edition, pp. 57-8.
3. Radzinowicz, *op. cit.*, pp. 100-107. **Mather, F. C.,** *Public Order in the Age of the Chartists*. Manchester U.P., 1959. pp. 90-95.
4. Smith, Adam, *The Wealth of Nations*, quoted in Radzinowicz, *op. cit.*, p. 421.
5. Radzinowicz, *op. cit.*, pp. 141-207.
6. Colquhoun's writings are analysed at length in Radzinowicz, *op. cit.*, p. 211 *et seq.*
7. Mather, F. C. *op. cit.*, pp. 186-7.
8. Bentham called for eight police departments, including police for the prevention of offences, calamities, and endemic diseases; also police of charity, of interior communications, of public amusements, a police for intelligence and information, and what might be called a registrar police for collecting statistical information of all kinds. Bentham marks the transition between lumping many sorts of public regulation together under the name 'police', and distinguishing the need for a specifically organised force for crime prevention and public order. Cf. Radzinowicz, *op. cit.*, pp. 431-47.
9. See **Bentham, J.,** *Introduction to the Principles of Morals and Legislation*, 1780; *Works*, John Bowring (ed.), Vol. 1, Edinburgh, 1843 or 1859, pp. 86-91.
10. Radzinowicz, *op. cit.*, p. 448 *et seq.*
11. See *First Report of the Constabulary Force Commissioners*, HMSO 1839, p. 184, signed by Chadwick, Charles Rowan and Charles Shaw Lefevre. The Commissioners were responding to a situation in which they believed that the efficient organisation of the Metropolitan Police had caused organised criminal gangs to migrate to the rural areas. **Hart, J.,** 'Reform of the Borough Police', *Econ. Hist. Review*, LXX, 1955, pp. 411-27. Mrs Hart argues that this was untrue, and the real motive behind the extension of the new police was fear of the Chartists. However, E. C. Midwinter doubts whether the extension can be accounted for by any one motive, but thinks the 1839 Act was inspired more by fear of robbery than of the Chartists. **Midwinter, E. C.,** *Social Administration in Lancashire 1830-1860*. Manchester U.P., 1969, pp. 138-9, 141-2.
12. **Reith, Charles,** *British Police and the Democratic Ideal*. O.U.P., 1943, *passim*.
13. The controversy is summarised by Midwinter, E. C., *op. cit.*, pp. 126-8.
14. Midwinter, *op. cit.*, pp. 149-52. Midwinter makes the point that the Home Office exerted very little power, or even influence over the local forces.
15. Midwinter, *op. cit.*, *passim*. Hart, *op. cit.*, p. 420.

16. See **Foster, John,** *Class Struggle and the Industrial Revolution.* Methuen, 1974, in which this is throughout implied. Midwinter argues pretty strongly against this kind of bias in his thesis, slightly modifying his attitude in his book.

17. The 1808 Act for the Better Care and Maintenance of Lunatics being Paupers or Criminals . . . (Wynn's Act) enabled Quarter Sessions to erect asylums, levy a county rate, and appoint Visiting Justices to inspect. The first county asylum was opened at Nottingham in 1810. By 1827 there were nine in operation. In 1845 the Lunacy Act made the building of county asylums compulsory. **Jones, Kathleen,** *Lunacy Law and Conscience, 1744–1845.* Routledge, 1955, pp. 75, 77, 116, and *passim.* **Parry Jones, William Ll.,** *The Trade in Lunacy: A Study of Private Madhouses in England in the Eighteenth and Nineteenth Centuries.* Routledge, 1972, p. 20.

18. The number of paupers exceeded the number of private patients. In 1844 there were 7,482 paupers to 3,790 private patients. See the tables given in Ch. VIII, Statistics of insanity, *Report of the Metropolitan Commissioners in Lunacy, to the Lord Chancellor.* Bradbury & Evans, 1844, p. 184.

19. Jones, K., *op. cit.,* pp. 1–8. This book is a useful and comprehensive standard work covering the growth of the county asylums and the development of inspection, as well as the law of criminal lunacy. Unfortunately it is not always accurate. E.g. Sir G. O. Paul, a pioneer of county asylums, as well as of the separate system of prison discipline (see p. 217) is mentioned as a supporter of Bentham's Panopticon.

20. Theories of the cause of mental illness were even more primitive than epidemiology. Improvements in the practical treatment of insanity were pioneered in such institutions as the Quaker Retreat at York, and consisted largely in kindness and common sense.

21. Parry Jones, William Ll. *op. cit.,* shows how attempts to improve the condition of pauper lunatics and stop using private asylums were constantly defeated by inadequacies of provision.

22. Protection of pauper lunatics was Ashley's first 'cause' as a young MP.

23. Jones, K., *op. cit.,* pp. 164–6.

24. Under the Private Madhouses Act of 1774, private madhouses were to be inspected and licensed by a Commission of Five elected annually by the Royal College of Physicians. But those outside London were inspected by Visiting Justices. This proved inadequate. Jones, K., *op. cit.,* p. 38. In 1828 the number of Commissioners was increased to 15, appointed by the Secretary of State for the Home Department and including 5 doctors who were paid £1 an hour for their services. *Ibid.,* pp. 142–4. In 1832 the Commissioners (of whom 2 had now to be barristers) were removed from the jurisdiction of the Home Office to that of the Lord Chancellor, doubtless because some scandalous cases had revealed the danger of imprisonment in asylums of some people at the instance of malicious relatives. In 1842 the Commissioners were increased to between 15 and 20, of whom 4 were to be lawyers and 6 or 7 physicians or surgeons. They were part-time, and were paid stipends of £1 an hour in London and 5 guineas outside. Two of them were to visit the madhouses licensed by the JPs outside London every six months. *Ibid.,* p. 173–5. At last under the Lunatics Act of 1845 the 3 medical and 3 legal Commissioners in a body of 11 became full-time and were paid £1,500 a year. But the 5 lay commissioners remained unpaid. *Ibid.,* p. 191.

25. In the public-private partnership field, note, for instance, the later agreement between the Local Government Department and the Charity Organisation Society.

26. **MacDonagh, Oliver,** *A Pattern of Government Growth, 1800–60: The Passenger Acts and their Enforcement.* MacGibbon and Kee, 1961, *passim.*

27. **Parris, Henry,** *Government and the Railways in Nineteenth Century Britain.* Routledge, 1965, *passim.*

28. This has been summarised in various works, e.g. **Parris, Henry,** *Constitutional Bureaucracy.* Allen and Unwin, 1969, Ch. IX. For a list of some of the articles in

the controversy, see **Henriques, U.,** 'Jeremy Bentham and the machinery of reform', *British Government and Administration*, p. 179, footnote 29. It was superfluous in that the contradictions were largely artificial; useful in so far as the controversy focused attention and led to increase in knowledge.

29. **Lubenow, William C.,** *The Politics of Government Growth.* David and Charles, 1971, *passim.* I call these disputes dichotomies not dialectics, since I doubt whether they will lead to an agreed synthesis – even after the present work!
   MacDonough, Oliver, *Early Victorian Government 1830-1870.* Weidenfeld and Nicolson, 1977, seems to be a return to the individualism-versus-collectivism thesis. I have suggested I think this to be an oversimplification. However, this interesting book appeared when my manuscript was virtually complete, and I regret I have been unable to make more than a few references to it.

30. Parris, *Constitutional Bureaucracy.* p. 282.

31. **Kitson Clark, G.,** 'Statesmen in disguise', *Historical Journal*, II, 1959, pp. 19-39.
   Kitson Clark, G., *An Expanding Society.* Melbourne U. P., 1967, pp. 133-50.

32. **Thomis, Malcolm I.,** *The Town Labourer and the Industrial Revolution.* Batsford, 1974, does something to check this tendency.

33. *Past and Present*, 1965, pp. 39-61. The argument was advanced in **MacDonagh, Oliver,** 'The nineteenth century revolution in government: a reappraisal', *Historical Journal*, I-II, 1958-9. It is much less strongly used in his book *Early Victorian Government.*

34. *Vide* the early formulation of the Separate System by Jonas Hanway, or the first attempts at the scientific ventilation of prisons in the plans for Ipswich gaol by the Unitarian ex-Cambridge don, John Jebb. The radical formula for democratic parliamentary reform later adopted by the Chartists, went back as far as the Duke of Richmond's Bill of 1780.

35. **Mill, James,** *Essay on Government.* Reprinted from the supplement to the *Encyclopaedia Britannica.* London, 1828.

36. 'The less unequal the distribution of the external instruments of felicity is – the greater, so as security be unshaken, will be the sum of felicity itself.' *Constitutional Code. Works*, Vol. IX, p. 272, para 32.

37. See **Himmelfarb, Gertrude,** 'The Haunted House of Jeremy Bentham', in *Victorian Minds.* Weidenfeld and Nicolson, 1968, pp. 32-81. Cf. p. 165 above.

38. Mary Carpenter, not at all a Benthamite, used it as the title of one of her books.

39. See Henriques, *op. cit.*, pp. 180-1. But Cf. p. 38 below, n. 107.

40. This has been partly done for Disraeli in **Smith, Paul,** *Disraelian Conservatism and Social Reform.* Routledge, 1967.

41. Friendly societies within one trade tended to turn into trade unions. It was sometimes difficult to distinguish them. **Gosden, P. H. J. H.,** *Self Help.* Batsford, 1973, p. 14.

42. This right was conferred by Rose's Act of 1793, and retained, subject to registration with the barrister appointed, to certify the rules of savings banks in the Act of 1834. He became the Registrar of Friendly Societies in 1846. Until 1850 friendly societies were also allowed to invest their funds with the National Debt Commissioners at a favourable and subsidised rate of interest. *Ibid.*, pp. 34-5, 63-8. The first Registrar of Friendly Societies, John Tidd Pratt, was greatly admired by Chadwick for his stern attitude towards defaulting subscribers.

43. *Ibid.*, p. 66.

44. Cf. **Harrison, J. F. C.,** *Learning and Living 1790-1960.* Routledge, 1961, pp. 42-3 *et seq.*

45. **Evans, L. W.,** *Education in Industrial Wales, 1700-1900.* Avalon Press, 1971, pp. 309-10.

46. The extent to which the Poor Law Unions and municipal public health and amenities committees were simply the footballs of local party (often middle-class party) politics has been explored in detail in **Fraser, Derek,** *Urban Politics in Victorian England.* Leicester U. P., 1976, *passim.*

47. Cf. **Gauldie, E.,** *Cruel Habitations.* George Allen and Unwin, 1974.
48. The expression was that of the Chartist Julian Harney.
49. See **Smith, Paul,** *op. cit., passim.*
50. Cf. **Rowbotham, Sheila,** 'The call to university extension teaching, 1873–1900', *Birmingham University Historical Journal,* XII, 1969–1970, pp. 57–71. Critics such as Jelinger Symons in the 1840s had called for the restoration of personal contact and paternal care of the higher for the lower orders. The university extension movement revealed signs of guilt by the educationally privileged at class inequalities.
51. The title of Prof. David Roberts' excellent book.
52. **Hay, J. R.,** *The Origins of the Liberal Welfare Reforms, 1906–1914.* The Economic History Society. Macmillan Press, 1975, p. 12. Hay quotes from **Briggs, A.,** 'The welfare state in historical perspective', *Archives Européennes de Sociologie,* **2,** 1961.
53. Based on the revived distinction between deserving and undeserving poor. Cf. the character of Mr Doolittle in Bernard Shaw's *Pygmalion.* The satire has become meaningless in modern terms, and is not amusing unless the contemporary distinction is fully understood.

Bibliographical note

My main contemporary source throughout this book has been the collection of Select Committee and Royal Commission reports, with their volumes of evidence, the returns to parliamentary inquiries, and the inspectors' reports which together make up the government Blue Books of the early nineteenth century. These sources have been much used by historians, but by no means exhausted. Their volume is enormous, they touch on every aspect of social life, and nothing can be done without them. Unfortunately they are difficult to refer to. Government papers were often published first as individual folio books on behalf of HMSO. They were then bound in the annual volumes of the *Parliamentary Papers*. In some instances, such as the oddly named 'Minutes' of the Committee of the Privy Council on Education, i.e. the Education Inspectors' Reports, they were also issued for HMSO in a quarto edition. In recent years the Irish University Press has produced a classified edition of the *Parliamentary Papers*, in which the different reports have been removed from the annual volumes and rebound together in topics. Finally, some of the most famous individual reports have been reprinted in modern editions with editorial introductions; e.g. S. G. and E. O. H. Checklands' edition of the *Poor Law Report* of 1834 (Pelican Paperback 1974, already out of print) and M. W. Flinn's edition of Chadwick's *Report on the Sanitary Condition of the Labouring Population of Great Britain*, 1842 (Edinburgh U. P., 1965). Unless you are within easy reach of one of the great copyright libraries such as the British Library, or the Bodleian Library at Oxford, where complete or nearly complete collections of the *Parliamentary Papers* are housed, it is almost impossible to maintain consistency in referring to them. It is possible when using the Irish University Press edition to identify the volume of the *Parliamentary Papers* from which each report was obtained, and I have tried so far as possible to keep the original title and printed page numbers, and to make clear from which edition each quotation or reference is taken.

I have supplemented the Blue Books with Hansard's Parliamentary Debates. I have utilised some of the correspondence between Inspectors of Factories and Prisons and the Home Office, now in the Public Record Office. But I have not attempted to investigate the voluminous correspondence and MS reports of the Poor Law Assistant Commissioners. Nor have I ventured into the vast field of the local record repositories, whose collections have enabled so much investigation of public administration to be carried out. Instead I have consulted a selection of the growing army of postgraduate theses, both doctoral and MA. These present a detailed picture of actual administration based on local archives which would otherwise not be available to the synthesiser; and I am most grateful to the authors for permission to use them. In several cases these dissertations have been subsequently re-written and published as books or articles, but the original thesis may contain details omitted from the later publication.

I have made considerable use of the Bowring edition of Bentham's *Works*, 1843 (the complete edition now being prepared in University College, London, not yet being far enough advanced), and have supplemented this from the Chadwick papers in the D.M.S. Watson Library, University College, London. Shaftesbury's diaries, kept in the Historical Manuscripts Commission, Chancery Lane, are also of great interest to students of nineteenth-century social administration.

I append a selection from some of the pamphlets and secondary works, contemporary and modern, roughly according to topic.

Bibliography

Chapter 1, Introduction; Chapter 12, The machinery of reform; Chapter 13, Conclusion

General books

Bamford, G. B. A. M., *England in the Eighteen Thirties.* Arnold, 1969.

Binney, J. E. D., *British Public Finance and Administration, 1774-92.* Clarendon Press, 1958.

Clokie, H. M. and Robinson, J. W., Royal Commissions of Inquiry, Stanford University, 1937.

Cullen, M. J., *The Statistical Movement in Early Victorian Britain.* Harvester Press, 1975.

Finer, S. E., *The Life and Times of Sir Edwin Chadwick.* Methuen, 1952.

Foster, John, *Class Struggle and The Industrial Revolution.* Methuen, 1974.

Hollis, Patricia, *Pressure from Without in Early Victorian England.* Edward Arnold, 1974.

Kitson Clark, G., *An Expanding Society.* Melbourne U. P., 1967.

Lubenow, William C., *The Politics of Government Growth.* David & Charles, 1971.

MacDonagh, O., *The Passenger Acts and their Enforcement.* MacGibbon & Kee, 1961.

MacDonagh, O., *Early Victorian Government.* Weidenfeld and Nicolson, 1977.

Moore, D. C., *The Politics of Deference.* Harvester Press, 1976.

Musson, A. E., *Trade Union and Social History.* Cass, 1974.

Parris, Henry, *Government and The Railways in Nineteenth Century Britain.* Routledge, 1965.

Parris, Henry, *Constitutional Bureaucracy.* Allen and Unwin, 1969.

Perkin, Harold, *The Origins of Modern English Society, 1780-1880.* Routledge, 1969.

Roberts, David, *Victorian Origins of the British Welfare State.* Yale U. P., 1960.

Thomis, Malcolm, *The Town Labourer and the Industrial Revolution.* Batsford, 1974.

Articles

Kitson Clark, G., 'Statesmen in disguise', *Historical Journal*, II, 1959.
Hart, Jennifer, 'Nineteenth-century social reform: a Tory interpretation of history', *Past and Present*, No. 31, July, 1965.
Henriques, U. R. Q., 'Jeremy Bentham and the machinery of social reform', H. Hearder and H. R. Loyn (ed.), *British Government and Administration*, University of Wales Press, 1974.
MacDonagh, Oliver, 'The nineteenth-century revolution in Government: a reappraisal', *Historical Journal*, I–II, 1958–59.

Specialised books and articles

Police

Bentham, J., *Works*, J. Bowring, (ed.), Edinburgh, 1843, Vol. I.
Hart, Jennifer, 'Reform of the Borough Police', *English Historical Review*, LXX 1955.
Mather, F. C., *Public Order in the Age of the Chartists.* Manchester U. P., 1959.
Midwinter, E. C., *Social Administration in Lancashire, 1830–1860*, Manchester U. P., 1969.
Radzinowicz, L., *History of Criminal Law.* Vol. 3, *The Reform of the Police.* Stevens, 1956.
Reith, Charles, *British Police and the Democratic Ideal*, O. U. P., 1943.

Thesis

Midwinter, E. C., 'Social Administration in Lancashire, 1830–1860: Poor Law, Public Health and Police.' York D. Phil., 1966.

Lunacy

Jones, Kathleen, *Lunacy Law and Conscience, 1744–1845.* Routledge, 1955.
Parry Jones, William Ll., *The Trade in Lunacy: a Study of Private Madhouses in England in the Eighteenth and Nineteenth Centuries.* Routledge, 1972.

Chapter 2, The old Poor Law; Chapter 3, The new Poor Law

Books

Brundage, Anthony, *The Making of the New Poor Law.* Rutgers U.P., 1978.
Chambers, J. D. and Mingay, G. E., *The Agricultural Revolution, 1750–1880.* Batsford, 1966.

Cowherd, Raymond, G., *Political Economists and the English Poor Laws.* Ohio U.P., 1978.
Edsall, Nicholas, *The Anti Poor Law Movement, 1833-44.* Manchester U. P., 1971.
Fraser, Derek, (ed.), *The New Poor Law in the Nineteenth Century,* Macmillan, 1976.
Gosden, P. H. J. H., *Self-Help.* Batsford, 1973.
Hampson, E. M., *The Treatment of Poverty in Cambridgeshire.* C. U. P., 1934.
Marshall, Dorothy, *The English Poor in the Eighteenth Century.* Routledge, 1926.
Poynter, J. R., *Society and Pauperism.* Routledge, 1969.
Redford, A., *Labour Migration in England, 1800-1850.* Manchester U. P., 1926.
Rose, M. E., *The English Poor Law, 1780-1930.* David & Charles, 1971.
Webb, Sidney and Beatrice, *English Poor Law History.* Part I, Part II, Vol. I, Longman, 1927-9.

Articles

Ashby, A. W., 'One Hundred Years of Poor Law Administration in a Warwickshire Village', in P. Vinogradoff (ed.), *Oxford Studies in Social and Legal History,* (V) 1912.
Barnett, D. C., 'Allotments and the Problem of Rural Poverty, 1780-1840', in Jones, E. L. and Mingay, G. E., (eds.), *Land, Labour and Population in the Industrial Revolution.* Edward Arnold, 1967.
Baugh, D. A., 'The cost of poor relief in S. E. England, 1790-1834', *Economic History Review,* 2nd series XXVIII, No. 1, Feb. 1975.
Blaug, Mark, 'The Myth of the old Poor Law', *Journal of Economic History,* Vol. 23, 1963.
Blaug, Mark, 'The Poor Law re-examined'. *Journal of Economic History,* Vol. 24, 1964.
Brundage, Anthony, 'The landed interest and the new Poor Law', *English Historical Review,* LXXXVII, 1972.
Brundage, Anthony, 'The English Poor Law of 1834 and "the cohesion" of agricultural society', *Agricultural History,* Vol. 48, 1974.
Digby, Anne, 'The labour market and the continuity of social policy after 1834', *Economic History Review,* 2nd series XXVIII, No. 1, 1975.
Dunkley, Peter, 'The landed interest and the new Poor Law: a critical note', *English Historical Review,* LXXXVIII, October, 1973.
Dunkley, Peter, 'The hungry forties – the new Poor Law, a case study', *Historical Journal,* XVII, 2, 1974.

Henriques, U. R. Q., 'Bastardy and the new Poor Law', *Past and Present*, No. 37, July 1967.

Henriques, U. R. Q., 'How cruel was The Victorian Poor Law?', *Historical Journal*, XI, 1968.

Lewis, R. A., 'William Day and the Poor Law Commissioners', *University of Birmingham Historical Journal*, Vol. 9, 1964.

McCord, N., 'The implementation of the Poor Law Amendment Act on Tyneside', *International Review of Social History*, XIV, 1969, Pt. 1.

Marshall, J. D., 'The Nottinghamshire reformers and their contribution to the new Poor Law', *Economic History Review*, II, 13, 1960-61.

Roberts, David, 'How cruel was the new Poor Law?', *Historical Journal*, VI, 1963.

Rose, M. E., 'The Allowance System under the new Poor Law', *Economic History Review*, 2nd series XIX, 1966.

Contemporary books and pamphlets

Bentham, Jeremy, *Works*, J. Bowring (ed), Edinburgh, 1843, Vol. VIII.

Bowen, John, *Refutation of the Charges against the Poor.* 2nd ed. 1837

Colquhoun, Patrick, *A Treatise on Indigence.* 1806.

Eden, F. M., *The State of the Poor.* 1797.

Liverpool, Earl of, *An Account of the Operation of the Poor Law Amendment in the Uckfield Union ... by The Earl of Liverpool, Chairman of that Union.* 1836.

Smith, Adam, *The Wealth of Nations* (1776). Clarendon Press, 1880.

Walter, John, *A Letter to the Electors of Berkshire, on the New System for the Management of the Poor proposed by the Government.* 1834.

Theses

Barnett, D. C., 'Ideas on Social Welfare, 1780-1834'. Nottingham M.A., 1961.

Brooks, Clive, 'The Poor in the Medway Towns of Kent, 1852-7'. Uncompleted London M.A.

Couth, William, 'The Development of the Town of Gainsborough'. Wales (Cardiff) M.A., 1975.

Christmas, E. A., 'The Administration of the Poor Law in some Gloucestershire Unions, 1815-1847'. Bristol M.Litt., 1973.

Froshaug, Ann, 'Poor Law Administration in Selected London Parishes between 1750 and 1850'. Nottingham M.A., 1969.

Hindley, M. D., 'Local Administration of the Poor Law in Great Boughton and Wirral Unions and the Chester Local Act Incorporation, 1834-71'. Wales (Bangor) M.A., 1969.

Hopkin, N. D., 'The Old and New Poor Law in East Yorkshire, *c.*1760-1850'. Leeds M.Phil., 1968.

Lane, Joan, 'Administration of the Poor Law in Butlers Marston, 1713-1822'. Wales (Cardiff) M.A., 1970.

Mawson, Pamela, 'Poor Law Administration in South Shields, 1830-1930'. Newcastle on Tyne M.A., 1971.

Mishra, R. C., 'A History of the Relieving Officer in England and Wales from 1834 to 1948'. London Ph.D., 1969. (Senate House).

Pack, L. F. C., 'A Study of the Evolution of the Methods of Poor Relief in the Winchester Area'. Southampton M.A., 1967.

Pike, Walter, 'Administration of the Poor Law in the Rural Areas of Surrey, 1830-1850'. London (Birkbeck) M.A., 1950.

Rose, M. E., 'Poor Law Administration in the West Riding of Yorkshire, 1820-1855'. Oxford D.Phil., 1965.

Thomas, J. E., 'Poor Law Administration in West Glamorgan from 1834-1930'. Wales (Swansea) M.A., 1951.

Chapters 4 and 5, Factory Acts

Books

There is a very large literature on the technical, economic and social aspects of the first Industrial Revolution. As 'background' books to the development particularly of textiles, I have picked out the following – by no means exhaustive – examples.

Bienefeld, M. A., *Working Hours in British Industry.* London School of Economics, 1972.

Bythell, Duncan, *The Handloom Weavers.* C. U. P. 1969.

Chapman, S. D., *The Early Factory Masters.* David and Charles, 1967.

Chapman, S. J., *The Lancashire Cotton Industry.* Manchester U. P., 1904.

Gayer, A. D., Rostow W. W. and Schwartz, A. J., *The Growth and Fluctuation of the British Economy, 1740-1850.* Clarendon Press, 1953, 2 Vols.

Harte, N. B. and Ponting, K. G., (eds.), *Textile History and Economic History.* Manchester U.P., 1973.

Pinchbeck, Ivy, *Women Workers and the Industrial Revolution, 1750-1850.* Routledge, 1930.

Rimmer, W. G., *Marshalls of Leeds, Flax Spinners 1788-1886.* C. U. P., 1960

Smelser, J. N., *Social Change in the Industrial Revolution.* Routledge, 1959.

Wadsworth, A. P. and Mann, M., *The Cotton Trade and Industrial Lancashire, 1600-1780.* Manchester U. P., 1931.

The factory movement and early Acts

Books

Driver, Cecil, *Tory Radical: A Life of Richard Oastler.* O. U. P., 1946.
Gill, J. C., *The Ten Hour Parson.* London, SPCK 1959.
Hodder, E., *The Life and Work of the Seventh Earl of Shaftesbury,* K. G.
  Cassell, 1886–87.
Kirby, R. G. and Musson, A. E., *The Voice of the People: John
  Doherty, 1798–1854, Trade Unionist, Radical and Factory
  Reformer.* Manchester U. P., 1975.
Thomas, M. W., *The Early Factory Legislation.* Thames Book
  Publishing Co., Leigh on Sea, 1947.
Ward, J. T., *The Factory Movement, 1830–1855.* Macmillan, 1962.

Articles

Henriques, U. R. Q., 'An early factory inspector: James Stuart of
  Dunearn', *Scottish Historical Review,* L.1, No. 149, 1971.
Martin, Bernice, 'Leonard Horner: a portrait of an inspector of
  factories', *International Review of Social History,* XIV, 1969, pt. 3.
Webb, R. K., 'A Whig Inspector', *Journal of Modern History,* XXVII,
  1955.

Contemporary books and pamphlets

Lord Ashley, 'The Factory System', *Quarterly Review,* LVII, 1836.
Lord Ashley, 'Infant Labour', *Quarterly Review,* LXVII, 1841.
Baines, Edward, Jnr, *History of the Cotton Manufacture in Great Britain.*
  Jackson, 1835.
Brown, John, *A Memoir of Robert Blincoe,* J. Doherty: Manchester,
  1832.
Oastler, Richard, *Slavery in Yorkshire.* 1835.
Senior, Nassau William, *Letters on the Factory Act.* 1837.
Trollope, Frances, *The Life and Adventures of Michael Armstrong, the
  Factory Boy.* 3 Vols. London, 1840.
Ure, Andrew, *The Philosophy of Manufactures.* Charles Knight, 1835.

Chapters 6 and 7, Public health

Books

Finer, S. E., *The Life and Times of Sir Edwin Chadwick.* Methuen,
  1952.
Flinn, M. W., (ed.), *Report on the Sanitary Condition of the Labouring
  Population of Great Britain,* by Edwin Chadwick, 1842, with
  Introduction. Edinburgh U. P., 1965.

Frazer, W. M., *Duncan of Liverpool.* Hamish Hamilton, 1947.
Gauldie, Enid, *Cruel Habitations.* George Allen and Unwin, 1974.
Gosden, P. H. J. H., *Self-Help.* Batsford, 1973.
Hennock, E. P., *Fit and Proper Persons: Ideal and Reality in Nineteenth Century Urban Government.* Edward Arnold, 1973.
Hodgkinson, Ruth, *The Origins of the National Health Service.* The Wellcome Historical Medical Library, 1967.
Lambert, Royston, *Sir John Simon, 1816-1904.* MacGibbon & Kee, 1963.
Large, D. and Round, F., *Public Health in mid-Victorian Bristol.* Bristol Historical Association, 1974.
Lewis, R. A., *Edwin Chadwick and the Public Health Movement, 1832-1854.* Longman, 1952.
Longmate, Norman, *King Cholera.* Hamish Hamilton, 1966.
Midwinter, E. C., *Social Administration in Lancashire 1830-1860.* Manchester U. P. 1969.
Morris, R. J., *Cholera, 1832.* Croom Helm, 1976.
Simon, Sir John, *English Sanitary Institutions.* Cassell, 1890.
Stedman Jones, Gareth, *Outcast London.* Clarendon Press, 1971.

Articles

Lambert, Royston, 'Central and local relations in mid-Victorian England: the Local Government Act Office, 1858-71', *Victorian Studies,* VI, No. 2, Dec. 1962.
Lambert, Royston, 'Commonsense and the Dwellings of the Poor', *Nineteenth Century,* XIV, July-Dec. 1883.
Linebaugh, Peter, 'The Tyburn Riot against the Surgeons', in Hay, D., Linebaugh, P. and Thompson, E. P., *Albion's Fatal Tree.* Allen Lane, 1975.
Penny, R. I., 'The Board of Health in Victorian Stratford-upon-Avon; aspects of environmental control', *Warwickshire History,* Vol. 1, No. 6, 1971.

Contemporary books and pamphlets

Engels, F., *The Condition of the Working Class in England,* Henderson, W. O. and Chaloner, W. H., (eds.), Blackwell, 1958.

Theses

Archer, Alan, 'A Study of Local Sanitary Administration in certain selected areas, 1848-75'. Wales (Bangor) M.A., 1967.
Davies Jones, Tydfil, 'Poor Law and Public Health Administration in the Area of Merthyr Tydfil Union, 1834-1894'. Wales (Cardiff), M.A., 1961.
Durey, M. J., 'A Social History of the First Cholera Epidemic in Britain, 1831-3'. York D.Phil., 1975.

Elliott, Malcolm, 'The Leicester Board of Health, 1849-1872'. Nottingham M.Phil., 1971.

Midwinter, E. C., 'Social Administration in Lancashire, 1830-1860, Poor Law, Public Health and Police'. York D.Phil., 1966.

Toft, Jean, 'Public Health in Leeds in the Nineteenth Century: a Study in the Growth of Local Government Responsibility, *c.*1815-1880'. Manchester M.A., 1966.

Townley, W. E., 'Urban Administration and Health: a Case Study on Hanley in the Mid Nineteenth Century'. Keele M.A., 1969.

Chapters 8 and 9, Prisons

Books

Barry, J. V., *Alexander Maconochie of Norfolk Island.* O. U. P. Melbourne, 1958.

Branch Johnson, W., *The English Prison Hulks.* Philimore Press, 1970.

Collins, Philip, *Dickens and Crime.* Indiana U. P., 1962.

Griffiths, Arthur, *Chronicles of Newgate,* Chapman and Hall, 1884.

Griffiths, Arthur, *Memorials of Millbank.* Chapman and Hall, 1884.

Hinde, R. S. E., *The British Penal System, 1773-1950.* Duckworth, 1951.

Pinchbeck I. and Hewett, M., *Children in English Society.* Vol. II, Routledge, 1973.

Radzinowicz, L., *A History of English Criminal Law.* Stevens and Sons, 1948, Vol. I.

Shaw, A. G. L., *Convicts and the Colonies.* Faber and Faber, 1966.

Thomas, J. E., *The English Prison Officer since 1850: a Study in Conflict.* Routledge, 1972.

Tobias, J. J., *Crime and Industrial Society in the Nineteenth Century.* Batsford, 1967.

Webb, S. and B., *English Prisons under Local Government* (1922). Cass, 1963.

Articles

Gatrell, V. A. C. and Hadden, T. B., 'Criminal statistics and their interpretation', in E. A. Wrigley, (ed.), *Nineteenth Century Society. Essays in the Use of Quantitative Methods.* C. U. P., 1972.

Henriques, U. R. Q., 'The rise and decline of the Separate System of prison discipline', *Past and Present,* No. 54, Feb. 1972.

Himmelfarb, Gertrude, 'The haunted house of Jeremy Bentham', *Victorian Minds,* Weidenfeld and Nicolson, 1968.

Contemporary books and pamphlets

Adshead, Joseph, *Prisons and Prisoners.* London, 1845.

Bentham, Jeremy, *Works,* Bowring, (ed.), 1843, Vol. I, IV.

Burt, J. T., *Pentonville Prison.* London, 1852.

Buxton, T. Fowell, *An Inquiry Whether Crime and Misery are Produced or Prevented by our Present System of Prison Discipline.* London, 1818.

Carlyle, Thomas, *Model Prisons.* London, 1850.

Carpenter, Mary, *Our Convicts.* Vols. I and II, London, 1864.

Carpenter, Mary, *Reformatory Schools for the Children of the Perishing and Dangerous Classes, and for Juvenile Offenders.* London, 1851.

Chesterton, G. L., *Revelations of Prison Life.* Vols I and II, London, 1856.

Clay, W. L., *The Prison Chaplain: a Memoir of the Rev. John Clay, B.D.* London, 1861.

Field, J. C., *Prison Discipline: The Advantages of the Separate System of Prison Discipline as Established in the New County gaol of Reading, etc.* London, 1846.

Hanway, Jonas, *Solitude in Imprisonment with Profitable Labour and a Spare Diet.* London, 1776.

Hanway, Jonas, *Distributive Justice and Mercy, etc.* London, 1781.

Hill, Rosamund and Florence, *The Recorder of Birmingham: a Memoir of Matthew Davenport Hill, etc.* Macmillan, 1878.

Holford, George, *Thoughts on the Criminal Prisons of this Country.* London, 1821.

Holford, George, *An Account of the Penitentiary at Millbank.* London, 1828.

Howard, John, *The State of the Prisons* (1777), Everyman Edition.

Col. Jebb, CB, *Report on the Discipline and Management of Convict Prisons.* HMSO, 1855.

Col. Jebb, CB, *Report on the Discipline of the Convict Prisons and the Operation of the Act of 16 and 17 Victoria c.99, 1854-55.* HMSO, 1856.

Kingsmill, Joseph, *Chapters on Prisons and Prisoners etc.* London, 1853.

Maconochie, A., *Report on the State of Prison Discipline in Van Diemen's Land,* 1837 appendix to Barry's *Alexander Maconochie of Norfolk Island.*

Maconochie, A., *Crime and Punishment: the Mark System.* London 1846.

Mayhew, Henry and Binny, John, *The Criminal Prisons of London, and Scenes of Prison Life.* Griffiths, Bohn & Co., 1862.

Paley, William, *Moral and Political Philosophy,* 1785, Ch. IX.

Smith, Sydney, 'Prisons', *Edinburgh Review,* XXXVI, 1822.

Symons, J., *Tactics for the Times as regards the Condition and Treatment of the Dangerous Classes.* London, 1849.

Wakefield, Edward Gibbon, *Facts Relating to the Punishment of Death in the Metropolis,* London 1831.

Wakefield, Edward Gibbon, *An Account of the Origin and Object of the Society for the Diffusion of Knowledge upon the Punishment of Death and the Improvement of Prison Discipline,* 1812, Montagu Tracts.
Wakefield, Edward Gibbon, *3rd Report of the Society etc.,* 1816.

Theses

Bartrip, P. W. J., 'The Career of Matthew Davenport Hill'. Wales (Cardiff) Ph.D., 1975.
Bell, E. P., 'A Social History of Salford New Bailey Prison'. Salford M.Sc., 1972.
Tomlinson, Margaret Heather, 'Victorian Prisons: Administration and Architecture, 1835-1877'. London Ph.D., 1975.
Whiting, G. R. S., 'Sir G. O. Paul's Reform of Gloucestershire Prisons, 1776-1820'. Geneva College, Indiana, D.Litt., 1973.
More theses have recently been completed.

Chapters 10 and 11, Elementary education

This is a small selection from the vast and growing literature on the subject.

Books

Adams, Francis, *History of the Elementary School Contest in England.* 1882.
Altick, R. D., *The English Common Reader.* University of Chicago Press, 1957.
Ball, Nancy, *Her Majesty's Inspectorate.* Oliver and Boyd, 1963.
Evans, L. Wynne, *Education in Industrial Wales, 1700-1900.* Cardiff Avalon Press, 1971.
Gosden, P. H. J. H., *The Development of Educational Administration in England and Wales.* Blackwell, 1966.
Hurt, John, *Education in Evolution.* Rupert Hart-Davis, 1971.
Johnson, Marion, *Derbyshire Village Schools in the Nineteenth Century.* David and Charles, 1970.
New, Chester, *The Life of Henry Brougham to 1830.* Clarendon Press, 1961.
Robson, A. H., *The Education of Children engaged in Industry in England, 1833-1876.* Kegan Paul, 1931.
Sellman, Roger, *Devon Village Schools in the Nineteenth Century.* David and Charles, 1967.
Silver, Harold, *The Concept of Popular Education.* MacGibbon and Kee, 1965.
Simon, Brian, *Studies in the History of Education.* Lawrence and Wishart, 1969.

Smith, Frank, *A History of English Elementary Education, 1760-1902,* University of London Press, 1931.
Smith, Frank, *The Life and Work of Sir James Kay-Shuttleworth.* John Murray, 1923.
Sturt, M., *The Education of the People.* Routledge, 1967.
Ward, W. G., *Religion and Society in England, 1790-1850.* Batsford, 1972.
Webb, R. K., *The British Working Class Reader, 1790-1848.* George Allen and Unwin, 1955.
West, E. G., *Education and the State.* Institute of Economic Affairs, 1965.

Articles

Coleman, B. I., 'The Incidence of Education in mid-century', in Wrigley, E. A. (ed.), *Nineteenth Century Society.* C. U. P., 1972.
Duke, Francis, 'Pauper Education', in Fraser, Derek, (ed.), *The New Poor Law in the Nineteenth Century.* Macmillan, 1976.
Goldstrom, J. M., 'Richard Whately and Political Economy in school books, 1833-80', *Irish Historical Studies,* XV, No. 58, Sept. 1966.
Roderick, G. W. and Stephens, M. D., 'Approaches to technical education in nineteenth century England, Pt. IV, The Liverpool Mechanics' Institution', *The Vocational Aspects of Secondary and Further Education,* XXV, No. 61, Aug. 1973.
Saunderson, Michael, 'Education and the Factory in Industrial Lancashire', *Economic History Review,* 2nd series XX, 1967.
Simon, Joan, 'Post-Restoration Developments: Schools in the County 1660-1700', in Simon, Brian, (ed.), *Education in Leicestershire 1540-1940.* Leicester University Press, 1968.
Stephens, M. D. and Roderick, G. W., 'National attitudes towards scientific education in early nineteenth century England', *The Vocational Aspect of Secondary and Further Education,* XXVI, No. 65, Dec. 1974.
Stones, E., 'The Growth of Technical Education in Nineteenth Century Accrington', *Vocational Aspects, etc.,* No. 18, Spring 1957.
Wadsworth, A. P., 'The first Manchester Sunday Schools', in Flinn, N. W. and Smout, T. C., (eds.), *Essays in Social History.* Clarendon Press, 1974.

Contemporary books and pamphlets

Baines, Edward, Jnr, *A Letter to the Rt. Hon. Lord John Russell on . . . State Education,* London 7th ed., 1847.
Bloomfield, B. C., (ed.), 'The Autobiography of Sir James Kay-Shuttleworth', *Education Libraries Bulletin,* Supplement 7, 1964.
Brougham, Henry, *Practical Observations on the Education of the People,*

Addressed to the Working Classes and their Employees. London, 1825.

Duppa, Baldwin Francis, 'Central Society of Education – Objects of the Society', *Central Social of Education.* First Publication of 1837, Woburn Press, 1968.

Hook, Walter Farquhar, *A Letter to the Lord Bishop of St Davids, on the Means of Rendering more efficient the Education of the People.* 9th ed. London, 1846.

Lovett, William, *Address from the Working Men's Association to the Working Classes on the Subject of National Education,* London.

Lovett, W. and Collins, J., *Chartism: a New Organisation of the People* (1840). Leicester U. P. 1969.

Owen, Robert, *A New View of Society,* 1812. Everyman Edition.

Shuttleworth, Sir James Kay, *Public Education as Affected by the Minutes of the Committee of the Privy Council from 1840-1852.* London 1853.

Symons, Jelinger, *Light and Life to the People.* London, 1843.

Temple, Frederick, 'National Education', in *Oxford Essays.* London 1856.

Vaughan, Robert, D. D., 'Popular Education in England', reprinted from *the British Quarterly Review* No. VIII with 'A Reply to the Letter of Mr Edward Baines Jnr on that Article', London, 1846.

Watson, Rev. Alexander *A Letter to Henry Lord Bishop of Exeter occasioned by a Letter from R. F. Hook.* London, 1846.

Theses

Bartrip, Peter W. J., 'The Career of M. D. Hill'. Wales (Cardiff) Ph.D., 1975.

Duke, Francis, 'The Education of Pauper Children: Policy and Administration, 1834-1855'. Manchester M.A., 1968.

Gilbert, Amy Margaret, 'The work of Lord Brougham for Education in England'. University of Pennsylvania Ph.D., 1922. Franklin Repository. A copy is in University College, Swansea, Library.

Gordon, Peter, 'The Elementary School Manager and the Management of Education, 1800-1902'. London Ph.D., 1970.

Handley, M. D., 'Local Administration of the Poor Law in Great Boughton and Wirral Unions and the Chester Local Act Incorporation, 1834-71'. Wales (Bangor) M.A, 1969.

Index